Canadian Writers and Their Works

CANADIAN WRITERS AND THEIR WORKS

FICTION SERIES · VOLUME FOUR

 EDITED BY

ROBERT LECKER, JACK DAVID, ELLEN QUIGLEY

INTRODUCED BY GEORGE WOODCOCK

ECW PRESS, 1991

CANADIAN CATALOGUING IN PUBLICATION DATA

Main entry under title:

Canadian writers and their works: essays on form,
context, and development : fiction

Includes bibliographies and indexes.
ISBN 0-920802-43-5 (set). — ISBN 1-55022-052-7 (v. 4)

1. Canadian fiction (English) — History and criticism.*
2. Authors, Canadian (English) — Biography.* I. Lecker,
Robert, 1951– . II. David, Jack, 1946– .
III. Quigley, Ellen, 1955– .

PS8187.C36 1991   C813′.009   C82-094801-2
PR9192.2.C36 1991

The publication of this series has been assisted by grants from the Ontario Arts
Council and The Canada Council.

This volume was typeset in Sabon by ECW Type & Art, Oakville, Ontario. Printed
and bound by University of Toronto Press, North York, Ontario.

Published by ECW PRESS, 307 Coxwell Avenue, Toronto, Ontario M4L 3B5.

The illustrations are by Isaac Bickerstaff.

CONTENTS

PREFACE

Canadian Writers and Their Works (CWTW) is a unique, twenty-volume collection of critical essays covering the development of Canadian fiction and poetry over the past two centuries. Ten volumes are devoted to fiction, and ten to poetry. Each volume contains a unifying Introduction by George Woodcock and four or five discrete critical essays on specific writers. Moreover, each critical essay includes a brief biography of the author, a discussion of the tradition and milieu influencing his/her work, a critical overview section which reviews published criticism on the author, a long section analyzing the author's works, and a selected bibliography listing primary and secondary material. The essays in each volume are arranged alphabetically according to last names of the writers under study.

This is Volume Four of the Fiction Series of *Canadian Writers and Their Works*. Other volumes in the series will be published as research is completed. The projected completion date for the entire series is 1991.

The editors wish to acknowledge the contributions of many people who have played an important part in creating this series. First, we wish to thank the critics who prepared the essays for this volume: Stan Atherton, Dick Harrison, W.J. Keith, Joy Kuropatwa, Morton Ross, and George Woodcock. We are also indebted to the production and design teams at both The Porcupine's Quill and ECW Type & Art, and to Pat Kenny and Stephanie Termeer, who keyboarded the manuscript in its initial typesetting phase.

RL/JD/EQ

Introduction

GEORGE WOODCOCK

IN THIS VOLUME we are probing down to the bedrock of significant Canadian fiction as we have known it for the past generation or so; a tradition founded in realism but ready to learn from modernist and post-modernist innovatory techniques in so far as they sustain that curious combination of goals — verisimilitude tempered by moralism and flavoured at times with Gothic fantasy and talltale exaggeration — that has distinguished the main line of Canadian fiction.

It was long a commonplace of literary history that the Canadian realist tradition emerged in the Prairies, and another commonplace that it represents the principal contribution to Canadian literature of the three provinces that lie between the Shield and the Rockies. And there is enough truth in both views to make them worth examination.

Four out of the five novelists discussed in this volume lived in and wrote of the Prairies, and between them Grove and Ross, Ostenso and Mitchell present in their works a notably large proportion of the interesting Canadian fiction being written between 1925, when Grove published *Settlers of the Marsh*, and 1947, when W.O. Mitchell's *Who Has Seen the Wind* appeared. Any list of Canadian literary classics inevitably includes these two titles as well as Ross's *As for Me and My House*, Ostenso's *Wild Geese*, and certainly at least two of Grove's other titles, *Over Prairie Trails*, his least flawed book, and *The Master of the Mill*. But, as the essayists in this volume have pointed out, these four writers represent a much larger range of novelists who wrote out of the Prairie experience during the same period.

Stanley Atherton, in his piece on Martha Ostenso, reminds us of the popularity of the Prairies in the earlier nineteenth century as a setting for romantic adventure, presented in novels by writers like Gilbert Parker and James Oliver Curwood, Harold Bindloss and Ralph Connor. And he also notes that:

Another interesting development in the decade preceding the publication of *Wild Geese* was an evolution in the *kind* of fiction produced by a number of Prairie writers. Both Douglas Durkin and Robert Stead began by writing romances, but were later able to make the transition to more serious realistic work.

In fact, the last two writers mentioned by Atherton bear serious comparison with the four Prairie writers selected for this volume; Durkin's *The Magpie* and Stead's *The Smoking Flax* and *Grain* are capable and even powerful works, not inferior to much of Grove or to Sinclair Ross's less successful novels. And Durkin — as Atherton reminds us and as Peter E. Rider originally revealed in introducing a 1974 reprint of *The Magpie* — must take at least part of the credit for *Wild Geese*, which was the result of a collaboration between him and Ostenso and was fraudulently presented as the latter's work to win a literary competition for unpublished writers and for which Durkin, whose major novel had already appeared, was ineligible.

Apart from the writers noted by Atherton, Dick Harrison in his piece on W.O. Mitchell also identifies "a more popular if generally less distinguished stream of Prairie fiction in the sentimental comedies of such writers as John Beames, Ross Annett, and Ralph Allen, which have logical antecedents in the sentimental romances of Nellie McClung," and he sees Mitchell's *Who Has Seen the Wind* "as the culmination of that type of fiction, a counterpart in the comic mode to Ross's . . . *As for Me and My House*."

This rich and complex pattern of Prairie fiction has, of course, continued into our own period with the work of writers as important in the general Canadian literary landscape as Margaret Laurence, Rudy Wiebe, and Robert Kroetsch. These younger writers openly acknowledge the importance of their predecessors and the way their own work has been influenced by Grove and Ostenso and Ross, so that there is the sense of a continuing and consciously sustained succession that changes and develops but retains certain basic elements, notably the varying combination of realism and romance that since the 1920s has been characteristic of the fictional genres in a western setting.

This tradition of Prairie fiction had undoubtedly contributed greatly to Canadian fiction, as a clearly defined regional tradition, and through its more important writers, like Sinclair Ross and Margaret Laurence, its influence has permeated far beyond the

Prairies. Academic critics, indeed, tend to become so fascinated by the phenomenon of the least urban area of the country making so impressive a contribution that they tend to exaggerate the importance of the writers who represent it. Perhaps the most striking instance is that of Frederick Philip Grove, about whom there is a curious division of views. Professional writers, being highly craft conscious, are inclined to see Grove's faults very clearly and to regard him at worst as a pretentious bore and at best — to use my own past words which W.J. Keith quotes in his excellent temperate essay — as "a fumbling giant among novelists," who presents us with "the problem of why a writer, so large in texture, so gigantic in his fumblings, never wrote a book that seemed completely to fulfill his possibilities."

Grove has become more interesting to writers since Douglas Spettigue's revelations of his past as Felix Paul Greve, the minor German decadent who faked suicide to escape from a life of crushing indebtedness and from the stigma of imprisonment, but it is as a complex and enigmatic personality that Greve-Grove appeals without the professional view of his quality as a writer having greatly changed.

Academic critics, on the other hand, have made surprising claims. Writing at the time of Grove's death in 1948, Northrop Frye expressed the opinion that "Frederick Philip Grove was certainly the most serious of Canadian prose writers, and may well have been the most important one also."[1] (One wonders in quite what way he was more "serious" as a prose writer than contemporaries like, say, Morley Callaghan or Hugh MacLennan, who were just as much involved in the problems of prose style and in their own ways equally philosophically inclined.) And as late as 1970, at a time when Canadian writing had shown an astonishing degree of vitality and a remarkable qualitative development, Desmond Pacey could still astonishingly remark: "I believe it is true to say that, at home, Grove is regarded as Canada's greatest novelist."[2]

Just as there has been a tendency to inflate Grove's merits largely because of the admirable grandeur of the ambitions he so imperfectly fulfilled in his novels, there is a tendency, I believe, to exaggerate the importance of Prairie fiction in the development of the special kind of realism that is the dominant mode of Canadian fiction. In fact, of course, the growingly recognized presence of Sara Jeannette Duncan, writing through the 1890s and the Edwardian era, undermines the claims that have been made for Grove as the first important Canadian novelist, while her sharp perceptions of Canadian small town life and of turn-of-the-century political practices in *The Imperialist* suggest that there were other sources as well as the Prairie experience for the development of a realist trend in Canada.

There is also, of course, the fifth writer represented in this volume, Raymond Knister, whose single successful novel, *White Narcissus*, dealt like the Prairie novelists with the farming life, and did so, like so many of them, with realism tempered with romantic sentiments. But Knister was writing not of the homesteads of Prairie pioneers, but of the long-established farms of Ontario. Knister was roughly Grove's contemporary in terms of publication, even if he was twenty years younger in terms of age, and like the older novelist he produced his share of novels too incompletely realized ever to achieve publication. Knister was a young writer of great brilliance and potentiality, and what he might have done if he had not achieved romantic status as Canada's own drowned poet, dead at 33, it is hard to prophesy. He might well have started a tradition of Ontario rural writing; he might have developed over a long life into a poet as important as his friend and contemporary, Dorothy Livesay. Apart from his fiction and poetry, he aspired to being the complete man-of-letters, and at times he showed a notable critical acuity.

Among Knister's essays is one on Grove, written in 1928, which is interesting because it gives us a cross reference between contemporaries and shows a writer who was himself struggling to master the novel as a form recognizing the problems that a fellow novelist encounters. Knister praised *Over Prairie Trails*, which must have appealed to his lyrical sensibility, as "a superb evocation of the prairie winter, sketched in appropriately huge strokes." But he then went on to say, in one of the best comments made by a contemporary:

It is surprising . . . to find Mr. Grove's novels on the whole so unsatisfactory. "Settlers of the Marsh" is powerfully conceived, the honesty and forthright intentions of the author are apparent, yet the book as a whole misses that finality of effect which it should have. In some instances it is downright awkward and childish, as when every few pages we are shown the depravity of the "fallen woman" the hero has married by the fact that she plasters her face with powder. One cannot help conclude that the novel is a strange harness to Mr. Grove's talent. He has to leave so many things unsaid, and forego the advantage of so many branches of his varied learning, that the finished novel must seem a very fragmentary thing.[3]

That last phrase — "that the finished novel must seem a very fragmentary thing" — is especially acute, for what strikes another writer about Grove is that, just as Lowry would spend years working on novels and yet be quite unable to complete them, so Grove would spend vast amounts of time writing and cutting and shaping, and yet could rarely end up with a book that seemed properly integrated. It was not merely a matter of a rough surface, such as some sculptors deliberately leave, but of structural problems unresolved and which for some deep inner reason Grove seems to have been incapable of resolving. But all this Knister expressed with gentleness and understanding, and in a very different way from the other cross reference between authors that immediately comes to mind in the context of this volume, when Grove, combining the arrogance and the envy that were his two besetting faults, burst out, when *Wild Geese* won its award and Ostenso-Durkin became a best-selling team almost overnight, "only trash wins a prize," which did not prevent him from enjoying his own Governor-General's Award.

Yet the fact that the role of Prairie novelists in Canadian fiction as a whole, and also the importance of some individual Prairie novelists, may have been overvalued by academic critics more impressed by a writer's themes than by his way with words, does not lessen the interest of the phenomenon of Prairie fiction. Why did so many good novelists, when one considers the whole succession from Stead to Kroetsch, come out of the Prairies? And why was prose fiction so attractive to Prairie writers, for so many years, to the virtual exclusion of poetry, so that there was no Prairie poet of any consequence between Charles Mair in the 1860s and Eli Mandel in the 1950s?

The two questions are clearly related, and a clue to answering them can perhaps be found in some remarks by Henry Kreisel, centring on Sinclair Ross's *As for Me and My House*, which Morton L. Ross quotes in the essay on his namesake here included. "All discussion of the literature produced in the Canadian west must of necessity begin with the impact of the landscape on the mind," says Kreisel, and he goes on: "It is because *As for Me and My House* contains the most uncompromising rendering of the puritan state of mind produced on the prairie that the novel has been accorded a central place in prairie literature."

The equation that produces puritan consciousness out of Prairie landscape is one with many and subtle ramifications, for there is no doubt that the best novels of all the four western writers discussed in this volume are haunted by the puritan state of mind, at times to the extent of nightmare. Grove's novels resemble Greek tragedies in the relentlessness of the retribution they offer for human flaws, whether these are mere sensual weaknesses or the lusts for power and wealth. In all Martha Ostenso's Canadian novels the negative and destructive — often ultimately self-destructive — power of the puritan will is evident, and the need to defy it is repeatedly proclaimed. In *As for Me and My House* both of the leading characters are potential artists whose creativity is in every way frustrated by the puritan attitude which affects them in two ways; first, it is part of their own inherited view of life from which they are never able — whatever their doubts and inner rebellions — to escape; beyond that it is the moving spirit of the cruel little town of Horizon in which, for the time of the novel at least, they are obliged to live. Even in the case of W.O. Mitchell, who deliberately turned his talents towards comedy for the greater part of his career, the dread of the natural and instinctual life that is characteristic of the puritan mind was there from the start in the deliberate presentation, even in *Who Has Seen the Wind*, of the passage from innocence to experience as a Fall, and the darker implications of this concept of man as a fallen being become much more strongly evident in Mitchell's late novel, *How I Spent My Summer Holidays*, where sexuality becomes an evil, death-ridden force, and the imagery suggests, as I remarked at the time of publication, "a vision that seems to have stepped straight out of the Puritan nightmare."

Perhaps the Prairie novel is the truest manifestation of Northrop Frye's idea of literature in a garrison society. In the vast spaces and the climatic extremes of the great plains, a large number of people, from mainly north European and North American backgrounds, settled in isolated farms or small villages and towns and conquered the land so that its primordial character of a vast open terrain where Indians and bison wandered freely was destroyed, as the survey lines netted it into squared-off farms and the ploughs destroyed the original Prairie vegetation in the same way as the introduction of firearms had destroyed the bison herds and forced the Indians by starvation into accepting a life on reservations.

To conceive such changes required a mentality that could defy nature without and discipline the natural and instinctive elements within men so that work would seem — at least on this earth — their everlasting duty. And the puritan outlook provided that mentality. Whether or not they belonged originally to the traditional puritan sects, those who succeeded on the Prairie were men and women driven by the urge to subdue the land and build a new life there, and in fulfilling that urge the puritan virtues of hard work, self-control, abstemiousness, thrift, were indispensable. It did not make any difference if a man were an Anglican from the English counties, a Scots Presbyterian, a Polish Catholic, or a Ukrainian Orthodox; his share of the puritan virtues was his basic equipment in accepting his tasks as a homesteader, as basic as his plough, and the more stubbornly he continued his struggle with the land, the more the puritan elements were likely to become dominant both in himself and in the society he created. This, I take it, is what Kreisel means by "the puritan state of mind" produced in the Prairie.

But the puritan state of mind in other parts of Canada — in the Maritimes where it flourished greatly and in Upper Canada — was not productive of notable fiction. This is because, I would suggest, nowhere else has it been so strongly involved in its antitheses. Nowhere else in Canada was the struggle with the land so formidable or the land itself, in its sheer open vastness and in the extremity of its natural forces, so antithetical to human desires and intents as in the great plains.

This is why the small towns of Prairie novels, the Manawakas and the Horizons, seem so much like precariously held outposts isolated in the vastness of the land, and why they are such ingrown settlements and so cruel to those who do not abide by the puritan virtues and in this way break the solidarity of the embattled human community. This is why the wind, so relentless in its blowing yet so filled with the scented intimations of another kind of living, plays such an important role in Prairie fiction and in Mitchell's and Ross's novels especially, and why the wild geese that open and close Ostenso's novel, as their haunting cries across the sky intimate the possibility of a free and proud life untrammeled by the puritan urges and inhibitions, stay so firmly in the mind as the guiding symbol as well as the title of the book. That is why the Prairie itself, and especially its untamed recesses, is at once a threat and a temptation.

Perhaps one can regard the realism that is the dominant mode of the Prairie novel as itself a manifestation of the puritan state of mind;

it parallels the other kind of "realism" that sets a man solving the practical problems of life with sense, diligence, and not too much sentiment. But there is something hubristic about this puritan "realism." It succeeds only by setting aside as irrelevant both the untamed processes of nature and the instinctual urges within man, and so it serves God by defying the gods. The consequence is that the very forces it had ignored in the end rise up against it. It was the recognition of this conflict, continuing even after the land had been tamed, between "realism" and reality, that set Prairie people writing novels rather than poems and gave those books the agony and intensity that, in the works of writers like Sinclair Ross and Margaret Laurence, have carried them to the forefront of Canadian fiction.

In the process, just as practical "realism" has been attacked, so literary realism has been modified. For the struggle between the instinctual and the dutiful, with all its perversions of tyranny and greed, inevitably tinges realism with romance, even if only in the Lawrencian sense, while the revenges of circumstance, the punishments for hubris, often make inevitable the intrusion of Gothic fantasy.

So we see the Prairie novel, at its best, as one of those mongrel breeds that often show so much more vitality then the purebred strains. It is realist in the sense that it consciously and conscientiously gives us the Godwinian picture of "things as they are," of the struggle to subdue the land and to survive in the process that is man's life on the Prairie, and the way that life shapes and often misshapes both communities and individuals. But it takes its own vitality from the tension between this "reality" and the emotions and aspirations and longings that rebel against it, whether they flourish in the loves frustrated by parental tyranny in Ostenso-Durkin's *Wild Geese* and *The Young May Moon*, or emerge in the frustrated desire to live a creative life that, despite their differences, unites the Bentleys in *As for Me and My House*. And in this sense we can certainly call the Prairie novel romantic.

But there are also elements in Prairie fiction that bring it very close to Gothic fantasy. Margot Northey in *The Haunted Wilderness: The Gothic and Grotesque in Canadian Fiction* has noted "the heightened depiction of life found in some of Frederick Philip Grove's fiction, such as *The Yoke of Life*,"[4] and has enlarged on "the sense of impending catastrophe"[5] that permeates *Wild Geese* and "the mood of menace and terror" induced in that novel by the combination of such factors as "the mysterious and destructive role of nature, and the willful evil of Caleb Gare."[6] Nothing could be more Gothic in its combination of horror, elemental justice, and underlying absurdity (requiring a hearty "suspension of unbelief") than Caleb's death, swallowed into the liquid mud of a muskeg he should have known well as he hurried to save his blue-flowered field of flax from the onrush of a Prairie fire. There is a touch of lurking menace even in a novel of the Prairies so apparently comic in intent as *Who Has Seen the Wind,* and this certainly deepens into "a mood of menace and terror" in Mitchell's later novel, *How I Spent My Summer Holidays,* while the kind of politically oriented Gothicism that flourished in Zamyatin's *We* and George Orwell's *Nineteen Eighty-Four* found a not unworthy congener on Grove's *The Master of the Mill,* where the mill becomes a sinister symbol of man's subordination to his own industrial and political systems.

There is a special kind of seriousness, a moral earnestness, in the more important Prairie novels, that tends to make critics treat them with a respect that demands more than mere formal analysis or aesthetic appreciation. These are writers out to tell us something about life and the way it should and/or should not be lived; their content emphatically demands our attention, even when they are not being tediously didactic, as they sometimes are. We read them with the sense that we are going to learn something as well as gaining imaginative satisfaction, and we are rarely disappointed. Grove was in a way the exception among them in starting off as the aesthete Greve, a devotee of Wilde and the other Decadents, but it would have surprised his early and rather dismissive acquaintance, André Gide, to see him turning into perhaps the most determined moralist, posing earnest questions about existence, of all the Prairie writers. The problem of freedom and determination lies at the heart of Grove's work, endlessly developed in changing permutations. In the first of his novels to be published, *Settlers of the Marsh,* he poses the question:

> Are there in us unsounded depths of which we do not know ourselves? Can things outside of us sway us in such a way as to change our very nature? Are we we? Or are we mere products of circumstance?[7]

It is a question that seems to have lurked in the minds of many of the Prairie novelists, deriving naturally from that "impact of the

landscape on the mind" to which Kreisel also attributes the prevalence of the puritan mentality in the Prairies. To this extent the
vestiges of the naturalist heritage are evident not only in Grove. But
they are balanced by the defiant sense that liberty is possible and
that, if it is not, the injustice is monstrous, so that whatever quasi-
naturalist presentation of existence-as-it-is we find among these
writers is balanced by the sense that even in the flat monotonies of
the Prairie, man can stand upright and free in the challenging wind.

It is, I believe, the recognition of this uncompromising seriousness
— which made even W.O. Mitchell seem in the end a tragic rather
than a comic novelist — that explains the careful and sensible quality
of the essays included in this volume. They all add notably to the
discussions carried on up to now in relation to the novelists they
concern.

W.J. Keith's sympathies for Grove are obvious and multiple in their
origins. Like Grove and Wyndham Lewis and I, he came out of a
European background into a Canadian literary world whose deni-
zens were not always welcoming. I remember the bitter attack made
on his excellent study of Charles G.D. Roberts by a nationalist
poetaster too paltry to name, merely because Keith was British by
origin. And so I see in context his excellent statement why we should
consider Grove seriously as introducing a new element into the
Canadian literary landscape.

> Instead of the standard classical education of, say, the "Con-
> federation Poets," Grove enjoyed a deeper understanding of the
> whole European tradition; instead of an America-based,
> contemporary-oriented narrowness of attitude, he brought a
> consciousness personally aware of the artistic achievements and
> experiments of continental Europe, a familiarity with other
> literary movements, an openness to new creative possibilities.

Keith's interest in rural literature, which had led to some excellent
studies in the English country-writing tradition, has given him a good
deal of insight into Grove as a kind of agrarian novelist, and the
admiration for Wordsworth he has often expressed also fits into
context, for Wordsworth too was one of those ponderous and
loquacious writers with broad philosophic content who form a large
image in the mind but whose air of the majestic is never completely
convincing because their way with words is never sharp or deft

enough. Both need the distillation neither was able to perform of his own works.

Perhaps it is the multiplicity of these sympathies that explains why Keith has been able to express his admiration for Grove, which is clearly considerable, in a temperate yet sympathetic way that consistently engages one's interest. Certainly he hits upon an important insight into the achievement of that notable liar paradoxically dedicated to the pursuit of artistic truth when at the end of his essay he talks of Desmond Pacey's use of the word "Integrity," at first sight rather surprisingly, in describing Grove.

> Integrity! The word seems strange after the revelations of the "sullied" European years. Yet it is a word that commentators on Grove constantly find themselves needing to use (similarly, I wrote of his "sincerity of purpose" three paragraphs back). Here, perhaps, a gleam of light is shed upon the artistic implications of the so-called Grove mystery. The firm literary integrity pervading the work of Frederick Philip Grove, though ironically including a deceiving account of his own development, seems to have been a massive act of redemption offered as personal penance for the moral shortcomings in the life of Felix Paul Greve. And Canadian fiction is richer as a consequence.

Perhaps, indeed, the process of redemption had already begun in Germany after the prison interlude, when Felix Paul Greve in fact initiated the career of Frederick Philip Grove by writing those early novels, *The Master Mason's House* and *Fanny Essler*, which in a number of important ways anticipated the fiction of the Canadian years.

Recent research has revealed unfamiliar aspects of Martha Ostenso's past as well as Frederick Philip Grove's, though the revelations in her case have not been so bizarre as in Greve-Grove's. Not long ago it was generally assumed that her novels were her own unaided work; the general ignorance about her was linked to an inclination to regard her as a novelist who wrote only one really successful work and at the same time only one novel of interest to Canadians. Even the entry on Ostenso in the 1983 *Oxford Companion to Canadian Literature* mentions only *Wild Geese*, though the author, Joy Kuropatwa, is aware of Ostenso's collaboration with Durkin and remarks that she published "over a dozen volumes of fiction."[8] In fact Ostenso and Durkin wrote sixteen novels, and three of them, beside *Wild Geese*, have Canadian settings, including what is probably the best of her later novels, *The Young May Moon*, also set in Manitoba, as well as *Prologue to Love* and *The White Reef*, both of which have British Columbian backgrounds. It is also clear that her Canadian experience and that of Durkin influenced notably the later novels published under Ostenso's name, even when their settings were American, and that Canada continued to attract her, so that there has been a certain injustice in her having been seen for so long by Canadians as if she were important merely for a single book. By examining her career as a whole, Stanley Atherton has not merely shown that some of her later works were a good deal more than pot-boilers; he has also restored to our attention one excellent novel about Canadian Prairie life, *The Young May Moon*, and one hopes his essay will be the beginning of a broader appreciation of the results of the Ostenso-Durkin joint work and perhaps a closer study of the real nature of the collaboration.

As Atherton convincingly argues, Ostenso-Durkin wrote at least two other books that can stand beside the better known *Wild Geese*. In the case of Sinclair Ross, it is harder to break the image of an essentially one-novel writer, for though Morton L. Ross has given fair treatment to all of Sinclair Ross's books, one is still left after reading his essay, as one is after repeatedly reading the Sinclair Ross *oeuvre*, with the knowledge that, apart from a few of his early short stories, Ross wrote nothing afterwards even nearly equal to *As for Me and My House*. Perhaps one can find the reason for this inability to repeat an early triumph in Ross's removal from his Prairie background almost from the time his first novel was published. But such creative intermittencies are as mysterious as the creative process itself, of which Sinclair Ross himself wrote cagily and sensibly in the 1970 essay quoted by Morton Ross and entitled "On Looking Back," in which he refused to talk about his "sensibility and creative processes," arguing that:

> . . . artists themselves as well as psychologists seem pretty well agreed that the "creative sources" are in the subconscious, and the psychologists are also agreed that self-analysis can seldom do more than scrape the surface . . . . So if I don't understand myself — my "creative processes" if you like, why I did this and that — how could I possibly write about them?

From personal experience and from observing many writers who are my friends, I can only agree with Ross. The so-called artists who can explain their creative impulses are usually at best artificers. And this is why I welcome Morton Ross's attempt to restore a measure of respect for the artist's lack of deliberation in his discussion of the aspect of *As for Me and My House* that the academic critics have worn threadbare — the reliability and, indeed, the integrity of the narrator of the novel, Mrs. Bentley.

I enter on this subject with some caution, since the matter was brought into the open by two critics who are my friends and were indeed my associates in editing *Canadian Literature*, Donald Stephens and W.H. New. Donald Stephens rightly warned us against accepting Mrs. Bentley's narrative at face value; in doing so he was laying an emphasis on the subjectivity of point of view with which one cannot disagree. W.H. New entered a more perilous area by arguing, in Morton Ross's words, "that the deliberate aim of the novel is ambivalence" emerging (and here we use New's own words) "out of a carefully constructed web of viewpoints, Mrs. Bentley's and ours, pitted ironically against each other so that we come to appreciate not only the depth and complexity of the narrator and her situation, but also the control in which Ross artistically holds his words." To that I must answer, with the suspicion that I would have Sinclair Ross's support, that the "deliberation" which critics often attribute to writers exists usually only in the critic's mind, and that the "carefully constructed web of viewpoints" is more likely to be a clustering of intuitive insights that comes together in the writer's mind as he is actually working, often fully formed, and is probably only in a slight degree a product of the deliberating intelligence. Novels are not mathematical propositions. Rather than seeking the origins of Mrs. Bentley's ambivalences in artifice, I would suggest they are the products of a writer's naturally ironic sensibility operating in a situation given by the imagination. Those who see Ross as exposing Mrs. Bentley to our contempt are mistaken; he is rather developing out of his natural awareness of human psychology the ways in which the mind can combine clear perception with self-deception without being entirely aware of the distinction. In Mrs. Bentley as in all of us weaknesses and virtues are combined, and in the confusion of them — and the occasional perception of that confusion — lies the ironic structure of the novel — of which, despite her preoccupations with her husband Philip, she remains the centre.

Morton Ross's debate with Mrs. Bentley's denigrators helps us understand this.

In more than one way, Mitchell is the most divided if not exactly the most complex of the novelists studied here. He belongs in appearance to the "popular" comic tradition of Prairie writing as distinct from the "serious" tragic one, and the corpus of his writing shows that curious combination of the passing and the permanent that develops with any writer who has committed himself over a long period to turning out radio and television scripts which, because of their very form, are unpublishable and — except in an archival sense — perishable.

What is perhaps most impressive about Mitchell, and what Harrison admirably traces, is the way in which, despite his comic beginnings, despite his popularity as a radio and television writer, despite his folksy public personality, Mitchell found himself drawn into the mainstream of Prairie writing, and in doing so allowed the tragic intimations that were always present in his work to surface and become dominant. Perhaps more strikingly than any other example the transformation of W.O. Mitchell shows the unity of Prairie fiction as a tradition of its own within Canadian literature.

NOTES

[1] Northrop Frye, "Canadian Dreiser," *The Canadian Forum*, Sept. 1948, p. 121.

[2] Desmond Pacey, Introd., *Frederick Philip Grove*, ed. Desmond Pacey (Toronto: Ryerson, 1970) p. 1.

[3] Raymond Knister, "Frederick Philip Grove," *Ontario Library Review*, 13 (1928), 62.

[4] Margot Northey, *The Haunted Wilderness: The Gothic and Grotesque in Canadian Fiction* (Toronto: Univ. of Toronto Press, 1976), p. 62.

[5] Northey, p. 63.

[6] Northey, p. 65.

[7] Frederick Philip Grove, *Settlers of the Marsh*, New Canadian Library, No. 50 (Toronto: McClelland and Stewart, 1966), p. 166.

[8] Joy Kuropatwa, "Ostenso, Martha" in *The Oxford Companion to Canadian Literature*, ed. William Toye (Toronto: Oxford Univ. Press, 1983), p. 626.

*Frederick Philip Grove
and His Works*

Frederick Philip Grove (1879–1948)

W.J. KEITH

Biography

IN OCTOBER 1971 Douglas O. Spettigue made a discovery in the British Museum Library in London that rendered out of date all that we thought we knew about the life of the Canadian novelist Frederick Philip Grove. After subsequent research, which confirmed the original revelation, he was able to announce that "Frederick Philip Grove" was in fact an *alias*: that his real name was Felix Paul Greve; that his numerous autobiographical statements were either fabrications or at best rearrangements of actual experience; and that he had made a separate literary reputation in Germany (and led a dramatic, even notorious life there) before coming to North America in the early part of this century. This new information is fascinating in itself, but it also casts light (some might say, shadow) on his Canadian writings which, we now see more clearly, are invariably concerned with the relation between fact and truth, between what seems and what is, between the mask that an individual assumes in public and his real self.

Felix Paul Greve, as I shall call him while he used the name, was born on 14 February 1879 at Radomno in what was then East Prussia and is now Poland. His parents, both German, were from Mecklenburg, his father — at that time an estate-manager — coming from traditional farming stock, while his mother (*née* Reichentrog) was descended from a family of millers. By the time Felix was two, the Greves (there was an elder daughter, who apparently died young) had moved to Hamburg where the father worked first as a tram-conductor and later as a minor clerk in the city transportation system. This was far from the early life of wealth and comfort to which Grove laid claim in his supposed autobiography *In Search of Myself* and by implication in the opening chapter of *A Search for America*, where Phil Branden is described as "the young Croesus."[1] The parents' marriage broke up while Felix was in his early teens.

Graduating from a Hamburg technical school in 1896 and from a classical grammar school two years later, he enrolled in philology at Friedrich-Wilhelms University in Bonn in April 1898. Within a few weeks of his entering university, his mother died.

We know infuriatingly little about Greve's financial position from the time of his parents' separation, but it would always have been precarious. He must have got increasingly into debt as a university student since he had expensive tastes and attempted to move in literary and artistic circles that were far beyond his means. Intent upon pursuing a literary career, he aspired towards entering the neo-Romantic circle gathered around the poet Stefan George, and came under the influence of *fin-de-siècle* writing in general, especially that of Oscar Wilde and, a little later, André Gide. In 1902 he published a slim volume of poems entitled *Wanderungen*, and this was soon followed by a verse-drama and articles and pamphlets of literary criticism (notably on Wilde). But his attempt to live by his pen depended for the most part on a battery of translations over the next seven years, mainly from English, French, and Spanish authors but also including the *Arabian Nights* adapted from the English version. Yet Greve's surviving correspondence makes it clear that his literary earnings fell pitifully short of his financial needs.

Moreover, Greve was involved at this time in a liaison with Elsa, the wife of August Endell, an architect whom Greve mentioned as a friend in his correspondence. After Elsa eloped with Greve in 1902, the couple travelled in Italy and Sicily, growing even deeper in debt. For some years Greve had been borrowing considerable sums of money from a wealthy university friend, Herman Kilian, apparently with the assurance that he had means that could eventually be tapped. But Kilian ultimately lost patience and discovered that Greve was in no position to repay what he had borrowed. On his return to Bonn in 1903, Greve was arrested and sentenced to a year's imprisonment for fraud.

While in prison he continued to translate at a furious pace, often using pseudonyms in an endeavour to evade enforced terms of repayment (he claims, indeed, to have translated forty volumes at this time). Immediately on his release from prison, he obtained an interview with André Gide, from whose account we derive Greve's first concerted attempt to construct a fictional autobiography. Within the next few years, moreover, he attempted to make a name for himself as a writer of naturalistic fiction, two novels subsequently being published, *Fanny Essler* (1905) and *Maurermeister Ihles Haus* (1906). Meanwhile Elsa's marriage had been annulled in 1904, while Greve was still in prison. He announced to Gide their intention to marry, though whether they legally did so is not known.

The pressure soon became unbearable. Translations continued to roll from Greve's pen, but their declining quality led to criticism, and he could hardly have paid off all his debts, much less maintained or improved his hopeless financial position. At last, Greve and Elsa agreed to a separation, at least temporarily. After gaining some quick cash by selling the same translation to two different publishers, Greve boarded a ship to Sweden in September 1909 — and disappeared. The scanty evidence available suggests that he faked a suicide with Elsa's co-operation. Little definite is known of his life in the United States, though recently discovered evidence reveals that Elsa followed him there. In December 1912, after a final separation from her, he emerges as "Fred Grove" in Manitoba.[2]

When Frederick Philip Grove published *A Search for America* in 1927, it was generally regarded as veiled autobiography. Devious as ever, Grove described it later as "to a certain extent, fiction."[3] Whether the book is based even in part on the author's personal experience remains uncertain. Many of the North American scenes contain a vividness of detail that appears genuine; on the other hand, close examination reveals it as a decidedly artful book, highly structured and full of covert allusions to literary models. From evidence of his mode of life during the years 1909–12 he is virtually non-existent. All we have are vague rumours about another marriage in the United States and the possibility that he may have had prior experience as a teacher before coming to Canada. Since he probably travelled under another *alias* in the United States, the difficulties of tracing his movements at this time are considerable. What can be said is that *A Search for America* ends with Branden embarking on a teaching career in the Canadian west, and at this point fiction and biography merge.

In a 1944 letter to Desmond Pacey, in answer to biographical queries, Grove wrote: "From then on (i.e., after 1914) the years are as it were certified."[4] He means, of course, that an account of his life in Canada is readily open to verification or challenge from external sources. Certainly *In Search of Myself* becomes more accurate (and, be it said, less interesting) when Grove comes to his Canadian years. Exaggerations and anomalous details remain, but its broad lines can be accepted. Grove's teaching career lasted from January 1913 until June 1924. He married Catherine Wiens, a fellow-teacher from a Mennonite background, in 1914 and they taught in a variety of schools, sometimes together, sometimes separately. Grove began by putting enormous energy and enthusiasm into his teaching, but his overbearing manner tended to lead to conflicts with the local school boards, and in consequence the Groves rarely spent more than one year in the same place. The impression derived from these years is that of a talented, restless man who has not yet found his proper vocation.

Grove began writing seriously in English in October 1919, and from that time was determined to devote his main energies to literary work. The order of composition of his novels is still in dispute, but it is clear that he wrote fast and furiously during the 1920s. Both *Over Prairie Trails* (1922) and *The Turn of the Year* (1923) are non-fiction in form, but the attraction of fiction had been latent ever since his German years (he apparently began *Settlers of the Marsh* in German some time during World War 1[5]), and he finds his true medium with *Settlers of the Marsh* (1925) and *A Search for America* (1927). For a brief period at the end of the 1920s, the latter book made him a celebrity and he embarked on a number of lecture-tours across Canada. His main address, along with other articles, was published in *It Needs to Be Said* (1929).

A combination of circumstances frustrated Grove's burgeoning ambitions. First, a daughter born in 1915 died with tragic suddenness in 1927; this was a crushing blow to the Groves, only partly redeemed by the birth of a son in 1930. Then the Wall Street crash and the economic depression of the 1930s affected sales and opportunities, and an attempt to find more congenial employment in the publishing industry failed in 1931. The same year, the Groves moved to Simcoe, Ontario, close to the shores of Lake Erie, where Grove dabbled with indifferent success in farming and his wife provided a modest degree of financial security through teaching. Grove continued to write and publish, but his work failed to attract the attention that it deserved. In 1942 he even made a brief foray into politics, standing unsuccessfully as CCF candidate at a provincial election.[6]

In these later years, however, literary honours began to come his way. In 1934 he had been awarded the Lorne Pierce Gold Medal by the Royal Society of Canada, and he was elected Fellow of the Society in 1941. An honorary degree was conferred upon him by the University of Manitoba in 1946, and in the same year *In Search of Myself* was published and won the Governor-General's Award for non-fiction. (Given the fictional nature of much of the book, and the official neglect of his novels, Grove must have relished the multiple ironies in the situation.) But he was by then a sick man. He had suffered a stroke in 1944 and was an invalid thereafter. He died on 19 August 1948 and was buried in Rapid City, Manitoba, where his daughter had been laid to rest twenty-one years before.[7]

⋈ Tradition and Milieu

There can be no doubt that Grove's German origins contributed in large measure to his anomalous position as a Canadian writer. He arrived in Canada not only as a mature adult but with the literary experience of an established author. *A Search for America* implies, however, that this was by no means an unmixed blessing; a recurrent theme in that book is the idea that education in the old world can be more of a liability than an asset in the new. While he could claim a broader intellectual perspective than most Canadian-born writers of his time, he also brought with him certain non-Canadian preconceptions not easily grafted on to a native stock (Margaret Stobie has offered his emphasis on patriarchy in the prairies as an example[8]). But his contribution could also be positive. Instead of the standard classical education of, say, the "Confederation Poets," Grove enjoyed a deeper understanding of the whole European tradition; instead of an America-based, contemporary-oriented narrowness of attitude, he brought a consciousness personally aware of the artistic achievements and experiments of continental Europe, a familiarity with other literary movements, an openness to new creative possibilities.

At the same time, his delicate position as a fugitive from the ruins of his old life set him apart. He may have come to the new world with previous literary experience but circumstances prevented him from admitting this fact. He intended to begin a new life, both personal and artistic, and he could not afford to display too obviously the traces of his earlier years as a man of letters. Above all, his knowledge of Europe was balanced by a corresponding ignorance about North America, and, whatever its percentages of truth and falsehood may be, *A Search for America* presents within the form of imaginative allegory a fascinating account of his *odi-et-amo* relationship with the continent in which he had decided to settle. The book is packed full of ironies, not the least of which is the implication that the real America for which Phil Branden is in search, beneath the surface of "graft, 'con,' politics, and bossdom" (*SA*, p. 315), is the embodiment of an essentially European tradition that Grove had been unable to discover in Europe itself.

The story of Phil Branden represents a conversion from a materialist to a spiritual way of life — in Grove's own words, "the movement away from the accidentals of life and towards the essentials" (*SA*, p. 248). It seems clear that Greve/Grove's debacle in Germany was a traumatic experience that impelled him into rethinking his moral attitudes and dedicating the rest of his life to higher principles. His well-known definition of the tragic in *It Needs to Be Said* takes on new meaning and a new poignancy when considered in the light of his painful transformation from Felix Paul Greve into Frederick Philip Grove: "To have greatly tried and to have failed; to have greatly wished and to be denied; to have greatly longed for purity and to be sullied; to have greatly craved for life and to receive death: all that is the common lot of greatness upon earth."[9] Although offered as a generalized statement, these remarks also constitute an intensely personal confession. Greve/Grove had failed and been sullied in Europe yet, coming to North America to make a new start, he still yearned for success in old-world terms.

Phil Branden's association with the criminal and illegal in the first two books of *A Search for America* may now be read as temptation towards a repetition of Greve's earlier transgressions; to resist this temptation Branden had to resist the materialist emphasis in American life that Grove recognized as a betrayal of the best in the European tradition, all the more so since it was materialist ambition that had led to his European downfall. But the American ideal continually eluded both Branden and Grove. Despite Branden's assertions about the significant differences between Europe and America — that European civilization is based upon original sin while America assumes "that the average American is honest," that "Europe regards the past [whereas] America regards the future" (*SA*, pp. 431, 436) — the America for which Branden and Grove are in search is essentially traditional. This is made explicit in *It Needs to Be Said* where Grove claims that in people living in certain districts of western Canada he "discovered a continuation of this old European tradition, as distinguished from the new-born American tradition which has not yet found its way to the fundamentals" (*INBS*, p. 157). Hence his impassioned appeal to the Canadian people to maintain its connection with "that older, grey-haired, yet fiery-hearted tradition of Britain" (which he defines as "itself part of the great European tradition"), rather than associating with "that glaringly new and purely material civilization of our neighbours to the south" (*INBS*, pp. 18, 144).

Europe, he believed, "still stands for the devotion to the so-called higher things of life" (*INBS*, p. 155), and this is implicit in *A Search for America*. When Branden leaves New York to explore the real America in the west, he takes with him a New Testament and a Greek *Odyssey* representing the two great intellectual and religious streams (Matthew Arnold's "Hebraism and Hellenism") which nurtured European civilization. We may compare this symbolic detail with the case for the European artistic tradition that Grove offers in *It Needs to Be Said* —

> that, being born from a blending of the greatest artistic urge which the world has seen, that of Greece, with the greatest religious urge which the world has seen, that of Judah, its aim is still that of a final evaluation of life; of a recognition of man's true place in nature; of a determination of the balance, so far attained, between man's beasthood and man's godhead. (*INBS*, p. 5)

This three-fold subject, discussed again and again in Grove's non-fiction writings, becomes an overriding preoccupation — the king-pin, one might say — of his fiction. Elsewhere Europe is described as representing "the fundamentally human tradition which looks at life with a fanatical, and almost Biblical seriousness even when it smiles or jests" (*INBS*, p. 156). Clearly, for good or ill, this is the tradition to which Grove's own work belongs. The creative tension (as well as some of the awkwardnesses) within his writings derives from the conflicting pulls of Europe and America which he found within himself and also, albeit in somewhat different form, within the Canadian people.

Perhaps his greatest strength as a writer in Canada during the early years of this century lay in his experience of a multiplicity of literary and intellectual movements. The translator of Balzac, Cervantes, Dumas, Flaubert, Gide, and Lesage (to name only non-English fictionists), who shows in his work a firm grounding in the Classical writers of Greece and Rome as well as a close acquaintance with, among others, Rousseau, Goethe, Baudelaire, and Tolstoy, and who freely discusses the philosophies of Plato, Nietzsche, and Bergson in his letters, can clearly draw upon a wide range of European art and thought. On the other hand, his interest in the work of his contemporaries seems limited. References in his letters to a belated study of the work of D.H. Lawrence, decidedly perfunctory allusions to Eliot and Joyce, his notorious neglect of contemporary American writing, suggest that his renunciation of his earlier literary life resulted in an impoverishing withdrawal. Part of this is explained, of course, by the inevitable circumstances of his situation in Canada. For years he was isolated from well-stocked libraries and could not afford to own many books himself. Since he was forced to rely on loans of books from friends, notably Watson Kirkconnell and Richard Crouch, his later reading tends to be spotty. His letters possibly exaggerate the comprehensiveness of his knowledge (one detects a propensity for name-dropping from time to time); nevertheless, even after all due allowances have been made, his learning and reading remain impressive and set him far ahead of his Canadian fiction-writing contemporaries.

Grove's situation, then, was unprecedented. In Canada, particularly in the west where the impact of European immigrants had been strongest, he discovered some of the ideals and spiritual rigour that he admired in Europe. But what he had to offer seemed alien to most of those who might have learned from him. They saw his example as leading back to a sterile imitativeness, a dependence upon old-world models they felt they had outgrown. In his own lifetime he was important as living proof that work of sustained power and intellectual substance could be produced in Canada. But Grove's way was too personal, too single-minded to be of much immediate assistance to others. However, his general position, unpopular at a time of "shallow optimism" (*INBS*, p. 153), appears more acceptable today. To many Canadian readers of the 1990s, his message, particularly his suspicion of the cultural and economic influence of the United States expressed in "Nationhood" (*INBS*, pp. 133–63), seems more urgent and more shrewd than it did half a century ago. It is therefore appropriate that a prominent contemporary novelist has acknowledged a practical debt to Grove, though the fact that Rudy Wiebe is a German-speaking son of immigrant prairie-settlers with a strong European heritage is not coincidental. What Grove has been able to offer Wiebe is support for the seriousness of the novelist's art, an example of ambitious aims and strong-minded heroes, and valuable hints towards the structuring of Wiebe's own imaginative creations.[10] Certainly Grove's virtues now appear decidedly more significant than his faults. He remains a lonely, aloof, austere figure, seemingly unapproachable, sometimes infuriating, but, whatever reservations we may have, he is the first Canadian novelist to attain classic status.

Critical Overview

In "Literary Criticism," one of the addresses collected in *It Needs to Be Said*, Grove asserted: "The critic is necessary, he is indispensable to the author because without him, barring fortunate accidents, that author speaks into a void, he does not even know to whose capacity to adjust his utterance" (*INBS*, p. 37). He was later to write, however, of "the utterly hopeless ineptitude prevailing in what is commonly called literary criticism in Canada" (*ISM*, p. 407). Given Grove's situation, it is easy to understand why he felt the need for a mature criticism. Because he was addressing an audience totally different from that to which his now unacknowledged work in Germany had been addressed, he was in special need of guidance. Nonetheless, even if literary criticism in Canada in the 1920s and 1930s had been in a more advanced state than it was, his particular circumstances rendered such help virtually impossible, since commentators were inhibited by the smokescreen of mystery that Grove set up between his work and the early experiences of the man who wrote it. Much of the richness of effect in *A Search for America*, for instance, depends upon an awareness of the ironic tensions between the story of Phil Branden and the carefully created authorial mask of "Frederick Philip Grove." Grove could hardly blame the reviewers and critics for failing to pick up clues that he had deliberately concealed.

At the same time, the contemporary reviews of his work make depressing reading. Most of them were either descriptive, perfunctory, or (especially in the case of non-Canadian reviews) condescending. They usually emphasized his "realism," and often found it uncongenial. Criticism was, for the most part, of an elementary sort, full of blanket-judgements about "character" or "style" with generalizations about his "philosophy." But, despite Grove's later self-encouraged myth of himself as representative of the neglected artist, they were by no means negative. His statement in *In Search of Myself* that the publication of *Settlers of the Marsh* "became a public scandal" (*ISM*, p. 381) overlooks the fact that the majority of the reviews of that novel were decidedly positive. While some reviewing-space was taken up by those who were shocked, much more was appropriated by defenders shocked at those who were shocked. From the start, Grove enjoyed the attention of regular, influential reviewers (notably W.A. Deacon and S. Morgan-Powell, to be joined later by Carleton Stanley) who recognized his importance and did their best to gain him a hearing. But inevitably, under the circumstances, their work was given over to popularization rather than to thoughtful and discriminating criticism.[11]

As far as academic scholarship is concerned, a clear dividing-line may be discerned between what can now be called the "innocent" literary commentary on Grove's work up to the late 1960s and subsequent criticism written after Spettigue's discoveries became known. Early discussion was hampered by what we now recognize as a naïve acceptance of Grove's biographical statements. Desmond Pacey deserves considerable credit for being the first scholar to write, and succeed in publishing, a full-length critical study, *Frederick Philip Grove* (1945). Unfortunately, however, he relied upon a manuscript version of Grove's not-yet-published autobiography and, apart from using a few phrases like "incredible as it may seem," he apparently accepted it without question. The opening biographical chapters are therefore hopelessly inadequate, but the discussions of individual works are also weakened since Pacey took over Grove's early dating of his work along with all his other "facts." As a result, Pacey claims Grove as a neglected literary innovator in a way that can no longer be accepted. For the most part, then, Pacey's book has not stood the test of time, though we should not fail to acknowledge its usefulness in insisting upon Grove's importance within the context of Canadian literature.

Much the same has to be said about Wilfrid Eggleston's chapter in Claude Bissell's *Our Living Tradition* (1957) and Ronald Sutherland's pamphlet in the New Canadian Library literary-critical series (1969). Although Eggleston had some suspicions about Grove's early years long before Spettigue began his researches, he refrained from active investigation out of deference to the feelings of Mrs. Grove.[12] The article ignores Grove's origins, and never mentions *In Search of Myself* by name though short passages are quoted. The accounts of the novels rely heavily on second-hand opinions. Sutherland's pamphlet retells Grove's own account of his life (though subsequent reprints revise the text to indicate doubts), and discusses individual books cogently but at a rather elementary level.

Douglas O. Spettigue's first book on Grove, in the Copp Clark "Studies in Canadian Writers" series (1969), though superseded to a considerable extent by his later discoveries, represents an important break-through. Here Spettigue does not yet know about Felix Paul Greve, but he submits Grove's own versions of autobiography to rigorous examination and finds them wanting. Much still remained a mystery, but Spettigue was able to prove that Grove was an inventor in his supposedly non-fiction writings, and this enabled him to approach the novels with a much greater appreciation of their creative qualities. He was also the first to make full use of Grove's unpublished materials which had been acquired by the University of Manitoba in 1962. As a result, his consideration of Grove's writings takes on a new dimension; for the first time Grove is seriously discussed as an important imaginative writer who deserves scholarly and sustained analysis.

Spettigue's subsequent identification of Grove as Felix Paul Greve (first announced in a brief report in *Queen's Quarterly* in 1972) not only opened up a new hoard of Grove material but produced the much-needed publicity and sense of academic excitement requisite to stimulate further research. The initial interest, of course, was biographical. Spettigue's fully argued case for the identification, *FPG: The European Years*, appeared in September 1973, a few months after Margaret R. Stobie's study in the Twayne series, *Frederick Philip Grove*, which provides easily the best biographical account of the Canadian years to date. But the excitement had other results. As early as 1963 Bruce Nesbitt had written of Grove's unfinished and unpublished novel-saga, "The Seasons," and further accounts of manuscript material soon followed. The University of Ottawa's Grove symposium in May 1973 (the occasion when the Grove-Greve connection was first openly discussed among scholars) contained no less than four papers on unpublished material, and a number of others have appeared since. Long before Spettigue's discoveries were made, Desmond Pacey, who published an important collection of Grove's short stories, *Tales from the Margin*, in 1971, had begun work on his edition of Grove's letters which eventually appeared (a few months after his own death) early in 1976. But all this scholarly activity has sparked off literary-critical responses as well. Perhaps the most substantial argument for a reconsideration of Grove's fictional artistry is to be found in a series of scattered articles by the present writer each devoted to a single text.

The revelations about Grove's life provided an unusually rich harvest of critical commentary in the 1970s and early 1980s. These items are too numerous to discuss here, but include Patricia Morley's study of *Over Prairie Trails*, Henry Makow's essay on *The Yoke of Life*, treatments of *The Master of the Mill* by R.D. Macdonald and Beverley Mitchell, and Margaret Stobie's analysis of *Consider Her Ways*. Other critical approaches have also proved fruitful. Laurence Ricou relates Grove's work to the whole context of prairie fiction in the appropriate chapter in *Vertical Man / Horizontal World*, D.J. Dooley offers a stimulating challenge to Grove's moral thought in a chapter on *Fruits of the Earth* in *Moral Vision in the Canadian Novel*, while Enn Raudsepp has initiated a more psychoanalytical probing of the relation between Grove as "pathological liar" and his literary creations in an article in *Canadian Literature*. More recently, *A Stranger to My Time*, Paul Hjartarson's edition of essays by and about Grove, is especially important for its revelations about the Greve-Elsa relationship in America, and for its publication of some hitherto unavailable Grove material, including a diary from the 1930s.

Grove criticism and scholarship, then, is in a tantalizing, if still fairly rudimentary state. His own secretiveness inhibited early research, and we have not yet had time to absorb fully the implications of the recent discoveries. Nonetheless, the lines of Grove's development now seem much clearer than they did before the early 1970s. Spettigue's discoveries have revealed him as a decidedly complex figure, and an equivalent complexity is readily visible in his writings. It is Grove's constantly evolving artistic procedures, his capacity to ring changes on various major themes in his novels, and his systematic use of fictional form to investigate the challenges and frustrations of life that I wish to explore in the following pages.

Grove's Works

Any attempt to deal comprehensively with Grove's writings at the present time inevitably encounters two stumbling-blocks. First, most of Felix Paul Greve's German work (with the exception of the two novels) is inaccessible to all save the most persistent and widely travelled; moreover, some of it, though believed to exist or to have existed, has not yet been tracked down. Second, a significant percentage of his Canadian writing remains unpublished — in several cases, indeed, either unfinished or not of a standard to justify publication. Most of this material is in the Grove Collection at the University of Manitoba, and once again is only available to specialists. The plain fact is that no one (not even Professor Spettigue) can yet see Grove whole. Since my space is limited, I shall confine my attention here, except for some brief asides, to the work that is both widely known and readily obtainable.

Greve's two published German novels, *Fanny Essler* (1905) and *Maurermeister Ihles Haus* (1906), had long sunk into oblivion, and would never have been translated into English if Frederick Philip Grove had not written his later novels in Canada and Spettigue's discoveries had not created an academic interest in Felix Paul Greve's work. We are invited to read them, then, not so much for themselves as for the light they shed on the author's own life and on his subsequent writings. This is especially true of *Fanny Essler*, an episodic novel in the standard Naturalistic style that follows the fortunes of its petit-bourgeois heroine from the night on which she takes (or is taken by) her first lover to the moment in which her death saves her from "the greatest disappointment of her life" — disillusionment with the last of her many lovers. She is an engaging if somewhat silly figure (in some respects, a cut-rate Emma Bovary), but the excessively detailed descriptions of her environment and Greve's earnest probing into her psychology never quite blend. The novel is fascinating for the hidden clues it may offer to Greve's early life and contacts (much of the detail is known to be based on Elsa's early life), but as a work of art it proves uneven, frustrating, and sometimes tedious.

On the other hand, the shorter and better controlled *Maurermeister Ihles Haus* (translated as *The Master Mason's House*), may be accepted as a modest but definite achievement in itself and deserves consideration on its own merits. Like *Fanny Essler*, it is a representative though rather late example of the German Naturalist novel. But it manages to portray in convincing but less exhaustive and exhausting detail a slice of bourgeois life in Pomerania in the last two decades of the nineteenth century. Told from the viewpoint (but not in the words) of the rebellious elder daughter, Susie Ihle, it records the fortunes of a master mason's family by means of a series of tableau-scenes rather than as a continuing narrative — what a contemporary reviewer described as "a series of photographic pictures held together through the consistency of the characters presented."[3] Though the text is divided symmetrically into three parts each containing three chapters, there is no step-by-step plot. Nothing extraordinary happens: the father is petty and tyrannical, the first wife cowed and increasingly unbalanced; she eventually goes mad and dies, and the father marries again; the two daughters grow up and become engaged. It is not so much a story as an impressionistic chronicle. We are given genre-paintings in words — a typical day in a girls' high school, family preparations for Christmas, a local ball — and these are offered as a representative selection rather than as a progressing sequence.

The individual scenes range from the amusing through the touching to the grotesque, but Greve presents a drab picture of a basically drab life. Indeed, he seems to be documenting a pervasive paralysis similar to that which James Joyce was brilliantly evoking at about the same time in *Dubliners*. Yet in saying that, one immediately senses the difference between major and minor art. Greve's work lacks the verbal precision and economy, the fastidious selection of the exactly right detail, that enables Joyce to find a paradoxical depth in the superficial ordinariness of his material. Similarly, there is none of the social range, the ambitious vitality, the sense of comprehensive amplitude that made Thomas Mann's *Buddenbrooks*, which had appeared five years earlier, an artistic triumph escaping the limitations of its realistic-naturalistic origins. *The Master Mason's House* is more conventional, sticking closer to the pattern of traditional Naturalism. Yet a consistent Naturalism may become self-defeating; when Greve presents scenes of domestic trivia, for instance, he runs the risk of becoming trivial himself. Nonetheless, there is a distinct assurance about the book that is impressive; we feel that the author has learned his craft.

It is natural, however, that we should read the book in search of clues to the mystery of Felix Paul Greve. But here, as elsewhere, Greve/Grove could have said: "I believe I have hidden myself fairly well" (*ISM*, p. 383). Individual details prove as frustrating as they are intriguing: a reference to "Reverend Greve" on the second page appears to be no more than a private joke since he is never mentioned again; a family called Kilian plays a small part in the book but has no discernible connection with the friend of that name who had been responsible for having Greve arrested and imprisoned three years earlier. More generally, the Pomeranian setting is of interest as the area where Greve's parents lived between 1876 and 1878, but there is no record of Felix Paul ever having lived there. However, it has recently been established that Elsa Endell, the girl who eloped with Greve in 1902 and with whom he lived during his post-prison years in Germany and later in the United States, was not only from Pomerania but the daughter of a master mason.[14] *The Master Mason's House* may therefore be based on her experiences and memories rather than Greve's. Indeed, since little is known of their movements between Greve's release from prison in 1904 and the publication of the novel, it seems possible (even, perhaps, likely) that they paid an extended visit to Elsa's native province at that time.

Viewed in relation to the later Canadian fiction, *The Master Mason's House* has much to offer in terms of both comparison and contrast. Spettigue has noted Grove's attraction to the chronicle-form, and the presentation of a family — especially the break-up of a family — over an extended period of time is a recurrent feature of his work. The relation between Ihle and his wife may be compared with similar situations in the Canadian novels, while Mrs. Ihle's grotesque behaviour after the ball (Book II, Chapter iii) connects not only with the account, whether factual or invented, of his mother in *In Search of Myself* (Part I, Section 2) but with the story of the dying Mrs. Elliot in *Our Daily Bread* (Book I, Chapter vi). In each case, neurotic behaviour when close to death is presented as the correlative of a life of emotional frustration. Other fairly obvious connections are thematic — the money-consciousness, the tension between generations, the unfulfilled and yearning women, the concern for regional specificity.

The inconsequential ending to the book can also be parallelled in Grove's later fiction. After her father's second marriage, Susie finds that she has no alternative but to marry Consul Blume, whom she does not love. This is at one with Grove's sense of the individual's helplessness in the face of the combined tyrannies of nature and human society. But in leaving Susie in the process of telling Blume that she accepts him, Greve produces a complex and perhaps deliberately unsatisfying effect: a variant of the conventional "happy ending"[15] which promises to be anything but happy to the protagonist, an ending that is no ending, the close of a phase without any

35

resolution of the tensions that generate the fictional interest. Commentators on Grove's Canadian novels frequently complain of endings that are either hurried (*A Search for America*) or anticlimactic (*Settlers of the Marsh, Fruits of the Earth*) or frustratingly ambiguous (*The Master of the Mill*). Such endings are clearly deliberate but they suggest that Grove was troubled by the incongruity of offering a clear-cut resolution to a novel written in a stringently realistic mode. The conclusion of *The Master Mason's House* is at one with his artistic principles at the time of writing, and traces of his naturalistic apprenticeship remain in his subsequent preference for "open" endings.

It is not difficult, then, to find points of similarity with the later fiction, but the differences are ultimately more striking. Most obvious (and on the credit side for this novel) is the variety and ease of female characterization. Here the women are more interesting and more subtly drawn than the men, and this contrasts oddly with the situation in the Canadian books. However, what is lacking in the world of this novel, and especially in Ihle himself, is a creative sense of purpose. In their introduction A.W. Riley and Douglas O. Spettigue maintain that "Richard Ihle is only the first of FPG's defeated strong men,"[16] but it is surely inadequate to see him as an early manifestation of Niels Lindstedt or Abe Spalding or Ralph Patterson. Ihle is defeated by a vulgar and domineering second wife rather than by nature and his environment; moreover, he is a tyrant with no compensating "vision." In the terms of Grove's later definition of "the tragic," already quoted, Ihle has "failed" but has not "greatly tried." The dynamism inherent in a vigorous if doomed attempt to create a world is absent here, and the lack points up the intellectual superiority of Grove's later work.

And here an interesting connection can be established between Grove's new start in North America and his renunciation of Naturalism. In his lecture, "Realism in Literature," Grove emphasizes the concern of Zola and the naturalistic movement to introduce scientific experimentation into literary work. He specifically dissociates himself from Zola, whom he sees as relating only to pseudo-science, but accepts Realism when defined as "the endeavour to reproduce nature or to describe real life just as it appears to the artist" (*INBS*, p. 59). The last phrase, of course, is crucial. Grove insists that the artist remain omnipresent in his work, though he agrees that his "vision" must be conveyed indirectly. In *The Master Mason's House*, as we have seen, personal and therefore moral judgement is suppressed. I believe that Grove came to associate the naturalistic approach with his own disgrace in Germany and determined, when creating a new literary reputation in North America, to practise a literary method firmly grounded in moral vision.

Given the nature of Felix Paul Greve's literary career, we may initially be surprised that Frederick Philip Grove's first published works in Canada, *Over Prairie Trails* and *The Turn of the Year*, belong to the category of non-fiction. But two factors need to be considered. First, Grove had suddenly found himself in a new country and a very different culture. Since he defined art — not only the novel but all art — as "that activity of the human mind and soul which awakens and directs an emotional response to what is not I" (*INBS*, p. 84), it was essential that he should make himself intimately acquainted with his new non-human environment. If he were to write fiction in Canada, he desperately needed a context within which to set his characters. In *In Search of Myself* he tells a story of being taken to see the schoolhouse at "Plymouth" (Falmouth, Manitoba) and excitedly recognizing in the local countryside "the landscape in which Niels Lindstedt had lived; Len Sterner; Mrs. Lund; and many other creatures of my brain" (*ISM*, p. 299). We need not accept his assertion that the novels had been planned (much less written) earlier, but the importance of his mastering the background for future stories cannot be gainsaid.

The second factor involves the whole complex relation between fiction and non-fiction in Grove's work. According to his own account, *Over Prairie Trails* consists of a selection of seven out of a total of seventy-two solitary journeys by buggy or cutter between Gladstone and Falmouth undertaken during the winter of 1917–18 when Grove and his wife were teaching in different schools. The basic facts can be accepted (though thirty-six journeys each way may be a characteristic exaggeration), but we need not assume that the adventures he recounts occurred in the precise order and form that he describes. The book can now be approached more rewardingly as a deliberate work of art — not fiction but structured, reorganized experience. It is not so much a memoir as an imaginative recreation offering essential truth rather than prosaic fact.

At the same time, both books reflect a passionate interest in natural history, in recording the minutest details of the visible scene. More specifically, they belong to the tradition of Thoreau and John

Burroughs, both of whom are frequently mentioned by Grove during this period. Like Thoreau he is "self-appointed inspector of snowstorms"; like Burroughs he appears to have been "born with a chronic anxiety about the weather."[17] Man against the elements, man in relation to his environment, I and what is not I: these are the basic concerns explored in the novels and they are explored here in non-fiction form. *Over Prairie Trails*, for instance, recounts journeys in thick fog, over virtually impassable snow-drifts, against dangerous winds and beneath the staggering beauty of the night-sky. But they are also journeys undertaken in mental states of intellectual curiosity, expectant high spirits, personal anguish and shattered nerves; the I changes as bewilderingly as the landscape.

Over Prairie Trails might best be described as a series of tone-poems communicated in a variety of styles, each appropriate to the mood of the individual incident. They continually tremble on the verge of fictional narrative. On the first journey, for example, Grove imagines the inhabitants of the farms and settlements that he passes, thus playing the part of an embryo novelist. Of one, which he calls the White Range Line House, he comments, "There hangs a story by this house. Maybe I shall one day tell it . . . ,"[18] evidence that, at the time of writing, *Settlers of the Marsh* was at least in the planning process. On a later trip he claims to have passed the body of a man frozen in his carriage, an image later to be developed in his best-known short story, "Snow." Thus what might be expected to prove repetitious — a succession of descriptions of the same terrain — becomes instead an artistic *tour de force*, a demonstration of creative versatility. A writer who can succeed in this self-imposed challenge is capable, we feel, of creating the appropriate (as well as accurate) background for any prairie story that he wishes to tell.

The Turn of the Year is looser in structure, consisting of a series of descriptive sketches in which personal impressions and fancies rub shoulders somewhat uncomfortably with a rather dry scientific-textbook prose. But these accounts of land and weather are interspersed with a number of sections involving human portraiture: "The Sower," "Harvest" (containing a companion figure), and three seasonal vignettes representing an idealized version of prairie settlement. Here we encounter Grove's first attempt to populate his newly-found Canadian landscape with human beings other than himself. The story of the sower, indeed, becomes a paradigm of Grove's later fiction. He is an Icelandic immigrant with a religious devotion to the land; but his wife and children are seduced by the "shallow ease"[9] of city life, reject his "vision" and ultimately desert him (his son eventually becomes a garage mechanic, anticipating the pattern of Norman Elliot in *Our Daily Bread* and Jim Spalding in *Fruits of the Earth*). Grove both sums up and articulates his philosophy: "This country is the granary of a world. To put it to that use for which it was meant is serving God" (*TV*, p. 64). Despite a touch of sentimentality, due perhaps to over-concentration, the sketch is effective in a raw sort of way and central to Grove's later development.

In all these sections — and the same can be said for many of Grove's fictional characters — the figures are less individuals than emblems. Thus the harvester is "the incarnation of all that is fine and noble in bodily labour" (*TV*, p. 210), a remark later applied to Ivan in *A Search for America* (p. 399). Ivan is so named because he reminds the narrator of a character in Tolstoy's *Anna Karenina*, and one of the pastoral vignettes here, in which John and Ellen work together to pitch and spread hay (*TV*, p. 117), is clearly modelled on a scene from the same novel (Book III, Chapter ii). This curious mixture of personal observation and literary allusion becomes a dominant mode of discourse in *A Search for America*.

In both *Over Prairie Trails* and *The Turn of the Year*, then, we discover distinct intimations of the later novels. In the former, the emphasis on action and achievement is characteristic; it is significant, however, that on the last ride Grove fails to complete his journey on the day on which he set out; instead, he is forced to beg shelter for the night before continuing in the morning. It is a comparatively minor defeat, but it reminds us, like all Grove's work, that man's aspirations are inevitably doomed to failure. Similarly, in *The Turn of the Year*, the sower's homestead is decaying around him, and we experience a faint foretaste of the fate of John Elliot, Sr., at the close of *Our Daily Bread*. The three vignettes involving John and Ellen link seasonal change to human aging and document the relentless passing of time which is a conspicuous feature of Grove's fiction, while the seasonal structure of the whole moves characteristically from the end of one winter to the beginning of another. Together the two books, though achievements in their own right (many commentators consider *Over Prairie Trails* his finest work), represent the successfully completed apprenticeship of the Canadian Grove.

Although *Settlers of the Marsh* (1925) was the next book to be published, it is convenient to consider *A Search for America* (1927) at this point. Grove now brings together the physical quest-journey that dominates *Over Prairie Trails* with the symbolic human figures and meaningful vignettes of *The Turn of the Year*. Moreover, we encounter here the first beginnings in his writings in English of Grove's myth concerning his earlier years that was later to be elaborated in the similarly titled *In Search of Myself*. Phil Branden is the leading character in a series of picaresque adventures that involve both allegory and social satire (we may recall at this point that Felix Paul Greve had been the translator of both *Don Quixote* and *Gil Blas*). Born into a life of wealth, culture and extensive travel, he is suddenly told that his father's fortune has come to an end; he thereupon sails to America to make his own way.

His subsequent adventures, absorbing in themselves, become even more rewarding when read with a knowledge of Grove's own story and his "lifetime of disguise" (*SA*, p. 8), to quote Branden on his father. He begins work as a busboy and waiter in a Toronto restaurant, and makes friends with a fellow-waiter named Frank who is eventually shown to be anything but frank. They have a conversation about "assuming a false name" and reference is made to "fraud" (*SA*, p. 89). Moving to New York, Branden is immediately involved in a confidence-trick and temporarily detained by the police. A later job as book salesman introduces him to a society of people who are not what they seem and, later still, to another form of confidence-trick: the selling of phony limited editions to rich collectors. Over the whole of the first two books (appropriately entitled "The Descent" and "The Relapse") hangs the aura of crime and deceit.

So far Branden's experience has been centred on Eastern cities. Believing, however, that the "real America was somewhere else" (*SA*, p. 163), he now heads towards the agricultural West. But, far from divesting his hero of sophisticated artifice and having him embrace the honest reality of active farm life, Grove presents Branden in a series of encounters that depend upon a wide range of literary antecedents. As Margaret Stobie was the first to point out, his meeting with the old couple who have lost their son (Book III, Chapter i) is modelled on Ovid's story of Baucis and Philemon in the *Metamorphoses*.[20] Later he constructs a raft and not only sails down a river in *Huckleberry Finn* fashion but meets a hermit with the face of Mark Twain. After a number of other parabolic adventures with sociopolitical overtones, he is literally railroaded to the West when an empty box-car in which he is sleeping is attached to a train and set off on its journey (commentators who claim that Grove had no humour should ponder the implications of this scene). There he becomes a hobo defined as "a coarser and de-sublimated Henry David Thoreau" (SA, p. 368) and meets the mentor who resembles Jesus, reminds him of a character in Anna Karenina, and conjures up the whole Tolstoyan mystique of rural labour. Few books with a reputation for thinly-veiled autobiography can be so dependent on literary allusion.

In the course of this long and varied narrative Branden is, in his own words, "cross-sectioning the life of a nation" (SA, pp. 248) and the book culminates in a discussion on the nature and politics of America with the owner of a vast bonanza-farm in his home appropriately named the White House. The subtitle of the book is "The Odyssey of an Immigrant" and by the end Branden's experience has "widened out . . . into the experience of a whole class of immigrants" (SA, pp. 439–40). He decides that his destiny is as a teacher of immigrants who will help them "build these partial views of America into total views" (SA, p. 448). But this destiny leads him into the area where human beings are still clearing and settling land. The American West has, he decides, become materialized, but he sees his "promised land" (grasping at allusion as always, Branden himself uses the Mosaic phrase [SA, p. 448]) in Canada.

A Search for America, prefaced from the fourth edition onwards by a characteristically elusive statement about the relation of fiction to fact and truth, is a rich gathering of Grove's major preoccupations. It is, first, a searching analysis of the subject seeing as well as the object seen; Grove/Branden asks not only, What is America?, but also, Who am I who go in search of America? The contrast between the relative values of old world and new is never far below the surface. The book represents a desperate attempt on Grove's part to accept the American democratic ideal while at the same time remaining true to his European faith in the superiority of "the man with vision" (SA, p. 76). In his own way, in moving from Europe to America, Branden is a pioneer but, to adapt a title of one of his later unfinished novel-cycles, he is very much a latter-day pioneer. One of his revelations, which provides the impetus for the prairie novels, is of "the town working for the country: the farmer . . . the real master of the world who would one day come into his own" (SA, p. 356).

Yet his journey to the West, and then from the United States to Canada, becomes a flight from increasing industrialism and urbanization. His later farm-heroes share the agricultural vision but are prevented from achieving it, and henceforward this becomes Grove's main theme. *A Search for America*, then, chronicles the experience of the man who by the close of the book is in a position to write the novels of the Canadian West.

With *Settlers of the Marsh* (1925) Grove initiates the full-scale fictional exploration of the immigrants, pioneers and farmers of the Canadian West that he was to describe, in his "Author's Note" to *Fruits of the Earth*, as "my (still largely unpublished) Prairie Series." Through a sequence of often interlinked novels and short stories, both published and unpublished, he attempts a *tragédie humaine* based upon his already-quoted personal definition of Realism: the presentation of real life as it appears to the artist. The advance in scope and creative ambition is considerable, but at the same time the work evolves through a kind of natural logic from his earlier writings. Thematic inter-relation is here more important than date of composition or publication, so I shall therefore discuss *Settlers of the Marsh* and *The Yoke of Life* (1930) together, two novels involving young protagonists that have been classified by Henry Makow, along with an unpublished work, "The Canyon," as Grove's " 'Platonic' tragedies."[21]

A first reading of *Settlers of the Marsh* is likely to reveal the realism before the Platonism. The novel opens with two Scandinavian immigrants making their way on foot not only "over prairie trails" but in the identical landscape, the Big Marsh country, that Grove had described so minutely and imaginatively in his first Canadian book. The emphasis from the start is on the pioneer's struggle with both the elements and the land; the detailed meteorological observations central to both *Over Prairie Trails* and *The Turn of the Year* now become subservient to Grove's fictional purpose, most dramatically in the wind and snow of the opening pages and the crucial scene in which an inner crisis involving Niels Lindstedt and Ellen Amundsen is played out, crudely but effectively, against a violent prairie storm (Chapter iii). The idealized vignettes of *The Turn of the Year* have here developed into realistic presentations of pioneer labour — digging wells, driving cattle, pitching hay — that not only convey a sense of active human settlement but take their place in a continuing fictional structure. We realize that Branden's vision of teaching immigrants at the close of *A Search for America* has been transformed into Grove's vision of communicating their struggles and frustrations to a sophisticated world that is benefiting from their example but often ignorant of their achievement.

Artistically, the most obvious feature of the book is its regional specificity and coherence. Within the context of Grove's whole *oeuvre*, it establishes not only the landscape of the Big Marsh but a set of inhabitants about whom numerous other stories can be told. Place names like Balfour, Minor, and Odensee recur elsewhere; settlers mentioned casually in this novel reappear later. Thus Kurtz, only referred to in passing here and in *The Yoke of Life* (where Niels Lindstedt is also mentioned), becomes a central figure in "Water," a short story in which Amundsen and the Lunds also appear briefly. Part of this interconnection is explained by the fact that *Settlers of the Marsh* itself and several of the short stories constitute part of Grove's "Latter-Day Pioneers" manuscript, that ultimately had to be split up for publication. But enough of Grove's original plan remains to show his concern to produce an inter-relating series that may owe something to his familiarity with Balzac and Hardy and reminds the modern reader of the plan of Faulkner's saga of Yoknapatawpha County.

Yet always, cutting across his emphasis on realistic portrayal and documentation, there is Grove's determination to write philosophical fiction — novels that embody his own vision of life as well as the life itself. Hence Makow's phrase, " 'Platonic' tragedies," since Grove's philosophical tenets are primarily derived from the Greek thinker. While he seems to have read Plato in some detail, three fairly well-known Platonic principles are most prominent as a basis for his fiction: first, drawing from the chariot-myth in the *Phaedrus*, that human beings are continually pulled between the dictates of passion and reason, between the senses and the spiritual faculties; second, from Aristophanes' famous speech in the *Symposium*, that male and female are split parts of an original whole and that each part is continually seeking reunion with its lost "soul-mate"; third, that the material world in which we live is no more than an imperfect reflection of an unchanging world of ideas (a belief that takes the form in Grove's work of a potentially tragic yearning for the unattainable).

All these tenets are discernible in *Settlers of the Marsh* and can be seen to have profound influence on the novel's structure. Niels

Lindstedt has a vision of domestic fulfillment, of a house built by himself on his own land and peopled by his wife and children. But although Lindstedt soon comes to believe that Ellen Amundsen is his destined soul-mate, the perpetual conflict between physical and spiritual defeats his purpose — partly because Ellen's insight into her parents' marriage has left her with a disgust for physical love, partly because his own sexual nature betrays him into a liaison with Clara Vogel whom he is too naïve to recognize as the local whore. Lindstedt achieves the material part of his vision, but the house is never transformed into a home. Despite the mutedly positive conclusion, his White Range Line House remains, like Abe Spalding's great house and barn in *Fruits of the Earth*, a symbol of his failure.

This philosophic dimension distinguishes Grove's Canadian novels from the "slice of life" photographic technique of *The Master Mason's House*, but its reconciliation with the accustomed emphasis of fiction on probability and verisimilitude is something that Grove never quite achieves. Although he may well have been influenced by the work of Thomas Hardy, whose novels, especially *Tess of the d'Urbervilles* and *Jude the Obscure*, are often structured on similar principles (Tess torn between the physical and spiritual in the persons of Alec d'Urberville and Angel Clare, Jude between Arabella Donn and Sue Bridehead), Hardy was more skilful in combining his philosophical attitudes and the narrative demands of his fiction. Platonic dualism too often shows through as rigid artifice in Grove's plots: Ellen and Clare are too obviously symbolic opposites, while Lindstedt's actions seem determined more by the needs of the phil-osophical structure than by the terms of his character. Nonetheless, *Settlers of the Marsh* contains scenes of great power that approach the awesomeness of tragedy, and the sympathetic reader is prepared to forgive certain crudities of design in the interest of moving situations and an overall seriousness of purpose. For all its faults, this novel matters.

A variant on the same pattern, also set in the Big Marsh country, is present in *The Yoke of Life*. It is important to realize, however, that, although he is constantly reworking his material, exploring situations from a new angle, extracting fresh insights from themes treated before, Grove never repeats himself. There is always an original twist to familiar subject matter. Len Sterner, like Lindstedt, is young, and like all Grove's protagonists "a dreamer of dreams,"[22] but he qualifies as a pioneer only in an intellectual sense, by way of metaphor. His "vision" is of knowledge, of academic success in the great world beyond the horizon of his limited prairie home, but like the visions of all Grove's protagonists it is doomed to failure because the possible achievements of the mind are betrayed by the insatiate demands of the body. The split manifests itself in childhood. When he overhears his stepfather making sexual demands upon his mother, we are reminded of Ellen's similar experience in *Settlers of the Marsh*, but it is entirely characteristic of Grove that he should this time chronicle a male response.

Len's soul-mate, Lydia Hausman, combines the aspects of Clara and Ellen in one body; she becomes the barrier rather than the means to Len's success. Len himself is constantly seeking an inner purity beneath her sensuality, while his own lust for Lydia clashes with his vision of her as a spiritual ideal. At the end of the novel he finds her again after she has become a prostitute in Winnipeg, and she nurses him during an illness. But the tensions are irresolvable, and Len engineers a double suicide in the wilderness retreat to which they have fled. The final image of their drowned bodies lashed together represents Grove's symbolic and tragic version of Aristophanes' less solemn presentation of the union of male and female.

The book has strong links with "The Canyon" (completed by 1926), where the hero is, perhaps significantly, the professor that Len Sterner failed to become. Here body and spirit are again totally opposed, the sexual drive again inhibits intellectual — in this case, poetic — development, and the solution (though now for only one of the partners) is again suicide. Grove's difficulty in reconciling the concrete-universal and abstract-philosophical aspects of this plot is at its most extreme in "The Canyon," and this doubtless explains the failure of that novel to find a publisher. Acceptable perhaps as an intellectual allegory, the plot grates against the realistic bedrock of the novel-form. Makow has shrewdly observed: "It is a measure of Grove's high-minded innocence that he submitted such a novel for mass publication without giving a hint of its philosophical basis."[23] *The Yoke of Life* occupies a position midway between the two poles, and the two fictional modes of realistic narrative and philosophical fable co-exist rather awkwardly side by side. By the end of the book, however, the latter has obviously gained the upper hand.

The fourth chapter conveniently demonstrates in small compass the larger challenge presented by the novel as a whole. The opening account of the devastating hail-storm — culminating in the one-sentence paragraph, "Man ventured out to look at his losses" (*YL*, p. 60) — is supreme, but it is followed by Len's embarrassingly unconvincing vision of a unicorn. Here, of course, the presentation of sexual feeling is involved, and Grove's awkwardness in writing on that topic (as distinct from his admirable recognition of it as an important subject that must not be avoided) is nowhere more evident than in this novel. But the chapter is symptomatic of an unresolved dichotomy that permeates the book. Len Sterner, exemplar as well as victim of Platonic dualism, is sometimes a credible prairie youth (he was modelled on a brilliant pupil whom Grove had taught), sometimes no more than a convenient peg on which the novelist can hang his philosophical generalizations. He moves from the magnificently realized world of subsistence farming at the opening to the "absolute wilderness" (*YL*, p. 315) of the close which, though based upon an actual locale on Lake Winnipegosis, is converted into a symbolic dream-landscape presented in heightened terms as an appropriate background to the emblematic human conflict.

Critical response to *The Yoke of Life* has reflected this split. Of all Grove's novels it has been the most extravagantly praised and, with *Two Generations*, the most unjustly neglected. (These are the only Grove novels that at the time of writing have not been made generally available in paperback). Commentators who have praised it highly seem to have ignored the distinction between intention and execution. This is perhaps Grove's most ambitious novel until *The Master of the Mill* but unfortunately it required a rigorous artistic control, an ability to conduct the reader through astonishing fluctuations of mood and tone, that Grove was never to possess. Part of this failure stems from the fact that he is rarely able to detach himself sufficiently from his characters. Len's assumptions and reactions are never adequately "placed," and readers become embarrassed when they find themselves wondering whether the novelist's viewpoint is as naïve as his protagonist's. As always in Grove, there are scenes of remarkable power and poignancy but recollection of the novel tends to concentrate on individually memorable scenes; like so many of Grove's books, and more obviously than most, it reads as the flawed product of a major novelist.

Grove is able to achieve a greater degree of objectivity when portraying older protagonists. Nonetheless, *Our Daily Bread* (1928) takes its origin from autobiographical experience since the engagement of Woodrow Ormond and Cathleen Elliot reproduces the circumstances under which Grove himself became engaged to Catherine Wiens while visiting her family at Rush Lake, Saskatchewan. The local area, the "short grass country," also becomes the setting of the novel, and once again the locale and its inhabitants form a focal point for a number of other fictions. Two unpublished novels, "The Weatherhead Fortunes" and to a lesser extent "Jane Atkinson," belong here, the links being either geographical or thematic or both.[24] A recurrent preoccupation in these stories, picking up a strand from *The Master Mason's House*, is the break-up of a family. Several short stories, including "The House of Many Eyes" that mentions Pete Harrington and Dr. Stanhope, cluster around the larger fictions; some, indeed, like "Lazybones" and "The Spendthrift," are alternative versions of parts of *Our Daily Bread*.

Grove seems to have been determined to produce in *Our Daily Bread* a Western novel as distinct as possible from *Settlers of the Marsh*. This is the story not of a youthful pioneer but of an aging farmer; it involves not active struggle but passive decline. In *Settlers of the Marsh* Lindstedt is denied the family he longs for; here John Elliot, Sr., has a large family but, as the epigraph from the First Book of Samuel indicates, they "walked not in his ways." Instead of a novel pared down to the minimum of principal characters and a single plot, we have in *Our Daily Bread* so complex a series of relationships and subjects that it is by no means easy to keep them all in mind and to distinguish the participants one from another.

Nonetheless, there are numerous resemblances. Lindstedt and Elliot are not so much opposites as complementary images of each other. Each is a dreamer possessing high moral principles but lacking in human understanding; each has a vision of domesticity in which his family is gathered around him; each is defeated by a combination of external circumstances and the terms of his own character. Each is associated with a house that becomes a symbol of his personal failure. Again, a chapter in *Our Daily Bread* entitled "The Leaven of Sex Is at Work" recalls Lindstedt's dilemma, though in this case the link is with the Elliot children rather than with the father.

This last connection between the two books introduces a theme which, though prominent in *The Master Mason's House*, becomes a major preoccupation in subsequent work: the gap between the generations. Elliot belongs to the old order; a son-in-law calls him "Lear of the prairie"[25] but he is also an American Abraham, a prairie patriarch vainly attempting to preserve the old ways in a new world.

His ideal is presented unequivocally: "To live honourably, to till the land, and to hand on life from generation to generation: that was man's duty; that, to him, in spite of all doubts, had meant and still meant serving God" (*ODB*, p. 189). His closeness to the sower in *The Turn of the Year* is obvious. And, like the sower, he finds that his family deserts him. A son, echoing the sower's, finds work in an urban garage; a daughter, married to an unscrupulous fraudulent businessman, Fred Sately (whose first name suggests that Grove may here be offering a masochistic portrait of his German life), believes that "You can eat your cake and have it, too" (*ODB*, p. 24).

Elliot, then, is presented throughout the book as at odds with his family, a fact that has implications for the structure of the novel. Much has been written of Grove's use of the chronicle-form, which is clearly discernible in the juxtaposed presentations of the lives of the Elliot children. Indeed, many of Grove's artistic effects in *Our Daily Bread* are the result of the narrator's shifting our attention dramatically from one sister or brother to another in order to point up the parallels or contrasts. At the same time, the father is indisputably the central figure in the novel. To the extent that the book partakes of "tragedy" it derives its quality from the presentation of the patriarch as tragic protagonist. And here we begin to recognize the pattern for later Grove "heroes": the concern with metaphysical questions, a fascinated preoccupation with the mysteries of life. Such questions had been briefly raised by Niels Lindstedt: "What was life anyway? . . . Who was God anyway?"[26] But in *Our Daily Bread* and the later novels (especially *Fruits of the Earth*) the questions get more urgent and more obsessive. The mystery of death is especially prominent here. Elliot's life descends into chaos at the death of his wife, and his lonely vigil at the death-bed of his son-in-law Pete Harrington is recognized as a prelude to his own death.

Once again, the battle is between materialism, a life devoted to "inessentials" rather than essentials, the impact of commercial assumptions upon the moral life. But Grove's portrait is not one-sided. Elliot's character is brilliantly illuminated in an exchange between his daughter Mary and his wife. To Mary's assertion, "Father is human," the wife replies, "He is upright" (*ODB*, p. 29). The whole novel focuses upon the questionable compatibility of the two terms.

The passing of time is invariably important in Grove's work, and nowhere more poignantly than here. In presenting Elliot's decline in a world that has rejected the principles on which his life is based, Grove offers a cogent comment on the dilemma of a modern world in which material power has outstripped spiritual growth. The point gets its most impressive treatment in a scene in Winnipeg where Elliot is visiting a daughter and son-in-law and finds himself in a sophisticated social gathering. A chance question from a young historian releases a stream of recollections, and soon the whole party is listening spell-bound to the spokesman of another age. The emphasis (and this is typical of Grove) is not so much on the details of the historical past as on the circumstances under which they are recalled. In creating a situation in which representatives of the modern world of urban industrialism listen to a practising farmer who remembers the days of the early settlers, Grove is offering, in essentially creative terms, a microcosm of Canadian historical evolution.

In *Fruits of the Earth* (1933) Grove reconsiders his main themes and rings more changes upon them. The result is, in many respects, the subtlest of his presentations of the pioneering character. In this novel the characteristic pattern is seen complete. *Settlers of the Marsh* had chronicled the initial struggle to wrest a living out of natural wilderness; *Our Daily Bread* had shown the speed with which an achieved family unit can break up. In *Fruits of the Earth* we see both the rise and the fall.

At first, it is tempting to draw comparisons between Abe Spalding and Elliot; indeed, some commentators have found them similar. But basically they are decidedly different. Spalding may ultimately rise to a position comparable with Elliot's, but at the opening of the novel, a young farmer ploughing his first furrow on virgin prairie, he is at the other extreme. Moreover, while Elliot persisted in the old ways, Spalding was lured by the attractions of machinery. While Elliot is proud that he never got into debt, Spalding is perfectly prepared to use "modern methods," though this results in his becoming a slave to the land in much the same way that Sam Clark later becomes the slave rather than the master of the mill. Although Spalding, like all Grove's protagonists, possesses a vision, we are told at the outset that it is an "economic vision."[27] He is out to dominate and conquer nature, as Elliot, who knows that "You can't fool the land" (*ODB*, p. 4), is not. The emphasis is on Spalding's materialism.

As a consequence his "conversion" (spiritual understanding develops as power and influence decline) is all the more dramatic. The book is appropriately divided into two parts. Basically, the first part represents Spalding's rise to position and power, while the second chronicles his defeat and withdrawal. But the respective titles, "Abe Spalding" and "The District," show that this pattern is related to a larger historical progression. The tragedy of Abe Spalding is not merely that his marriage is unsatisfactory, that his perfect house begins to decay (literally and symbolically) as soon as it is completed, and that he loses his children through death and quarrels; it is, rather, the inevitable tragedy of a pioneer who survives after pioneer conditions have been replaced. The brand of leadership effective and, indeed, essential in the early stage of the historical process becomes oppressive and doomed to defeat in newer conditions. Grove is able to tap deep springs of emotion because Spalding, as a victim of historical circumstances, has helped to create the society that defeats him.

Grove originally called the book "The Chronicles of Spalding District," but it is decidedly a novel as well as a chronicle. Spalding is a convincing character who develops credibly — one might say, inexorably — in the course of the narrative. The account of his deteriorating relations with his wife is presented with a Lawrentian intensity and directness, and the extended time-span (which so often provides Grove with the epic scope that he needs) is carefully managed so that a balance is maintained between personal development and communal growth. The novel has been criticized for its anticlimactic ending, but this (despite Grove's original attempt at heroic tragedy that resulted in fustian melodrama[28]) is the inevitable result of the theme. Grove's conclusion is in fact subtly ambiguous. In his prefatory author's note he describes how he once discovered an "outwardly palatial house" in which only two or three rooms were occupied and "a barn built for half a hundred horses" that contained "a team of sorry nags." The image (though not technically a part of the fiction) hangs as a shadow over the whole story, and although the book ends with Abe's first attempt to regain his authority by leading a campaign against the local teenage gang, we know that he will ultimately fail in his efforts to maintain his great farm. Here fictional probability, the sanctioned pattern of tragedy, and Grove's particular form of realism are held in a precarious but artistically acceptable balance.

The Groves had left Manitoba for Ottawa in 1929, and by the time *Fruits of the Earth* was published they were settled in Simcoe, Ontario. The next novel, *Two Generations* (1939), is set in the area of their new home and initiates what might have become another fictional series linked by recurring characters and a common locale. Grove had plans at this time for an ambitious novel called "The Seasons" in which Phil and Alice Patterson of *Two Generations* were also to appear. He described it as "a panoramic novel of Canadian life, with town, city, and open countryside" and hoped that it would become his *magnum opus*;[29] unfortunately, it was never completed.

Two Generations itself, as the title suggests, returns to the same themes that preoccupied him in his earlier work. The protagonist, Ralph Patterson, resembles Elliot and Spalding in being a pioneer who has outlived the historical conditions in which pioneers can flourish. But we see Patterson only in his displaced state, and the emphasis is on the younger generation that will not walk in his ways. As his wife explains to her children, "he is living through a crisis; he is being superseded."[30] But the book is by no means all repetition. Grove accurately describes its subject in his autobiography as "the transition, in Ontario, from pioneer conditions to an urbanized rural life which brought about a conflict between fathers and sons" (*ISM*, p. 440). Although Patterson echoes Phil Branden's vision of agricultural America ("It's the purpose of the city to serve the country" [*TG*, p. 257; cf. *SA*, p. 356]), the novel reflects Grove's awareness in his later years that he is living in an age of rapidly increasing industrialization and that as a thoughtful novelist he must turn his attention to the social and psychological effects of this development.

This is, however, a distinctly mellower book than its predecessors, and although it lacks the imaginative expansiveness and energy of the earlier work, it has greater unity and poise. The philosophizing is less overt (though the close brother-and-sister relationship of Phil and Alice owes much to Grove's Platonism); assertion by narrator or protagonist gives way — particularly in the last chapter — to discussion among equals. Indeed, a significant development in this novel is Grove's ability to create other characters besides Patterson so that a balanced argument becomes possible. Grove always denied that his sympathies were with the men rather than the women in his pioneering books, insisting that he merely reproduced the situation in that particular stage of society, but only in *Two Generations*, where Mrs. Patterson is both a strong, rounded character and more than a match for her husband, does his text support his intention. Mrs. Patterson and her children (the second generation) are forces in the novel capable not only of arguing with Patterson but of winning the argument. Like the earlier protagonists, Patterson asks himself whether he had, "by following the bent of his nature, missed something in life that was infinitely precious" (*TG*, p. 175); unlike them he is able to acknowledge the fact and attempt to adapt to a new world. Although the conclusion of the novel can hardly be described, in the phrase that was an anathema to Grove, as a "happy ending," it at least ends on the establishment of an emerging harmony.

Two Generations, though successful in its own right, has all the hall-marks of a transitional work. The pattern of the earlier prairie-series is still discernible but it is handled with a new artistic assurance. Because the characters are more evenly matched, the fictional tension can arise from internal rather than external sources. There is less melodramatic action than in any other Grove novel. Above all, Grove has widened his range of subject. The worlds of industry, commerce and finance are more evident here. This new material, though hinted at, is not fully developed, but *Two Generations* contains the seeds of a greater subject than Grove had yet tackled. Spettigue notes that, at the peak of his success, Patterson has " 'nothing to do'; his farm empire is self-sustaining."[31] This idea combines with Grove's growing concern with the future of industrialism to form the basis for the far more ambitious novel he was planning at about this time: *The Master of the Mill*.

Grove's last conventional novel, *The Master of the Mill* (1944) represents both a culmination of his earlier work and a challenging new departure. The mill in question is a flour-mill, and with this account of processing grain the whole cycle that began with pioneers breaking soil is now complete. The novel shows the growth of the Langholm mill and the Clark family fortunes until the time when Sam Clark, the central figure, feels impelled to do some painful moral accounting. It is a continuation of Grove's earlier interests insofar as the Clarks may reasonably be considered pioneers, albeit in an industrial rather than an agricultural context. There is yet another clash between fathers and sons, but the generations are now extended to three and we come to realize that, whatever disagreements are involved, all are slaves rather than masters of the omnipotent mill.

In this novel Grove expands his interests from the more regional concerns of prairie-fiction to issues that are national in scope. Certainly the book reflects in quasi-allegorical form the development of Canada from a predominantly rural to an unequivocally urban society. "Control of the mill, in the long-run," we are told, "means control of the country,"[32] and a Canadian Prime Minister makes a brief appearance among the dramatis personae. But, as Grove remarked in a letter to Lorne Pierce, "the theme is world-wide, not merely Canadian."[33] The mill itself is a highly complex, universal symbol — a thing of beauty and a thing of terror, both a blessing and a curse, a brilliant creation as well as a frightening automation. Throughout the book, appreciation of its magnificence is qualified by awareness of the ruthlessness of the process it represents. As emblem of the Industrial Revolution, it is a human invention that gets out of human control.

Yet, lurking beneath the surface of the text, there is an even more disturbing idea that has been latent in Grove's fiction from the beginning: the suggestion that the whole process is part of the nature of things and that human beings have no power to alter it. As early as *Settlers of the Marsh* Grove as narrator had remarked of Niels Lindstedt: "the farm owned him; not he the farm . . . . It grew accordingly to laws of its own" (*SM*, p. 174). And in *A Search for America* Phil Branden, working in another kind of mill (a veneer-factory), "saw the mill as a thing alive — as a living organism" (*SA*, p. 339). Here Sam Clark comes to believe that "the mill was not a man-made thing: it was an outgrowth of the soil, the rock, the earth, subject to laws of growth of its own" (*MM*, p. 51). By the close of *The Master of the Mill* "it seemed as if . . . , even though the whole population of the earth perished, it would go on producing flour till it had smothered the globe" (*MM*, p. 213). The mill then comes to represent Process itself. No one can be "the master of the mill"; Sam Clark, like those he employs, like novelist and reader, is merely "a cog in the machine" (*MM*, p. 68).

What makes the novel startlingly original in the Grove canon is the technical experimentation involved. Like the earlier pioneers, Sam Clark asks, "What was the meaning of it all?" (*MM*, p. 93), but the question becomes the mainspring that not only sets off memories and regrets but determines the particular form of the novel. Perhaps Sam Clark's excessive introspection is to be seen as one of the consequences of an urban-industrial society. At all events, Grove discovered in the course of writing that the subject demanded what was for him a radically new technical approach. The dying Sam Clark "was no longer remembering the past, he was reliving it" (*MM*, p. 97), and the book therefore fluctuates violently between present and past as the old man finds it increasingly difficult to distinguish the two. A character from one part of his experience suddenly blends into another, and the fact that the three chief women in his life are all named Maud adds to the old man's (and often enough the reader's) puzzlement. Sam Clark's entrapment in events is itself symbolized by the context in which his recollections take place — the interminable drives around "the Loop," a road that relentlessly encircles the area of the mill and so emphasizes both spatial and temporal recurrence.

Grove employs a battery of modernist devices — diary-recollections, extracts from a history, stories within stories, discussions by other characters parallelling the course of the old man's memories, juxtapositions that highlight thematic connections — in an endeavour to catch the sense of personal and psychological time. For readers accustomed to the methods of Joyce or Proust or Virginia Woolf or Faulkner, Grove's experiments may seem obvious enough in themselves and somewhat clumsily executed. We should remember, however, that the Canadian novel was decidedly traditional at this time, and that Grove's methods here qualify as fictional pioneering. It is easy to fault the novel for its stiffness and to regret that Grove did not carry his experiments further; stylistic variety, for example, is lacking — Captain Stevens' history of Langholm Mill and Odette Charlebois' long discourses are both indistinguishable from each other or from the habitual prose of the narrator. But the ordering of information as it comes to the reader and the structuring of the whole narrative are managed with considerable skill, and, whatever reservations we may have, we feel we are in the presence of a richly-textured work of art.

Grove's last two books, though very different in themselves, may both be seen as attempts to round off his life's work, to sum up his lifelong preoccupation with the distinction between I and what is not I. *In Search of Myself* (1946), ostensibly his autobiography, looks inward in order to present the final and most elaborate version of his carefully-constructed mask. *Consider Her Ways* (1947), a difficult book to categorize but best summed up by Spettigue as an "encyclopedic satire,"[34] turns outwards once more and offers his detached view of the nature of mankind.

In Search of Myself has already been quoted and discussed, so needs little further consideration here. Half fiction and half non-fiction, it uses autobiographical experience, like *Over Prairie Trails* but more blatantly, as the basis for an artfully patterned structure.

Once again, Europe is set against America, a fantasy of wealth contrasted with prosaic poverty; like *A Search for America* and so much of the fiction it is, in Grove's own words, "the story of a conflict between material and spiritual things" (*ISM*, p. 370). If approached as a mere container for information it will be found unsatisfactory; Margaret Stobie, from an exclusively biographical standpoint, calls it "disappointingly empty," "thin and unrewarding."[35] But if read as an imaginative construct, as Grove wished it to be read, not so much the presentation of an authentic past as the creation of an ideal author for his already achieved work, the book is absorbing and fascinating — a portrait (in Joyce's sense) of the artist in Canada.

Consider Her Ways is the completed (and imaginatively adapted) version of a manuscript entitled *MAN: His Habits, Social Organization, and Outlook* upon which Grove was working as early as the 1920s.[36] It is one more indication of the philosophical underpinning of his novels, of the way in which his attitude to human beings and human behaviour, generalized in his non-fiction writings, is embodied in particular instances in his fiction. Here Grove pretends to look at mankind from an ant's eye view. The human editor claims to get into communicative contact in Venezuela with a wise ant, Wawaquee, who dictates to him an account of a scientific journey to observe the behaviour of human beings in the United States — in other words, an ant's *Search for America*. The device is, of course, a Utopian *jeu d'esprit* that enables Grove, in the sanctioned tradition of satire, to view human activity from an unusual, withdrawn perspective (cf. More's *Utopia*, Swift's *Gulliver's Travels*, Samuel Butler's *Erewhon*).

It is a witty, civilized, well-poised book, different in tone if not in content from anything else that Grove produced. "Here," wrote Robertson Davies on its first appearance, "we have a fine mind amusing itself."[37] That, I think, strikes the right note. The book combines at least three different literary modes. First, there is the "science fiction" aspect: the imaginative account of establishing contact with the ant world (which is well done) and the construction of the narrative so that human achievements are described without using the human terminology that has developed around them (a device which, in my opinion, gets tedious by the end). Then there is the satire, the excuse for ridiculing human practices — political arrangements, philosophical and theological beliefs, scientific and literary activity, etc. — which is the main purpose of the book. And finally there is the verbal comedy that the device makes possible; the ants communicate through scents rather than words, and Grove is able to exploit to the full the punning verbal consequences: "she was as good as her scent," "a number of scentures on our travels," "I conscented."[38]

The original reviewers were understandably surprised by the book's lightheartedness. There is, however, a deeply serious purpose at its core. The imaginative, creative framework is in itself highly entertaining and the philosophical centre might well seem ponderous without it, but it would be a mistake to neglect Grove's overall intention. Personally, I am not convinced that he has quite succeeded in combining the many strands of the book into a unifying "anatomy," but the relevance of the material to the total significance of Grove's work is not in dispute. Spettigue's eloquent case for *Consider Her Ways* as a fitting conclusion to Grove's writings cannot be improved upon:

> At the end of his creative life, as I read it, FPG was completing his expression of the vision that, whether he had seen it earlier or not, he now could see unfolded in his books. *Consider Her Ways* was intended to show us how to read them as a whole: man struggling to transcend the limitations imposed by nature and himself, man approaching the ideal agricultural mode, man degenerating into the slavery of the materialist state.[39]

A dour vision characteristic of all Grove's work receives in *Consider Her Ways* an unusually inventive treatment.

The case for Frederick Philip Grove as a literary figure can be stated very simply: he was Canada's first important novelist. His claims to importance rest on four main qualities. First, his fiction, instead of being a mere conglomeration of stories, constitutes a clear and recognizable *oeuvre* with a discernible progression from beginning to end. Second, his preoccupations, and the viewpoint from which he presented them, offer a unique insight into the cultural and psychological history of Canada. Third, he displays a basic seriousness (by which I do not mean either pomposity or undue solemnity) concerning the nature of art in general and the importance of the novel in particular. Fourth, although his prose is that of a foreigner and his work is rarely noted for verbal dexterity, he makes up for this by a remarkable structural imagination, by sheer critical intelligence, by an enviable steadiness and sincerity of purpose.

On the other hand, he laboured under many disadvantages, and displayed a number of weaknesses that might well have been considered crippling. To the traditionalist, his plots are often slow-moving and straggling, while his characterization (apart from a dominating central figure) is either conventional to the point of stereotype or vague and undistinguished. His style — particularly his dialogue — must often be criticized as ponderous and clumsy, and although he was never one to stress his own limitations Grove himself admitted: "I had at bottom no language which was peculiarly my own . . . . All my struggles were with words" (*ISM*, p. 338). From the viewpoint of the modernist, moreover, until *The Master of the Mill* he showed little interest in the radical experiments in fictional technique that were so prominent a feature of the novel-writing of his time in both Europe and America.

Under the circumstances, it is hardly surprising that even our best critics have found Grove puzzling, elusive, difficult to "place." For George Woodcock, for example, he is "The Hamhanded Master," "that fumbling giant among novelists," and Woodcock shrewdly isolates, in a passage that we cannot afford to brush aside, what he calls "the real problem of Grove — the problem of why a writer so large in texture, so gigantic in his fumblings, never wrote a book that seemed completely to fulfil his possibilities."[40] The last passage first appeared in 1966, before Spettigue's biographical discoveries that help to explain, though not perhaps to excuse, some of the oddities surrounding Grove's life and work. Much of the problem was undoubtedly personal, part of the historical circumstances in which he found himself. The solidity of his writings can sometimes become oppressive but it was badly needed in its time. Hitherto no one in Canada had approached the art of fiction so single-mindedly and with such determined creative energy. The difficulties were enormous, and emphasis should be laid less on the inevitable blemishes than on the remarkable success achieved. Desmond Pacey's summing-up as early as 1945 remains surprisingly just: "The steady uniformity of his vision gives to his work an organic unity of effect: its total bulk presents itself to us with a massive integrity."[41]

Integrity! The word seems strange after the revelations of the "sullied" European years. Yet it is a word that commentators on Grove constantly find themselves needing to use (similarly, I wrote of his "sincerity of purpose" three paragraphs back). Here, perhaps, a gleam of light is shed upon the artistic implications of the so-called

Grove mystery. The firm literary integrity pervading the work of Frederick Philip Grove, though ironically including a deceiving account of his own development, seems to have been a massive act of redemption offered as personal penance for the moral short-comings in the life of Felix Paul Greve. And Canadian fiction is richer as a consequence.

NOTES

[1] Frederick Philip Grove, *A Search for America* (Ottawa: Graphic, [1927]), p. 2. All further references to this work (*SA*) appear in the text.

[2] The biographical information about Felix Paul Greve is derived from Douglas O. Spettigue's *FPG: The European Years* (Ottawa: Oberon, 1973), supplemented by information on Elsa Endell in Desmond Pacey, ed., *The Letters of Frederick Philip Grove* (Toronto: Univ. of Toronto Press, 1976), pp. 524, 554. For information on Greve and Elsa in the United States, see Paul Hjartarson, "Of Greve, Grove, and Other Strangers: The Autobiography of the Baroness Elsa von Freytag-Loringhoven," in his ed., *A Stranger to My Time: Essays by and about Frederick Philip Grove* (Edmonton: NeWest, 1986), pp. 269–84.

[3] Frederick Philip Grove, *In Search of Myself* (Toronto: Macmillan, 1946), p. 181. All further references to this work (*ISM*) appear in the text.

[4] *The Letters of Frederick Philip Grove*, p. 437.

[5] See Henry Makow, ed., "Letters from Eden: Grove's Creative Rebirth," *University of Toronto Quarterly*, 49 (Fall 1979), 59, 60.

[6] For a brief memoir of Grove at this time, see Bernard Webber, "Grove in Politics," *Canadian Literature*, No. 63 (Winter 1975), pp. 126–27.

[7] For biographical information on Grove's Canadian years I am indebted to Margaret R. Stobie, *Frederick Philip Grove* (New York: Twayne, 1973).

[8] See Stobie, p. 27.

[9] Frederick Philip Grove, *It Needs to Be Said* (Toronto: Macmillan, 1929), p. 87. All further references to this work (*INBS*) appear in the text.

[10] See Rudy Wiebe, "A Novelist's Personal Notes on Frederick Philip Grove," *University of Toronto Quarterly*, 47 (Spring 1978), 189–99.

[11] For a convenient gathering of many of the original reviews of Grove's books, see Desmond Pacey, ed., *Frederick Philip Grove*. Critical Views of Canadian Writers (Toronto: Ryerson, 1970), pp. 99–184.

[12] See Wilfrid Eggleston's interesting account, "In Search of F.P. Grove," in his *Literary Friends* (Ottawa: Borealis, 1980), pp. 79–105.

[13] Quoted in (and translated by) Spettigue, *FPG: The European Years*, p. 148.

[14] See the introduction, by A.W. Riley and Douglas O. Spettigue, to Frederick Philip Grove, *The Master Mason's House*, trans. Paul Gubbins (Ottawa: Oberon, 1976), p. 6, and *The Letters of Frederick Philip Grove*, p. 552.

[15] See Grove's essay, "The Happy Ending," in *It Needs to Be Said*.

[16] Riley and Spettigue, Introduction to *The Master Mason's House*, p. 7.

[17] Henry David Thoreau, *Walden* [1854], Volume 2 of *The Writings of Henry David Thoreau* (Boston: Houghton Mifflin, 1906), p. 19; John Burroughs, *Locusts and Wild Honey* [1879], Volume 4 of *The Writings of John Burroughs* (Boston: Houghton Mifflin, 1904), p. 73.

[18] Frederick Philip Grove, *Over Prairie Trails* (Toronto: McClelland and Stewart, 1922), p. 33.

[19] Frederick Philip Grove, *The Turn of the Year* (Toronto: McClelland and Stewart, 1923), p. 59. All further references to this work (*TY*) appear in the text.

[20] See Stobie, p. 65.

[21] Henry Makow, "Grove's 'The Canyon,'" *Canadian Literature*, No. 82 (Autumn 1979), p. 142.

[22] Frederick Philip Grove, *The Yoke of Life* (Toronto: Macmillan, 1930), p. 66. All further references to this work (*YL*) appear in the text.

[23] Makow, "Grove's 'The Canyon,'" p. 141.

[24] For a discussion of these manuscripts, see Peter Noel-Bentley, "The Position of the Unpublished *Jane Atkinson* and *The Weatherhead Fortunes*," in John Nause, ed., *The Grove Symposium* (Ottawa: Univ. of Ottawa Press, 1974), pp. 13–33.

[25] Frederick Philip Grove, *Our Daily Bread* (Toronto: Macmillan, 1928), p. 258. All further references to this work (*ODB*) appear in the text.

[26] Frederick Philip Grove, *Settlers of the Marsh* (Toronto: Ryerson, 1925), p. 152. All further references to this work (*SM*) appear in the text.

[27] Frederick Philip Grove, *Fruits of the Earth* (Toronto: Dent, 1933), p. 5.

[28] For an account and discussion of the original manuscript ending, see Douglas O. Spettigue, *Frederick Philip Grove* (Toronto: Copp Clark, 1969), pp. 113–15.

[29] *The Letters of Frederick Philip Grove*, pp. 386, 401. For an account of "The Seasons," see Bruce Nesbitt, "'The Seasons,' Grove's Unfinished Novel," *Canadian Literature*, No. 18 (Autumn 1963), pp. 47–51.

[30] Frederick Philip Grove, *Two Generations* (Toronto: Ryerson, 1939), p. 48. All further references to this work (*TG*) appear in the text.

[31] Spettigue, *Frederick Philip Grove*, p. 116.

[32] Frederick Philip Grove, *The Master of the Mill* (Toronto: Macmillan, 1944), p. 251. All further references to this work (*MM*) appear in the text.

[33] *The Letters of Frederick Philip Grove*, p. 346.

[34] Douglas O. Spettigue, "Introduction," *Consider Her Ways*, by Frederick Philip Grove, New Canadian Library, No. 101 (Toronto: McClelland and Stewart, 1977), p. xv.

[35] Stobie, pp. 176, 177.

[36] For a useful discussion of this manuscript and its relevance to Grove's later work, see Birk Sproxton, "Grove's Unpublished *MAN* and its Relation to *The Master of the Mill*" in Nause, ed., *The Grove Symposium*, pp. 34-54.

[37] Robertson Davies, quoted in Pacey, ed., *Frederick Philip Grove* (Critical Views of Canadian Writers), p. 181.

[38] Frederick Philip Grove, *Consider Her Ways* (Toronto: Macmillan, 1947), pp. 17, 46, 237.

[39] Spettigue, *FPG: The European Years*, p. 211.

[40] George Woodcock, "Editorial," *Canadian Literature*, No. 29 (Spring 1966), p. 4; *Odysseus Ever Returning: Essays on Canadian Writers and Writing* (Toronto: McClelland and Stewart, 1970), pp. 3-4, 149.

[41] Desmond Pacey, *Frederick Philip Grove* (Toronto: Ryerson, 1945), p. 130.

SELECTED BIBLIOGRAPHY

Note: The works of Felix Paul Greve are confined to those translated into English. For the most complete bibliography of Grove's writings up to 1980, see John Miska's compilation listed below.

Primary Sources

Books

Greve, Felix Paul. *Oscar Wilde* [1903]. Trans. Barry Asker. Vancouver: William Hoffer, 1984.

———. *Fanny Essler* [1905]. Trans. Christine Helmers, A.W. Riley, and Douglas O. Spettigue. 2 vols. Ottawa: Oberon, 1984.

———. *The Master Mason's House* [1906]. Trans. Paul Gubbins. Ottawa: Oberon, 1976. [Published in German as *Maurermeister Ihles Haus.*]

Grove, Frederick Philip. *Over Prairie Trails.* Toronto: McClelland and Stewart, 1922.

———. *The Turn of the Year.* Toronto: McClelland and Stewart, 1923.

———. *Settlers of the Marsh.* Toronto: Ryerson, 1925.

———. *A Search for America.* Ottawa: Graphic, [1927].

———. *Our Daily Bread.* Toronto: Macmillan, 1928.

———. *It Needs to Be Said.* Toronto: Macmillan, 1929.

———. *The Yoke of Life.* Toronto: Macmillan, 1930.

———. *Fruits of the Earth.* Toronto: Dent, 1933.

———. *Two Generations: A Story of Present-Day Ontario.* Toronto: Ryerson, 1939.

———. *The Master of the Mill.* Toronto: Macmillan, 1944.

———. *In Search of Myself.* Toronto: Macmillan, 1946.

———. *Consider Her Ways.* Toronto: Macmillan, 1947.

———. *Tales from the Margin: The Selected Short Stories of Frederick Philip Grove.* Ed. Desmond Pacey. Toronto: McGraw-Hill Ryerson, 1971.

————. *The Letters of Frederick Philip Grove.* Ed. Desmond Pacey. Toronto: Univ. of Toronto Press, 1976.

————. *The Adventure of Leonard Broadus.* Ed. Mary Rubio. Guelph, Ont.: Canadian Children's Press, 1983.

Contributions to Periodicals

Grove, Frederick Philip. "Canadians Old and New." *Maclean's,* 15 March 1928, pp. 2, 55–56.

————. "Realism and After." *Canadian Bookman,* Nov. 1928, pp. 389–402.

————. "Assimilation." *Maclean's,* 1 Sept. 1929, pp. 7, 74–75, 78–79.

————. "Apologia pro Vita et Opere Suo." *The Canadian Forum,* Aug. 1931, pp. 420–22.

————. "A Writer's Classification of Writers and Their Work." *University of Toronto Quarterly,* 1 (Jan. 1932), 236–53.

————. "Thomas Hardy: A Critical Examination of a Typical Novel [*The Return of the Native*] and His Shorter Poems." *University of Toronto Quarterly,* 1 (July 1932), 490–507.

————. "The Rockies Versus the Alps." *Canadian Geographical Journal,* 7 (Dec. 1933), 261–74.

————. "The Plight of Canadian Fiction? A Reply [to Morley Callaghan]." *University of Toronto Quarterly,* 7 (July 1938), 451–67.

————. "Postscript to *A Search for America.*" *Queen's Quarterly,* 49 (Autumn 1942), 197–213.

————. "Democracy and Education." *University of Toronto Quarterly,* 12 (July 1943), 389–402.

————. "Peasant Poetry and Fiction from Hesiod to Hémon." *Proceedings and Transactions of the Royal Society of Canada,* 3rd ser., 38 (1944), 89–98.

————. "Morality in the Forsyte Saga." *University of Toronto Quarterly,* 15 (Oct. 1945), 54–64.

Secondary Sources

Ayre, Robert. "Canadian Writers of Today, IV: Frederick Philip Grove." *The Canadian Forum,* April 1932, pp. 255–57. Rpt. as "A Solitary Giant." In *Frederick Philip Grove.* Ed. Desmond Pacey, pp. 17–24.

Bader, Rudolf. "Frederick Philip Grove and Naturalism Reconsidered." In

Gaining Ground: European Critics on Canadian Literature. Ed. Robert Kroetsch and Reingard M. Nischik. Edmonton: NeWest, 1985, pp. 222–33.

Bailey, Nancy I. "F.P.G. and the Empty House." *Journal of Canadian Fiction,* Nos. 31–32 (1981), 177–93.

Birbalsingh, Frank. "Grove and Existentialism." *Canadian Literature,* No. 43 (Winter 1970), pp. 67–76. Rpt. in *Writers of the Prairies.* Ed. Donald G. Stephens. Vancouver: Univ. of British Columbia Press, 1973, pp. 57–66.

Blodgett, E.D. "*Alias* Grove: Variations in Disguise." In his *Configuration: Essays in the Canadian Literatures.* Downsview, Ont.: ECW, 1982, pp. 112–53. Revised and abridged as "Ersatz Feminism in F.P.G.'s German Novels" in Hjartarson, ed., *A Stranger to My Time,* pp. 21–46.

Boeschenstein, Herman. "Frederick Philip Grove: Lehrer, Dichter und Pionier, 1871–1946 [*sic*]." In *Festgabe fur Eduard Berend.* Ed. Hans Werner Seiffert and Bernhard Zeller. Weimar: Hermann Böhlaus Nachfolge, 1959, pp. 257–71.

Bonheim, Helmut. "F.P. Grove's 'Snow' and Sinclair Ross' 'The Painted Door' — The Rhetoric of the Prairie." In *Encounters and Explorations: Canadian Writers and European Critics.* Ed. Frank K. Stanzel and Waldemar Zacharasiewicz. Würzburg: Königshausen & Neumann, 1986, pp. 58–72.

Brown, E.K. "Frederick Philip Grove: In Memoriam." *Winnipeg Free Press,* 28 Aug. 1948. Rpt. in his *Responses and Evaluations: Essays on Canada.* Ed. David Staines. Toronto: McClelland and Stewart, 1977, pp. 304–06.

Cohn-Sfectu, Ofelia. "At the Mercy of Winds and Waves? — *Over Prairie Trails* by F.P. Grove." *University of Windsor Review,* 11 (Spring-Summer 1976), 49–56.

Collin, W.E. "La tragique ironie de Frederick Philip Grove." *Gants du Ceil,* 4 (hiver 1946), 15–40. Rpt. in his *The White Savannahs.* Ed. Germaine Warkentin. Toronto: Univ. of Toronto Press, 1975, pp. 304–29.

Collins, Alexandra. "An Audience in Mind When I Speak: Grove's *In Search of Myself.*" *Studies in Canadian Literature,* 8, No. 2 (1983), 181–93.

Craig, Terrence, ed. "Frederick Philip Grove's 'Poems.'" *Canadian Poetry: Studies, Documents, Reviews,* No. 10 (Spring–Summer 1982), pp. 58–90.

———, ed. "Frederick Philip Grove's 'The Dirge.'" *Canadian Poetry: Studies, Documents, Reviews,* No. 16 (Spring–Summer 1985), pp. 55–73.

———. "F.P. Grove and the 'Alien' Immigrant in the West." *Journal of Canadian Studies,* 20 (Summer 1985), 92–100.

Dewar, Kenneth C. "Technology and the Pastoral Ideal in Frederick Philip Grove." *Journal of Canadian Studies,* 8 (Feb. 1973), 19–28. Rpt. in Hjartarson, ed., *A Stranger to My Time,* pp. 211–25.

Dooley, D.J. "Puzzled by Immensities: Grove's Double Vision in *Fruits of the*

Earth." In his *Moral Vision in the Canadian Novel.* Toronto: Clarke, Irwin, 1979, pp. 13–23.

Dudek, Louis. "The Literary Significance of Grove's Search." In Nause, ed., *Grove Symposium*, pp. 89–99. Rpt. in Dudek, *Selected Essays and Criticism.* Ottawa: Tecumseh, 1978, pp. 336–48.

Eggleston, Wilfrid. "Frederick Philip Grove." *In Our Living Tradition: Seven Canadians.* Ed. Claude T. Bissell. Toronto: Univ. of Toronto Press, 1957, pp. 105–27.

———. "F.P.G.: The Ottawa Interlude." In Nause, ed., *Grove Symposium*, pp. 101–10.

———. "In Search of F.P. Grove." In his *Literary Friends.* Ottawa: Borealis, 1980, pp. 79–105.

Fetherling, Doug. "F.P. Grove Versus F.P. Greve." In his *The Blue Notebook: Reports on Canadian Culture.* Oakville, Ont.: Mosaic, 1985, pp. 11–19.

[Frye, Northrop.] "Canadian Dreiser." *The Canadian Forum*, Sept. 1948, pp. 121–22. Rpt. in Pacey, ed., *Frederick Philip Grove*, pp. 186–87.

Gide, André. "Conversation avec un Allemand quelques années avant la guerre." In his *Incidences.* Paris: Gallimard, 1925, pp. 134–45. Rpt. in his *Oeuvres Complètes.* Vol. 9. Ed. L. Martin Chauffer. Paris: Nouvelle revue française, 1935, pp. 133–43. Trans. Blanche A. Price in Gide, *Pretexts: Reflections on Literature and Morality.* Ed. Justin O'Brien. London: Secker and Warburg, 1959, pp. 234–42.

Giltrow, Janet. "Grove in Search of an Audience." *Canadian Literature*, No. 90 (Autumn 1981), pp. 92–107.

Healey, J.J. "Grove and the Matter of Germany. The Warkentin Letters and the Art of Liminal Disengagement." *Studies in Canadian Literature*, 6, No. 2 (1981), 170–87. Rpt. in Hjartarson, ed., *A Stranger to My Time*, pp. 89–105.

Heidenreich, Rosmarin. "The Search for FPG." *Canadian Literature*, No. 80 (Spring 1979), pp. 63–70.

Hind-Smith, Joan. "Frederick Philip Grove." In her *Three Voices: The Lives of Margaret Laurence, Gabrielle Roy, Frederick Philip Grove.* Toronto: Clarke, Irwin, 1975, pp. 131–209.

Hjartarson, Paul. "Design and Truth in Grove's *In Search of Myself.*" *Canadian Literature*, No. 90 (Autumn 1981), pp. 73–90.

———, ed. *A Stranger to My Time: Essays by and about Frederick Philip Grove.* Edmonton: NeWest, 1986.

———. "Of Greve, Grove, and Other Strangers: The Autobiography of the Baroness Elsa von Freytag-Loringhoven." In his *A Stranger to My Time*, pp. 269–84.

Holliday, W.B. "Frederick Philip Grove: An Impression." *Canadian Literature*, No. 3 (Winter 1960), pp. 17–22.

Kaye, Frances W. "Hamlin Garland and Frederick Philip Grove: Self-Conscious Chroniclers of the Pioneers." *Canadian Review of American Studies*, 10 (Spring 1979), 31–39.

Keith, W.J. "Grove's *Over Prairie Trails*: A Re-Examination." *Literary Half-Yearly*, 13 (July 1972), 76–85. Rpt. in Hjartarson, ed., *A Stranger to My Time*, pp. 127–34.

———. "F.P. Grove's 'Difficult' Novel: *The Master of the Mill*." *Ariel*, 4 (April 1973), 34–48.

———. "Grove's Search for America." *Canadian Literature*, No. 59 (Winter 1974), pp. 57–66.

———. "The Art of Frederick Philip Grove: *Settlers of the Marsh* as an Example." *Journal of Canadian Studies*, 9 (Aug. 1974), 26–36.

———. "Grove's 'Magnificent Failure': *The Yoke of Life* Reconsidered." *Canadian Literature*, No. 89 (Summer 1981), pp. 104–17.

Knister, Raymond. "Frederick Philip Grove." *Ontario Library Review*, 13 (Nov. 1928), 60–62. Rpt. as "A Canadian of Canadians" in Pacey, ed., *Frederick Philip Grove*, pp. 11–17, and, combining both titles, in Knister, *The First Day of Spring: Stories and Other Prose*. Ed. Peter Stevens. Toronto: Univ. of Toronto Press, 1976, pp. 435–39.

Kroenagel, Axel. "Greve's First Translation." *Canadian Literature*, No. 111 (Winter 1986), pp. 214–20.

Kroetsch, Robert. "The Grammar of Silence: Narrative Pattern in Ethnic Writing." *Canadian Literature*, No. 106 (Fall 1985), pp. 65–74.

La Bossière, Camille R. "Of Words and Understanding in Grove's *Settlers of the Marsh*." *University of Toronto Quarterly*, 54 (Winter 1984–85), 148–62. Rpt. in Hjartarson, ed., *A Stranger to My Time*, pp. 139–55.

MacDonald, R.D. "The Power of F.P. Grove's *The Master of the Mill*." *Mosaic*, 7 (Winter 1974), 89–100. Rpt. in Hjartarson, ed., *A Stranger to My Time*, pp. 255–68.

Makow, Henry. "Grove's Treatment of Sex: Platonic Love in *The Yoke of Life*." *Dalhousie Review*, 58 (Autumn 1978), 528–40.

———. "Grove's 'The Canyon.'" *Canadian Literature*, No. 82 (Autumn 1979), pp. 141–48.

———, ed. "Letters from Eden: Grove's Creative Rebirth." *University of Toronto Quarterly*, 49 (Fall 1979), 48–64. Rpt. in Hjartarson, ed., *A Stranger to My Time*, pp. 107–26.

———. "Frederick Philip Grove." In *Profiles in Canadian Literature*, Ed.

Jeffrey M. Heath. Toronto: Dundurn, 1980, pp. 49–56.

———. "Grove's 'Garbled Extract': The Bibliographical Origins of *Settlers of the Marsh*." In *The Canadian Novel: Modern Times*. Ed. John Moss. Toronto: NC, 1982, pp. 38–54.

———. "An Edition of Selected Unpublished Essays and Lectures by Frederick Philip Grove Bearing on His Theory of Art." Diss. Toronto 1982.

———. " 'Ellen Lindstedt': The Unpublished Sequel to Grove's *Settlers of the Marsh*." *Studies in Canadian Literature*, 8, No. 2 (1983), 270–76.

Mathews, Robin. "Frederick P. Grove: The Tragic Vision." In his *Canadian Literature: Surrender or Revolution*. Toronto: Steel Rail, 1978, pp. 63–74.

———. "F.P. Grove: An Important Version of *The Master of the Mill* Discovered." *Studies in Canadian Literature*, 7, No. 2 (1982), 241–57.

McCourt, E.A. "Spokesman of a Race?" In his *The Canadian West in Fiction*. Toronto: Ryerson, 1949, pp. 56–70. Rpt. in Pacey, ed., *Frederick Philip Grove*, pp. 59–73.

McKenna, Isobel. "As They Really Were: Women in the Novels of Grove." *English Studies in Canada*, 2 (Spring 1976), 109–16.

McMullen, Lorraine. "Women in Grove's Novels." In Nause, ed., *Grove Symposium*, pp. 67–76.

McMullin, Stanley E. "Grove and the Promised Land." *Canadian Literature*, No. 49 (Summer 1971), pp. 10–19. Rpt. in *Writers of the Prairies*. Ed. Donald G. Stephens. Vancouver: Univ. of British Columbia Press, 1973, pp. 67–76, and in *The Canadian Novel in the Twentieth Century*. Ed. George Woodcock. Toronto: McClelland and Stewart, 1975, pp. 28–37.

———. "Evolution Versus Revolution: Grove's Perception of History." In Nause, ed., *Grove Symposium*, pp. 77–88.

Middlebro', Tom. "Animals, Darwin, and Science Fiction: Some Thoughts on Grove's *Consider Her Ways*." *Canadian Fiction Magazine*, No. 7 (Summer 1972), pp. 55–57.

Miska, John. *Frederick Philip Grove: A Bibliography of Primary and Secondary Materials*. Ottawa: Microform Biblios, 1984.

Mitchell, Beverley. "The 'Message' and the 'Inevitable Form' in *The Master of the Mill*." *Journal of Canadian Fiction*, 3, No. 3 (1974), 74–79.

Morley, Patricia. "*Over Prairie Trails*: 'a poem woven of impressions.' " *Humanities Association Review*, 25 (Summer 1974), 225–31.

Moss, John. "Grove." In his *Patterns of Isolation in English Canadian Fiction*. Toronto: McClelland and Stewart, 1974, pp. 199–209.

———. "Grove, Frederick Philip." In his *A Reader's Guide to the Canadian Novel*. Toronto: McClelland and Stewart, 1981, pp. 106–13.

Nause, John, ed. *The Frederick Philip Grove Symposium.* Ottawa: Univ. of Ottawa Press, 1974. (Originally published earlier in 1974 as a special issue of *Inscape.*)

Nesbitt, Bruce. " 'The Seasons,' Grove's Unfinished Novel." *Canadian Literature,* No. 18 (Autumn 1963), pp. 47–51.

Noel-Bentley, Peter. "The Position of the Unpublished *Jane Atkinson* and *The Weatherhead Fortunes.*" In Nause, ed., *Grove Symposium,* pp. 13–33.

Pacey, Desmond. "Frederick Philip Grove." *Manitoba Arts Review,* 3 (Spring 1943), 28–41. Rpt. in his *Essays in Canadian Criticism, 1938–1968.* Toronto: Ryerson, 1969, pp. 5–21.

———. *Frederick Philip Grove.* Toronto: Ryerson, 1945.

———. "Frederick Philip Grove: A Group of Letters." *Canadian Literature,* No. 11 (Winter 1962), pp. 28–38.

———, ed. *Frederick Philip Grove.* Critical Views of Canadian Writers. Toronto: Ryerson, 1970.

———. "In Search of Grove in Sweden: A Progress Report." *Journal of Canadian Fiction,* 1 (Winter 1972), 69–73.

———, and J.C. Mahanti. "Frederick Philip Grove: An International Novelist." *International Fiction Review,* 1, No. 1 (Jan. 1974), 17–26.

———. "On Editing the Letters of Frederick Philip Grove." In *Editing Canadian Texts.* Ed. Francess Halpenny. Toronto: A.M. Hakkert, 1975, pp. 49–73.

Pache, Walter. "Der Fall Grove — Vorleben und Nachleben des Schriftsellers Felix Paul Greve." *Deutschkanadische Jahrbuch/German Canadian Yearbook,* 5 (1979), 121–36.

———. "The Dilettante in Exile: Grove at the Centenary of His Birth." *Canadian Literature,* No. 90 (Autumn 1981), pp. 187–91.

———. "Frederick Philip Grove's Loneliness — Comparative Perspectives." In *Symposium 83*: Annals of German Canadian Studies, 4. Ed. M. Batts, W. Riedel, and R. Symington. Vancouver: CAUTG, 1983, pp. 185–96. Rpt. as "Frederick Philip Grove: Comparative Perspectives" in Hjartarson, ed., *A Stranger to My Time,* pp. 11–20.

Phelps, A.L. "Frederick Philip Grove." In his *Canadian Writers.* Toronto: McClelland and Stewart, 1951, pp. 36–42.

Pierce, Lorne. "Frederick Philip Grove (1871 [sic] –1948)." *Proceedings and Transactions of the Royal Society of Canada,* 3rd ser., 43 (1949), 113–19. Rpt. in Pacey, ed., *Frederick Philip Grove,* pp. 188–94.

Raths, Deborah, comp. *Register of the Frederick Philip Grove Collection.* Winnipeg: Dept. of Archives, Manuscripts, and Rare Books, Elizabeth Dafoe Library, University of Manitoba, 1979.

Raudsepp, Enn. "Grove and the Wellsprings of Fantasy." *Canadian Literature*, No. 84 (Spring 1980), pp. 131–37.

Ricou, Laurence. "The Implacable Prairie: The Fiction of Frederick Philip Grove." In his *Vertical Man/Horizontal World: Man and Landscape in Canadian Prairie Fiction*. Vancouver: Univ. of British Columbia Press, 1973, pp. 38–64.

Riley, Anthony W. "The German Novels of Frederick Philip Grove." In Nause, ed., *Grove Symposium*, pp. 55–66.

———. "The Case of Greve/Grove: The European Roots of a Canadian Writer." In *The Old World and the New: Literary Perspectives of German-Speaking Canadians*. Ed. Walter E. Riedel. Toronto: Univ. of Toronto Press, 1984, pp. 37–58.

Rowe, Kay. "Here He Lies Where He Longed . . . ." *Manitoba Arts Review*, 6 (Spring 1949), 62–64. Rpt. in Pacey, ed., *Frederick Philip Grove*, pp. 195–99.

Rubio, Mary. "Grove's Search for the Artist." *Journal of Canadian Fiction*, No. 16 (1976), pp. 163–67.

Sandwell, B.K. "Frederick Philip Grove and the Culture of Canada." *Saturday Night*, 24 Nov. 1945, p. 18. Rpt. in Pacey, ed., *Frederick Philip Grove*, pp. 56–59.

Saunders, Doris B. "The Grove Collection of Papers in the University of Manitoba: A Tentative Evaluation." *Papers of the Bibliographical Society of Canada*, 2 (1963), 7–20.

Saunders, Thomas. "The Grove Papers." *Queen's Quarterly*, 70 (Spring 1963), 22–29.

———. "A Novelist as Poet: Frederick Philip Grove." *Dalhousie Review*, 43 (Summer 1963), 235–41. Rpt. in Pacey, ed., *Frederick Philip Grove*, pp. 86–96.

Scobie, Stephen. "The Invisible City of Lund: The Absent Origin and the Place of Canadian Writing." In Jørn Carlsen and Bengt Streijffert, ed., *Canada and the Nordic Countries: Proceedings from the Second International Conference of the Nordic Association for Canadian Studies, University of Lund, 1987*. Lund: Lund Univ. Press, 1988, pp. 299–306.

Siemens, Reynold, and Peter Brown. "Frederick Philip Grove among the Mennonites." *Journal of Mennonite Studies*, 5 (1987), 37–43.

Sirois, Antoine. "Grove et Ringuet: Témoins d'une époque." *Canadian Literature*, No. 49 (Summer 1971), pp. 20–27.

Skelton, Isabel. "Frederick Philip Grove." *Dalhousie Review*, 19 (July 1939), 147–63. Rpt. as "One Speaking into a Void" in Pacey, ed., *Frederick Philip Grove*, pp. 24–44.

Spettigue, Douglas O. *Frederick Philip Grove*. Toronto: Copp Clark, 1969.

————. "Frederick Philip Grove in Manitoba." *Mosaic*, 3 (Spring 1970), 19–33.

————. "'Frederick Philip Grove.'" *Queen's Quarterly*, 78 (Winter 1971), 614–15.

————. "The Grove Enigma Resolved." *Queen's Quarterly*, 79 (Spring 1972), 1–2.

————. *FPG: The European Years*. Ottawa: Oberon, 1973.

————, and A.W. Riley. "Felix Paul Greve *redivivus*. Zum früheren Leben des kanadischen Schriftstellers Frederick Philip Grove." *Seminar*, 9 (June 1973), 148–55.

————. "Fanny Essler and the Master." In Hjartarson, ed., *A Stranger to My Time*, pp. 47–64.

Sproxton, Birk. "Grove's Unpublished MAN and Its Relation to *The Master of the Mill*." In Nause, ed., *Grove Symposium*, pp. 35–54.

Stensberg, Peter A. "Translating the Translatable: A Note on Practical Problems with F.P. Grove's *Wanderungen*." *Canadian Review of Comparative Literature*, 7 (Spring 1980), 206–12.

Stich, K.P. "F.P. Grove's Language of Choice." *Journal of Commonwealth Literature*, 14 (Aug. 1979), 9–17.

————. "Grove's New World Bluff." *Canadian Literature*, No. 90 (Autumn 1981), pp. 111–23.

————. "Extravagant Expression of Travel and Growth: Grove's Quest for America." *Studies in Canadian Literature*, 6, No. 2 (1981), 155–69.

————. "The Memory of Masters in Grove's Self-Portraits." *Études Canadiennes*, 12 (June 1982), 153–64.

————. "Grove's 'Stella.'" *Canadian Literature*, Nos. 113–14 (Summer–Fall 1987), pp. 258–62.

Stobie, Margaret R. "'Frederick Philip Grove' and the Canadianism Movement." *Studies in the Novel*, 4 (Summer 1972), 173–85.

————. *Frederick Philip Grove*. New York: Twayne, 1973.

————, ed. "Grove's Letters from the Mennonite Reserve." *Canadian Literature*, No. 59 (Winter 1974), pp. 67–80.

————. "Grove and the Ants." *Dalhousie Review*, 58 (Autumn 1978), 418–33. Rpt. in Hjartarson, ed., *A Stranger to My Time*, pp. 227–42.

————. "Grove in Simcoe." *Canadian Literature*, No. 111 (Winter 1986), 130–42.

Sutherland, Ronald. *Frederick Philip Grove*. Toronto: McClelland and Stewart, 1969.

————. "What Was Frederick Philip Grove?" In Nause, ed., *Grove Symposium*, pp. 1–11.

Thomas, Clara, and John Lennox. "Grove's Maps." *Essays on Canadian Writing*, No. 26 (Summer 1983), pp. 75–79.

Thompson, Eric. "Grove's Vision of Prairie Man." *Ariel*, 10 (Oct. 1979), 15–33.

Thompson, J. Lee. "In Search of Order: The Structure of Grove's *Settlers of the Marsh*." *Journal of Canadian Fiction*, 3, No. 3 (1974), 65–74. Rev. and rpt. in *The Canadian Novel: Modern Times*. Ed. John Moss. Toronto: NC, 1982, pp. 19–37.

Webber, Bernard. "Grove in Politics." *Canadian Literature*, No. 63 (Winter 1975), pp. 126–27.

Wiebe, Rudy. "A Novelist's Personal Notes on Frederick Philip Grove." *University of Toronto Quarterly*, 47 (Spring 1978), 189–99. Rpt. in *A Voice in the Land: Essays by and about Rudy Wiebe*. Ed. W.J. Keith. Edmonton: NeWest, 1981, pp. 212–25.

Raymond Knister
and His Works

Raymond Knister (1899–1932)

JOY KUROPATWA

Biography

JOHN RAYMOND KNISTER was born in Ruscom,[1] near Stoney Point on Lake St. Clair, in Essex County, Ontario, on 27 May 1899. His mother was a teacher, his father a farmer "extremely active in the social and political life of Ontario farmers."[2] What is probably a fictionalized account of this activity is found in Knister's still unpublished novel "Turning Loam." Reading and writing appealed to Knister from the first; he kept a record of his reading between late 1914 and mid-1924 in which over a thousand works are listed,[3] and he started writing as a teenager. There is evidence that much of his poetry was written in the early 1920s,[4] and his first published story, "The One Thing," appeared in the January 1922 issue of the American publication *The Midland*,[5] a magazine that H.L. Mencken described as "perhaps the most important magazine ever founded in America."[6]

In 1919 Knister attended the University of Toronto, until he was hospitalized for pneumonia (Waddington, p. 176). While at the university, he contributed to his college's publication *Acta Victoriana*,[7] and was the student of Pelham Edgar, author of *Henry James, Man and Author* (1927).

From 1920 to 1923 he wrote while working on his father's farm near Blenheim, Ontario. It was during this time that "Mist-Green Oats," probably his best-known short story, appeared (O'Halloran, p. 195). By the autumn of 1922, Knister turned his attention to novel writing; he also began reviewing books for a Windsor newspaper, *The Border Cities Star*, and "within a year earned for the *Star* the reputation of printing one of Canada's outstanding Literary Pages" (Waddington, p. 179).

In the autumn of 1923 Knister moved to Iowa City:

Knister began his work with *The Midland* in October, 1923 as the Associate Editor. This was a special new position representing a kind of scholarship Frederick [the editor] had created for young writers of exceptional promise. Ruth Suckow had been the first appointed to the position a year before. Knister's duties ranged through almost every aspect of *Midland* work, and included reading and judging manuscripts, proofreading them and participating in editorial decisions. He was entitled to choose his own hours, perhaps two or three a day, so as to have substantial leisure for his own creative work. (Waddington, p. 179)

Knister attended courses at Iowa University and completed two still-unpublished novels, "Group Portrait" and "Turning Loam," while working on *The Midland*.[8] After his term as associate editor ended in June 1924, he went to Chicago, where he wrote during the day and drove taxi by night. Chicago would become the setting for more than one work: the short story "Hackman's Night," the published novella "Innocent Man," and the unpublished novella "Cab Driver" (which surfaced only in January 1984). In October 1924 Knister left Chicago to return to Canada; this homecoming is considered to be the background to the poem "After Exile" (Waddington, p. 181).

By 1925 his work appeared in *This Quarter*, an American expatriate magazine published in Paris, in which the work of Djuna Barnes, e.e. cummings, Ernest Hemingway, James Joyce, and Carl Sandburg also appeared (Waddington, p. 182). In a letter from Ernest Walsh, editor of *This Quarter*, Knister was told, "Your stuff is real."[9]

Knister wrote many reviews, articles, and sketches for popular magazines and newspapers, but a 1925 letter suggests that he tolerated rather than rejoiced in bread-and-butter composition:

You will be interested to know that I have taken on the job of turning out a story a week . . . . a series of rural character sketches — *Toronto Star Weekly*'s request . . . . Loth to have anything to do with Can. (or any other kind of) journalism, I says, How much? 2 c. per word, quoth 'e. Aweel, says I, you've brought it on yourself.[10]

In 1926 Knister moved to Toronto, where he wrote full-time. The literati included Morley Callaghan, Dorothy Livesay, Wilson MacDonald, Charles G.D. Roberts, Mazo de la Roche, and Duncan Campbell Scott. It was also during the Toronto years that Knister became the mentor of Thomas Murtha, whose short stories were not published in book form until 1980.[11]

Knister married Myrtle Gamble in 1927, and the couple spent the summer at the "Poplars," a cottage at Hanlan's Point, Toronto Island. Here Knister completed the final draft of *White Narcissus*, his only novel to be published during his lifetime. In September 1927, Macmillan accepted the novel for publication and in October commissioned him to edit an anthology of Canadian short stories (Waddington, p. 186). *Canadian Short Stories*, dedicated to Duncan Campbell Scott, was published in 1928 and is thought to be the first anthology of its kind. Knister's Introduction to the collection is still considered a helpful discussion of the Canadian short story. In 1929 *White Narcissus* was published in Canada, England, and the United States.

In the spring of 1929 Knister and his wife moved to a farmhouse on the lake road near Port Dover, Ontario; here he wrote *My Star Predominant*, a well-researched novel based on the life of John Keats. A daughter, Imogen, was born in Port Dover in 1930. *Show Me Death*, a World War 1 novel, appeared in 1930 under the name of W. Redvers Dent, but was actually, to a currently unknown extent, ghost-written by Knister. Frederick Philip Grove encouraged Knister to submit *My Star Predominant* to the Graphic Publishers' Canadian Novel Contest; Grove was chairman of the committee adjudicating the award, the other committee members being W.T. Allison, who taught English at the University of Manitoba, and Barker Fairley, who taught German at the University of Toronto.[12] The novel won the $2,500 first prize in 1931, but Graphic went bankrupt and the novel did not appear until 1934, when it was published in Canada and England. Knister had written *My Star Predominant* between 1929 and 1931; the dates of composition of other works overlap with the time of writing the novel: "Innocent Man" was written between 1927 and 1931, while "Cab Driver" was written between 1927 and 1930.[13] The novella, "There Was a Mr. Cristi," became available in February 1986; the typescript ends with the notation, "May–June, 1928, Toronto — December, 1930, Port Dover."[14]

In 1931 and 1932 Knister lived in Quebec, first in Montreal and then in Ste. Anne de Bellevue; it was while in Quebec that his friendship with Leo Kennedy was established.[15] Knister's last novel, "Soil in Smoke," was written between 1931 and 1932; it is a revised version of his first novel, "Group Portrait."[16] Both remain unpublished. During the same period, Knister wrote a number of short stories and the novella "Peaches, Peaches" (O'Halloran, p. 198). He returned to Ontario in 1932 and was offered a job on the editorial staff of Ryerson Press that would allow him time for his own writing.

Raymond Knister drowned while swimming off Stoney Point, Lake St. Clair, on 29 August 1932. An account of this last day has been published.[17] He was thirty-three at the time of his death.

Knister was a writer of short stories, poems, novels, and novellas, and a playwright, as well as being a critic and editor. Much of his writing remains unpublished, and therefore unknown. Moreover, during the 1970s some works were published for the first time, and some reprinted, and with this revival of interest emerged a reevaluation of his role in Canadian letters as being that of an interesting but minor author. An important contribution to this reevaluation is the Knister issue of the *Journal of Canadian Fiction* (1975), also published in book form as *Raymond Knister: Poems, Stories and Essays*, edited and introduced by David Arnason, in which work by and about Knister appears.

A selection of Knister's poetry, edited by Dorothy Livesay, was published as *Collected Poems of Raymond Knister* (1949). Further poems, many previously unpublished, appear in *Raymond Knister: Poems, Stories and Essays* and *Windfalls for Cider: The Poems of Raymond Knister* (1983). There is no collected edition of Knister's short stories, but a few appear in *Selected Stories of Raymond Knister* (1972), and many can be found in *Raymond Knister: Poems, Stories and Essays* and *The First Day of Spring: Stories and Other Prose* (1976). Of Knister's nine currently known works of longer prose fiction, five remain unpublished. A 1990 reprint of *White Narcissus* includes an Afterword by Morley Callaghan (in McClelland and Stewart's New Canadian Library series).

Tradition and Milieu

It is difficult to associate Knister's work strictly with any single literary tradition and maintain an accurate sense of his work as a whole. Knister has usually been described as working within the tradition of literary realism, but the complexity and range of his writing suggest that his work could receive more careful attention than it has in the past. In his own critical writing there is cross-

reference between forms: for example, he observes that the short
story has an "adaptability to poetical interpretation";[18] elsewhere,
that Edwin Arlington Robinson is "the Conrad of the narrative
poem," as Browning "had been its Henry James."[19] Furthermore,
Knister read widely, tended to be experimental, valued the artist who
had the courage to express his personal vision, and felt the appeal
of the eclectic. He considered himself a Canadian writer and saw
Canada as a place where "we have room for all schools, space to be
free of all schools."[20] But his view was not isolationist: "Criticism
on the part of readers, yes, by all means. But not the kind which
assumes that a book is going to be good or bad because it is
Canadian."[21]

Yeats remarked that after "established things were shaken by the
Great War," there arose the feeling that

> poetry must resemble prose, and both must accept the vocabu-
> lary of their time; nor must there be any special subject-matter.
> Tristram and Isoult were not a more suitable theme than
> Paddington Railway Station.[22]

Knister's work exhibits the thematic range that Yeats speaks of: the
"ill-starred lovers of romance, Tristram and Isoult," are mentioned
in *White Narcissus*,[23] and in the Foreword intended for "Windfalls
for Cider," a proposed selection of his poems, Knister writes, "Birds
and flowers and dreams are real as sweating men and swilling pigs."[24]
Knister did not divorce theory from practice; if he is usually remembered for his observant and evocative nature poetry, he is also the
author of prose fiction depicting acute psychological tension,
imprisonment, racial hostility, and sexual politics.

Knister describes the Canadian writers "Scott, Roberts, Carman,
E.W. Thomson, W.W. Campbell, and Lampman" as having to work
in a situation in which ".... the normal response of a writer to his
environment was that of a more or less thoroughly transplanted
Englishman."[25] He adds that the Canadian poet sometimes

> did not even keep his eye accurately upon the object, and too
> often he lapsed into a weak-kneed banality of line and a depen-
> dence upon the quality of recognition in his reader. "That is
> good verse, it reminds me of Shelley." It is not to be supposed
> that a poet of Lampman's gifts would now begin a sonnet,
> "Beautiful are thy hills, Wayagamack" .... (p. 457)

The Imagist movement has been considered the greatest single influence on Knister's poetry. Knister's evaluation of the importance of the technical aspects of writing reflects Imagist concerns. In his "Credo," Pound writes, "I think ... that some poems may have form as a tree has form, some as water poured into a vase" and refers to "technique of surface and technique of content."[26] Knister observes,

> Now technique is not merely an exterior matter; or even if it be that it is as the bark of a tree is exterior — and essential. Your subject will be changed, added to, weakened, heightened, or diminished, by a change of method.[27]

A comment of Knister's (made in the course of his essay on Lampman's poetry) has been described by Livesay as a statement of his aesthetic: " 'Poetry is to make things real — those of the imagination, and those of the tangible world.' "[28] Elsewhere Knister writes, "... poetry must have, or rather has a connection with life" ("Canadian Letter," p. 381). And, again in his essay on Lampman, he defines the "basic and enduring qualities" of poetry as being "truth of thought, integrity of feeling, and tempered expression" (pp. 457–58).

Marcus Waddington points out that Knister, like Poe, thought in terms of some continuity between poetry and the short story (Waddington, Thesis, p. 20). Knister refers to one of his short stories (likely "The Strawstack") as being "obviously derived from Poe" ("Canadian Literati," p. 166), and he writes of the short story as "the ark and covenant of Maupassant, Tchekov and Poe" ("Democracy and the Short Story," p. 146). But it is Chekhov who is seen as the master: "... since he is to the short story what Shakespeare is to the poetic drama, the form can never be quite the same again."[29] Waddington calls this "symbolic form" and describes Knister's short stories as influenced by Chekhov's technique:

> It involves the art of infusing a story with an inner radiance by virtue of which every word, every object and action, every aspect of character, situation and landscape reflects upon and reveals the significance of every other. (Waddington, Thesis, p. 31)

Knister notes that the "modern novelist" has "concerns deriving from James and Flaubert,"[30] and that "... it is his view of the world which the artist seeks to impart as Henry James has said."[31] In his Introduction to *Canadian Short Stories*, Knister states:

When Flaubert is bringing some undeniable picture to your recognition, he is doing it only to impose upon you some emotion which is part of his plan and the outgrowth of his own emotion. What is known as realism is only a means to an end, the end being a personal projection of the world.[32]

Henry James refers to Flaubert in the same preface in which he defines his understanding of the literary label "romance,"[33] a definition generally helpful in considering the work of American nineteenth-century writers of romance.[34] Knister refers to James, Melville, and Poe in his critical work, and in *White Narcissus*, as the crisis of the novel nears, the protagonist reaches for Hawthorne's *The Scarlet Letter*.[35] In Knister's remark that the best "American short story writers . . . care more for emotional authenticity than for ingenuity of plot, or for too explicit realism" ("Democracy and the Short Story," p. 148), perhaps there is some empathy with Hawthorne's observation that the writer of romance ought not "swerve aside from the truth of the human heart."[36]

Certainly Knister had little use for the type of romance that celebrates "times when gentlemen carried swords and yearned to use them, if possible on pretext of a lady's honour."[37] He was interested in the possibilities of literary realism, although he refers to going "beyond realism"[38] as moving in a positive direction. "Perhaps," speculates Knister,

it is because of the difficulties attending upon the discovery of the interesting and the heroic in everyday reality that our novelists have tended to shirk the task . . . .[39]

If Knister's view of realism was highly positive, it was not unqualified: "Realism is not . . . to be accepted as an end in itself, nor, at its best, as an unmixed good, but as bringing a depth of knowledge and conviction and authenticity of feeling together with a more revealing portrayal of our inner life."[40] Although Knister employs the techniques of literary realism, his work can be viewed as open to the influence of more than one tradition.

Knister expresses a definite aversion to an author distrusting, misrepresenting, or violating "experienced reality" ("The Poetry of Archibald Lampman," p. 458); characters in fiction, he writes, "may transcend the people we see about us, but they must be true to them, and true to type."[41] He rejects the attitude that caused the editor of the *Toronto Star Weekly* to "expostulate earnestly . . . 'Mr. Knister, you make your people too real. Our readers don't want to read about real things. They want to be amused. Try to put more plot into your stories' " ("Canadian Literati," p. 164). Knister had little patience for any "yea-saying protagonist of all's-wellness."[42] Despite the fact that he "was sure that there were some thousands of readers of the paper who would like to see their life pictured more or less as it was" ("Canadian Literati," p. 165), such potential readers were, as David Arnason points out, "protected from Knister by conservative editors."[43] In summing up the essay "Canadian Literati," Knister remarks, "I am only pointing out that we probably will have to come to grips with reality before we shall have a literature . . ." (p. 167).

Knister's milieu included many of the Toronto literati of his day (see "Biography" above); correspondents included Harriet Monroe, Pelham Edgar, Frederick Philip Grove, Leo Kennedy, A.J.M. Smith, Thomas Murtha, Morley Callaghan, John T. Frederick, Dorothy Livesay, Duncan Campbell Scott, and Ruth Suckow. Letters between Knister and Murtha, and Knister's correspondence with various publishing houses, provide windows through which to glimpse the literary life of the era. Letters from Grove to Knister have been published,[44] and correspondence with Knister is quoted, and his connection with *Saturday Night* briefly discussed, in a biography of William Arthur Deacon.[45] William Murtha discusses the relationship between Thomas Murtha and Knister in his Introduction to *Short Stories of Thomas Murtha*.[46]

Knister is remembered in various forms of memoir and memorial. The dedication of Leo Kennedy's *The Shrouding* reads "For / Raymond Knister / one year dead."[47] A large proportion of *Collected Poems of Raymond Knister* (1949) consists of Dorothy Livesay's memoir, an abridged version of which is reprinted in *Right Hand Left Hand*.[48] Another Livesay memoir of Knister appeared in the April 1987 issue of *Books in Canada*. Letters by Imogen Knister Givens and Alice Munro appear in the August–September 1987 issue of *Books in Canada*: both writers cast the accuracy of Livesay's version of events in some doubt. A subsequent Livesay "Reminiscence" seems to contradict the impression the 1987 piece leaves (*Newest Review*, 15, No. 2 [Dec. 1989–Jan. 1990], 10–14). A CBC Radio program about Knister included contributions from Nathaniel Benson, Morley Callaghan, Philip Child, Wilfrid Eggleston, Wilson

MacDonald, James Reaney, and Knister's wife.[49] In 1976 a memoir by Leo Kennedy appeared,[50] and meeting Knister at Pelham Edgar's home is recollected in Earle Birney's *Spreading Time*.[51]

In "Raymond Knister — Man or Myth?" Imogen Knister Givens discusses her father's life and career, quotes a diary entry of her mother's describing the day of Knister's death, and refutes Livesay's "suicide theory" concerning Knister.[52]

Dorothy Livesay, James Reaney, and David Arnason have all pointed to the power of Knister's writing, but most critics of Knister's work have not explored either the literary roots or branches of Knister's work to any great extent, and there has been slight discussion of Knister in the context of his cultural era. However, Knister's letters include, for example, references to Lawren Harris and A.Y. Jackson,[53] to Emma Goldman,[54] and to his visiting, while in New York, "Greenwich Village where the artists and writers (used to) hang out."[55] The totality of Knister's work, much of which remains unpublished or unreprinted, and the Knister papers and letters suggest that Knister has been overlooked as a major Canadian writer — if not the major Canadian writer — of the 1920s.

Critical Overview and Context

No encompassing view of Knister as poet, writer of prose fiction, and critic has yet emerged, which may be fortunate, as the fragments, versions, and miscellaneous documents held in different archival collections of Knister papers have yet to be collated and become the basis of reliable editions of Knister's work. Interestingly enough, among the critics whose work is most helpful on the subject of Knister — David Arnason, Dorothy Livesay, James Reaney, and Marcus Waddington — are creative writers.

The line taken in English and American reviews of *White Narcissus* may be summed up in the expression with which Cyril Connolly describes the novel — "mildly sophisticated."[56] J.D. Robins — like Pelham Edgar, Robins had taught Knister at Victoria College (Waddington, p. 166) — argues, in his 1929 *Canadian Forum* review, that the novel shows the influence of Nathaniel Hawthorne.[57]

Desmond Pacey notes the regionalism of and the American influence upon Knister's work. As Knister "had lived for a time in the American mid-west," he would have "come in contact with the work of . . . Sherwood Anderson and Sinclair Lewis." Pacey adds that Knister's "stories are set . . . in rural Ontario, and it is in the fresh description of the life and scenery of that part of Canada that the chief virtue of his better novel, *White Narcissus,* is to be found."[58] In his Introduction to the 1962 New Canadian Library edition of *White Narcissus,* Philip Child takes a similar view of the strength of Knister's work: "The depicting of the Ontario country landscape and the life and manners and atmosphere of living in the farmland are the staples of his best writing."[59] According to Child, "though the White Narcissus is meant to be the central symbol of the novel and though it gives the book its title, it is static"; he also claims, "Once planted in the story it does not grow and help to move the plot forward or deepen its significance." The "description of nature making its impact on . . . Milne's mind" is seen as more successful. While finding that "Knister's originality" resides in creating "an atmosphere in which realism . . . is combined with realism's own kind of poetry" (p. 13), Child concludes that Knister's contribution to Canadian literature is "a real achievement though it is not a major one" (p. 16).

In his 1978 article, "Beyond Realism: Raymond Knister's *White Narcissus,*" Paul Denham argues that "Realism is not an adequate category to describe either of Knister's [published] novels."[60] Denham remarks that Knister's protagonist "eventually abandons his romanticism," but if it can be assumed that Knister upholds "a more 'realistic' view," precisely what "this realistic view is to consist of . . . is not entirely clear" (pp. 71–72). Denham notes that the mythological associations of the "narcissus, the various descriptions of Ada, and the name Lethen itself all contribute to the sense of a dark and threatening underworld" (pp. 72–73), but that a "major weakness of the novel" is "a failure to sustain the duality of the daylit world and the dark one which Knister establishes at the beginning of the novel" (p. 76). Although Denham discusses various intriguing points of contact between Hawthorne's fiction and *White Narcissus,* he sees no ongoing "parallel" at work (pp. 75–76). Denham concludes that "Knister's strength is in his willingness to make use of several modes to suggest a complex vision of the world." If "we are not used to looking for gothic elements and mythological allusions in the realistic Canadian novel," *White Narcissus* "is a novel of southwestern Ontario, a region whose writers — from Major John Richardson to James Reaney, Graeme Gibson, and Alice Munro — display a continuing interest in the gothic" (p. 77).

Glenn Clever, in his 1978 "Point of View in *White Narcissus*," maintains that Knister "has little control over point of view,"[61] and claims that "viewpoint fails to keep its focus," especially "in passages on Richard and Ada" (p. 121). Clever concludes that the work "deserves to be admired as a fine novel of mood and poetic description and as a turning point in the course of the Canadian novel from external to internal viewpoint," but finds "one of the main reasons" for reader "dissatisfaction" to be "lack of adequate control over point of view" (p. 123).

In *A Reader's Guide to the Canadian Novel* (1981), John Moss points to the symbolism of the name Lethen,[62] and sees the novel as "essentially realistic" (p. 145). Moss identifies the treatment of "imagery of the rural world" as "the source of the novel's lasting importance," and finds that despite its "major flaws," *White Narcissus* "is not as pretentious or contrived as *My Star Predominant*" (pp. 145–46).

Robert Ayre's 1934 *Saturday Night* review of *My Star Predominant* describes the novel as being, "in the richest meaning of the word, a recreation." He states that "Knister has brought John Keats to life."[63] However, *The Globe*'s anonymous 1934 review, "Keats and His Ailment," declares, "Never squeamish, Mr. Knister does not hesitate to introduce the baser frailties of the Victorian age, nor yet does he spare the reader in the matter of his hero's disease." Knister's "fictionalized life of John Keats" is said to be "thoroughly readable and instructive," if "not satisfying."[64]

Some interesting remarks about *My Star Predominant* occur in discussions that focus on other Knister works. Waddington notes that "Structurally the novel divides into four themes: Friends, Poetry, Love and Death," and that these "interweave" (Thesis, p. 218). He sees the "paradoxes" present in Knister's earlier work — "good and evil, growth and decay, hopefulness and futility, and beauty and dreariness" — reappear in *My Star Predominant*, and describes the work as "a summation" of Knister's "stylistic and thematic development" (Thesis, p. 219). In the context of his discussion of Knister's poetry, Don Precosky cites both *White Narcissus* and *My Star Predominant* in coming to the conclusion that "The process through which his writer-heroes go is undoubtedly based upon Knister's own development." Precosky sees Knister's Keats as going from "sentimentality to a desire for direct contact with life and from ignorance to self-knowledge."[65] Desmond Pacey, in *Literary History of Canada*, finds *My Star Predominant* to compare unfavourably with *White Narcissus*. Pacey defines Knister's accomplishment as "describing honestly the rural Ontario scene."[66]

The 1972 *Selected Stories of Raymond Knister* reprints six of Knister's early short stories. In his Introduction, editor Michael Gnarowski suggests that "archetypal elements" should be taken into account in considering Knister's work.[67] Gnarowski views "The One Thing" as a study in isolation; "Mist-Green Oats," "The Strawstack," and "The Loading" as "studies in initiation"; "Elaine" and "The Fate of Mrs Lucier" as "psychological or 'state-of-mind' stories" (p. 13); and poses the question of whether Knister may have "gone on . . . to create along a progressively more experimental line" (p. 11).

Dorothy Livesay's 1974 "Knister's Stories" is both a review of *Selected Stories of Raymond Knister* and a discussion of Knister as a prose fiction writer. Livesay notes that Knister's "chief desire . . . was to write fiction,"[68] and comments that Gnarowski's "emphasis on the mythopoeic aspect of the stories is provocative, yet in my view it runs contrary to Knister's own intention." Livesay explains,

All writers make some use of myth but with some moderns such as Malcolm Lowry . . . there is a conscious structure, a schema of symbols. I do not feel this to be the case in Knister's fiction. (p. 81)

The selected six stories are said to share the presence of "a lonely, introspective key character who identifies with 'one thing,' one person, one animal, one object; usually because he cannot fit into the norms of the community" (pp. 81–82).

Knister's fiction is seen as being "strongly influenced by what we might now call the 'magic' realism of Sherwood Anderson," in the sense that Knister found in Anderson's work "a confirmation of his own views: start with precise observation, but see behind it into the nature of things" (p. 80). Livesay writes that "Knister is less facile and obvious than Anderson," and "more profoundly concerned with the loneliness of man"; the "magic realism" enters because "whereas Knister sought for a simple realistic effect he possessed, in addition, an intensity and sensitivity by which he was able to make the ordinary extraordinary" (p. 81).

84

Knister is described as a "stylist of the first order": his "prose must be read slowly, savoured, for each sentence has weight and thickness, its rhythms carefully balanced." Knister's vocabulary, as an aspect of his style, is said to be "recherché sometimes to the point of obscurity," but more frequently "pays off," and the power of his imagery is noted (p. 82). Livesay concludes,

This evocation of landscape through all the pores of the senses is what makes Knister's short stories so memorable. The other haunting element is the structure of the stories: their movement with great ease from the authorial-objective point of view to the subjective inner eye of the protagonist. And finally there is the effect of the inconsequential, ambiguous series of endings to the stories. Here Knister could offer a lesson to Callaghan, who presses home his point *ad nauseum*. Knister's "point" is hard to come by. We are left with the question: just what does the story mean? And that is perhaps why there will be many more interpretations beyond mine, and beyond Gnarowski's. (p. 81)

David Arnason's edition of works by and about Knister, *Raymond Knister: Poems, Stories and Essays*, appeared as Number 14 of *Journal of Canadian Fiction*, Special Knister Edition, and as a book, in 1975. It includes Knister poems, short stories and essays, a biographical essay by Marcus Waddington, a chronology, and Arnason's Preface, which discusses Knister in the context of his era:

Canada, like the rest of the western world, entered the modern age, and Raymond Knister, a child of the century, entered it at the same time. Behind all the hoopla, the crazes that swept the country, the jazzy superficialities, a new sensibility was emerging, and in Canada during the nineteen-twenties its most articulate spokesman was an intense, desperately hard working youth with a stutter, Raymond Knister. The form that the new sensibility took in literature was an increasing concern for psychological truth and realist techniques, and those elements are at the heart of Knister's work.
. . . Knister was in perfect tune with the new, emerging sensibility, and it appalled him that he could not make others see it. He read widely and he thought a great deal about his art and the nature of art in general. He found a few kindred spirits . . .

85

and he describes the intense joy of finding someone who agreed with him on all the important points.[69]

Leo Kennedy, in his 1976 review of *Journal of Canadian Fiction*'s Special Knister Edition, comments that "Knister's horses have more diverse personalities, and are observed more vividly and acutely than are many human fictional characters that I've stumbled over or gagged at recently."[70] Kennedy describes Knister as a "resolute, greatly gifted writer handicapped by the economics and prejudices of the times he worked in," one "resolved to get the Ontario rural scene onto paper in convincing terms that would hammer on the consciousness of his fellow countrymen," "a writer determined, as so many still are, to make Canadians aware of the Canadian written word."[71]

By the mid-seventies a revival of interest in Knister's work was underway: Livesay's discussion of Knister's prose fiction appeared in 1974, Arnason's *Raymond Knister: Poems, Stories and Essays* in 1975, *The First Day of Spring: Stories and Other Prose*, edited by Peter Stevens, in 1976, and Waddington's thesis in 1977.

In his Introduction, Stevens states that "Knister has never been given the recognition that he deserves as one of the first truly modern writers in Canadian literature."[72] Stevens views Knister as "not merely a direct realist," and refers to Knister's "belief that the realistic surface of a story should contain a symbolic depth" (p. xvii). Stevens finds "Innocent Man" to include "a kind of Kafka-like allegory" (p. xxi), and sees in Knister's fictional treatment of animals "Omens of *Animal Farm*" (p. xviii).

Reaction to *The First Day of Spring* varied. Michael Darling dismisses it, finding "about six per cent of the text" better than "dross."[73] Margot Northey joins Livesay in referring to Knister's "magic realism," and states that his stories move us "beyond the surface to more private and mysterious levels of experience."[74] Barry Cameron finds Knister "knowledgeable about world literature, and his criticism of both Canadian and non-Canadian writers evolves out of that knowledge"; "Knister's own poetry and fiction also evolve out of his knowledge of world literature." Cameron describes Knister as "an important Canadian writer."[75]

Knister's fiction is the subject of more than one thesis. Doris Everard's 1972 M.A. thesis, "Tragic Dimensions in Selected Stories of Raymond Knister," argues a "tragic development" in his work.[76]

Marcus Waddington's 1977 "Raymond Knister and the Canadian Short Story" is an extensively researched study that includes discussion, based on Knister papers as well as published material, of Knister's life and work. Waddington assigns dates for Knister's works, which is of especial value as Knister revised repeatedly — in the case of "Mist-Green Oats" even after publication — and there is no strict correspondence between the order of writing and the sequence of publication. Knister as writer, editor, and critic of the Canadian short story is the focus of Waddington's study.

Waddington notes that Knister "looked upon Chekhov as the greatest writer of the short story and the artist most responsible for its modern form" (Thesis, p. 18). Knister is said to have "absorbed Chekhov's technique" of using what "might be termed symbolic form" (Thesis, p. 31). In Waddington's view, "by taking the consciousness of his characters for his theme, Knister carried the tradition of the Canadian story into the realm of modern experimental prose being created by Joyce, Woolf and Mansfield" (Thesis, p. 80). Although, Waddington notes, Knister chose to forego including his own work in *Canadian Short Stories*, his short story "The Fate of Mrs. Lucier," "the first Canadian story to employ the technique of interior monologue, is remarkable as an experiment in psychological realism" (Thesis, p. 55).

In a CBC program about Knister, James Reaney remarks,

P.K. Page and the Montreal crowd *Preview* group — they think Knister was just hopelessly pastoral and sort of funny — you know — writing about pigs and horses and so on — "Who the Hell does that any more?" they would probably say. They were interested in Rilke though, and he was interested in Rilke and that's where they meet — because in Rilke, that's where you get those images that you get in *White Narcissus*. And in P.K. Page you get these weird images — which sort of combine outside nature with things inside the mind.[77]

As Reaney points out, it is unfortunate to typecast Knister's work as "hopelessly pastoral" — the tone of dismissal critics may employ when referring to Knister as a writer of things pastoral or regional is seen in perspective if one were to imagine dismissal of Thomas Hardy's work for similar reasons. In Raymond Knister's fiction, tangible reality — "pigs and horses and so on" — is as real as intangible reality — "things inside the mind." One of the very reasons Knister's work endures the test of time is that his writing acknowledges realities more and less tangible — imaginary and "experienced reality" ("Lampman," p. 458).

Two very diverging views emerge in the context of more recent discussions of Knister's work. Doug Smith's 1985 omnibus review, "The Fine and Patient Hand," includes discussion of *Windfalls for Cider*. Smith states, "I would venture to say that Knister is one of the important, if not *the* most important of Canadian poets" and gives three reasons for saying so: Knister's understanding of the image, Knister's recognition that "poetry could be about *anything*," and Knister being "the first Canadian poet to use a modern idiom."[78] Smith mentions concepts of Keats (p. 205) and D.H. Lawrence (p. 206) in relation to the work of Knister, comments that Knister's "prose does not show the same weaknesses" as his poetry, and concludes,

> Raymond Knister was a genius, all right, if we can agree that by genius we mean someone who can wake his audience up to a world of inherently multiple and simultaneous possibilities, making them recognize and appreciate the tension between as is and as if, that energy which fruitfully unites imagination and life. (p. 207)

George Woodcock, in his 1987 introduction to Volume III of the Poetry Series of *Canadian Writers and Their Works*, takes a much dimmer view of Knister's work. Woodcock describes Knister as "an ambitious writer who died while his powers were still maturing."[79] Interestingly enough, the views of Smith and Woodcock regarding Knister seem to be in close to perfect opposition. Smith claims that Knister learned from "his reading of Pound and Eliot" (p. 203) while Woodcock claims that Knister's poetry was "innocent . . . of the great mainstream modernist masters like Eliot and Pound" (p. 11). Smith and Woodcock both associate Knister's work with Lawrence's (p. 11). Nevertheless, Woodcock's essential view of Knister is opposite to Smith's: Woodcock maintains,

> Of his two novels that were published, *White Narcissus* is an engaging liaison between romance and realism, but no master-

piece, while *My Star Predominant,* his novel about John Keats (another poet who died young), is a clumsily architectured monument to careful research. Knister wrote some shrewd, but not profound, criticism and some very good short stories, but so far as his actual achievement — as distinct from his ambitions — is concerned, his reputation is likely to stand or fall on his poetry .... (p. 11)

In contrast to Smith, Woodcock concludes that "one cannot claim him [Knister] as one of the more important Canadian writers" (p. 11).

The sheer disparity, amounting to virtual polar opposition, of even descriptions of Knister's work suggests how much critical opinion of Knister's writing currently varies; the fluidity of the situation likely reflects concurrent interest in Knister's work and the fact that much of what Knister wrote still remains an archival proposition.

Knister's Works

The fiction of Raymond Knister celebrates "experienced reality" with power and integrity. Broadly inclusive vision and a willingness to experiment mark Knister's stories, novellas, and novels. To enter the world of Knister's fiction can mean considering published and unpublished novels and novellas, looking at a sampling of unpublished avant-garde stories, and examining documentation that reveals traces of an interesting dispute. Raymond Knister defended an assertion which, as a basis for his writing and a position he actively argued, helps explain what makes his role in the development of Canadian literature crucial.

When the word "experience" appears in Knister's non-fiction, the context he provides for the term generally constitutes a comment which can be applied to his own fiction. For example, Knister's work frequently acknowledges "inward experience" ("Katherine Mansfield," p. 431). Knister, in his non-fiction, writes of the importance of "search and the possibility of discoveries"[80]; he also describes Sandburg's poetry as serving as a reminder that "man must go on exploring his many provinces, that his only hope is a truthful and honest search for beauty in what *experience* is given him, in daily life and vision"[81] (italics added). And Knister's declared interest in

Sandburg's work at least partly stems from Sandburg's ability to draw on his own experience:

> Had we the courage of our experience, we might have produced a Burns; by which I mean a poet drawing his inspiration from the soil.... Carl Sandburg finds beauty and majesty in Chicago, but he was not born there. His very name I feel sure, arouses a shudder among my readers. That is why we have no Burns, no Sandburg; the fallacy that only certain traditionally sanctified objects are poetical would make progress impossible. Nothing, not poetry or dreams, can exist except on the basis of reality. As long as we flinch from contact with the actual, we shall go without great poetry, and our verses will become more and more nearly dead matter.[82]

In his Preface to "Windfalls for Cider" (1926), Knister refers to the possibility of "we in Canada" having "the courage of our experience," and the latter phrase also appears in Knister's 1928 remarks about Sandburg. The expression implies an underlying view of reality, for to have "the courage of our experience" is to acknowledge more than the material conditions of reality as existing. More than regionalism as local colour or vibrant landscape is in question. For example, like Sandburg, Knister made space for politics and religion in his work. What appears to intrigue Knister about Sandburg is that the latter draws on his own experience — be it of place or perceptions of politics — in his writing. The reality of geographical place just provides the ground for beginning to write of "reality," or, in Knister's words, the "experience" of "daily life and vision."

A preference for literature that reflects experienced reality emerges from Knister's reference to writers "not vigorous enough to deal with experienced reality as a whole" ("Lampman," p. 458). Knister calls for a Canadian literature engaged with "what is actually being lived among us" ("Canadian Letter," p. 379) — and makes it plain that more than material reality is in question. As Livesay notes, for Knister, "poetry is to make things real — those of the imagination, and of the tangible world" ("Lampman," p. 464). It follows that Knister sees the art of fiction as involving more than accurate reproduction of surface or material reality, or what Knister calls "photographic realism."[83] In a letter of 16 October 1922, Knister remarks, "I did not mean to speak from behind the rampart of the

90

dominant (whatever the ultra-intelligentsia may say) cult of realism of a more or less photographic sort."[84]

Knister's repeatedly reveals a limited interest in a "photographic" type of verisimilitude:

> Realistic experience does not weigh so vastly according to purely literary values. Gun-playing West and North or chimes-auraëd cathedral towns may be absurd; but it is not so necessary that art should portray a reality which we can identify without going farther than the window or the mirror, as that it should embody a life of its own. ("Canadian Letter," p. 380)

Knister's chary sense of "photographic" realism informs his critical statements about "realism." As the photograph, the window, and the mirror reveal only appearances, Knister's point seems to be that a realism concerned exclusively with appearances is not really a means of coming to an engagement with reality at all.

Knister recounts that an

> editor would expostulate earnestly with me: 'Mr. Knister, you make your people too real. Our readers don't want to read about real things. They want to be amused. Try to put more plot into your stories.' ("Canadian Literati," p. 164)

The suggestion is that Knister himself has an interest in capturing the "real" in his fiction, although by the "real" he does *not* mean an utter servitude to empirically verifiable detail. If the artist may, according to Knister, legitimately "create his own world" ("Canadian Literati," p. 168), such a world would not necessarily rely upon a photographic verisimilitude or semblance of actuality. As the title *White Narcissus* implies, Knister's sense of the realities to be treated in literature admits the kind of truths that myth and metaphor can embody. Dorothy Livesay observes that Knister's

> first literary influences . . . were those found in the American mid-west. But if I assert that Raymond Knister was strongly influenced by . . . Sherwood Anderson, this is to say that he found in him a confirmation of his own views: start with precise observation, but see behind it into the nature of things. As . . . in . . . Goethe's Confessions, the special quality of the artist is

that it is given to him to perceive the metaphysical real — *das Ding an Sich*. ("Knister's Stories," pp. 79–80)

For Knister, "there are many truths in the world," and the "question for the artist is, will they bring imagination to white heat."[85] What Knister calls "photographic realism" may conjure the material conditions of reality, but possibly little else, and the "many truths" — or possibly the tangible and intangible realities — acknowledged in Knister's fiction begin, but are not bound by, the ground of material reality.

Knister's belief in the power of literature based on (rather than being bounded by or denying) experience, seems to have been the basis of a dispute between Knister and Morley Callaghan. Documentation suggests that the source of the dispute is somewhat biographical, the nature of the disagreement in part ideological, and the expression of the controversy partly fictional.

Knister spent some of 1924 — between finishing work at *The Midland* in the spring and returning to Canada in the autumn — in Chicago. He worked as a taxi driver while in Chicago, and as Imogen Knister Givens point out, "When his taxi was commandeered by some criminals, he was temporarily thrown in jail along with them."[86] Knister's novella, "Innocent Man," includes a taxi driver who is in jail for similar reasons, although this episode takes up relatively little volume in the work, most of which is set in a Chicago jail cell. However, such an inclusion supports Knister's assertion that the genesis of "Innocent Man" lies in "observed" reality. In a letter of 12 January 1928 to a publishing company, Knister describes his novella as "based on the actual."[87] Knister elaborates, in a letter of 4 October 1929 to his friend Thomas Murtha, "The underworld of *Innocent Man* was observed by the author more nearly first-hand, I bet, than that of *Strange Fugitive*."[88] In the context of an essay Knister makes some pointed remarks about Callaghan's 1928 *Strange Fugitive*:

> Canadian life, Callaghan held, was more like American life than anything else, and his first novel, *Strange Fugitive*, dealt with a typically American figure, a bootlegger. He was delighted to find in the files of newspapers record of the fact that there really had been in Toronto as many bootleg killings as there were in his novel. But few Toronto people would admit that he gave a

faithful picture of life in the city. He seems to have suffered a nostalgia for Pittsburgh and Chicago, which he had scarcely seen . . . . Nevertheless he wrote in terms of his own experience, and a pivotal scene of his novel where rival bootleg kings come to conference to decide whether it shall be peace or war, shows these underworld big guns talking precisely like the boys on a street corner discussing a game of pool. ("Canadian Literati," p. 166)

In explaining that Callaghan's "rival bootleg kings" talk "precisely like the boys on a street corner discussing a game of pool," Knister is pointing out that Callaghan "wrote in terms of his own" — and, in context, limited — "experience." Knister, in a letter to his parents, reiterates his objection to Callaghan's treatment of subject matter: Knister writes that Callaghan's "bootleg kings . . . holding a conference" actually "talk like the teen age boys on any corner disputing who won that game of pool." When Knister continues, his comment can be taken as a concise description of the nature of his disagreement with Callaghan's approach: "The only trouble with Morley's underworld is that he never saw it."[89]

Eventually, Knister and Callaghan came to loggerheads in print. In Knister's Introduction to the 1928 anthology that he also edited, *Canadian Short Stories*, he comments that little Canadian work has been done in drama or the novel because these, like their "writers, must be rooted in the soil. Shakespeare might write of Rome or Denmark, but his imagination was England, and the people responded."[90] Callaghan took exception to Knister's view of Canadian writing. In a letter of 15 August 1928, Callaghan tells Knister,

Today I got a copy of the Canadian Stories [sic]. I read the Introduction . . . . What is the matter with you?
. . . I am sore. Your really know better. Then why do it? Are you thinking of retiring definitely?
Why do you do it? Since you know better and are willing to put your name on the book. Or is it the mellowing effect of the soil?[91]

The letter's closing question is a formulation of Callaghan's disagreement with Knister's view of Canadian literature, and Callaghan expresses much the same sentiment, in similar terms, in a story published in 1929.

Callaghan's 1929 *A Native Argosy* consists of fourteen short stories and two novellas. In one of the short stories in the book, "Settling Down," a young man called Burg or Burgess, who initially desires to be a writer, after being fired from his job as a reporter, finds his niche in selling magazines. When Burgess first applies for a job selling magazines,

> The red-headed sales manager took off his glasses and told Burg how his magazine was developing a national literature. All the women in the province ought to have the magazine in their homes, he said. Burg got the point and talked to him about books and his ambition to write stuff that would come right out of the soil. (p. 156)[92]

The possibility exists that Callaghan's ironic description of Burg's ambition is a veiled attack on the view Knister expresses in his 1928 Introduction to *Canadian Short Stories*. This possibility becomes more likely when Callaghan has Burgess become "convinced that people along rural routes weren't interested in developing a national literature" (p. 157). Knister writes of a literature "rooted in the soil," whereas Callaghan refers to the "mellowing effect of the soil" and "stuff that would come right out of the soil." Callaghan implies that the writer of fiction should ferret out topics of interest, while Knister suggests that fiction can discover what is of inherent interest in a given time and place.

The basic point of contention between Callaghan and Knister is the validity of the aim of a literature "rooted in the soil." Callaghan's work, unlike Knister's, can be relatively unanchored in time and place. The body of Knister's work suggests that he sometimes wrote of rural life at least partly because the idea of literature arising from the ground of material (and often everyday) reality fascinated him. As Knister bluntly explains, in a 1930 article, he rejects the notion of "people who say that a field of daffodils is as real as a garbage can, but who won't admit that daffodils grow in anything so material as earth and manure."[93] For Knister, recognition of the continuity between tangible realities and intangible realities is vital, as the very title *White Narcissus* suggests, for, in nature, apparently no purely white narcissus exists. Callaghan, who had written a novel depicting crime, did not empathize with Knister's view of the relationship between external, material reality and fiction; Knister gave a pragmatic response to a theoretical proposition in writing "Innocent

Man," a novella of prison life, after the experience of being a prisoner himself.

The sources cited imply the origins, nature, and chosen arenas of a disagreement; other sources hint that the dispute between Knister and Callaghan was neither strictly personal nor entirely private. In a letter of 4 October 1928, Knister explains to his mother that "Sat Night"

> had Morley Callaghan do an article on Canadian Prose, and it was so terrible they couldn't print it. It had heavy slams on Mazo de la and Grove, and referred to "critics with jobs" (Deacon) and "hack-writers in good standing locally" (me, I suppose). I wish to goodness they'd printed it. The ideas were all right, but he sure swung the shillalah in expressing 'em.[94]

The humour, directness, and precision of Knister's remarks typify some of his finest work, while also revealing that his dispute with Callaghan was not personal; in addition, Knister's use of the word "locally" might serve as a reminder of his basic disagreement with Callaghan. An omnibus review that appeared in *The Canadian Forum* in 1929 hints that the difference of opinion between Knister and Callaghan was not private. J.D. Robins, in a review entitled "Essentials and Accidentals," discusses works by Grove, de la Roche, *A Native Argosy*, and *White Narcissus*. Robins, who remarks "I cannot quite see Mr. Callaghan as the stylistic devil," states that Callaghan "may go to Paris, but it is only because he regards Paris as American, as the cultural capital of America. It is the literary suburb of New York."[95] What Robins states of Callaghan's geographical-cultural stance is similar to what Knister says, in "Canadian Literati," of Callaghan's seeming "nostalgia for Pittsburgh and Chicago, which he had scarcely seen." Robins overtly compares Knister's fiction to Callaghan's:

> Mr. Knister's book is a good antidote to Mr. Callaghan's. . . . He does select characters which allow us to hope that there are more good and worthy men than are to be found in the world of Mr. Callaghan's creation. There are stories of Mr. Knister's which show his competent knowledge of the so-called real world. His choice is deliberate.[96]

Robins depicts Knister as capable of making choices in his fiction precisely because he has "competent knowledge of the so-called real world." If what Robins declares is partisan, in terms of the disagreement between Knister and Callaghan, it accords with what Knister writes in his non-fiction. Knister's theoretical allegiance to "experienced reality" being acknowledged in literature accompanies a recognition that fictional characters "may transcend the people we see about us, but they must be true to them, and true to type." Knister's non-fiction delineates what he wanted in fiction, and clarifies the experimental impulse which underlies the choice of subject matter and the diversity of technique which mark Knister's fiction. The variously toned and richly coloured spectrum of Knister's fictional world suggests that Knister made theory and practice continuous.

"Group Portrait," Raymond Knister's first novel, was written between 1922 and 1923. The novel concentrates on the Nebblin family, who raise tobacco, but two of the Nebblin children dominate the story: twenty-five-year-old Del, and his teenaged sister, Robina or Roby. In their shared scorn of everyday life and thirst for urban adventure, Del and Robina also hold their rural environment in contempt. The final failure of the Nebblin's tobacco crop to fetch more than a minimal price, because the price of tobacco declines, is a descent that parallels the final situations of Del and Robina. "Group Portrait" includes verisimilitude which is less a matter of unalloyed "photographic realism" than contribution to moving portraits of people who feel trapped in their environment.

Knister's description of Del's contempt, for the town near the Nebblin farm, appears as a handwritten addition in the typescript of "Group Portrait."[97] As Del enters the town, driving a wagon freighted with barrels of apples, he contemplates with distaste the sight of himself in his current environment: "Slower than ever through town, with the rigs and aimless people. His thick-coated figure slid along green blinds of the store windows. Some burg!"[98] Knister's image of Del seeing himself repeatedly gliding by shop windows that serve somewhat as a series of repeating mirrors suggests the infinitely reflexive, and perhaps functions as a reflection of Del's vision. He travels in a world of mirrors. Del observes serial reflections of himself, and in being metaphorically unable to see beyond such limits, Del is implied to have an impaired vision of the world he inhabits.

Robina first appears in the novel, seen from a distance by Del, as

RAYMOND KNISTER

"a small figure of a girl, smaller beside the trees that leaned over the road" (p. 11). As she lies in bed she thinks that "the apple orchard seemed never to go away; it leaned black above her" (p. 76). If trees repeatedly dwarf her, she also repeatedly sees trees as being black; for her, peach trees "make the land so black" (p. 73), and in the winter the trees she sees from a window look "like tiny black ferns" (p. 275). Robina's view of trees as dark, or even darkly threatening, represents her view of local landscape and local life.

Benny Slooman's view of the local landscape opens the novel (p. 1) and, in his attraction to Robina, he dismisses malicious local gossip about her kleptomania (p. 29). Benny enjoys the quality of rural life; he takes pleasure in such things as wood fires (p. 119), and likes horses, while acknowledging that automobiles are becoming more popular than horses (p. 35). Eventually Benny comes to court Robina, whom he newly sees as a "creature of flashes, turnings, burnings" (p. 120). Sharp differences of vision distinguish Benny from Robina. While Benny sees in Robina "beauty . . . so near to him" (p. 121), Robina yearns for urban or distant "beauty." Robina thinks, "There *was* beauty, more sweet than sin, where people wore the clothes, and lived in the houses, and did the things you read about" (p. 125). (This sentence appears as a handwritten addition in the typescript of "Group Portrait.") Benny can find "beauty" in his immediate environment, while Robina's conception of "beauty" involves the "things" of the city. She steals a "silver mesh purse" (pp. 255–56); her vision is one of glittering materialism. The difference in the visions of Benny and Robina emerges in their different views of urban life; Benny finds Robina's "enthusiasm" for the city, where he has spent three winters, "puzzling" (p. 122). Robina craves the "things which put the gilding on life" (p. 125), and assumes she can find such things in the city. She overlooks inherent or natural beauty; Robina thinks "how dull everything" is, even as she sees a field that is "a lake of golden-rod, with spray, whitecaps" (p. 73). She finally rejects Benny because she sees him as someone who has "been to the city" and was "foolish enough" to leave the place (p. 126).

Robina rejects Benny is favour of Stanley, whose family is prosperous, and whom she associates with his "long car" (p. 44). As Robina drifts into sleep, memories of an evening with Stanley blend into her sense of the orchard near her bedroom being a black presence leaning over her. (This scene exists only in rudimentary form in the earlier versions of "Group Portrait.") As the scene closes, she remembers

Stanley saying he cannot see a resemblance between Del and Robina, and she falls asleep wondering,

> What did his lying mean? He was nearly four years older than she, must be twenty-one or more. Long, lank brown face flat with features which were no part of it, stuck out like ornaments, scrollings. (p. 78)

As Robina falls asleep, Stanley's face becomes a gargoyle mocking her desire for "beauty, more sweet than sin." In the final scene of the novel, Robina goes to a dance with Stanley, where she becomes attracted to a stranger called Albert, implicitly agrees to sleep with Stanley, and steals an ermine stole from the cloak room before leaving (pp. 281–90). At the dance, Robina sees people "in the galleries" as "strange quivering ornaments" (p. 281), while earlier she associates Stanley's face with "ornaments" as she falls asleep (p. 78). Robina's yearning for beauty can be related to denial; Robina has difficulty seeing others as more than "ornaments" to her own existence.

Knister's short story, "Mist-Green Oats," appeared in the August–September issue of *The Midland* in 1922,[99] likely while "Group Portrait" was in progress. Both works have a central character or characters immensely dissatisfied with everyday rural life, while at some level being capable of dismissing the beauty of the natural world. In "Mist-Green Oats," the young Len Brinder becomes increasingly impatient with the unrelenting work of the family farm. However, his irritation with farm work coexists with his appreciation of the rural environment:

> The green of an oats field beyond was visible under the apple-boughs. It was even now beginning to take on a gray misty tinge. Soon the oats field would seem an unbelievable blue-gray cloud, glimpsed from beneath the apple trees . . . fields of wheat would bow and surge in amber-lit crests. The rows of young corn would be arching to either side and touching, black-green and healthy. The smell of it, as he cultivated and the horses nipped off pieces of the heavy leaves, would be more sweet than that of flowers . . . . (pp. 268–69)

In the context of "Mist-Green Oats," celebration of the natural world is the touchstone of tranquillity. When tired of ploughing, Len notes that "In the orchard the sunlight seemed to pack the heat down below the boughs and above the earth," and the boughs trap heat of "broiling" intensity. He wonders, "Could it be as hot as this in the city, where one might go into the ice-cream parlors and the movie theatres?" (p. 259). Later, Len yearns for the time when "he should have reached the city and entered on some transcendently congenial and remunerative occupation" — and envisions as an alternative "his going to sea" (p. 267). Knister's presentation of Len's disgust with the work of the farm is telling: "The fatal impressibility of youth was lapping chains about him" (p. 271). "Mist-Green Oats" presents the idea of escape to the city as a quintessential delusion, and a conceivably dangerous one. Robina overlooks the natural beauty of her environment in yearning for a distant "beauty, *more sweet* than sin" — Len similarly falls victim to an entrapping delusion, which loops "chains about him," in his desire to escape an environment where the scent of the crops he helps raise is "*more sweet* than that of flowers" (italics added). Perception of what is "more sweet" than the immediate environment directs and may help delude these characters; Knister provides continuity between their dreams, desires, aesthetics, and visions.

"Turning Loam," Knister's second novel, was written in 1924, and is still unpublished. The novel includes elements that are of general interest in terms of Canadian literary history: the presentation of French-Canadians in English Canada, and a main character who is a successful writer, critic, and is outspoken on the subject of Canadian writing. Howard Winters, the protagonist of "Turning Loam," lives on his family's farm in Essex County, Ontario; he is a recent graduate of the "Agricultural College" in Guelph. The action of the novel largely consists of Howard's vacillation in his choice of a mate. His choice is between Rosemary Count, who comes from London, Ontario, is a materialist, and has contempt for rural life, and the artist Dell Greene, who was raised and lives on a nearby farm, and who cherishes and tries to interpret the everyday life of the countryside. In the course of the novel, Howard's interest in cultivating the land becomes the counterpart of Dell's interest, as a writer and critic, in cultivating Canadian literature.[100]

Only fragments are currently available of the early versions of "Turning Loam." In one such fragment, Howard, temporarily soured toward farm life while under Rosemary's influence, imagines, of "young men" leaving "farms" for "the cities" — "They did it as Madame Blatavsky [sic] said people sold their souls to the devil, to have someone on their side." The passage continues, "On the side of the city was youth, gaiety, leisure, even an illusion at least of beauty." Knister omits these remarks in "Turning Loam" (p. 211), possibly because they are more directly relevant to the symbolic level of "Group Portrait." Robina's search for beauty has an analogue in Len Brinder's partial recognition of the beauty of the natural world, while Howard's vision leads to his union with Dell, who has a writer's dedication to and a critic's concern with the subject of beauty. "Turning Loam" is Knister's fable of the search for an aesthetic.

In the course of "Turning Loam," Howard refers to Sinclair Lewis' 1922 novel, *Babbitt*, while Dell refers to Lewis' 1920 novel, *Main Street* (pp. 269–70). In context, these references suggest the feasibility and viability of ordinary life and a sense of place as subject matter. But the works Knister alludes to, like "Turning Loam" itself, involve psychological and visionary realities, as well as material reality.

In his 1923 review of *Babbitt*, Knister attacks the notion that the work is "photographic," and notes that "it has somehow been taken for granted" that *Main Street* and *Babbitt* respectively "present an exact reproduction of the manners of Gopher Prairie and Zenith." Knister notes that, if Lewis felt "obliged to live up to 'realism,' "

nothing could exceed the gusto with which he unfolds the tale of Babbitt's foibles and adventures, the joyous satire of all the institutions of the hundred percenter and the Solid Citizen.

For Knister, Lewis' *Main Street* and *Babbitt* are not works of "photographic" verisimilitude, but works in which Lewis uses a "combination of the snap-shot and cartoon method."[101] Knister's description of Lewis' method, in both *Main Street* and *Babbitt*, of alternating or combining realistic passages with satirical ones, is exceptionally accurate; Knister's 1923 description of Lewis as being interested in realities beyond the bounds of "photographic" realism anticipates the flamboyant colours of Lewis' portrait of Sharon Falconer in the 1927 novel, *Elmer Gantry*. Both of the main characters of "Turning Loam" making positive references to Lewis' works invite the reader to consider just how distant the world of "Turning Loam" is from the flat verisimilitude of a photograph.

The major feature of Knister's portrait of Howard Winters is Howard's desire to view rural life in the light of a clarifying vision. Howard desires to know the abstract realities that the details and concerns of everyday life may mask or muddy. As his appreciation of *Poetry* (Chicago), Turgenev, and Stravinsky indicates, Howard would like knowledge of what is to be found "beneath the surface of toil and calculation" (p. 175), or what experience tells him exists but may not occur in tangible form, or receive clear everyday manifestation.

What Dell can offer Howard, and Rosemary cannot, is a means of moving toward defining the vision he seeks:

> She sighed. "Yes; when all is said it is a different world — in books." Dell pondered. "It used to be that only the great masters let themselves go. Now there are many who tear through whatever inhibitions they think bind them, and try to tell what they know. But for us — our obsession with constraints — that makes it natural perhaps that our novels have ended where those of other countries begin."
>
> "You may say that," he replied with brutal abruptness, "Yet if I were to put my arm around you now you'd — "
>
> "Yes but you see that is where the confusion comes, between art and life. As though art were made as a photograph, instead of as a vision."
>
> Howard saw this and did not see it. (p. 135)

Howard copes well with the details of everyday life — he has scientific and practical knowledge of farming; he can see the "surface of toil and calculation," but knows that, in order to achieve a vision of everyday life, he must go beyond the "surface" of appearances. Dell is "literary" and claims that "art" is "made . . . as a vision." Despite his struggle toward a vision, Howard cannot quite fully grasp Dell's comment. At the symbolic level, it would make sense that in "Turning Loam" the union of Howard and Dell occur, for, if Howard can "see" the reality of daily life as a "photograph," he seeks a visionary understanding of daily life, while Dell can "see" the reality of "vision" that art expresses, but also recognizes the reality of daily experience.

Howard initially flirts with Rosemary Count and materialism, but ultimately he develops a passion for the artist Dell Greene. The union of Howard and Dell represents the uniting of the two elements that, in dynamic relationship, constitute the aesthetic "Turning Loam" suggests: verisimilitude, or recognition of tangible reality, and symbolism, or recognition of intangible reality. It is, so to speak, not

Rosemary Count and a pot of gold, but Dell Greene and an aesthetic position, that Howard finds at the end of the rainbow appearing toward the close of "Turning Loam."

White Narcissus is continuous with "Turning Loam" insofar as the former is a treatment of different ways of seeing. The first edition of White Narcissus ends with Knister's notation of the places and dates of composition: "Northwood, Ontario, Oct.–Dec. 1925 — Hanlan's Point, June–Aug. 1927." Chronology, technique, and subject matter make White Narcissus a central Knister fiction, but the novel is elusive because questions of vision are at the core of the work.

The protagonist, Richard Milne, a successful writer of novels and advertisements, returns to visit the rural area in which he grew up, determined to make a final attempt to win the hand of Ada Lethen. Ada, however, hesitates to leave her farm home because her parents are not on speaking terms. As Ada can communicate with both parents, she feels it her duty to remain at the Lethen farm. In the course of the novel, Richard boards at two farms in the area. At first, Richard stays with Carson Hymerson and his wife. However, Carson's wish to foreclose the mortgage on the Lethen farm alienates Richard, who leaves the Hymerson farm to stay with the Burnstiles. Bill Burnstile, a longstanding friend of Richard's, is conspicuously more relaxed and good-natured than Carson Hymerson. White Narcissus ends with the removal of barriers to the departure of Ada with Richard.

In terms of the context of White Narcissus, Knister's short story, "The Strawstack," is significant. Edward J. O'Brien's annual devoted to the short story placed "The Strawstack" on the "Roll of Honor" for stories published in North America between October 1923 and September 1924. "The Strawstack" appeared in the October issue of The Canadian Forum in 1923, and in his essay, "Canadian Literati," Knister refers to his story published in The Canadian Forum as being "obviously derived from Poe" (p. 166). "Canadian Literati" was not published until 1975, but the essay can be roughly dated, as it includes a reference to a 1929 Callaghan work, A Native Argosy (p. 166). Knister, therefore, had a work he explicitly stated to be "derived from Poe" singled out for recognition at the time he started writing White Narcissus, and Knister acknowledged the influence of American romance on his work at roughly the time White Narcissus was published.

The protagonist of "The Strawstack" is a man who flees to the family farm after his years of crime culminate in murder; he returns to find the farmhouse abandoned, and the story consists of his memories, "old despair" (p. 194),[102] current "despair" (p. 192), and the final implication that he commits suicide. His criminal career began when, at fifteen, he mistakenly believed that an accident he was involved in caused his sister's death. While the story is a portrait of an individual's despair, Knister's protagonist has a conception of what might rescue him: an elusive "sharp beauty" that "would tear apart the curtain that stood . . . between himself and life" — "The search alone would steady him, set him again upon his feet" (pp. 192–93). However, as he cannot concentrate on contemplating his future, so can he not confront his past: "His first homesickness had been a sandbar only from which he soon floated away not free" (p. 186). Psychological states, suggestion, and metaphor mark Poe's work, appear in "The Strawstack," and occur in *White Narcissus*. In nineteenth-century American romance, Knister could discover a literature which included effective strategies for recognizing intangible realities.

Evidence points to Knister's general interest in nineteenth-century American romance. Knister's reading list for the years 1914 to 1924 reveals a consistent interest in the work of Henry James and Nathaniel Hawthorne. By the time he wrote "Canadian Literati," Knister would refer positively to the writing of Melville and Poe, and associate the highly symbolic work of American romance writers with coming "to grips with reality."

Textual evidence suggests that the central tension in *White Narcissus* is between the narrowly obsessive vision, which becomes associated with the myth of Narcissus, and the broadly inclusive vision that works of nineteenth-century American romance, as exemplified by *The Scarlet Letter*, celebrate. Knister's treatment of landscape introduces the subject of vision, while allusion to romance brings the subject of vision into focus.

White Narcissus begins, "Richard Milne was only two hours away from the city," but he finds the road he follows "incredibly foreign," and the road leads him to "the centre of lost wastes screened by scattered and fretful trees."[103] He soon feels "lost in this too-familiar country" (p. 19). Richard sees the road he follows as leading to "lost wastes" and feels himself "lost." The first paragraph of the novel hints that the protagonist's view of the landscape determines its presentation. As Richard questions the good of his return, he sees the "fields, river banks" and the "sky" as similarly questioning him (p. 20). Again, the landscape Richard sees becomes a reflection of his own mood. In the course of *White Narcissus*, the landscape Richard sees reflects his changing feelings. The colouration of the physical world of the novel becomes dependent upon the likely "outcome of his quest" for Ada's hand (p. 36).

As Richard's hopes stagnate, the summer passes, and

Along the river . . . the rank vegetation smothered the raw outlines of the ground. In a swamp a forest, a pond of nettles higher than a man's head waved acridly, wavered and bowed like long trees, fern-like, in the light breeze, some recoiling more quickly than others, jostling and bowing back and forth to each other. They had a symbolic malevolence, a blue-green sea of fire, and Richard Milne watched it for moments without thinking. (p. 104)

The image of enormous nettles may reflect, with "symbolic malevolence," Richard's consciousness of his recourse to inaction, in response to Ada's rejection. Knister's use of the Biblical (Rev. 15.2) phrase "sea of fire" suggests that the landscape described is the environment Richard's experience colours, a landscape that the terms and techniques of "photographic realism" might not necessarily express. In the nettles image, as elsewhere in the novel, an over-powering natural fertility mocks Richard, as Ada's denial foils him:

Sumach grew densely along moist ditches, rank, with stalks as thick as a man's arm, little groves towering branchless twenty feet, at that height to spread a thick thatch of green which withstood light showers: it was like tropical vegetation. That year the elderberries grew thick and weighty on brittle stalks, changing from discs of cream frothiness to dark, pendulous spheres of fruit, purple, which almost seemed to swell with the increasing rains.

This richness of greenery and bitter yellow, blue-grey stems, purple fruit, stretched above his head, seeming to bury his consciousness as he walked about . . . . The man would stop and sit . . . under the canopy of sumach and stare at the ground, black earth strewn with rusty stems of the sumach leaves of other years, thinking of those times and of Ada Lethen, while the rain began to patter unheeded above him. (pp. 104–05)

The season's smothering wealth of vegetation is another choking reminder of the poverty of his prospects; at his initial meeting with Ada on this visit, Richard thinks of the "few . . . vistas" she has seen as he asks her, " 'What is it holds you, Ada?' . . . in a choking tone" (p. 36), and he sees the landscape as "A place of choked vistas" (p. 20). As the rain patters "unheeded above him," he thinks first of Ada, and then of his being immobilized by indecision, showing himself "a veritable Hamlet" (p. 105); presumably for similar reasons his vision causes him to see "a cliff of cloud the shape of the map of Denmark" (p. 114). Richard's frustration shapes the very clouds he sees. As he tries to lose himself in work by helping on the Burnstile farm, he sees the "oats field and the gloomy light" as "curiously lethargic in their tranquillity," and "even the forests seemed to toss with a heavy, slow resignation" (p. 115). Catching sight of Ada, he stops her; as soon as Ada's "musical voice" greets him, it becomes a "glorious day" (p. 116). Following Ada's confession of her love for him, when they walk in the forest, "every leaf" moves "in ecstasy" (p. 120). After they consummate their love, Richard no longer sees clouds the shape of Denmark, but a sky "blue with thronging white clouds" (p. 127). Instead of stagnation, Richard sees "fulfilment" in the "passing of the summer" (p. 127).

Richard's state of mind colours the landscape he sees, and introduces the subject of vision, which receives further attention in the serial presentation of obsessive characters. The most prominently obsessive character in *White Narcissus* is Mrs. Lethen. In her obsession with narcissi, which fill the house, Mrs. Lethen channels her emotions toward them. Mrs. Lethen may have "burnt-out eyes" (p. 68) because hers is a minimal vision, which admits narcissi as fitting recipients of attention. Knister's choice of the narcissus as Mrs. Lethen's object of obsession draws on the myth of Narcissus, for the narcissus as symbol, and the essential meaning of the myth — the harmful consequences of self-absorption or obsessive selfishness.

Another obsessed character in *White Narcissus* is Carson Hymerson, a "small figure of a man," a local farmer who first appears in the story carrying "dripping swill pails." As Richard approaches Carson's house, he walks "over a series of long, warped boards" (p. 25); there is more "warped" about Carson than initially meets the eye.

Early in the novel Carson rants on about Mr. Lethen (pp. 27–28). Richard initially does not know that any "change" (p. 56) has made

Carson obsessed with his grievances against Mr. Lethen, and so for the first part of the summer Richard finds himself boarding at the farm of a man who has, for Richard, a particularly irksome axe to grind. Carson becomes increasingly obsessed with the idea that Mr. Lethen is maltreating him.

Carson's obsession with Mr. Lethen eventually erupts in physical violence (p. 91). Richard's subsequent description of Carson as a "well-known psychological type" (p. 93) associates the obsessed Carson and the obsessed Mrs. Lethen, for Richard similarly describes the latter's relationship to narcissi as "pathological" (p. 41). Carson turns his fury on Richard, making it plain that he cares neither for Mr. Lethen nor "all his friends with him" (p. 107). Towards the end of the novel, Richard learns that Carson

> flew into a rage about something, and finally they got the police, and it took a bunch of them. . . . It appears he got violent. He kept hollering something about everybody being in a conspiracy against him. (p. 128)

Carson's obsession intensifies, while Mrs. Lethen's dissolves. However, the resolution of his obsession, like that of Mrs. Lethen, is a preliminary to the disentanglement of Ada.

Mrs. Lethen and Carson both preoccupy themselves with one thing; Knister's short story, "The One Thing," was published in *The Midland* in 1922, and *White Narcissus* was not published until 1929, but documentation shows that Knister worked on drafts of these works in the same year, 1925. In "The One Thing," "the one thing" that the main character, Billy Dulckington, "cares about's his horses" (p. 152);[104] he has an "obsession with his horses" (p. 154). Billy tends to worship his horses, with his regard for them being greater than that "for his own soul" (p. 163), just as Mrs. Lethen "worships" (p. 41) her narcissi. Carson is a "small figure of a man" (p. 25), while Knister notes Billy's "shortness" (p. 153). When the local veterinarian and Billy's brother show an enthusiasm for horses unequal to Billy's, he finds himself unable "to dispel a latent impression that the two larger men were somehow siding against him" (p. 160), just as Carson Hymerson seems unable to dispel the initially latent impression that "everybody" is "in a conspiracy against him" (p. 128). Billy has an "obsession" (p. 154) with one thing. All three of these Knister characters have obsessions, and have impaired vision: Billy has "little eyes" (p. 156), Mrs. Lethen "burnt-out eyes" (p. 68), and Carson Hymerson "little" eyes (p. 30).

In *White Narcissus*, obsessive vision denies the broad recognition of reality that characterizes American nineteenth-century romance. As the climax of the novel nears, Richard reads *The Scarlet Letter: A Romance*, a choice he makes from a selection of magazines and other books:

> after looking through a haphazard pile of popular magazines, he took up *The Scarlet Letter*, one of the three books, along with Bunin's stories and *Wilhelm Meister's Wanderjahre*, which he had brought with him. (pp. 107–08)

In his non-fiction, Knister discusses the works Richard rejects. Knister refers to the "strolling player" of long ago as being considered "at best an intellectual valet to whom the count and the baron could unburden their minds as they could not to their more materialistic equals, as in *Wilhelm Meister*."[105] Knister implies that Goethe's *Wilhelm Meister* recognizes the intangible realities that the "materialistic" — one recalls "Turning Loam" — might miss.

In his review of Ivan Bunin's *The Gentleman from San Francisco and Other Stories*, Knister states,

> The Gentleman from San Francisco is one of those essentially simple souls who devote themselves to the acquisition of property: simple, because the instinct for acquisition is one of the primary ones, common to animals and to prehistoric man. It was only when thoughts and more complicated feelings came to man that the . . . arts to which they gave rise could make man what he ideally should be, and what in many cases he is now. Well, this Gentleman, with an overdose of his primitive obsession, was able to gather together a great amount of property in the course of years.[106]

Knister suggests that, if *Wilhelm Meister* veers away from "materialistic" concerns, Bunin's story demonstrates the "primitive" nature of an "obsession" with materialism. Richard, who early in *White Narcissus* rejects materialism (p. 44), likely rejects these works because he already knows what it is that they have to tell him. Knister describes Richard's response to *The Scarlet Letter*:

> But he could not sleep. Phrases and images from *The Scarlet Letter* floated in his mind. He was expiating Dimmesdale's secret sin yet, after two centuries. Love could not be free yet for men and women who had taken civilization as an armour which had changed to fetters upon them. What was his whole piacular story but that of Dimmesdale — prophetic name — a delusion no longer a delusion of sin, but of impotence and analysis which belied action and love? It was the conflict of the conscious ones of his whole generation, this confusion of outer freedom and inner doubt. (p. 108)

Richard considers the applicability of *The Scarlet Letter* to his own situation, which seems to amount to a state of indecision. Richard's being frozen in indecision would also account for Richard seeing himself "a veritable Hamlet" (p. 105), and seeing "a cliff of cloud the shape of the map of Denmark" (p. 114). It dawns on Richard that his vision has been too confined for, like Dimmesdale, he has allowed delusion to rob him, and, like Hamlet, he has prolonged introspection and analysis. Richard, being an author, presumably knows that Hamlet and Dimmesdale have visions and circumstances that cost them their lives.

What might be an oblique reference to Henry James's 1903 novel, *The Ambassadors*, clarifies Richard's approach to the question of vision. A major character in *The Ambassadors*, Chad Newsome, is a young American who visits Europe but seems unable to benefit from travel: he is last seen expressing an intention to return to America, where he will pursue his interest in "the art of advertisement." Chad asserts, "It's an art like any other, and infinite like all the arts." He concludes, "With the right man to work it *c'est un monde*."[107] Richard is a "poetical novelist" *and* a writer "of mail-order advertising matter."[108] The function of this possible allusion would parallel the function of reference to *The Scarlet Letter*; Richard can see the importance of a vision of multiplicity, as these works explore reality from the position of such a vision, but Richard has difficulty in translating such a vision into action; he may think with Hawthorne and James, but he runs the risk of acting as Chad and Dimmesdale do, and both of these characters rely on what convention dictates for insight.

Knister remarks, in a letter of 29 January 1929,

> I treated . . . aberrant characters in *White Narcissus* . . . . A girl who would not leave her mother because the latter had not spoken to her father for years. The mother obsessed with (symbolically) white narcissus bulbs. But the story is more that of the oft-returning suitor.[109]

Knister suggests that Richard's role is central, and textual evidence implies that his role is central because his vision, which increasingly becomes associated with the unfettered vision nineteenth-century American romance celebrates, comes to balance the narcissistic vision collectively held by the negative characters in *White Narcissus*. (Interestingly enough, the language of contemporary psychiatry includes the expression "malignant narcissism.")

There are several resemblances between *White Narcissus* and *The Scarlet Letter*, resemblances of both theme and technique. These similarities point to the ultimate importance of a vision broad enough to admit the complexity of reality. Both novels include a writer who works at something else; the writer in *The Scarlet Letter* has worked as a "Custom-House officer,"[110] while Richard works at an "advertising agency" (p. 29). While the writer in "The Custom-House" refers to "the deep and aged roots which my family has struck into the soil" (p. 8), but mentions that "frequent transplantation is perhaps better for the stock" (p. 9), Richard notes that "he could never be freed from the hold of this soil" except by "a forfeit of love which . . . he had come to redeem or tear from its roots forever" (p. 21). In "The Custom-House," the Preface to a work subtitled "A Romance," the writer admits that the "page of life . . . before me seemed dull and commonplace, only because I had not fathomed its deeper import" (p. 37). Richard sees the "commonplace of romance" as "quartz-glitter in the dust" (p. 54). Were Richard obsessively to pursue his habit of seeing in the landscape reflections of his own feelings, he would presumably, like Hawthorne's Chillingworth, look "like a man chiefly accustomed to look inward, and to whom external matters are of little value and import, unless they bear relation to something within his mind" (p. 61). Interestingly enough, Chillingworth tells Hester, "I know not Lethe" (p. 72). Neither Hawthorne's nor Knister's obsessed characters can easily renounce their obsession, and so cannot "know" Lethe, the river of forgetfulness in Greek mythology.

The titles of the two works function in similar ways, as both reflect a sense of the rich multiplicity of possibility. The "scarlet letter" is, in material terms, a red letter "A" Hester is to wear to signify that she has committed adultery. When Dimmesdale sees a red letter "A" appear in the sky, he gives it the "shape" of his "guilty imagination," although "another's guilt might have seen another symbol in it" (p. 155). But the Puritans who see a "great red letter in the sky — the letter A, —" "interpret" it to "stand for Angel" (p. 158). Eventually, Hester's helpfulness causes "many people" to interpret her scarlet letter as standing for "Able" (p. 161). Hawthorne's title explicitly encompasses very different possible meanings.

The title *White Narcissus* also represents a range of meaning. If there is emphasis on the "narcissus" of the title, the sinister aspects of the novel receive emphasis: obsessive and self-involved behaviour and its consequences. The "white" of the title has very different connotations. In the context of nineteenth-century American romance, *Moby Dick* looms large, and the narcissism of obsession is important in *Moby Dick*: Ahab has an "intense bigotry of purpose."[11] Melville explains, of his white whale, "in essence whiteness is not so much a color as the visible absence of color, and at the same time the concrete of all colors . . ." (p. 169). In a work Knister was aware of, Melville uses the colour white as a symbol of many things, if not multiplicity itself. The first word of Knister's title may refer to the kind of encompassing vision Richard favours, while the second half of Knister's title can be a reminder of the narrow, narcissistic vision that the negative characters in *White Narcissus* share. Finally, the title *White Narcissus* reflects the central tension of Knister's novel.

Knister's novella, "Innocent Man," written between 1927 and 1931, consists of three sections. In the first section, the protagonist, Jack Dolson, marries Grace; they leave Metropole, Michigan, for a honeymoon trip, but Jack's sudden arrest occurs just after they arrive in Chicago. The second section, which is longer than the other two sections combined, deals briefly with Jack's arrest and describes in detail the events and environment of his imprisonment. The final section further describes Jack's imprisonment, and concludes with a brief account of Jack's release and reunion with Grace.

In "Innocent Man," the movement from a personal, rural environment to an impersonal, urban environment, and the significant use of images of sound and sight, trace the protagonist's growing consciousness of others and the value of everyday life.

In a letter of 28 August 1929 to Thomas Murtha, Knister writes of "Innocent Man,"

> the start . . . doubtless does not give off the note of the main part. However my idea was to start from a credible and even mundane world so as to heighten as well as make credible what was to follow."[112]

Knister's letter refers to a shift in "Innocent Man" from a "credible" and relatively "mundane world" to another order of reality, that serves to "heighten" the latter. Jack's prison environment involves "a heightening that was a denial of life."[113] "Innocent Man," like other Knister works of longer prose fiction, celebrates the ordinary or "commonplace" (p. 237) world. Knister's treatment of the prison environment, like his drawing on the Narcissus myth in *White Narcissus*, evokes the extraordinary nature of the so-called ordinary.

Knister's novella, "Cab Driver," became available in January 1984; the only known extant copy is a typescript of 118 pages, which comes to a grinding halt, rather than a smooth conclusion. Evidence provided by letters indicates that roughly the last twenty pages of the novella are missing, that Knister worked on "Cab Driver" between 1927 and 1930, and that at least one version of "Innocent Man" was finished by the time work on "Cab Driver" was in progress.

"Cab Driver" presents twenty-four hours in the life of Jerry Berwind, a cab driver who works during the night in the Chicago of the 1920s. Over the course of a night Berwind moves through the city in increasing suspicion and fear. The relative freedom and pleasure of Berwind on the following day become a mockery under the influence of his night-time experience, for he absorbs the brutality of the streets of the city. Echoes of the protagonist's past slightly alleviate the gloom of the novella's atmosphere, without ameliorating the hell through which Berwind moves.

A character named Berwind appears elsewhere in Knister's fiction, in the short story "Hackman's Night." Chicago is the setting of the story, in which Knister balances attention to action and atmosphere. The protagonist, Berwind, drives a taxi during the crime-rife Chicago night. In "Hackman's Night," the atmosphere of the story lends an immediacy to the work. For example, Knister gives a sharp sense of environment in relation to character, in his description of Berwind's reaction to a sudden and severe underworld attack on his cab.[114] Waddington notes that Knister wrote "Hackman's Night" in early 1929 (pp. 186–87), which would mean that Knister was working on "Hackman's Night" while working on "Cab Driver."

Knister's novella explores one of the currents running through "Group Portrait," and especially through the novel's later version, "Soil in Smoke": "Cab Driver" follows a night in the life of a character who might, like Del or Robina, have once thought in terms of escaping to a city. "Cab Driver" is a work of six sections, and the division of the novella reflects the gradual erosion of Berwind's better impulses. As a physical setting, the city of Chicago is a place of dirt, noise, and stench. As a social setting, the city is even worse. In cabs, the "glass behind the driver" is "reinforced with wire netting" because violence is a real possibility.[115]

On "Sixty-third Street," the "doubtful second and third storey windows fronting on the L" or Elevated railway are the windows of "Speakeasies, furnished rooms, gang headquarters, whatnot" (p. 76):

> And one could bet that the windows opening directly upon the railway would not be unshaded. One saw strange sights from the window of an Elevated train, but one did not see actual murder, gambling, shooting, rape. There was a residue of caution left to the openness of the underworld. (p. 77)

It is through "the Babylon of the Chicago night" (p. 11) that Knister's protagonist moves. The *Oxford English Dictionary* defines "Babylon" as "any . . . vicious city," and "vicious city" is a concise description of Knister's Chicago. The filth, noise, stench, fear, suspicion, and violence of Knister's Chicago make it a Babylon.

In the first section of "Cab Driver," Berwind's passenger is a hunter, while in the second part of the story his passenger is a hunted person, and by the third section of the story Berwind himself becomes hunted. The implication arises that Berwind himself is a sort of quarry.

In the final section, Berwind "sauntered into the Century Cafe" to seek out Elyria, a waitress; Berwind initially teases Elyria in a friendly fashion, but his "general sense of well-being made him careless of everyone else in the place, in the city. They could go to hell. She could too" (p. 107). As Berwind speaks to Elyria, he smiles "inwardly" because she is "submissive." He thinks, "Doubtless if he were less unreasonable, she would tell him to go chase himself, and retire to the counter, with a mocking smile" (p. 108). Just as Berwind becomes the victim of the random brutality of the Chicago night, Elyria becomes the victim of Berwind's emotional brutality; both become victims of forms of violence that the city inculcates. Berwind's pretence of being "unreasonable" while with Elyria reflects his expectation of similar treatment as a cab driver in the "Babylon of the Chicago night" (p. 11); "The role of the conventional cab-driver demanded that he ignore advances from people in full possession of their faculties" (p. 12).

In leaving the restaurant, Berwind almost gives Elyria a "tip," but decides that he has "hurt her enough" (p. 112). Part of his pain is his rage at his own brutality; as he goes, Elyria is busy, "beginning to gather his dishes together and put them on a tray. He paused and turned to look at her. 'Be yourself,' he muttered" (p. 113). Berwind's self-knowledge leads him to hope that Elyria can withstand the influence of the Babylon that is Chicago.

Pastoral references in the novella serve as a reminder that there exist alternatives to the brutalizing hell of Chicago, while the urban degradation of the pastoral illustrates the extent to which the city of Chicago is a hell. In the absence of either a conclusion to "Cab Driver" or clearer reasons as to why Berwind rejects his past, it is difficult to arrive at conclusions about Berwind's final position. Perhaps the extent of his brutalization is such that he can no longer even conceive of partaking of pastoral pleasures beyond those feeble few offered within the limits of Babylon. A more cynical reading might be that — like the protagonist of Orwell's *Nineteen Eighty-Four* — he becomes brutalized to the point that he relishes his oppression. If such is the case, the point about Berwind is ultimately that the hell of Chicago reduces him to a satisfied inhabitant of Babylon.

Documentation suggests that Knister worked on three novellas between 1927 and 1931: "Innocent Man," "Cab Driver," and "There Was a Mr. Cristi," which became available in 1986, as a typescript of one hundred and twenty-nine pages. "There Was a Mr. Cristi" differs in tone from the stark and allegorical world of "Innocent Man" and the sharply depicted world of "Cab Driver," which simmers with the continual possibility of swift and random violence. "There Was a Mr. Cristi" is often comic, depicts everyday urban life in some detail, and ultimately refuses to rest upon belief in conventional views of society. Textual evidence suggests that "There Was a Mr. Cristi" presents the Toronto of the 1920s as an environment in which people routinely consider others as commodities, to be treated according to the dictates of personal gratification. bill bissett, in a 1983 interview, makes an observation that, although made in a very different context, characterizes Knister's novella well:

> There's a kind of poetry that happens in the Toronto area which is very concerned with people's relationships with each other in terms of personal exploitation, personal negotiation. Margaret Atwood's *Power Politics* is a supreme example of that, yet it could have been written anywhere.[16]

David Arnason provides reasons for Knister's poem "The Hawk" being able to "stand with anything written by any poet in the twentieth century, whatever his country."[17] Knister's *My Star Predominant* defies time and place in presenting a writer of another era.

My Star Predominant covers the last years in the life of John Keats, describing the illness and death of the poet's brother, Tom, as a result of consumption; the relationship of Keats and Fanny Brawne; and the poet's last days, as consumption claims him, in Italy. Knister devoted a good deal of research to his subject — as *The Times Literary Supplement* 1934 review of the novel notes, Knister makes "liberal use of Keats's own letters."[18] But Knister chose to write a fiction based on biographical fact about Keats, rather than a biography. The final focus of Knister's portrait of Keats involves the central use of images, which play a vital role in *My Star Predominant*, a novel which is a poet's homage to one particular poet, and a celebration of the timeless power of an artist's vision.

Images of central importance in *My Star Predominant* fall into three related groups. The first group or wave of images presents Keats as an image-maker, an artist who considers poetry to consist of the making of evocative images, and the source of these images is his immediate social and physical environment. This initial wave of images culminates in the image of Keats's delight at the sight of the "tide" created by the wind rippling a field of barley.[19] The second wave of images is connected with Tom, and suggests the growth of Keats's consciousness or the growth of his vision. This second wave culminates in the image of a rabbit upon Hampstead Heath that

Keats thinks might somehow embody the spirit of Tom (pp. 196–97). The third wave of images consists of a movement toward the synthesis of the implications of the previous waves; this third and final wave of centrally important images consists of images associated with Dante's *Divine Comedy*, and invoke the power of any great artist's vision. While central images reflect the genesis and growth of Keats's personal vision, they are associated with immediate reality, and when central images reflect the strength of artistic vision *per se*, they are also associated with a great artist of another era. The second wave of images in *My Star Predominant* is related to the third wave of images when Keats thinks, of the difference between Tom in the earlier stages of his fatal illness and Tom being gravely ill, "Purgatory blind! But this, then, was the Inferno. A sharp chill crossed his heart to think of the corresponding difference in Tom's health" (p. 152). *My Star Predominant* suggests that the vision of the artist defies time, and therefore the personal vision of a Keats or a Dante lives forever.

Central images are not the only source of structural unity in Knister's novel. *My Star Predominant* is divided into four sections of roughly equal length, and these divisions repeat the suggestions images evoke. Each "Book" of *My Star Predominant* has its own epigraph, and title taken from the epigraph. Book I, "While We Are Laughing," and Book II, "Something Real in the World," each begin with a quotation from a Keats letter, while Book III, "Too Many Tears for Lovers," and Book IV, "Yet, Do Not Grieve," both open with a quotation from a Keats poem. The sources for the epigraphs being first letters and then poems makes a transition which suggests the development of Keats as an artist, or the growth of his visionary power, and also repeats the suggestion that the basis of Keats's art is his daily life. The series composed of the openings of the four sections also evokes the growth of Keats as an artist. Book I opens "on a day in May" (p. 9) with Keats waiting to meet Leigh Hunt, who has published a Keats poem less "than a month ago" (p. 10). Book II begins with a description of Keats's brothers helping him prepare to leave for the country where he hopes to be able to concentrate on writing poetry. The third Book opens with Keats contemplating his treatment by the critics and worrying about his having become, at least in the eyes of others, "attached to Hunt's fortunes" (p. 159). However, there is also mention of Keats's "effort to get rid of a sore throat" (p. 159). Book IV opens with Keats trying to reconcile his knowledge of being a victim of consumption with his strong desire to live and be a poet. He thinks that "His death would burn with a fiercer flame into the minds of men than his life and works had done" and, as he considers that his death might make his work of interest, he cannot help smiling "at this grotesque victory" (p. 251). The openings of the four sections of *My Star Predominant* collectively trace the writing career of Keats, recording his struggle to get his work published, his efforts to write, his attempt to achieve intellectual independence, and his final struggle to accept the fact that his writing days will soon cease.

The title of *My Star Predominant* reflects the central concerns of the work. Knister's Keats uses the phrase "my star predominant" as a reference to his luck. When he finds Fanny Brawne at home and alone, he declares "All as though ordained for me. There is my star predominant!" (p. 237). But by the time he is in Italy, Keats uses forms of the expression in reference to his bad luck: "Before dawn he woke and watched the coming of the new day and cursed his star" (p. 316). It is also in Italy that Keats asks Severn, "You think I don't know my unlucky star, and how it has been predominant from the first?" (p. 314).

The phrase "my star predominant" occurs in a 30 November 1820 letter of Keats to his close friend Charles Brown, a letter that, in Forman's 1931 edition of Keats's letters, appears as the last that Keats wrote.[120] The context of the remark can be traced. When Keats and Severn left England for Italy, bad weather conditions delayed their departure, and from 19 September to 21 October 1820 their ship, the "Maria Crowther," had to remain in the vicinity of the coast of England.[121] During these weeks, the passengers of the "Maria Crowther" had opportunities to go ashore, and on two occasions Brown and Keats narrowly missed the chance to see each other for the last time. Keats deplores the ill-luck of these vanished opportunities when he writes, "There was my star predominant!"[122] Insofar as Keats uses the phrase to refer to his luck, Knister's use of the phrase "my star predominant" parallels Keats's. Alternately, Knister's choice of title may refer to the ironic truth that Keats's "star" was a fortunate one, in the sense that Keats wrote enduring work. The title of Knister's novel is fitting because it points to the longevity of the phrase "my star predominant" in relation to the man who coined it and died at the age of twenty-five — Knister's title celebrates the timelessness of the work of an artist of vision.

"Peaches, Peaches," a novella Knister worked on in 1931 and 1932, was submitted to the New York publishing house of Charles Scribner's Sons; although the work as it stood was rejected, Scribner's suggested Knister think of rewriting the work as a novel. The letter, making this suggestion, was written only about three months before Knister drowned.

The protagonist of "Peaches, Peaches," Ed Burkin, is a young unmarried man who works on his family's farm; his retired father has turned the operation of the farm over to his older son, Amos. Ed works with Murray March, an agricultural college student. The adults with whom Ed has daily contact are Amos, Amos's wife, Eleanor, and Murray. Over the course of a peach season, Ed's awareness of the liaison between Murray and Eleanor grows. The novella also describes the relationships of Ed and Murray to Florine and May, who work as seasonal help, at the Burkin farm, for the duration of the peach harvest. An inundation of peaches causes a frantic working pace at the Burkin farm, as Ed becomes increasingly conscious of the sexuality of relationships he witnesses and participates in. With the abrupt cessation of the peach harvest, dissolved relationships cause Ed, Eleanor, and May to reap a bitter harvest of regret. The novella includes a lush, almost entranced, atmosphere.

"Peaches, Peaches" also includes hints suggesting that D.H. Lawrence's 1921 novel, Women in Love, is a possible influence on the novella. The name of Lawrence's protagonist is Rupert Birkin, Knister's protagonist is Ed Burkin, and both works concentrate on the subject of consciousness of sexuality. Toward the end of Women in Love, Birkin thinks how, confronted by misery, "the heart would break,"[23] and how regret can be enough "to break the heart" (p. 540); toward the end of "Peaches, Peaches," Burkin thinks of Murray as a "heartbreaker."[24] Both Women in Love and "Peaches, Peaches" deal with the implications of relationships, and both works make reference, if obliquely, to the tree of knowledge. Rupert Birkin tells a secondary character, Hermione Roddice, "There is only one tree, there is only one fruit, in your mouth," and he elaborates "in exasperation," "The eternal apple" (pp. 43–44). In the course of "Peaches, Peaches," the peach tree becomes tantamount to a tree of knowledge, symbolizing Burkin's growing consciousness of sexuality. "Peaches, Peaches" also includes a character called March, as does Lawrence's novella The Fox, and both works concentrate on changing consciousness, especially of sexuality. While there appears to be no direct evidence that Knister read Women in Love, he was aware of Lawrence's work. In the opening paragraph of the essay "The Lost Gentleman," Knister writes, "I have just been reading D.H. Lawrence's *The Lost Girl*."[125] (Lawrence's 1920 novel, *The Lost Girl*, tells the story of an English nurse who finds herself repulsed by the lack of passion in English society; she eventually marries and leaves England for Italy.) A possible reason for Knister's interest in Lawrence's work is the simultaneous and detailed attention Lawrence pays to the emotional lives of his characters and the natural world. Lawrence's *Women in Love* assimilates both attention to the natural world and exploration of emotional truths (Gerald's death in the snow of the Alps serves as an example) and these elements are significant in Knister's work.

"Peaches, Peaches" has affinities of theme and technique with certain of Knister's short stories, especially the 1922 "Grapes" (Waddington, p. 178) and "Cherry Time." Titles alone suggest the possibility of a family resemblance among these works. Peter Stevens describes "Grapes" as depicting characters "caught in a state of unconsciousness about their relations."[126] "Peaches, Peaches," at least initially, also concerns "unconsciousness about . . . relations." Another link between the works is the common significance of their titles. In "Grapes," an eccentric "hired man" has the habit of stealing into his employer's kitchen during the night and gorging himself with cream, a habit that even attempts at "hiding the milk-pans" from him cannot discourage.[127] When grapes appear at the supper table, the hired man admits, "I never want to look at a grape again," and adds that he once "ate a six-quart basket" (p. 102) of grapes. His relations with people parallel his preferences in food; his employer jokingly remarks that the hired hand can probably sate his attraction to a person in the same fashion as he can sate his appetite for a food, so will overcome "his cream fever, like he got over his grape fever" (p. 105). In "Grapes," grapes represent the hired man's propensity toward transient but intense attraction, or his predisposition toward seasonal affinities. As in the case of "Peaches, Peaches," the title of "Grapes" draws attention to a symbol of changing consciousness, and especially consciousness of sexuality, and the title of "Cherry Time" has a similar function. For several reasons, the influence of Chekhov can also be associated with this group of Knister fictions; Chekhov's story "Gooseberries" has a teacher named Burkin,[128] *Women in Love* a school inspector called Birkin, and "Peaches, Peaches" a student named Burkin. "Grapes," "Cherry Time," and "Peaches, Peaches" all deal with a changing consciousness of sexuality over a brief season, and all are set in rural Ontario.

"Peaches, Peaches" evokes Ed's increasing consciousness of sexuality and the harmful consequences of sexual politics, and he learns to see the people around him in the revealing light of brief but telling sights and sounds: a discussion of sex beneath peach boughs (p. 22), Eleanor serving fig pie (p. 45), her final cries of grief (p. 57). Knister's images evoke truths of Ed's "ordinary" life, but these are truths that realism cannot necessarily convey, and an image in the novella calls particular attention to the limits of "photographic realism." On the day of an excursion, a photograph is taken:

> . . . May was beaming brightly enough to ruin the negative; Murray had adopted an easy hands-in-pocket pose of a well-dressed-young-man-with-his-hat-on. Ed held his hands down stiffly at his sides, and tried to outstare the low sun, while Florine was smiling with pursed lips, leaning forward a little, her head bent a little with an intimate look. (p. 51)

Knister's evocation of the four photographed characters, as presented over the course of the novella, in comparison makes their camera appearances relatively frozen and false. Cameras give limited representations, if empirically accurate ones. Knister's image of what the camera captures suggests that photography — and by extension photographic realism — gives an accurate impression of what it captures, but that what it captures is only part of a larger and much more complex picture or reality. As George Levine remarks, in *The Realistic Imagination,* for Joseph Conrad

> The reality he finds, or intimates, is a world in which the surfaces with which realism was preoccupied and which it largely tried to take as the reality itself merely disguise the truth, or repress it.[129]

For Knister, as Levine suggests of Conrad, "surfaces" cannot convey in full the discoverable "truth" of "experienced reality." Knister's use of intensely evocative images of everyday life is a fictional strategy that enables acknowledgement of intangible realities, without denial of the realities that photographic realism recognizes. The image of the "photograph" of Ed, Murray, Florine, and

May suggests the limitations of a photographic approach in fiction. This image of Knister's, which appears in one of the last works he wrote, helps explain why Knister made central use of evocative images of ordinary life; such images enable the acknowledgement of the realities that appearances may suggest, but do not necessarily reveal. In the second section of "Peaches, Peaches," when Ed, Murray, and Dave, a student working at a nearby farm, go swimming, during the others' chat about sex, Murray remains "silent," causing the others to look "at him in the dark, following in the narrow path overhung with peach boughs" (p. 22). This image reveals more about the three than any photograph could, as Knister's later image of a photograph demonstrates.

The peach season, and a season in Ed's life, end with his discoveries; the novella covers a dual season that fades into "A long, long fall until the end of November, there by the southern tip of Lake Erie" (p. 57). The protagonist finally is conscious enough, of what can be seductive, to imagine another's "dreams of summer delights through a winter of loneliness and longing" (p. 57). In "Peaches, Peaches," emotional states can be as real and as ephemeral as the brief peach season.

"Soil in Smoke" is Raymond Knister's last novel; as Waddington points out, "in 1931 and 1932 Knister had been reworking his first novel, "Group Portrait," which he now entitled 'Soil in Smoke'" (Thesis, p. 223). The polarity between those who cherish and those who despise ordinary life, if important in "Group Portrait," becomes more intense in "Soil in Smoke."

"Soil in Smoke" focuses on Roland, Milton (or Mil), and Robina (or Roby) Nebblin, three of the older children of the Nebblin family. Outlook divides the novel's cast of characters, who either appreciate the countryside or long to leave for the city, and who either discover pleasure in everyday life or yearn for pleasure in escape from daily life.

Mil Nebblin's portrait is more sharply drawn than was Del Nebblin's in "Group Portrait." During a scene at a beach dance pavilion, as Mil and a girl begin to dance, he notes

the way she turned, on the floor, and put up her arms. Liked it — her? His luck was dizzying. She was the swellest girl he had ever put his arms about. But who was she?

"My name's Nebblin, Milton Nebblin."

"Milton John, Paradise Regained or Lost?"

"Say, paradise, you said it. But I didn't say my name was John. My first name's Milton."

She didn't care to talk, it seemed.[130]

The girl refers to two of Milton's poems, but Mil is oblivious to these literary allusions. In context, the point is that Mil Nebblin cannot easily distinguish between the nature of an earthly paradise and exile from one.

The image of a scrap of leftover food as a nauseating bit of dead flesh captures Robina's view of ordinary life, or at least her momentary view (p. 109). Like Mil, Roby perceives her problem not as partly a matter of vision, but as the place she happens to be stuck in. Materialism becomes part of the problem because money becomes a means of escape. When a neighbour asks Mil where he has been, Mil replies,

"The city. Just back for a kind of holiday."

"Toronto or Detroit?"

"Hell, do I look as though I'd been to Toronto?" (p. 144)

Similarly, at a dance, the sight of a handsome stranger causes Robina to think that if she "could . . . regularly, go to all the city dances, she might meet a few fellows like that. But of course the snappy ones were not here, you had to go to Detroit" (p. 296). The yearning of Mil and Robina for Detroit is ominous because, in the context of "Soil in Smoke," such a yearning expresses a desire to escape from an environment that holds or genuinely promises the possibility of an earthly paradise. However, the oldest of the Nebblin children, Roland, who has the most patience with the work of the farm, has a vision of an earthly paradise.

Suitably enough, it is Roland who leads the massive work of tobacco growing on the Nebblin farm, work undertaken in Mil's absence (pp. 186–87). Roland's leading the work of growing tobacco plants in a peat bed "more garden-like than any garden" implies that he has a place in Eden, or recognizes the presence or possibility of an earthly paradise in the world around him. Given Knister's explicit reference to *Paradise Lost*, the suggestion that Roland can see the Edenic in the world around him becomes stronger when Roland crushes a snake (p. 201).

Roland has a vision of the intense beauty of the natural world, a vision of an earthly paradise (pp. 211–12). Human presence is an integral part of this earthly paradise; Roland envisions a girl emerging from the ground, "ankles growing from the thin moss and ferns, from the dried pool of long-drowned leaves." In isolation, the fact that the girl is actually Robina has ambiguous implications. A possible reading is that the girl of Roland's dreams is, in actuality, his seventeen-year old sister. An alternate reading is that Roland's vision redeems Robina from her misery, and so she literally appears to grow out of an Eden or arise from an earthly paradise.

The title "Soil in Smoke" hints that Robina's immediate hopes of an earthly paradise disappear in the "smoke" of delusion. Leaving a dance with a stolen fox stole, Robina feels "like a sparkmote in the blast of a locomotive's smoke-chimney. When the fire-box is opened the smoke is seen high above in its light. The sparks vanish. A spark in the light vanishing" (p. 299). When Mil first appears in the novel, he emerges from a farmyard building, from which "Blue jets of smoke chased one another from the roof, swept away to vanish in the light wind" (p. 3). Knister associates both Mil and Robina with vanishing or dissipating smoke, which in context suggests that both believe in delusory values.

In "Group Portrait," Robina steals a purse from her employer; in "Soil in Smoke," Robina steals, in addition to a purse, various articles (pp. 55, 257–58). While Robina implicitly agrees to sleep with Stanley in the last scene of "Group Portrait," in the later version of the novel Stanley repeatedly seduces Robina. In "Soil in Smoke," Stanley resumes his friendliness toward Robina, and subsequently his sexual relations with her, when they encounter each other one evening at the dance pavilion on the beach; between dances, Stanley drives Robina away in his new car, seduces her, and takes her back to the pavilion before the evening's dancing is over (pp. 213–21). Robina impulsively steals a fur stole in the final scene of "Group Portrait" but, in the concluding dance scene of "Soil in Smoke," she steals a fur stole belonging to a girl Stanley has paid attention to (pp. 290, 297). The later version of the novel therefore clarifies Robina's dual seduction by materialism: her faith in materialistic pleasure, on a presumably infinitely mounting scale, accounts both for her theft and her attraction to the unattractive (p. 299) but relatively wealthy Stanley.

In comparison to "Group Portrait," "Soil in Smoke" presents a more intense polarity between those who would create and those who prefer to consume, or those who can value their immediate environment, and those who tend to deplore it. This intensification occurs as Knister makes increased use of direct and oblique biblical allusions. Changing Del's name to Mil enables the unobtrusive inclusion of a reference to Milton's *Paradise Lost* in the later version of the novel. In "Group Portrait," Roland hears from Del that he would like to raise "Hob" when he spends his money (p. 18); in "Soil in Smoke," when Roland refers to Mil's raising "Hob," Mil replies, " 'Me? Raise Cain and put a prop under him!' Mil clutched his brother's arm" (p. 15). In clasping his "brother's" arm as he speaks of raising "Cain," Mil becomes a more sinister character than he was in his earlier incarnation as Del. Del jokes about returning to the Nebblin farm after being in "Hell" (p. 185); Mil, however, refers to "Hell" as "my old home town" (p. 207).

As well as heightening the visions of Mil and Robina, the revisions that distinguish "Soil in Smoke" from "Group Portrait" intensify Roland's vision. Roland crushes a "writhing" (p. 201) snake in "Soil in Smoke," while it is his brother, Frank, who strikes at an already "apparently dead" (p. 178) snake in the earlier "Group Portrait." "Group Portrait" includes only a brief discussion of Roland shovelling peat to be used for raising tobacco seedlings (p. 161), while "Soil in Smoke" additionally describes, in lush detail, Roland directing the construction of peat-filled hot-beds which, in being "more garden-like than any garden" (pp. 186–87), have an Edenic perfection.

A small but significant revision exemplifies how Knister heightens the polarity of vision found in the later version of the work. Del, recovering from venereal disease, watches his brothers build a garage, and sees the road near the farm as bleak: "Blue sand was the track, and blue ice lined it in streaks. The sun might melt it" (p. 267). Mil, similarly recovering from illness, sees the road in less hopeful terms: "Sulphury blue sand the track, blue ice lined it in streaks. The sun wouldn't melt it" (p. 276). While Del thinks the sun "might" melt the ice on the road, Mil thinks the sun "wouldn't" have a thawing effect. The added word, "Sulphury," also implies that Mil has a more hellishly despairing view than Del. The change and addition that occur in this passage imply that Mil's vision — he *watches* the road as these thoughts cross his mind — helps pave the metaphorical road to his private hell. Robina is last seen as a passenger in Stanley's car, and in "Group Portrait" (p. 298), as in

"Soil in Smoke," "The hazy sulphur road spun away beneath" (p. 299). However, only in the later version does Mil perceive the road as "sulphury." The later version of the novel suggests that Robina, like Mil, has a vision which paves the road to a private hell. Knister's increased use of biblical references, direct and not, sharpens focus on the central tension between the visions of those who can and those who cannot perceive the possibility of an earthly paradise. The real horror, in "Soil in Smoke," is the hideous waste of possibility with which Mil and Robina become associated, and there is evidence that they become artist *manqué* figures. In Knister's first novel, Robina Nebblin desires "beauty, more sweet than sin" — in Knister's last novel, Robina Nebblin's vision and circumstances make her desire for beauty futile.

"Soil in Smoke" presents the raising of crops and the raising of visions as being, in a sense, one. As Knister writes elsewhere, "Nothing, not poetry or dreams, can exist except on the basis of reality."[131] The title "Soil in Smoke" evokes an image that characterizes the direction of the novel as a whole, for it implies that the further consciousness moves from an awareness of the land, or the ground of ordinary life, the further the distance from genuine dreams, including those of the possibility of an earthly paradise. Raymond Knister's prose fiction culminates with a treatment of cultivation — cultivation of the land and of the various "dreams" that "can exist" in "reality."

Two unpublished short stories in the Knister papers indicate how *avant garde* his work could be. One short story, about a writer who attends a meeting of "the Guild of Authors" (a writer who will do such things as "test her own theories of writing"), has the protagonist wonder in the form of a one-sentence paragraph, "Why, just why had she come?"[132] The title, "The Judgment of Her Peers," functions as a delicious irony. Another unpublished story, "A Man for All That," is highly ironic, set in a "wild free scene"[133] and filled with very macho doings: in the "idyllic district" depicted, "a man is always a Man" to such an extent that one male character is "only stunned, having been shot in the head" (p. 10). A local "mighty likely young woman" poses for a painter and dies after the experience (p. 4). The story presents "Dollie Mewer with his fiancé Sammy Bane" (p. 6); as Dollie is male and Sammy female, it follows that Sammy is "taller than Dollie," "her chosen betrothed" (p. 11), in a world of fixed stereotypes becoming unglued. Sammy, who can speak with "feminine intuition" (p. 14), is "so large, so clean, so unsophisticated, so physically perfect!" (p. 6). Sammy takes "lessons on being a lady" from a poet (a stranger with "mellow" eyes and "tailored" clothes), so that she might have "an artistic awakening" (p. 6); in "The Judgment of Her Peers" the female writer-protagonist thinks of visiting a friend "able to talk of" Thomas Mann (p. 10), who won the Nobel Prize in 1929. In the world of Knister's fiction, conventional roles, rigid positions, obsessive outlook, and fixed ideas are the source, at best, of comedy: "choice," as stated in the Preface, entitled "Introductory," to "A Man for All That," is the source of fiction.

Knister's writing has its genesis in a vision that explores and charts a course from "experienced reality" to fiction; as bill bissett observes, "it's the only planet we're likely to experience," and "art is a bridge to life. It can be that."[34]

NOTES

The knowledge and encouragement of David Arnason and James Reaney made the writing of this essay possible. Imogen Knister Givens patiently and kindly answered numerous questions about her father's life and work, and permitted quotation from unpublished material. Thanks to William Murtha for discussions of, and permission to quote from, letters between Thomas Murtha and Raymond Knister.

Thanks to the "centralian great lakes picnicking societee."

[1] For this and subsequent information, I am indebted to Imogen Knister Givens.

[2] Marcus Waddington, "Raymond Knister: A Biographical Note," *Journal of Canadian Fiction*, No. 14 (1975) [Raymond Knister issue], p. 175. All further references to this work (Waddington) appear in the text.

[3] Imogen Givens courteously provided a copy of this list.

[4] "Raymond Knister," an unpublished essay, kindly made available by Imogen Givens. It may have been written by Knister and seems to form the basis for Leo Kennedy's "Raymond Knister," *The Canadian Forum*, Sept. 1932, pp. 459–61.

[5] Anne Burke, "Raymond Knister: An Annotated Bibliography," in *The Annotated Bibliography of Canada's Major Authors*, ed. Robert Lecker and Jack David, III (Downsview, Ont.: ECW, 1981), 292.

[6] David Arnason, "Canadian Poetry: The Interregnum," *CV/II*, 1, No. 1 (Spring 1975), 31. All further references to this work appear in the text.

[7] Bonita O'Halloran, "Chronological History of Raymond Knister," *Journal of Canadian Fiction*, No. 14 (1975) [Raymond Knister issue], p. 194. All further references to this work (O'Halloran) appear in the text.

[8] Raymond Knister, Letter to Elizabeth Frankfurth [copy], 11 April 1924, Raymond Knister Papers, Queen's Univ. Archives, Kingston, Ont.

[9] Ernest Walsh, Letter to Raymond Knister, 23 April 1925, Raymond Knister Papers, Queen's Univ. Archives, Kingston, Ont.

[10] Raymond Knister, Letter to Elizabeth Frankfurth [copy], 19 Nov. 1925, Raymond Knister Papers, Queen's Univ. Archives, Kingston, Ont.

[11] William Murtha, ed. and introd., *Short Stories of Thomas Murtha* (Ottawa: Univ. of Ottawa Press, 1980). The Introduction discusses the friendship of Murtha and Knister.

[12] Desmond Pacey, ed. and introd., *The Letters of Frederick Philip Grove* (Toronto: Univ. of Toronto Press, 1976), pp. 283–84.

[13] Joy Kuropatwa, "A Handbook to Raymond Knister's Longer Prose Fiction," Diss. Western Ontario 1985, pp. 135, 162.

[14] Raymond Knister, "There Was a Mr. Cristi," p. 129. Knister Family Papers. Imogen Knister Givens kindly provided a copy of the typescript, and permitted quotation from the work in this essay. All further references to this work appear in the text.

[15] Leo Kennedy, "A Poet's Memoirs," rev. of *Journal of Canadian Fiction*, No. 14 (1975) [Raymond Knister issue], *CV/II*, 2, No. 2 (May 1976), 23–24.

[16] Marcus Waddington, "Raymond Knister and the Canadian Short Story," M.A. Thesis Carleton 1977, p. 223. All further references to this work (Waddington, Thesis) appear in the text.

[17] Imogen Givens, "Raymond Knister — Man or Myth?" *Essays on Canadian Writing*, No. 16 (Fall–Winter 1979–80), pp. 5–19.

[18] Raymond Knister, "Democracy and the Short Story," *Journal of Canadian Fiction*, No. 14 (1975) [Raymond Knister issue], p. 148. All further references to this work appear in the text.

[19] Raymond Knister, "A Great Poet of To-Day, Edwin Arlington Robinson, Author of 'The Man against the Sky,' " *The New Outlook*, 30 June 1926, pp. 6, 27; rpt. in his *The First Day of Spring: Stories and Other Prose*, ed. and introd. Peter Stevens, Literature of Canada: Poetry and Prose in Reprint, No. 17 (Toronto: Univ. of Toronto Press, 1976), p. 417.

[20] Raymond Knister, "Canadian Letter," in Stevens, ed., *The First Day of Spring*, p. 380. All further references to this work appear in the text.

[21] Raymond Knister, "Canadian Literati," *Journal of Canadian Fiction*, No.

14 (1975) [Raymond Knister issue], p. 167. All further references to this work appear in the text.

²² William Butler Yeats, "Modern Poetry: A Broadcast," in his *Essays and Introductions* (New York: Collier, 1968), p. 499.

²³ Raymond Knister, *White Narcissus* (New York: Harcourt, Brace, 1929), p. 189.

²⁴ Raymond Knister, Foreword, *Windfalls for Cider: The Poems of Raymond Knister*, ed. and introd. Joy Kuropatwa, Preface by James Reaney (Windsor, Ont.: Black Moss, 1983), p. 15.

²⁵ Raymond Knister, "The Poetry of Archibald Lampman," *The Dalhousie Review*, 7 (Oct. 1927), 348–61; rpt. in Stevens, ed., *The First Day of Spring*, p. 456. All further references to this work appear in the text.

²⁶ Ezra Pound, "Credo," in *Literary Essays of Ezra Pound*, ed. and introd. T.S. Eliot (New York: New Directions, 1968), pp. 9, 10.

²⁷ Raymond Knister, "The Canadian Short Story," *The Canadian Bookman*, 5 (Aug. 1923), 203–04; rpt. in Stevens, ed., *The First Day of Spring*, p. 390.

²⁸ Quoted in Dorothy Livesay, "Raymond Knister: A Memoir," in *Collected Poems of Raymond Knister*, ed. Dorothy Livesay (Toronto: Ryerson, 1949), p. xxi. All further references to this work appear in the text.

²⁹ Raymond Knister, "Katherine Mansfield," in Stevens, ed., *The First Day of Spring*, p. 428. All further references to this work appear in the text.

³⁰ Rev. of *The Poetical Works of Wilfred Campbell*, ed. W.J. Sykes, *Queen's Quarterly*, 31 (May 1924), 435–39; rpt. "The Poetical Works of Wilfred Campbell," in Stevens, ed., *The First Day of Spring*, p. 450.

³¹ Knister, "The Canadian Short Story," p. 389.

³² Raymond Knister, Introd., *Canadian Short Stories* (Toronto: Macmillan, 1928), pp. xi–xix; rpt. in Stevens, ed., *The First Day of Spring*, p. 394.

³³ Henry James, "Preface to 'The American,' " in *The Art of the Novel*, introd. Richard P. Blackmur (New York: Scribner's, 1962), p. 32.

³⁴ I am indebted to Dr. G. Rans for this observation, and I would like to express my thanks to him for his introduction to, and guidance within, the world of the theory and the practice of nineteenth-century American romance.

³⁵ Knister, *White Narcissus*, pp. 194–95.

³⁶ Nathaniel Hawthorne, Preface, *The House of the Seven Gables* (New York: New American Library, 1961), p. vii.

³⁷ Raymond Knister, "The Lost Gentleman," *Journal of Canadian Fiction*, No. 14 (1975) [Raymond Knister issue], p. 152. All further references to this work appear in the text.

³⁸ Knister, Introd., *Canadian Short Stories*, p. xiv.

³⁹ Raymond Knister, "The Canadian Girl," *Journal of Canadian Fiction*, No.

14 (1975) [Raymond Knister issue], p. 159.

[40] Raymond Knister, "Canadian Literature: A General Impression," *Journal of Canadian Fiction*, No. 14 (1975) [Raymond Knister issue], p. 171. All further references to this work appear in the text.

[41] Knister, "The Canadian Girl," p. 159.

[42] Raymond Knister, "A Shropshire Lad," in Stevens, ed., *The First Day of Spring*, p. 420.

[43] David Arnason, "The Development of Prairie Realism: Robert J. Stead, Douglas Durkin, Martha Ostenso and Frederick Philip Grove," Diss. New Brunswick 1980, p. 223.

[44] See above, note 12.

[45] Clara Thomas and John Lennox, *William Arthur Deacon: A Literary Life* (Toronto: Univ. of Toronto Press, 1982). See pages 41, 42, 56, 57, 89–92, 144, and 229.

[46] See above, note 11.

[47] Leo Kennedy, *The Shrouding* (Toronto: Macmillan, 1933).

[48] Dorothy Livesay, *Right Hand Left Hand*, ed. David Arnason and Kim Todd (Erin, Ont.: Porcépic, 1977), pp. 48–58.

[49] *The Poet Who Was Farmer Too: A Profile of Raymond Knister*, prod. John Wood and Allan Anderson, CBC Radio, 19 July 1964.

[50] See above, note 15.

[51] Earle Birney, *Spreading Time: Remarks on Canadian Writing and Writers, Book I: 1904–1949* (Montreal: Véhicule, 1980), p. 24.

[52] See above, note 17.

[53] Raymond Knister, Letter to his parents, 29 Oct. 1928, Raymond Knister Collection, Mills Memorial Library, McMaster Univ., Hamilton, Ont.

[54] Raymond Knister, Letter to his father, 8 Feb. 1928, Raymond Knister Collection, Mills Memorial Library, McMaster Univ., Hamilton, Ont.

[55] Raymond Knister, Letter to Myrtle Knister, 11 May 1928, Raymond Knister Collection, Mills Memorial Library, McMaster Univ., Hamilton, Ont.

[56] Cyril Connelly, "New Novels," rev. of eleven novels including *White Narcissus*, by Raymond Knister, *The New Statesman*, 23 Feb. 1929, p. 637.

[57] J.D. Robins, "Essentials and Accidentals," *The Canadian Forum*, Aug. 1929, p. 390.

[58] Desmond Pacey, *A Short History of English Canadian Literature: Creative Writing in Canada* (Toronto: Ryerson, 1961).

[59] Philip Child, Introd., *White Narcissus*, New Canadian Library, No. 32 (Toronto: McClelland and Stewart, 1962), p. 7.

[60] Paul Denham, "Beyond Realism: Raymond Knister's *White Narcissus*," *Studies in Canadian Literature*, 3, No. 1 (1978), 70.

[61] Glenn Clever, "Point of View in *White Narcissus*," *Studies in Canadian Literature*, 3, No. 1 (1978), 119.

[62] John Moss, *A Reader's Guide to the Canadian Novel* (Toronto: McClelland and Stewart, 1981), p. 146.

[63] Robert Ayre, "Biography Without Footnotes," rev. of *My Star Predominant*, by Raymond Knister, *Saturday Night*, 8 Dec. 1934, p. 8.

[64] "Keats and His Ailment," rev. of *My Star Predominant*, by Raymond Knister, *The Globe* [Toronto], 29 Dec. 1934, p. 8.

[65] Don Precosky, "Ever with Discontent: Some Comments on Raymond Knister and His Poetry," *CV/II*, 4, No. 4 (Spring 1980), 9.

[66] Desmond Pacey, "Fiction 1920–1940," in *Literary History of Canada: Canadian Literature in English*, ed. Carl F. Klinck (1965; rpt. Toronto: Univ. of Toronto Press, 1970), p. 685.

[67] Michael Gnarowski, Introd., *Selected Stories of Raymond Knister* (Ottawa: Univ. of Ottawa Press, 1972), p. 12.

[68] Dorothy Livesay, "Knister's Stories," rev. of *Selected Stories of Raymond Knister*, *Canadian Literature*, No. 62 (Autumn 1974), p. 79. All further references to this work appear in the text.

[69] David Arnason, Preface, *Journal of Canadian Fiction*, No. 14 (1975) [Raymond Knister issue], p. 8.

[70] Kennedy, "A Poet's Memoirs," p. 24.

[71] Kennedy, "A Poet's Memoirs," p. 23.

[72] Stevens, Introd., *The First Day of Spring*, p. xiii.

[73] Michael Darling, "Knister Redivivus," rev. of *The First Day of Spring*, by Raymond Knister, ed. and introd. Peter Stevens, *Essays on Canadian Writing*, No. 6 (Spring 1977), p. 147.

[74] Margot Northey, rev. of *The First Day of Spring*, by Raymond Knister, ed. and introd. Peter Stevens, *The Canadian Forum*, June–July 1977, p. 45.

[75] Barry Cameron, "The Rediscovery of Raymond Knister," rev. of *The First Day of Spring*, by Raymond Knister, ed. and introd. Peter Stevens, *The Ontario Review*, No. 7 (1977–78), p. 108.

[76] Doris Everard, "Tragic Dimensions in Selected Short Stories of Raymond Knister," M.A. Thesis Sir George Williams 1972, p. 22.

[77] *The Poet Who Was Farmer Too: A Profile of Raymond Knister*. CBC Radio, 19 July 1964.

[78] Doug Smith, "The Fine and Patient Hand," rev. of *Mountain Tea and Other Poems*, by Peter van Toorn; *Russian Poetry: A Personal Anthology*, ed. and trans. R.A.D. Ford; and *Windfalls for Cider: The Poems of Raymond Knister*, ed. and introd. Joy Kuropatwa, *The Antigonish Review*, Nos. 62–63 (1985), p. 203. All further references to this work appear in the text.

[79] George Woodcock, introd., *Canadian Writers and Their Works*, Poetry Series, III, Ed. Robert Lecker, Jack David, Ellen Quigley (Toronto: ECW, 1987), p. 10.

[80] Raymond Knister, "The Wonders of Man," *The New Outlook*, 9 Feb. 1927, p. 15.

[81] Raymond Knister, "On Reading Aloud," *The New Outlook*, 27 Oct. 1926, p. 14.

[82] Raymond Knister, "The Poetic Muse in Canada," *Saturday Night*, 6 Oct. 1928, p. 3.

[83] Raymond Knister, "Duncan Campbell Scott," in Stevens, ed., *The First Day of Spring*, p. 402.

[84] Raymond Knister, Letter to Henry Goodman, 16 Oct. 1922, Raymond Knister Collection, Mills Memorial Library, McMaster Univ., Hamilton, Ont.

[85] Raymond Knister, "Letter to Miss Frankfurth," in Stevens, ed., *The First Day of Spring*, p. 405.

[86] Givens, "Raymond Knister — Man or Myth?" p. 7.

[87] Raymond Knister, Letter to Bobbs Merrill Publishing Company, 12 Jan. 1928, Raymond Knister Collection, Mills Memorial Library, McMaster Univ., Hamilton, Ont.

[88] Raymond Knister, Letter to Thomas Murtha, 4 Dec. 1929. Courteously made available by, and quoted with the permission of, William Murtha.

[89] Raymond Knister, Letter to his parents, 30 July 1929, Raymond Knister Collection, Mills Memorial Library, McMaster Univ., Hamilton, Ont.

[90] Knister, Introd., *Canadian Short Stories*, p. xv.

[91] Morley Callaghan, Letter to Raymond Knister, 15 Aug. 1928, Raymond Knister Collection, Mills Memorial Library, McMaster Univ., Hamilton, Ont.

[92] Morley Callaghan, *A Native Argosy* (New York: Scribner's, 1929). All further references to this work appear in the text.

[93] Raymond Knister, "Dissecting the 'T.B.M.': A Reply to S. Laycock's 'Why Be True to Life' and a Ruthless Investigation of a Certain Mental Viewpoint," *Saturday Night*, 6 Sept. 1930, p. 5.

[94] Raymond Knister, Letter to his mother, 4 Oct. 1928, Raymond Knister Collection, Mills Memorial Library, McMaster Univ., Hamilton, Ont.

[95] Robins, p. 389.

[96] Robins, p. 390.

[97] Discussion of versions of this work, and others, is based on Kuropatwa, "A Handbook to Raymond Knister's Longer Prose Ficiton."

[98] Raymond Knister, "Group Portrait," TS, Raymond Knister Papers, Queen's Univ. Archives, Kingston, Ont. All further references to this work appear in the text.

[99] Raymond Knister, "Mist-Green Oats," *The Midland: A Magazine of the Middle West*, 8, Nos. 8–9 (1922), 254–76. All further references to this work appear in the text.

[100] Raymond Knister, "Turning Loam," TS, Folders 37–45, Raymond Knister Collection, Pratt Library, Victoria Univ., Toronto, Ont. All further references to this work appear in the text.

[101] Raymond Knister, "The Unrealism of Sinclair Lewis's 'Babbitt,' " rev. of *Babbitt*, by Sinclair Lewis, *The Border Cities Star* [Windsor, Ont.], 14 April 1923, p. 2.

[102] Raymond Knister, "The Strawstack," in Stevens, ed., *The First Day of Spring*. All further references to this work appear in the text.

[103] Raymond Knister, *White Narcissus*, introd. Philip Child, New Canadian Library, No. 32 (Toronto: McClelland and Stewart, 1962), p. 19. All further references to this work appear in the text.

[104] Raymond Knister, "The One Thing," in Stevens, ed., *The First Day of Spring*. All further references to this work appear in the text.

[105] Raymond Knister, "The Lost Gentleman," *Journal of Canadian Fiction*, No. 14 (1975) [Raymond Knister issue], p. 150.

[106] Raymond Knister, "Bunin Does Story That Is Regarded by Critics as One of Greatest of Age," rev. of *The Gentleman from San Francisco and Other Stories*, by Ivan A. Bunin, *The Border Cities Star* [Windsor, Ont.], 14 July 1923, p. 9.

[107] Henry James, *The Ambassadors*, ed. and introd. Leon Edel (Boston: Houghton Mifflin, 1960), p. 359.

[108] James, p. 78.

[109] Raymond Knister, Letter to Dr. J. Guthrie, 29 Jan. 1929. Courtesy of Imogen Givens.

[110] Nathaniel Hawthorne, *The Scarlett Letter*, ed. William Charvat et al. (Columbus: Ohio State Univ. Press, 1962), p. 26. All further references to this work appear in the text.

[111] Herman Melville, *Moby Dick*, ed. Harrison Hayford and Herschel Parker (New York: Norton, 1967), p. 14. All further references to this work appear in the text.

[112] Raymond Knister, Letter to Thomas Murtha, 28 Aug. 1929. Courteously made available by, and quoted with the permission of, William Murtha.

[113] Raymond Knister, "Innocent Man," in Stevens, ed., *The First Day of Spring*, p. 281.

[114] Raymond Knister, "Hackman's Night," in Stevens, ed., *The First Day of Spring*, p. 208.

[115] Raymond Knister, "Cab Driver," TS, Box 11, p. 19, Raymond Knister

Collection, Mills Memorial Library, McMaster Univ., Hamilton, Ont. All further references to this work appear in the text.

[116] bill bissett, "Interview with bill bissett," with Maidie Hilmo, *Essays on Canadian Writing*, No. 32 (Summer 1986), p. 140.

[117] Arnason, "Canadian Poetry: The Interregnum," p. 32.

[118] Rev. of *My Star Predominant*, by Raymond Knister, *Times Literary Supplement*, 25 Oct. 1934, p. 732.

[119] Raymond Knister, *My Star Predominant* (Toronto: Ryerson, 1934), p. 107. All further references to this work appear in the text.

[120] John Keats, *The Letters of John Keats*, ed. M.B. Forman (Oxford: Oxford Univ. Press, 1931), II, 572.

[121] Amy Lowell, *John Keats* (Boston: Houghton Mifflin, 1925), II, 468–83.

[122] Keats, *The Letters of John Keats*, II, p. 572.

[123] D.H. Lawrence, *Women in Love* (Harmondsworth: Penguin, 1976), p. 538. All further references to this work appear in the text.

[124] Raymond Knister, "Peaches, Peaches," in Stevens, ed., *The First Day of Spring*, p. 57. All further references to this work appear in the text.

[125] Knister, "The Lost Gentleman," p. 149.

[126] Stevens, Introd., *The First Day of Spring*, p. xxiii.

[127] Raymond Knister, "Grapes," in Stevens, ed., *The First Day of Spring*, p. 99.

[128] Anton Chekhov, "Gooseberries," in *Anton Chekhov's Short Stories*, ed. R. Matlaw (New York: Norton, 1979), pp. 185–94.

[129] George Levine, *The Realistic Imagination* (Chicago: Univ. of Chicago Press, 1981), p. 318.

[130] Raymond Knister, "Soil in Smoke," TS, Folders 27–36, p. 28, Raymond Knister Collection, Pratt Library, Victoria Univ., Toronto, Ont. All further references to this work appear in the text.

[131] Knister, "The Poetic Muse in Canada," p. 3.

[132] Raymond Knister, "The Judgement of Her Peers," TS, Box 5, Raymond Knister Collection, Mills Memorial Library, McMaster Univ., Hamilton, Ont.

[133] Raymond Knister, "A Man for All That," TS, Box 6, Raymond Knister Collection, Mills Memorial Library, McMaster Univ., Hamilton, Ont.

[134] bissett, "Interview with bill bissett," p. 141.

SELECTED BIBLIOGRAPHY

Primary Sources

Letters

Knister, Raymond. Letter to Henry Goodman. 16 Oct. 1922. Raymond Knister
Collection. Mills Memorial Library, McMaster Univ., Hamilton, Ont.
——— . Letter to Elizabeth Frankfurth [copy]. 11 April 1924. Raymond Knister
Papers. Queen's Univ. Archives, Kingston, Ont.
——— . Letter to Elizabeth Frankfurth [copy]. 19 Nov. 1925. Raymond Knister
Papers. Queen's Univ. Archives, Kingston, Ont.
——— . Letter to Bobbs Merrill Publishing Co. 12 Jan. 1928. Raymond Knister
Collection. Mills Memorial Library, McMaster Univ., Hamilton, Ont.
——— . Letter to his father. 8 Feb. 1928. Raymond Knister Collection. Mills
Memorial Library, McMaster Univ., Hamilton, Ont.
——— . Letter to Myrtle Knister. 11 May 1928. Raymond Knister Collection.
Mills Memorial Library, McMaster Univ., Hamilton, Ont.
——— . Letter to his mother. 4 Oct. 1928. Raymond Knister Collection. Mills
Memorial Library, McMaster Univ., Hamilton, Ont.
——— . Letter to his parents. 29 Oct. 1928. Raymond Knister Collection. Mills
Memorial Library, McMaster Univ., Hamilton, Ont.
——— . Letter to his parents. 30 July 1929. Raymond Knister Collection. Mills
Memorial Library, McMaster Univ., Hamilton, Ont.

Unpublished Work

Knister, Raymond. "Cab Driver." TS. Box 11. Raymond Knister Collection. Mills
Memorial Library, McMaster Univ., Hamilton, Ont.
——— . "Group Portrait." TS. Raymond Knister Papers. Queen's Univ.
Archives, Kingston, Ont.

———. "The Judgement of Her Peers." TS. Box 5. Raymond Knister Collection. Mills Memorial Library, McMaster Univ., Hamilton, Ont.

———. "A Man for All That." TS. Box 6. Raymond Knister Collection. Mills Memorial Library, McMaster Univ., Hamilton, Ont.

———. "Soil in Smoke." TS. Folders 27–36. Raymond Knister Collection. Pratt Library, Victoria Univ., Toronto, Ont.

———. "Turning Loam." TS. Folders 37–45. Raymond Knister Collection. Pratt Library, Victoria Univ., Toronto, Ont.

Books

Knister, Raymond, ed. and introd. *Canadian Short Stories*. Toronto: Macmillan, 1928.

———. *White Narcissus*. New York: Harcourt, Brace, 1929; rpt. New Canadian Library, No. 32. Introd. Philip Child. Toronto: McClelland and Stewart, 1962; rpt. New Canadian Library. Afterword Morley Callaghan. Toronto: McClelland and Stewart, 1990.

———. *My Star Predominant*. Toronto: Ryerson, 1934.

———. *Collected Poems of Raymond Knister*. Ed. with a Memoir by Dorothy Livesay. Toronto: Ryerson, 1949.

———. *Journal of Canadian Fiction*, No. 14 (1975) [Raymond Knister issue]. Ed. David Arnason; rpt. *Raymond Knister: Poems, Stories and Essays*. Ed. and introd. David Arnason. Montreal: Bellrock, 1975.

———. *The First Day of Spring: Stories and Other Prose*. Ed. and introd. Peter Stevens. Literature of Canada: Poetry and Prose in Reprint, No. 17. Toronto: Univ. of Toronto Press, 1976.

———. *Windfalls for Cider: The Poems of Raymond Knister*. Ed. and introd. Joy Kuropatwa. Pref. James Reaney. Windsor, Ont.: Black Moss, 1983.

Contributions to Periodicals and Books

Knister, Raymond. "Mist-Green Oats." *The Midland: A Magazine of the Middle West*, 8, Nos. 8–9 (1922), 254–76.

———. "The Unrealism of Sinclair Lewis's *Babbitt*." Rev. of *Babbitt*, by Sinclair Lewis. *The Border Cities Star* [Windsor, Ont.], 14 April 1923, p. 2.

———. "Bunin Does Story That Is Regarded by Critics as One of Greatest of Age." Rev. of *The Gentleman from San Francisco and Other Stories*, by Ivan

A. Bunin. *The Border Cities Star* [Windsor, Ont.], 14 July 1923, p. 9.

———. "On Reading Aloud." *The New Outlook*, 27 Oct. 1926, p. 14.

———. "The Wonders of Man." *The New Outlook*, 9 Feb. 1927, p. 15.

———. "The Poetic Muse in Canada." *Saturday Night*, 6 Oct. 1928, pp. 3, 22.

———. "Dissecting the 'T.B.M.': A Reply to S. Laycock's 'Why Be True to Life' and a Ruthless Investigation of a Certain Mental Viewpoint." *Saturday Night*, 6 Sept. 1930, p. 5.

Secondary Sources

Arnason, David. "Canadian Poetry: The Interregnum." *CV/II*, 1, No. 1 (Spring 1975), 28–32.

———. "The Development of Prairie Realism: Robert J. Stead, Douglas Durkin, Martha Ostenso and Frederick Philip Grove." Diss. New Brunswick 1980.

Ayre, Robert. "Biography without Footnotes." *Saturday Night*, 8 Dec. 1934, p. 8.

bissett, bill. "Interview with bill bissett." With Maidie Hilmo. *Essays on Canadian Writing*, No. 32 (Summer 1986), pp. 134–46.

Burke, Anne. "Raymond Knister: An Annotated Bibliography." In *The Annotated Bibliography of Canada's Major Authors*. Ed. Robert Lecker and Jack David. Vol. III. Downsview, Ont.: ECW, 1981, 281–322.

Callaghan, Morley. Letter to Raymond Knister. 15 Aug. 1928. Raymond Knister Collection. Mills Memorial Library, McMaster Univ., Hamilton, Ont.

———. *A Native Argosy*. New York: Scribner's, 1929.

Cameron, Barry. Rev. of *The First Day of Spring*, by Raymond Knister. *The Ontario Review*, No. 7 (1977–78), pp. 106–08.

Chekhov, Anton. *Anton Chekhov's Short Stories*. Ed. R. Matlaw. Norton Critical Edition. New York: Norton, 1979.

Clever, Glenn. "Point of View in *White Narcissus*." *Studies in Canadian Literature*, 3, No. 1 (Winter 1978), 119–23.

Connolly, Cyril. "New Novels." Rev. of eleven novels, including *White Narcissus*, by Raymond Knister. *The New Statesman*, 23 Feb. 1929, p. 637.

Darling, Michael. "Knister Redivivus." Rev. of *The First Day of Spring*, by Raymond Knister. *Essays on Canadian Writing*, No. 6 (Spring 1977), pp. 144–47.

Denham, Paul. "Beyond Realism: Raymond Knister's *White Narcissus*." *Studies in Canadian Literature*, 3, No. 1 (Winter 1978), 70–77.

Everard, Doris. "Tragic Dimensions in Selected Short Stories of Raymond Knister." M.A. Thesis Sir George Williams 1972.

Givens, Imogen. "Raymond Knister — Man or Myth?" *Essays on Canadian Writing*, No. 16 (Fall–Winter 1979–80), pp. 5–19.

──────. Letter [commenting on Dorothy Livesay's "Death by Drowning."]. *Books in Canada*, Aug.–Sept. 1987, pp. 38–39.

Hawthorne, Nathaniel, preface. *The House of the Seven Gables*. New York: New American Library, 1961, pp. vii–ix.

──────. *The Scarlet Letter*. Ed. William Charvat et al. The Centenary Edition of the Works of Nathaniel Hawthorne, I. Columbus: Ohio State Univ. Press, 1962.

James, Henry. *The Ambassadors*. Ed. and introd. Leon Edel. Boston: Houghton Mifflin, 1960.

──────. "Preface to 'The American.'" In *The Art of the Novel*. Introd. Richard P. Blackmur. New York: Scribner's, 1962, pp. 20–39.

Keats, John. *The Letters of John Keats*. Ed. M.B. Forman. 2 vols. Oxford: Oxford Univ. Press, 1931.

"Keats and His Ailment." Rev. of *My Star Predominant*, by Raymond Knister. *The Globe* [Toronto], 29 Dec. 1934, p. 8.

Kennedy, Leo. *The Shrouding*. Toronto: Macmillan, 1933.

──────. "A Poet's Memoirs." Rev. of *Journal of Canadian Fiction*, No. 14 (1975) [Raymond Knister issue]. *CV/II*, 2, No. 2 (May 1976), 23–24.

Kuropatwa, Joy. "A Handbook to Raymond Knister's Longer Prose Fiction." Diss. Western Ontario 1985.

Lawrence, D.H. *Women in Love*. Harmondsworth: Penguin, 1976.

Levine, George. *The Realistic Imagination: English Fiction from "Frankenstein" to "Lady Chatterley."* Chicago: Univ. of Chicago Press, 1981.

Livesay, Dorothy. "Knister's Stories." Rev. of *Selected Stories of Raymond Knister*. *Canadian Literature*, No. 62 (Autumn 1974), pp. 79–83.

──────. "Raymond Knister: A Memoir." In *Collected Poems of Raymond Knister*. Ed. Dorothy Livesay. Toronto: Ryerson, 1949, pp. xi–xli. Rpt. (revised) in *Right Hand Left Hand*. Ed. David Arnason and Kim Todd. Erin, Ont.: Porcépic, 1977, pp. 48–58.

──────. "Death by Drowning." *Books in Canada*, April 1987, pp. 15–16.

──────. "On Being in Love: A Reminiscence." *NeWest Review*, 15, No. 2 (Dec. 1989–Jan. 1990), 10–14.

Lowell, Amy. *John Keats*. 2 vols. Boston: Houghton Mifflin, 1925.

Melville, Herman. *Moby Dick*. Ed. Harrison Hayford and Herschel Parker. Norton Critical Edition. New York: Norton, 1967.

Moss, John. *A Reader's Guide to the Canadian Novel*. Toronto: McClelland and Stewart, 1981.

Munro, Alice. Letter [commenting on Dorothy Livesay's "Death by Drowning."]. *Books in Canada*, Aug.–Sept. 1987, pp. 38–39.

Murtha, William, ed. and introd. *Short Stories of Thomas Murtha*. Ottawa: Univ. of Ottawa Press, 1980, pp. 13–31.

Northey, Margot. Rev. of *The First Day of Spring*, by Raymond Knister. *The Canadian Forum*, June–July 1977, pp. 44–45.

O'Halloran, Bonita. "Chronological History of Raymond Knister." *Journal of Canadian Fiction*, No. 14 (1975) [Raymond Knister issue], pp. 194–99.

Pacey, Desmond. *A Short History of English-Canadian Literature: Creative Writing in Canada*. Toronto: Ryerson, 1961.

———. "Fiction 1920–1940." In *Literary History of Canada*. Ed. Carl F. Klinck. Toronto: Univ. of Toronto Press, 1965, pp. 658–93.

———, ed. and introd. *The Letters of Frederick Philip Grove*. Toronto: Univ. of Toronto Press, 1976.

Precosky, Don. "Ever with Discontent: Some Comments on Raymond Knister and His Poetry." *CV/II*, 4, No. 4 (Spring 1980), 3–9.

Rev. of *My Star Predominant*, by Raymond Knister. *Times Literary Supplement*, 25 Oct. 1934, p. 732.

Robins, J.D. "Essentials and Accidentals." *The Canadian Forum*, Aug. 1929, pp. 388–90.

Smith, Doug. "The Fine and Patient Hand." Rev. of poetry books, including *Windfalls for Cider: The Poems of Raymond Knister*. *The Antigonish Review*, No. 62–63 (1985), pp. 193–207.

Thomas, Clara, and John Lennox. *William Arthur Deacon: A Literary Life*. Toronto: Univ. of Toronto Press, 1982.

Waddington, Marcus. "Raymond Knister: A Biographical Note." *Journal of Canadian Fiction*, No. 14 (1975) [Raymond Knister issue], pp. 175–92.

———. "Raymond Knister and the Canadian Short Story." M.A. Thesis Carleton 1977.

Walsh, Ernest. Letter to Raymond Knister. 23 April 1925. Raymond Knister Papers. Queen's Univ. Archives, Kingston, Ont.

Yeats, William Butler. "Modern Poetry: A Broadcast." In *Essays and Introductions*. New York: Collier, 1968, pp. 491–508.

*W.O. Mitchell
and His Works*

W.O. Mitchell (1914–   )

DICK HARRISON

Biography

W.O. MITCHELL's life invites comparison with his fiction to an extent uncommon among major Canadian authors. This is in part because Mitchell is a public figure, probably familiar to more Canadians on radio and television than on the page. His first widespread popularity was not as novelist but as writer of the "Jake and the Kid" radio dramas. His public readings, in the tradition of Dickens, Twain, and Leacock, are performances; he acts his way into his fiction in the eyes of his audience. The public persona he often affects — the old prairie gopher — is carefully chosen to complement his writings. Within Mitchell's fiction there are circumstances which parallel his Prairie childhood, and his theories of artistic creation further encourage the comparison. Mitchell stresses the importance to the artist of the vivid experiences of childhood, the "litmus" years which colour the imagination, and in his advice to young writers he speaks of the need to draw from the well of subconscious memory which is replenished by the flow of personal experience.

William Ormond Mitchell was born in Weyburn, Saskatchewan, 13 March 1914, second of four sons of Ormond S. Mitchell, a druggist from Waterdown, Ontario, and Maggie MacMurray, a nurse from Clinton, Ontario. In 1921 his father died, and his grandmother MacMurray moved in with the family. The boy was strongly influenced by her and by an uncle who farmed nearby.[1] Even these basic facts are a strong temptation to a biographical reading of Mitchell's first novel and of his "Jake" stories. But though Mitchell's Prairie childhood does undoubtedly underlie his fiction in an enduring way, the rest of his early life should alert the reader to the usual dangers of making simple biographical connections. From 1927 to 1931, Mitchell was sent to school in Long Beach, California, and St. Petersburg, Florida. This adolescent period of usually turbulent growth is almost untouched in his fiction until *Ladybug, Ladybug*

... (1988). His next three years, spent in the study of philosophy and psychology at the University of Manitoba, 1931 to 1934, have yet to appear in fictional form though they must have been important to his intellectual development. Since he spent some time there developing a talent for acting earlier discovered in St. Petersburg, the years could be seen as preparation for Mitchell as playwright, and they included the publication of his first piece of writing, "A Panacea for Panhandlers," excerpts from a diary kept while working his way around Europe in the summer of 1932. Mitchell's next six years, 1934 to 1940, look like the stock preparation of a young man of his generation for a writing career: an assortment of jobs in Seattle and, after 1936, in Calgary, predominantly in sales (insurance, magazines, and encyclopedias), journalism, and radio. His taking a course in play writing and the short story at the University of Washington suggests that the jobs were intended to be temporary.

By the time Mitchell enroled in the University of Alberta in 1940, he was writing but not publishing. He received a B.A. and a teaching certificate in 1943, but the importance of his Edmonton years was personal and artistic. He continued his acting; he met and, in 1942, married Merna Hirtle, who has been a mainstay of his life. He also came under the guidance of Professor F.M. Salter, a celebrated teacher of creative writing who had a strong influence on a number of Alberta writers. Salter encouraged Mitchell in the discovery of his subject and the development of his craftsmanship and theories of creation. As part of an association which was to continue after Mitchell left the university, Salter helped to arrange for the publication of three of Mitchell's short stories in 1942: "But as Yesterday" in *Queen's Quarterly*, and "You Gotta Teeter" and "Elbow Room" in *Maclean's*.[2] It was with the stimulation of Salter's teaching that Mitchell began the series of "Jake and the Kid" stories and conceived his first and most popular novel, *Who Has Seen the Wind*.

From 1942 until 1947 Mitchell combined his writing with teaching in a number of small Alberta communities: Castor, New Dayton, High River, and the Eden Valley Reserve west of High River, where he gathered experience that would serve him in *The Alien* (1953) and *The Vanishing Point* (1973). During this period his sons Ormond (1943) and Hugh (1946) were born, and his writing culminated in the publication in 1947 of *Who Has Seen the Wind*.

With the success of *Who Has Seen the Wind*, Mitchell moved out into a wider world, which in Canada in 1948 meant Toronto, for three years as fiction editor of *Maclean's* and for the inception of the "Jake and the Kid" radio series. The series ran through some 320 episodes from 1950 to 1956, with twelve of the episodes adapted for television.[3]

In 1951, Mitchell returned to settle in High River, where he would make his home base for the next seventeen years. They were years of great productivity but mixed success. The continuing "Jake and the Kid" episodes were immensely popular, and the selection published in 1961 won the Stephen Leacock medal for humour. Dozens of other Mitchell radio dramas were produced, including *The Black Bonspiel of Wullie MacCrimmon* (1951). The musical, *Wild Rose*, was performed in Calgary for the 1967 Centennial Celebration by the semi-professional group, "Mac 14," which became Theatre Calgary. Mitchell also wrote at least twenty-one television plays and programs and three screen plays as well as articles for magazines. A novel, *The Alien*, won the *Maclean's* award for fiction in 1953 and was serialized in an abridged version in *Maclean's* in 1953 and 1954, but Mitchell himself regards it as an artistic failure. Another novel, *The Kite* (1962), enjoyed little of the popular success or critical recognition accorded to *Who Has Seen the Wind*. A third novel of this period, *Roses Are Difficult Here* (1964), remains unpublished. All of this while Mitchell was cultivating an active home life (and various strains of orchids) in his foothills home. His daughter, Willa, was born in 1954.

The latest phase of Mitchell's career, 1968 to the present, is characterized by a succession of university appointments, four novels, a collection of stories, *According to Jake and the Kid* (1989), writing for the stage, and honours and awards too numerous to list. He has taught creative writing at the University of Alberta (1971–73) and been writer-in-residence at the University of Calgary (1968–71), Massey College (1973–74), and the University of Windsor from 1979 to 1987. The novels represent significant developments in his fiction. *The Vanishing Point* (1973), which incorporates portions of the unsuccessful *The Alien*, has earned critical acclaim, if not general popularity, to rival *Who Has Seen the Wind*. In *How I Spent My Summer Holidays* (1981), Mitchell departs from the comic form, though not the humour, of his earlier novels. In *Since Daisy Creek* (1984) and *Ladybug, Ladybug . . .* (1988), Mitchell explores his fundamental themes with older protagonists.

With the production of *The Devil's Instrument* in Peterborough in

1972, Mitchell began moving his dramatic writings to the live stage and attracting increasing recognition as a playwright. Just as many of his early radio dramas were adapted from his fiction, Mitchell's plays have usually moved from one medium to another. The five plays the author selected for *Dramatic W.O. Mitchell* (1982), *The Devil's Instrument*, *Back to Beulah*, *The Black Bonspiel of Wullie MacCrimmon*, *The Kite*, and *For Those in Peril on the Sea*, all had a previous form or precursor in radio, television, or fiction.

Official recognition of W.O. Mitchell's contribution to Canadian culture has included honourary degrees from the Universities of Ottawa, Brandon, Regina, Calgary, and Windsor, and appointment as an Officer of the Order of Canada. As he approaches eighty, Mitchell remains a prolific and intensely active artist. His remark that he would like to play the role of the irascible old Daddy Sherry in *The Kite* suggests his determination to remain that way.

Tradition and Milieu

W.O. Mitchell has made valuable contributions to Canadian literature whether he is looked upon as novelist, playwright, humorist, or regional writer. Yet it is difficult to assign him a place in the Canadian literary tradition central enough to reflect those contributions and the excellence of his art. The fact that a coherent tradition of Canadian literature has yet to be clearly articulated is only part of the difficulty. Mitchell's work has not been intimately related to other national literary activities before or during his writing career.

Mitchell's fiction is thoroughly regional, not simply because it is all nominally set within a small area of Saskatchewan prairie and Alberta foothills, but because the fictional region he creates and the metaphorical significance with which he invests it are vital elements in his novels. His work clearly forms an increasingly important part of Prairie fiction, but just where it belongs in the official tradition of that fiction is not as clear. Because he emerged in the 1940s creating vividly realized characters and settings, he could be expected to belong in the line of Prairie Realists with Frederick Philip Grove, Sinclair Ross, and Edward McCourt. But Mitchell, as a writer of comedy, did not project the tragic view of humanity's alienation from the land which characterizes Prairie Realism. For some years, though the most read of Prairie writers, he was treated as peripheral to the tradition.

The anomaly arose, of course, in the tradition rather than the writer. The ascendancy of the tragic view of Prairie life outlined by Grove and Ross has been largely the work of critics and the academic community over the past thirty years. Novels like Grove's *Settlers of the Marsh* and Ross's *As for Me and My House* were all but forgotten until they were revived by New Canadian Library reprints and subsequently taught in university courses and written about in journals.[4] The central "tradition" of Prairie fiction, then, has been academically and rather narrowly defined. To understand Mitchell's place it is useful to recognize a more popular if generally less distinguished stream of Prairie fiction in the sentimental comedies of such writers as John Beames, Ross Annett, and Ralph Allen, which have logical antecedents in the sentimental romances of Nellie McClung. While Mitchell would not be flattered by the comparison, *Who Has Seen the Wind* can be seen as the culmination of that type of fiction, a counterpart in the comic mode to Ross's critically acclaimed *As for Me and My House*.

Ironically, Mitchell has been the more difficult to place because he is that rarity in Canadian literature, a writer who appeals to a popular market yet earns the respect of critics. In most literatures, where the popular shades imperceptibly into the "serious" or literary, his achievement would not generate a critical dilemma; witness, for example, the popularity of Walter Clark's *The Oxbow Incident* and that writer's acceptance as a central creator of the serious novel of the American West. The gulf between popular and serious fiction has no doubt been widened by the fact that Canada failed to sustain an indigenous tradition of popular fiction after the 1920s.[5] Mitchell emerged at a time when Canadian literature, for those who read it, was a serious literature without the leaven of a popular tradition. A popular writer was not easy to place. Literary judgement, in fact, went beyond artistic seriousness toward a preference for grimness. As a humorist, Mitchell suffered the effects of a national trait Robertson Davies describes as hampering Stephen Leacock's reputation: "We can laugh, but we are a little ashamed of doing so, and we think less of the man who has moved us to mirth. We retain a sour Caledonian conviction that a man who sees life in humorous terms is necessarily a trifler."[6]

Mitchell does not acknowledge direct influence on his work by other Canadian writers, and the grounds for conjecture are not rich. He speaks of discovering Grove's work, only to have his excitement cooled by learning that Grove was at the end rather than the beginning of his career.[7] He was impressed by Sinclair Ross's story "Cornet at Night," and there is a remote parallel in Mitchell's use of the mouth organ in *The Devil's Instrument*, but neither Grove nor Ross could have provided models for intrinsic features of form or technique. As a humorist Mitchell has more in common with Ross Annett, whose "Babe" stories, about a motherless girl raised by her father on the drought-stricken prairie, began appearing in the *Saturday Evening Post* some four years before the publication of the first "Jake and the Kid" story. Mitchell acknowledges that he was probably influenced by Annett, but in much the same way he was influenced by the whole group of successful contributors to *Post* at the time. Nor does Mitchell's work exhibit obvious influence from earlier Canadian humorists. Though he has won the Leacock medal twice, his humour is very different from Leacock's. It thrives on hyperbolic character and anecdote and on artfully constructed dramatic ironies rather than the intense, self-conscious verbal ironies which vitalize a Leacock sketch. Mitchell is closer in form to Haliburton's creation of the dramatic persona of Sam Slick, but without Haliburton's didactic purpose. The only Canadian Mitchell credits with profoundly influencing his writing is not another author, but the creative writing teacher, F.M. Salter.

Mitchell has not felt any special community of interest with his contemporaries in Canadian writing. Hugh MacLennan, for example, has held nothing for him, but he reads intently the work of such writers as Margaret Laurence, Adele Wiseman, and Alice Munro. As author, teacher, and editor, Mitchell must have had a powerful influence on a generation of writers, but no obvious followers can be identified among prominent younger writers. When fiction editor for *Maclean's*, he gave early encouragement and/or direction to Ray Bradbury, Farley Mowat, Hugh Garner, and Ernest Buckler, but none could be considered a protégé. To younger writers of comedy in the West, such as Robert Kroetsch, Mitchell's traditional theories of fiction are unappealing. His insistence upon sustained illusion clashes directly with their Post-Realist convictions.

When Mitchell does speak of writers from whom he has learned, they are usually British or American: William Blake, William Wordsworth, Lewis Carroll, Joseph Conrad, Virginia Woolf, Katherine

Mansfield, Mark Twain, Willa Cather, John Steinbeck, Wallace Stegner.[8] He also recalls discovering the great Russian writers just before he succeeded in writing publishable fiction. It is discouraging to look for specific influences in all that diversity of gifts, especially when Mitchell holds that reading influences the writer much as it does the non-writer; if it changes him it presumably changes his writing. References and allusions to Blake, Wordsworth, and Conrad appear in Mitchell's novels, those to Blake assuming considerable importance in *The Vanishing Point*, but pervasive influences have yet to be convincingly traced. Mitchell consistently returns to Twain, and analogies there are easily seen. Brian O'Connal is like a Canadian Huck Finn journeying toward adulthood and awareness of a moral world, with the Young Ben as his shadowy Nigger Jim. *How I Spent My Summer Holidays* invites more comparisons: Hughie and Peter Dean Cooper, as they hide the fugitive mental patient in their cave, has a Huck Finn-Tom Sawyer relationship, and the novel's movement from innocence to a steadily darkening perception of humanity is reminiscent of Twain's later works. A number of characteristic features of Mitchell's work could, in fact, be traced to the traditions of American humour, including his version of the tall tale — never a very common form in the life or literature of the Canadian West. Here again the search would have to begin, and possibly end, with textual analogies. Mitchell himself has been conscious of a kinship with American writers not so much by direct influence as in the sense of a shared New World experience which goes back as far as Twain.

Not that this removes Mitchell's work from the mainstream of Canadian literature. Until very recently Canadian writers have typically experienced their most important direct influence from beyond rather than within Canada, especially in matters of form and technique. Thus what Eli Mandel calls "the necessarily unfavourable balance of payments in literature."[9] In this respect the Canadian "tradition" has been more than usually external, and whatever has been nationally distinctive must be sought in the transformation undergone by exotic forms in a Canadian context. The comparison of Mitchell and Twain is instructive. It is typically Canadian, for example, that Brian O'Connal's voyage toward adulthood is structured not over space but over time and Brian must gather a sober wisdom about his world; he is not, like Huck, allowed to retain an heroic innocence.[10] The two authors' shared questions are fundamental but their answers are distinctive.

As a dramatist, Mitchell's place in the literary tradition is less prominent yet more easily defined. The bulk of his work in radio and television drama remains unpublished and therefore removed from literature. The stage plays selected for publication in *Dramatic W.O. Mitchell* grow out of that wealth of earlier experience, but increasingly they are related to his fiction in ways which give them a strong literary interest. The most obvious example is the conversion of *The Kite* from novel to play.[11] Mitchell's plays have been produced across the country but are usually identified with the growth in Canadian drama during the 1970s and early 1980s through the development of regional theatre. Though his plays are less consistently dependent on a Prairie setting than his novels, Mitchell is usually regarded as a Prairie playwright.

Mitchell's strong regional identification should not diminish the importance of his work any more than it does that of Thomas Hardy or William Faulkner. When first applied to his writing, "regional" implied a merely local rather than universal significance, and Mitchell naturally resisted its dismissive overtones. As the term has matured in our critical vocabulary, it has become easier to see that through the particularity of his place, Mitchell explores aspects of humanity unconfined by any region. Prairie fiction itself has a primary place in the development of Canadian fiction as a whole, and in a national literature which can often be best understood as an aggregate of regional literatures, how central a writer is may even be a misleading question. We know from the responses of readers and critics that Mitchell is among the best of Canadian novelists. At least one of his novels, *Who Has Seen the Wind*, has stood the tests of enduring popularity and sustained critical scrutiny. It is one of a very few novels often referred to as a classic of Canadian literature.

Critical Overview and Context

With the publication of *Who Has Seen the Wind* in 1947, Mitchell won immediate and wide popularity, but it was sixteen years before a critical essay was devoted to his work, and more than twenty before anything like a critical dialogue developed. Recently Mitchell has been given more attention — more, in fact, in 1981 than in the first quarter century of his career — but still much less than is devoted to other major Canadian novelists.

It is possible to distinguish at least four phases of critical attention to Mitchell's work, all roughly, but not strictly, chronological. This first phase includes early reviews and initial academic responses. Most reviewers received *Who Has Seen the Wind* enthusiastically, the most unreserved judgements being Robertson Davies' "the best novel about life in Canada" to come his way in a long time,[12] and William Arthur Deacon's "one of the finest Canadian novels ever written."[13] Reviewers' judgements were generally on mimetic or thematic grounds: sensitive portrayal of childhood on the prairies, a penetrating vision of Canadian life. Many gave some attention to stylistic excellence, the most extensive by Richard Sullivan in *The New York Times*, who describes the book as "a piece of brilliantly sustained prose, a very beautiful, keen, perceptive rendering of human beings engaged in the ordinary yet profoundly meaningful drama of every day."[14] Sullivan's was one of at least seven generally favourable reviews appearing in major newspapers and magazines across the United States, reflecting a degree of international attention none of Mitchell's other novels would enjoy. There were, of course, dissenting voices, like that of James Bannerman, who judged the novel of interest only to people who "like Canada and want to be entertained by an all-Canadian peep-show set in a relatively unfamiliar scene."[15]

In contrast to the reviews, initial academic response was slight and condescending. Edward McCourt, in his *The Canadian West in Fiction* (1949), does include Mitchell in a chapter entitled "Some Others." Desmond Pacey treats Mitchell in less than a paragraph in *Creative Writing in Canada* (1952).[16] Arthur Phelps, in *Canadian Writers* (1951), felt obliged to explain why he "bothers with" *Who Has Seen the Wind*, because "Admittedly, this book of Mr. Mitchell's is of little general intrinsic importance."[17] All credit Mitchell with, in McCourt's words, "a prose style which, for subtle cadence and freshness of imagery, is a delight to the mind and the ear."[18] Claude Bissell, in "Letters in Canada: 1947," provides a balanced, scholarly review, arguing that the novel's thematic unity compensates for its looseness of structure.[19] While none of the initial responses can contribute much to current dialogue, collectively they anticipated some of the critical questions which would occupy later scholars: regionalism versus universality, the role of farcical humour, and the structural unity of the novel.

The second phase of critical attention including the first full academic essay followed by more than a decade, but the interval must be seen in perspective. Until that time, critical study of Canadian literature had been scattered and sporadic. Pacey's *Creative Writing in Canada* (1952) had been a pioneering effort at synthesis. The first enduring critical journal, *Canadian Literature*, had not been founded until 1959. Since few Canadian writers had been the subjects of any substantial commentary, the second phase of attention to Mitchell was not conspicuously late in coming. It coincided with the publication of *Jake and the Kid* (1961) and *The Kite* (1962). The first of these attracted favourable reviews from the popular press but little attention from the literary world. Most reviewers of *The Kite* were disappointed that it lacked the power of Mitchell's first novel. They applauded the creation of Daddy Sherry, but criticized the novel's loose, anecdotal structure.

W.H. New's essay, "A Feeling of Completion: Aspects of W.O. Mitchell" (1963), while it does not penetrate Mitchell's fiction beyond the level of psychological realism, set an example of taking Mitchell seriously in an academic context. New interprets *Who Has Seen the Wind* and *The Kite* as complementary approaches to the theme of maturation, seen as human adjustment to time and mortality. He argues that *Who Has Seen the Wind* is unified around Brian's growth from the egocentric completeness of childhood to a more mature, sociocentric completeness of participating in a larger whole. It exhibits "the sensitive boy balancing emotion with intellect," while *The Kite* shows "the man in limbo balancing intellect with emotion."[20] *The Kite* is seen as disunified, not merely by its anecdotal form, but by the tendency of the anecdotes to shift the focus to Daddy Sherry and away from David Lang, the character who must undergo change and maturation through the action.

The second phase included two other examples of serious academic attention. Patricia Barclay's "Regionalism and the Writer: A Talk with W.O. Mitchell" (1962) is a report on an interview in which Mitchell advances an early form of his argument for universality in regional fiction. Warren Tallman uses *Who Has Seen the Wind* as one of five novels exemplifying the state of Canadian fiction in "Wolf in the Snow" (1960). Provocative and idiosyncratic, Tallman's essay is an interesting contrast to New's. It draws attention to a darker side of the novel which New glosses over, "the human viciousness and natural desolation which characterize the town and the prairie."[21] Because his thesis concerns isolation, alienation, and the stifling of the self, Tallman dwells only on the dark side, seeing the humour and the comic resolution of the action as a mere protective screen, a sign of the "failure of the novel to confront the actuality which it suggests."[22]

The third phase of Mitchell criticism, a critical dialogue, or at least a variety of interpretative approaches continuing over a period of years, did not begin until the 1970s. Here the interval is not as easily explained. In the 1960s much had been written on other Canadian writers, even Prairie writers such as Grove, and Mitchell's *Who Has Seen the Wind* was a popular text for Canadian literature courses. It can only be assumed that the critics underestimated Mitchell's work or found it less tractable to their methods than some others, possibly because it does not belong to the mode of Realism which commanded literary attention at mid-century.

Most discussions of Mitchell continued to appear as segments of studies advancing theses about Canadian literature. These include some of the most valuable insights, but can expose the text to what might be called "thesis warp." D.G. Jones, in *Butterfly on Rock: A Study of Themes and Images in Canadian Literature* (1970) interprets *Who Has Seen the Wind* as a "struggle between a garrison culture and the land" in which the social outcasts represent a potential "authentic culture."[23] Mitchell is prominent in Eli Mandel's "Images of Prairie Man" because regional literature is said to depend on a myth of childhood as a vision of innocence, a lost Eden.[24] Typically, Mandel opens a way to the heart of the novel without staying to elaborate upon it. One critic who does pursue the implications of a lost Eden does serious violence to the text of *Who Has Seen the Wind*. Ronald Sutherland's thesis in "Children of the Changing Wind" is that "the typical child in Canadian literature is born disillusioned." Brian, he says, "develops a cynical attitude, as a result of bitter experiences."[25]

The two book-length studies of Prairie fiction during this phase are less constricted by their theses. Laurence Ricou devotes a chapter of *Vertical Man/Horizontal World: Man and Landscape in Canadian Prairie Fiction* (1973) to Mitchell's fiction.[26] Because the theme of his study is the interaction of man and landscape, he takes little account of the half of *Who Has Seen the Wind* set in town, but he provides one of the most perceptive interpretations of Brian's search for God and Mitchell's use of the prairie as metaphor. Ricou identifies Daddy Sherry as the central figure of *The Kite*; his comments on *Jake and the Kid* assign it a minor place in Mitchell's fiction. In my *Unnamed Country: The Struggle for a Canadian Prairie Fiction* (1977) I attempt to establish *Who Has Seen the Wind* as the culmination of a tradition of sentimental comedy in Prairie fiction.[27]

Two recent studies of the Indian in Canadian fiction have included interpretations of *The Vanishing Point*, David Williams' "The Indian Our Ancestor" (1978) and Leslie Monkman's *A Native Heritage* (1981). Williams sees Carlyle Sinclair as overcoming his false ancestors (Aunt Pearl and Old Kacky) to seek his true connection with the living whole through the Indian people. Monkman emphasizes Carlyle's release from "his prison of civilized rationalism." Both interpret the ending as total fulfilment.

Full-length essays during this third phase include the beginnings of substantial attention to Mitchell's second and third novels and one article that gives substantial attention to the short stories: Ormond Mitchell's "Tall Tales in the Fiction of W.O. Mitchell" (1986). Catherine McLay's "W.O. Mitchell's *The Kite*: A Study in Immortality" (1973) and "*The Vanishing Point*: From Alienation to Faith," while they make some general structural points, are basic interpretive readings useful to undergraduate students, though McLay does not always handle textual evidence with sufficient care. Donald Bartlett's "Dumplings and Dignity" (1978) is a slight piece devoted mainly to explicating three thematic images in *The Vanishing Point*: excrement, the vanishing point, and bridges. Arnold Davidson's "Lessons on Perspective: W.O. Mitchell's *The Vanishing Point*" (1981) is a more penetrating study. Davidson elaborates on the extensions of the idea of perspective to include points of view and modes of perception.

The best developed critical commentary continues to be on Mitchell's first novel. Ken Mitchell, in "The Universality of W.O. Mitchell's *Who Has Seen the Wind*" (1971) argues that "there is a balance maintained between positive and negative (good and evil; creation and destruction) both in the social community and in the natural one.[28] For Brian the conflict between good and evil is reconciled in his "vision of the cyclical pattern of the birth and death of seasons, days, and people — its inevitability and its beauty. . . ."[29] Robin Mathews, in "W.O. Mitchell: Epic Comedy" (1978), argues for a more pervasive balance within *Who Has Seen the Wind*, drawing together the dark and light aspects, the transcendent visions and the humorous excesses. He is concerned not so much with comic form as with a distinctively Canadian comic perspective shared by

Haliburton and Leacock which values civility and order but acknowledges that "the dark forces have an insistent presence, a legitimacy even, an attractive power and energy."[30] Brian learns acceptance of the human condition, of the struggle for a balance which "puts natural justice, social justice, and divine justice into relation."[31]

Through the period of this third phase a steady stream of interviews with Mitchell has been published. Probably the most informative have been Donald Cameron's "W.O. Mitchell: Sea Caves and Creative Partners" (1973) and David O'Rourke's "An Interview with W.O. Mitchell" (1980–81). Reviews of *The Vanishing Point* (1973) were mixed and generally less favourable than subsequent articles. One review article deserves attention. Don Gutteridge, in "Surviving Paradise" (1974), argues that the real power of *The Vanishing Point* lies in the Indian characters and that Mitchell blurs the focus by his compulsion to explain Carlyle's dilemma "in *psychological* terms, and hoary old Freudian ones at that."[32] Reviewers of *How I Spent My Summer Holidays* (1981) seem inclined to view it as Mitchell's attempt to return to his Prairie childhood without repeating *Who Has Seen the Wind*, though George Woodcock judges it as Mitchell's second most significant novel.[33] Productions of Mitchell's plays have been extensively reviewed, though few of the reviews have any strong literary implications. Among commentaries on Mitchell's drama, the most useful to students of literature is Diane Bessai's "A Literary Perspective on the Plays of W.O. Mitchell."

Finally, it may be possible to discern the beginnings of a fourth phase of Mitchell criticism which moves beyond theme, paraphrase, and interpretation. Many of the essays already mentioned, of course, do present important observations on form and technique. Tallman's judgement upon *Who Has Seen the Wind*, for example, is essentially structural, but some essays have begun to appear which approach Mitchell's fiction primarily through technique. Laurence Ricou, in "Notes on Language and Learning in *Who Has Seen the Wind*" (1977–78) and S.A. Gingell-Beckman, in "The Lyricism of W.O. Mitchell's *Who Has Seen the Wind*" (1981), both undertake close rhetorical analysis of the text. Barbara Mitchell's "The Long and the Short of It: Two Versions of *Who Has Seen the Wind*" (1988) is a close comparison of the author's original text, published only in the 1947 hardback by Macmillan of Canada, with the edited Little, Brown text which has been used for all subsequent editions. She analyses the deletions and recounts Mitchell's struggle to preserve those elements that raise the novel from the idyllic to a mature, ambivalent view of human mortality. This article offers not only the best available evidence of the author's intentions but also an insightful guide to the consistency of design in the novel. W.J. Keith devotes a brief chapter of his *A Sense of Style: Studies in the Art of Fiction in English-Speaking Canada* (1989) to Mitchell. He praises *Who Has Seen the Wind* as a "masterpiece" with "the confident eloquence of major art,"[34] crediting especially the power of Mitchell's style to unify a range of elements from the mystical to the ordinary and from the profoundly serious to the entertainingly popular. Yet it is just this balance, Keith contends, that Mitchell fails to sustain elsewhere in his fiction. On the basis of rather slight analysis of the later works, Keith concludes that "Mitchell seems to have cast in his lot with the crudely popular against the subtly permanent."[35] Michael Peterman's "'The Good Game': The Charm of Willa Cather's *My Antonia* and W.O. Mitchell's *Who Has Seen the Wind*" (1981) may be another sign of maturity in the critical dialogue. The essay offers no startling new insights, but its balanced interpretations and judgements clearly show the benefit of previous commentary on Mitchell's novel. One invaluable resource for the study of Mitchell's work is Sheila Latham's "W.O. Mitchell: An Annotated Bibliography."

Mitchell's Works

The narrator of *How I Spent My Summer Holidays* declares his motive for the long reminiscence which is the body of the novel: "I mourn the loss of an age of innocence."[36] The statement could introduce all of W.O. Mitchell's fiction. Not that Mitchell is mournful; his previous novels are all comedies, and even *How I Spent My Summer Holidays* is lightened by humorous episodes. To a degree, his serious intent is the victim of his own success as a humorist. The broad humour of the early novels can easily obscure the fact that they are relatively sophisticated comedies, enriched by their nearness to the depths of tragedy. As Robin Mathews points out, Mitchell's humour belongs in the tradition Stephen Leacock describes as voicing "sorrow for our human lot and reconciliation with it."[37] And in Mitchell's fiction, the central fact of our human lot is the tragic inevitability of our fall from innocence, a fall which occurs with maturity and which Mitchell equates explicitly with Adam's fall.

In Mitchell, feeling compelled to acknowledge a fallen world and yet, as he puts it, "to say 'yes' to man" are not contradictory impulses. They are, however, a source of tensions within his work, tensions between the tragic implications that surround the fall into mortality and Mitchell's choice of the comic form, or between the hilarity of his humour and the darker reaches of his vision. At best they can be generative; at worst they can create the strains that caused the failure of *The Alien*, which apparently moved inexorably toward saying "No" in spite of its author. Reconciling the potentially divergent forces in Mitchell's art would seem to be a question of "balance," a term Mitchell himself applies to both life and art.[38] It is probably due to the delicacy of such a balance that at the centre of the critical dialogue about Mitchell's art we find disagreements about structural soundness and uncertainty about interpretation. Both can best be approached through a careful examination of some aspects of technique and structure in his novels.

Ironically, Mitchell's stylistic brilliance was an early obstacle to balanced interpretation of *Who Has Seen the Wind*. Though *Who Has Seen the Wind* has only recently been subject to close textual analysis, it has long been an acknowledged *tour de force* of poetic, evocative style. Mitchell's descriptive language is sensuous, not only visual but strongly aural and tactile. His young protagonist, on his first visit to the prairie, hears "The hum of telephone wires along the road, the ring of hidden crickets, the stitching sound of grasshoppers, the sudden relief of a meadow lark's song"; he feels "a rock warm to the backs of his thighs." The scene has a vivid concreteness, a freshness of imagery generated by a profusion and freedom of metaphor more common in verse than in prose. It evokes convincingly the world of an unusually sensitive child with a wholeness of perception not yet conditioned by the civilized tyranny of the visual sense. Some of the metaphors, like that of the wind "warm and living against his face," introduce a romantic animism to the scene, while others, like the "haloed fox-tails" and the gopher watching from his "pulpit" hole, suggests a spiritual presence in nature.[39]

S.A. Gingell-Beckman, in "The Lyricism of W.O. Mitchell's *Who Has Seen the Wind*," identifies other "poetic" qualities of the style, including rhythms of pitch, stress, and juncture, repetitive patterns of assonance, consonance, and rhyme, and recurrent images, like those of the wind, related as motifs. To the extent that these qualities excite expectations appropriate to the lyric mode, they tend to draw the narrative into the child's subjective experience and free it from the logic of the prosaic adult world. The child's sensuous response to the prairie is free to expand into an almost mystic receptiveness to realities beyond the actual world. The reader is also tempted by this lyricism to accept the novel as an idyll of childhood on the Prairies.

The early idyll is, of course, only a part of the novel's concern with a boy's search for meaning in life, including spiritual meaning. Mitchell's poetic style is particularly effective in creating those moments of ecstatic awareness that provide Brian with intuitive glimpses of a meaning and order in life which eludes his conscious understanding. Those epiphanic moments which Brian refers to as "the feeling" Mitchell prudently leaves undefined. Excited most often and most intensely by Brian's sense of the numinous in nature, they are the tantalizing gleams that Brian follows in his search and also a measure of the boy's changing understanding. At first described as no more than "a soft explosion of feeling" of "completion and culmination," they develop into a feeling of ultimate harmony and an intuition of cosmic unity and beauty. The most fully articulated of Brian's "feelings" is excited by the very common sight of dew on spirea leaves:

> . . . the new, flake leaves of the spirea were starred in the sunshine — on every leaf were drops that had gathered during the night. He got up. They lay limpid, cradled in the curve of the leaves, each with a dark lip of shadow under its curving side and a star's cold light in its pure heart. As he bent more closely over one, he saw the veins of the leaf magnified under the perfect crystal curve of the drop. The barest breath of a wind stirred at his face, and its caress was part of the strange enchantment too.
>
> Within him something was opening, releasing shyly as the petals of a flower open, with such gradualness that he was hardly aware of it. But it was happening: an alchemy imperceptible as the morning wind, a growing elation of such fleeting delicacy and poignancy that he dared not turn his mind to it for fear that he might spoil it, that it might be carried away as lightly as one strand of spider web on a sigh of a wind. (pp. 107–08)

This scene is a microcosm of Mitchell's imagery: sunshine and the vegetable world, wind and the suggestion of sentience and will, roundness and the cyclical patterns of nature, the leaf veins and the connectedness of natural order, the opening petals and organic growth, all perceived in the "fleeting delicacy" of the boy's harmony with natural process. The cold and warmth, the light and dark, the perfection of the crystal sphere, the star's cold light, all render the image microcosmic in a larger sense. It is difficult not to suspect that Mitchell had been reading the transcendentalist essay "Nature," in which Emerson says, "Herein is especially apprehended the unity of Nature, — the unity in variety, — which meets us everywhere. . . . A leaf, a drop, a crystal, a moment of time, is related to the whole, and partakes of the perfection of the whole. Each particle is a microcosm, and faithfully renders the likeness of the world."[40] Brian's "feeling" is, in effect, a transcendental experience, an apocalyptic moment of contact with the divine. In Wordsworthian terms, it might be one of those intimations of immortality to which the school principal, Digby, refers much later in the novel. Like those intimations, it is destined to be withdrawn.

Mitchell is stylistically so successful in evoking the child's early intimations of cosmic harmony that readers have been inclined to give too little weight to later scenes exhibiting Brian's changing perception of human, natural, and divine order. In extreme instances, the boy is seen as growing up under the tutelage of a benign Nature.[41] Brian's continuing encounters with cruelty, death, and deformity, his experiences in town as well as on the prairie, are equally formative influences on the understanding he emerges with at the end of the novel. He is not merely shaken by the sight of the two-headed calf, the slaughter of the prolific rabbits, or the death of his dog and later of his father. He is changed. The incident of the tail-less gopher is a conveniently explicit example. Brian is revolted by Artie's unnatural cruelty in jerking the tail off the gopher. When the Young Ben mercifully kills the gopher and savagely attacks Arty, Brian is moved by his natural cruelty. He is filled with the feeling and with "a sense of the justness, the rightness, the completeness of what the Young Ben had done — what he himself would like to have done" (pp. 127–28). He identifies with the Young Ben's efforts to sustain the completeness of the natural world, taking its symmetry (aesthetic) for rightness (ethical). What must be remembered is that when he later sees the actual completion of the natural process in the gopher's body being consumed by flies and ants, his response is very different. The feeling is in him again, but fiercely, "with wild and unbidden power, with a new, frightening quality" (p. 128). The feeling still carries an intimation of a transcendent order in the universe, but now it lacks any warm sense of harmony with human moral order:

> Prairie's awful, thought Brian, and in his mind there loomed vaguely fearful images of a still and brooding spirit, a quiescent power unsmiling from everlasting to everlasting to which the coming and passing of the prairie's creatures was but incidental. He looked out over the spreading land under intensely blue sky. The Young Ben was part of all this. (pp. 128–29)

Brian is not, like the Young Ben, a part of all that but a civilized boy with an ingrained commitment to a moral order. His attraction to the prairie is not, of course, destroyed at a stroke; he continues to respond to its primal energies, but his sense of humanity's relation to the natural and divine orders is permanently altered.

The changes in Brian's perception should come as no surprise. The epiphany of the dew-drops on the spirea leaves is juxtaposed with a scene in church the same day, and the pair of scenes is set off at the end of a chapter and introduced with a faintly ironic authorial comment: "The Sunday that the Ben was received into Knox congregation was in a way a turning point in Brian O'Connal's spiritual life too" (p. 106). In the human community of the congregation, Brian thinks he sees a counterpart to the divine unity he has intuited in nature. He sees everyone sitting together in the House of the Lord, including the China kids and the Bens; when Mrs. Abercrombie sings "Holy, Holy, Holy," he associates it with "a holy holy holy drop lying holy on a leaf" (p. 111). The dramatic irony is only partly humorous. Unlike Brian, the reader knows the Reverend Powelly is a spiteful hypocrite, Mrs. Abercrombie the leader of intolerance and repression in the town, the China kids the objects of persecution which will ultimately drive old Wong to his death, and the Ben a totally amoral, asocial being harbouring in the church only for a place to conceal his still. The way in which Mitchell exploits the humorous potential of the Ben's welcome into the church is a clear example of the strength and the dangers of his craft. With rich incongruity, the pious hypocrite is placed in tension with the devious old moonshiner. A full page before the end of the scene, the reader becomes aware of the cud of tobacco in the Ben's mouth. There can be no doubt that it will play a crucial part in the climax of the anecdote, no surprise, only the pure enjoyment of how the story-teller will bring it into play. The danger, here as in so many of the humorous set-pieces of the novel, is that the broad humour of the anecdote, the partly chewed wad of Old Stag tobacco in the minister's white hand, may obscure the larger value of juxtaposing these scenes. They draw attention to the child's innocence and the inevitability of his disillusionment with regard to both worlds.

The unusual structure of *Who Has Seen the Wind* has also contributed to certain difficulties in interpretation. The novel's narrative structure is complex because of narrative problems inherent in its subject. Mitchell's protagonist is sensitive but inevitably inarticulate. His experiences, especially in the community, are limited by his age, and his conceptual powers cannot realistically comprehend all that the reader is expected to understand about those experiences. Mitchell's strategy of placing Brian within a third-person, omniscient point of view in turn raises the problems of narrative distance and unity. The scene of the dewdrops testifies to Mitchell's unusual success in keeping his protagonist expressive yet plausibly childlike and distanced from the authorial voice. On the other hand, readers could legitimately question the translation of Brian's "vaguely fearful images" at the sight of the rotting gopher into "a quiescent power unsmiling from everlasting to everlasting." Ricou, in his "Notes on Language and Learning in *Who Has Seen the Wind*," confirms Mitchell's authentic use of child language, but remarks on Brian's startlingly intellectual precocity.[42] The question is more of narrative consistency than plausibility. That Brian is intended to be an extraordinary child can be confirmed by comparing him with his playmates and with his thoughtlessly well-adjusted younger brother. And with few exceptions, Mitchell succeeds in maintaining that delicate balance of narrative distance even when conveying the insights of experience as opposed to those of innocent intuition.

Brian's age poses a further problem. While the child's active part in the affairs of the town is necessarily limited, the significance of his maturing into a social being is defined by the community. Mitchell creates that community in scenes among adult townspeople: the conversations of Digby, Hislop, and Palmer, the persecution of the Wongs and the Bens, the romance of Digby and Miss Thompson and their crusade for social justice. It is not often recognized that most of the novel's action is, in fact, set in town; in more than half of it Brian's consciousness is not the focus of narration; in about a third he is not present even as a spectator. Mitchell's way of meeting the resultant challenge to narrative unity is not to make his protagonist aware of the events which bear indirectly upon him, but to alternate his narrative focus rapidly. The average duration of viewpoint is about two pages. At times the structure is like a cinematic montage, as at the beginning of chapter seven, where the focus shifts from Uncle Sean to Mr. Hislop to Brian in one page. Coherence depends more on juxtaposition and association than on the logic of linear narrative. For much of the town action Digby also serves as a surrogate protagonist who bears his acquired understanding into Brian's life at crucial points. Mitchell's strategy is sufficient to preserve narrative coherence and to set up a counterpoint between child and adult worlds, nature and society, but not to discourage a tendency among readers to interpret Brian's development without giving due weight to the events of the town.

Other factors probably contribute to this tendency. The social drama and comedy of the town are less memorable than the lyricism of the prairie. The fact that so many of the townspeople are created as stereotyped comic characters, almost "humour" characters in the Jonsonian sense, would encourage D.G. Jones, for example, to cast the town as a kind of straw man. There is also that slightly misleading statement in the book's epigraph which Mitchell added only reluctantly at his publisher's insistence: "This is the story of a boy and the wind." Mitchell's protagonist is not, like the Young Ben, a creature of the prairie, and his growth can only be fully understood in relation to his family and community.

The plot structure of *Who Has Seen the Wind* introduces no such complications, but it must be clearly understood. The four sections of the novel, each separated by about two years of Brian's life, all end with deaths and with the new understanding the boy derives from them. The sequence of deaths — pigeon, dog, father, grandmother — may be puzzling if a climactic order is expected. The father's death is, quite naturally, the climactic one, not only in human terms, but also in the structure of the plot. It is at this point that the complications of action developed in the community and through the boy's contacts with the prairie force Brian into a scene of recognition and reversal. The final section which follows is a resolution of conflicts in the light of Brian's suddenly matured understanding. Note that the last death, the grandmother's, is the only one to take place in the natural course of life.

The recognition scene, the climax of the novel, is commonly overlooked, as it is by Ricou and Mathews, or misunderstood, as it is by Ken Mitchell.[43] It takes place the night of Brian's father's death, and again the coherence is by juxtaposition because the boy does not discover until the following morning that his father has died. Unlike most of Brian's contacts with the prairie, it takes place not on the symbolic border with the town, but in the open, at night, after he has fled from his uncle's farm. He takes refuge from the unobstructed wind in a straw-stack.

> Lying there he looked up to the dark face of the sky pricked out with stars. He was filled now with a feeling of nakedness and vulnerability that terrified him. As the wind mounted in intensity, so too the feeling of defenselessness rose in him. It was as though he listened to the drearing wind and in the spread darkness of the prairie night was being drained of his very self. He was trying to hold together something within himself, that the wind demanded and was relentlessly leaching from him. (p. 236)

Here is a prairie as menacing as any in the sombre pages of Sinclair Ross. The imaginative temperament which has made Brian sensitive to the creative and destructive aspects of nature exposes him to its power to annihilate. But more, the wind threatens specifically his *self*. After successfully resisting its demands he has in the morning "an experience of apartness much more vivid than that of the afternoon before" accompanied by "a singing return of the feeling that had possessed him so many times in the past" (p. 237). The "feeling" which has marked his glimpses of a transcendent order is still doing so, and in the process revealing to him his "apartness." He senses that his "self" or individuality separates him irretrievably from the flow of nature represented by the wind. That is why, after his father's funeral, he sees the prairie in cyclical terms but not humanity: "Winter came and spring and fall, then summer and winter again; the sun rose and set again, and everything that was once — was again — forever and forever. But for man, the prairie whispered — never — never. For Brian's father — never" (pp. 246–47). Brian senses in his individuality the source and essence of human mortality. People will not, like the undifferentiated grasses, return with the cycling of the seasons. Mitchell himself has said in an interview in *Canadian Heritage*, "Erich Fromm is right, I think, when he says consciousness of self is the phenomenon which separates man from the living whole. . . ."[44] Mitchell identifies this as a constant theme in his work.

Brian's attempt to articulate his insight after his father's death is given importance by some critics, but they make unexpected use of it. W.H. New, with his emphasis on the gradualness of Brian's passage from childhood, identifies no structural nexus in the plot.[45] It is more surprising that Mathews, who voices an interest in the novel's structure, does nothing with the passage.[46] Ken Mitchell quotes it but stops, conveniently, before the last two lines which say "for man, . . . never." He can then use the passage as evidence of Brian's acceptance of his father's death as part of the eternal cycles of nature.[47] Ricou recognizes the importance of Brian's discovery of human apartness. He quotes the "forever — never" passage in its entirety, but then, strangely, concludes that the prairie offers a "reassuring permanence," evidence that "Just as death is permanent, so is renewal and rebirth."[48] He seems to forget the "never."

The importance of Brian's discovery is reinforced by action in the adult world. The questions to which he gains intuitive access are addressed intellectually by the town's philosophers. Hislop muses, "Self and not-self; what was the relationship?" (p. 26). Milt Palmer rejects the philosophies of Aquinas and Berkeley, contending that he'd rather be a tree than a man because trees don't make any mistakes. Digby reminds him that he is inevitably separated from the tree because as a human being he cannot avoid thinking (p. 136). The philosophical centre of the discussion is the separation between the self and the non-self induced by the individual consciousness. And thinking has moral implications; Palmer does not want to make mistakes and he does not want to be "a critter like the Reverend Powelly" (p. 137). Brian's recognition scene also coincides roughly with Digby's recognition of what he calls "the heart of darkness" in Powelly's moralizing about the Bens.

Brian's sense of his "apartness" comes at a fateful moment in his life. At the time of his father's death, the boy's independent self-hood must emerge, and to be conscious of self is to be conscious of moral choice. His encounters with deformity, decay, and untimely death have stirred a growing awareness of the disparity between natural and ethical process. Like individuality, the dawning of moral awareness separates humanity from the natural order. He must recognize that human, natural, and divine orders are not in harmony. This is

Brian's final transcendental vision; after the day of his father's funeral, he no longer gets "the feeling." It is a time of passage, a passage the more painful because it is without rites, to a condition of moral responsibility; as Brian says after the funeral, his mother needs him now.

What Brian experiences is a fall from innocence roughly analogous to the Fall in orthodox Judaeo-Christian doctrine. It brings into his life the consciousness of good and evil, of mortality, of death, which excludes him from the Eden of cosmic harmony. Mitchell makes the analogy more explicit in *The Vanishing Point* when Carlyle Sinclair explains humanity's moral consciousness in terms of Adam and Eve, and again in *How I Spent My Summer Holidays* when the narrator explains his loss of innocence in terms of serpents.[49] The pattern of related themes which unites all of Mitchell's fiction is grounded in this recognition of the fall.

Recognition of how basic Mitchell's conception of the fall is to an understanding of Brian's maturity is inhibited by what might be called the dramatic structure of *Who Has Seen the Wind*. Particularly in Part IV of the novel, the disparity between a potentially tragic awareness and a comic form is hard to reconcile, and *Who Has Seen the Wind* has the classic shape of comedy. It begins with the good people, Digby, Miss Thompson, Hislop, excluded from their proper community, and Brian especially seeking a way into the communities of both humanity and nature. The human community is at first too bigoted, petty, and hypocritical to join, but the events of Part (or Act) IV of the comedy remove the major obstacles, and in the schoolboard meeting, Mrs. Abercrombie is ritually driven out, a scapegoat with all the sins of the town loaded upon her. The community thus purged is a fit place to welcome the sympathetic characters. In parallel action, the prairie is humanized in the comic scene of Saint Sammy calling down the wrath of God on the hypocrite Bent Candy. The impending marriage of Digby and Miss Thompson is the conventional comic conclusion symbolizing ultimate community, and Brian's resolve to become a "dirt doctor" promises to unite both communities.

The comic resolution is emotionally appealing, and testifies unmistakably to the resilience of the human spirit and the possibility of renewal. But to read it as naïve romantic comedy celebrating the redemption of the fictional world from its fallen state would do an injustice to the depth and sophistication of Mitchell's novel. The events of Part IV must be understood in the light of the climactic movement in Part III toward a recognition of humanity's fallen state which is confirmed in the novel's concluding passage. Brian's sense of "apartness," of isolation and alienation, is relieved in Part IV by his association with his grandmother. Through their ritual activities they forge a bond of community between the beginning and end of life and between generations. The boy is discovering the strength of community, with which the individual offsets isolation, and the sense of continuity through others, which tempers fear of the transitory nature of human life. Note that these are measures to reconcile the individual with mortality, not to overcome or transcend it. During the grandmother's last days there is a surprising absence of the usual Christian reassurances about the afterlife, the resurrection or the immortality of the soul. The only overt references to God are in the mouths of the Reverend Powelly and Saint Sammy, and theirs is a vengeful Old Testament God.

In the closing scene on the prairie after the grandmother's death, humanity remains essentially alone, transitory, and alienated from nature. The tone of the ending is often misapprehended because the scene is the most sustained example in the novel of the poetically evocative style which heightens the early scenes of innocent harmony with nature. The imagery is rich, the language sonorous, and the rhythms fall into regular metric cadences. The last two pages could easily be set as blank verse. At the same time, the scene is a winter prairie, cold, grey, and austere. The only living thing the boy sees is a solitary rabbit. There is a chilly echo of the earlier dewdrops in the hoarfrost on the rosebushes. The boy's reflections are upon death, which has been his usual access to an understanding of life. Humanity's place in this bleak landscape is represented by two things; one is the town: "dim — gray and low upon the horizon, it lay, not real, swathed in bodiless mist — quite sunless in the rest of the dazzling prairie" (p. 299). The other is the telephone wires: "He looked up at rime-white wires, following them from pole to pole to the prairie's rim. From each person stretched back a long line — hundreds and hundreds of years — each person stuck up" (p. 299). Even with the continuity of generations, humanity remains this alien thing on the landscape, a series of isolated occurrences loosely joined in a linear progression across the cyclical face of nature.[50]

The last page of the novel shifts to a timeless present tense describing the cycle of the prairie seasons. "High above the prairie, platter-flat, the wind wings on, bereft and wild its lonely song"

(p. 300). Human presence is now represented by faint light and sound emanating from the town and by graves: "Where spindling poplars lift their dusty leaves and wild sunflowers stare, the gravestones stand among the prairie grasses. Over them a rapt and endless silence lies. This soil is rich" (p. 300). It would appear that humanity participates in the eternity of the prairie only in a creatural sense, one's elements returning to fertilize the soil. For human consciousness, intellectual and spiritual being, the prairie still whispers "never." There is no suggestion of rebirth in the "rapt and endless silence" over the graves. The final image is given to nature's eternal cycles: "The wind turns in silent frenzy upon itself, whirling into a smoking funnel, breathing up topsoil and tumbleweed skeletons to carry them on its spinning way over the prairie, out and out to the far line of the sky" (p. 33). This is the sombre note upon which the novel ends. If the God Brian once set out in search of is to be found, as some commentators argue, in the wind, then that God is as indifferent to individual consciousness and moral order as nature itself.

Most critics, including New and Ricou, have been inclined to project a degree of optimism on the ending of *Who Has Seen the Wind* which the text will not support.[51] Some have evidently been misled by the comic resolution in Part IV. In *Unnamed Country*, I misinterpret it to mean that "man was never seriously alienated from his natural environment."[52] Ken Mitchell, in "The Universality of W.O. Mitchell's *Who Has Seen the Wind*," describes the storm which flattens Bent Candy's barn as a deliberate act of a just God and Saint Sammy as a "visionary madman." In effect, he sees the storm in the same way Sammy does. So does Robin Mathews, in "W.O. Mitchell: Epic Comedy," but the basis of his argument is more involved.

Mathews provides a very apt description of the protagonist's state at the end of the novel: "Brian acquiesces in the human condition, in community, in the struggle for balance."[53] Mathews' whole commentary on Brian's quest and Mitchell's humour is the most illuminating one published to date, but his contention that the novel presents the correlation of social, natural, and divine justice is based, in part, on a misunderstanding of the comic resolution. Mathews sees an expression of natural justice in the Young Ben. Unquestionably, the Young Ben represents vital elemental forces which need no justification beyond themselves. Brian learns from him, as from the prairie, about a side of himself which the spirit of the town would suppress and which is essential to his wholeness. The Young Ben is capable of natural affection and compassion, but to say that he embodies "a moral energy in the natural order" is to confuse the moral perspective of the novel.[54] Morality or "rightness," as Brian discovers in the tail-less gopher episode, is a peculiarly human preoccupation. Digby likens the Young Ben to the older Ben, who has "about as much moral conscience as the prairie wind" (p. 31). Later Digby reflects that the Bens are "as naked of right and wrong as a coyote howling on a still fall night" (p. 99). At the same time Digby recognizes that the natural order cannot be confined within the human moral order. The Young Ben should be allowed to steal a rifle and be set free from the socializing process of the school system. There is nothing in the role the Young Ben plays in the novel to contradict Brian's growing perception that moral awareness separates him from the natural world.

Mathews' argument for divine justice raises the vexed question of how Saint Sammy fits into the structure of *Who Has Seen the Wind*. For Mitchell to give such prominence to the character merely for comic relief would, as McCourt contends, be irresponsible.[55] Mathews contends that the final conflict between Saint Sammy and Bent Candy is the structural triumph of the novel, bringing together the three kinds of justice. But to see the storm scene as "a demonstration of divine justice" is to overlook the irony which gives the scene its point. If the storm is the wrath of God, called down by Sammy to restore justice, then Sammy is not insane but merely possessed. Candy, when he says "amen" to Sammy's tirade, is not behaving ridiculously but prudently. When Powelly and Mrs. Abercrombie fall to their knees during the storm, they are not fools but repentant sinners with a sound underlying perception of the divine. Brian, witnessing the storm, would presumably sense the restoration of that cosmic unity he intuited some years earlier, but he feels only a "ringing awareness of himself" (p. 308), the sensation which accompanied his recognition of his "apartness" from nature. A reader would have to conclude that Mitchell had either subjected several of his characters to miraculous transformations or carelessly misrepresented them in the first place.

The humour of the scene, and its far-reaching irony within the novel, depend upon the storm being sheer coincidence, a cosmic joke played those who try to see the world ordered in their own image. The storm is a normal manifestation of amoral energies in nature; it happens to damage the Abercrombie's house but also to blow down the MacDougall implement shed and brain Gaffer Thomas with a falling branch. It also happens to invigorate Brian's grandmother, rather than kill her, because even older people can respond well to primal energies. Sammy's prophecy, like all his Jeremiads, is a comic parody of the religious teachings Brian hears in church, as credible as Powelly's implication that the Ben's imprisonment is divine retribution.

Mathews hedges his bet by concluding that the three forms of justice are expressions of faith on the part of the perceivers. This seems not only to undercut his own previous arguments, but also to betray a lack of faith in the comic genre he is analyzing. In sophisticated comedy, the reader is given an ironic awareness that the purification of the world is ritual rather than actual. The scapegoat is not the very evil which has plagued the community but a ceremonial figure.[56] In a comedy such as *Who Has Seen the Wind*, preoccupied with human mortality, the driving out of figures such as Bent Candy and Mrs. Abercrombie signifies not that humanity is redeemed but that the fallen state is to be viewed comically.

E.D. Blodgett, who takes exception to my earlier interpretation in his "Gone West to Geometry's Country," is the only critic to recognize in the imagery of the closing passage of *Who Has Seen the Wind* the emphasis on the finality of death. His conclusion is that "With 'the feeling' gone, the act that mediates man and nature, it is difficult to perceive the boy other than 'separated from himself' (p. 235), as *other*, within a schematic and elemental universe."[57] *Other*, Brian evidently is, but isolated *by* rather than *from* self. Blodgett is mistaken, I would argue, in interpreting the climactic recognition scene in which Brian feels he is "being drained of his very self" as the centre of a progression toward loss of his "self" in a "schematic and elemental universe" represented by the wind. Brian's sense of vulnerability, like his earlier feeling of being "separated from himself" and subsequent feeling of "apartness," are effects of a dawning awareness of self which isolates him from that elemental universe. They are closely related to the "ringing awareness of himself" inspired by Saint Sammy's storm. His next recognition, after his father's funeral, is of human separateness; his next decisive act to move back toward the human world of moral responsibility, because his mother needs him. When Blodgett says that "it is unclear from the final pages whether, as Mr. Digby suggests, he has reached maturity and wisdom or whether he has moved 'out and out to the far line of the sky,' " he appropriately draws attention to the closing image of death and dissolution, but the sense of mortality it conveys is firmly rooted in Brian's maturing awareness of self.[58]

Who Has Seen the Wind retains its potentially tragic overtones to the end. The last section ends with a death. In the final scene, Brian still does not know what place humanity in the fallen state has in the natural and divine orders. Any divine order which may be inferred from the last vision of the prairie remains remote and inscrutable. As Mitchell himself says, *Who Has Seen the Wind* articulates only questions, not answers.[59] Brian dedicates himself to finding answers, but considering the purely secular terms he is given to pursue the search, his prospects are not particularly good. An obvious juxtaposition in the last page of the novel is not encouraging:

> Some day. The thing could not hide from him forever.
> A startled jack rabbit leaped suddenly into the air ahead of him. Ears ridiculously erect, in seeking spurts now to one side, now to the other, it went bounding idiotically out over the prairie. (pp. 299–300)

These are the last four lines in which the narrative occupies the boy's consciousness. Brian will go on seeking.

The Kite (1962) was the second of Mitchell's novels to be published in book form. Interviewed shortly after, Mitchell said, "When I wrote *Who Has Seen the Wind*, I didn't have an answer. It was just a question, which is a perfectly fine reason for writing a novel. In *The Kite*, there is an answer. . . ."[60] It would be unfair, of course, to expect of this short novel the answers to all the questions about God and "the ultimate meaning of the cycle of life"[61] raised in *Who Has Seen the Wind*. What it does offer is one answer to the more limited question of how humanity is to be reconciled with mortality. Instead of a child falling from innocence to an awareness of his mortality, it depicts a man in middle years who has allowed his spirit to be imprisoned within the limits of his mortal existence.

The plot is simple and appealing. David Lang is a journalist sent from Toronto to the Alberta foothills of his childhood to prepare a feature on the world's oldest man, 111-year-old Daddy Sherry. His research quickly becomes a quest for the secret of Daddy's longevity and youthful vitality. In addition to interviewing the old man, Lang hears a succession of anecdotes cherished by the townspeople: Daddy taking up the trapeze at 108, Daddy rejecting a fortune in oil revenue to preserve the sanctity of his Paradise Valley ranch, Daddy riding his house down the flooding Spray River across the international boundary. Lang also becomes involved with the widow, Helen Maclean, and her eleven-year-old son Keith, who is the old man's descendant and closest friend. Lang's changed understanding of life grows out of these experiences and his direct involvement in Daddy's latest escapade, his plan to die to spite those who would make history out of him.

Two leitmotifs run through the story: time and flight. Lang is single, prematurely aged, ulcerated, conventional, and time-bound. He travels west by air to save time though he fears flying. He evidently has much to learn from Daddy, an irreverent free spirit, stubbornly asserting his independence in the face of age, and enjoying his ability to shock and torment his conventional friends. Lang comes to see Daddy as a life force, a spirit of the Western past, and a centre of community with something of the magic of a tribal shaman. His smashing the antique grandfather clock presented to him for his 111th birthday dramatizes his triumph over time. His secret is partly his orientation toward natural time with its eternal cycles of regeneration rather than linear clock time. When he wilfully sets out to die before his 111th birthday, Lang and Keith are able to convince him that spring is an inappropriate time to die.

Mitchell again associates mortality with maturity, though in this novel the individual life is potentially cyclical. Lang is placed between Keith, who has not yet reached maturity, and the child-like Daddy, who has gone beyond it. The boy is both an access to Lang's own childhood and an opportunity to play a father's role. Daddy, who can represent all the lost fathers in Mitchell's fiction (including Lang's, Helen's, and Keith's), can supply the wisdom to reconcile both Lang and Keith to their maturity and consequent mortality. The old man is as indifferent to death as the child is oblivious of it. As Daddy says, "Get to ninety-five an' you're immortal agin. . . ."[62] Like Brian O'Connal, Lang learns that individual mortality is offset by participation in the cycle of generations, and Helen and Keith's remote blood connection with the native people unites the continuity of generations with the eternal cycles of the land, an idea Mitchell develops more fully in The Vanishing Point.

The other half of Daddy's secret is represented by flight, particularly in the central symbol of the kite, but by extension in the old man's unfailing appetite for surprise, adventure, and danger in life.

Lang's fear of flying, his celibacy, his careful calculation of time, all constitute efforts to evade his mortality which involve denying life. Daddy's awareness of his mortality comprehends the paradox; as he says, "Live loose an' soople an' you'll come through without a scratch. Live careful an' you'll break your goddam neck" (p. 191). What is missing in Lang's character is suggested by his having lost the opportunity to fly a kite in childhood. Kite-flying appears as a ritual assertion of the spirit's need to transcend time and earth-bound necessities. By making a kite with Keith, Lang restores that opportunity for himself, and when they give the kite to Daddy they share his appreciation of its natural symbolism of the soaring spirit and the balance of freedom and control needed to maintain its brief and tenuous connection with the earth. David Lang is at least tempted to risk a little flight, possibly by loving Helen Maclean or writing a novel instead of his ephemeral journalism. He sees "the astonishingly simple thing the old man had to say . . . knowing always that the string was thin — that it could be dropped — that it could be snapped. He had lived always with the awareness of his own mortality" (p. 209).

Sympathetic readers of Mitchell's work are left wondering why the answer is so much less compelling than the question. Mitchell's language remains fresh and vivid, though it lacks the lyric intensities which liberate the child's vision in *Who Has Seen the Wind*. His mastery of the story-teller's art of illusion and craft of shaping and pacing an anecdote is still as sure. His invention of comic character is at its height in Daddy Sherry. Yet somehow, as McCourt says, the parts are greater than the whole.[63] Most commentators have criticized the novel's narrative structure. The long anecdotes draw the narrative focus away from David Lang, who is, as W.H. New says, the character who must undergo development and discover the answer.[64] The condition is aggravated, according to Catherine McLay, by anecdotes ostensibly related by the townspeople being presented in third-person omniscient narration. They become autonomous structures isolated from Lang's experience. McLay also contends that only the first three of seven anecdotes are vital to the novel.[65] Even for Laurence Ricou, who identifies Daddy as the central character of the novel, the anecdotes weaken narrative coherence.[66]

The problem may be less a weakness in specific structures than a pervasive quality of form. *The Kite* is deficient in those tensions which generate vital action and develop resonances within the novel.

The regular and frequent shifts of narrative focus in *Who Has Seen the Wind* sustain a counterpoint between related experiences of prairie and town, of Brian and the adult world. The anecdotes in Daddy Sherry's past, as McLay points out, do not all have that inevitable relationship to the present action. Some, such as the goose hunt, do develop a rich interplay with the story as a whole. Daddy at the age of 99, attended by the doctor, the undertaker and the minister, is interred in his rocker in a goose blind for a shot at "Old Croaker," an ancient gander known throughout the West for his survival. The old man resurrects himself from beneath the artificial grave grass not to fire at the old goose but to identify with its stubborn life spirit and to laugh at the official attendants of mortality. McLay identifies this as the turning-point in the action from death-to life-directed movement.[67] Other anecdotes, such as Daddy's voyage to Montana in his house, are delightful but linked to the present action only because they expand upon the old man's character. Nor do such episodes have the tension which enlivens the anecdotes of *Jake and the Kid*, between an innocent first-person narrator and the world of life and illusion he witnesses.

The present scenes of the novel lack specifically dramatic tensions. Mortality is a rather nebulous opponent to set against the old man's vitality, and the conflicts between Daddy and his keepers are in large measure contrived. Because Daddy is neither senile nor self-destructive, he is not basically in opposition to his well-intentioned keepers. His perverse resolve to die is not the same thing as indifference to death; it is hard to believe that a man with such a proven appetite for life would ever go through with it. It seems rather like another of Daddy's peevish, spiteful tricks played on those who love him.[68] In terms of Mitchell's comic form, the obstacles to a happy resolution do not seem sufficiently great or inevitable to generate strong dramatic tensions.

Diane Bessai, in "A Literary Perspective on the Plays of W.O. Mitchell," suggests that the novel suffers from a "genre conflict." The Daddy Sherry character and anecdotes reflect the "basic structure and characterization of folk parable" Mitchell developed in his radio drama. They cannot be satisfactorily assimilated into the reflective, "psychologically naturalistic context Mitchell the novelist strives to establish through David Lang."[69] The success with which Mitchell moves that material into a purely dramatic context in the play, *The Kite*, is strong evidence for Bessai's argument.

It may also be that in the area of Mitchell's subject, the questions are ultimately more significant than any answers that can be formulated. Questions about the central mysteries of life and death can be rich with implications; answers tend to define, to limit, even to violate those mysteries. And in framing his answers, Mitchell limits himself to purely secular, psychological terms, a disadvantage especially when he is clearly looking for affirmative answers.

In *The Vanishing Point* (1973) both the questions and the answers about human mortality are better articulated in a more complex, sophisticated form of fiction. Mitchell is here reworking a plot drafted some nineteen years earlier for *The Alien*, and comparisons between the two novels are illuminating. *The Alien* Mitchell regards as a failure, one of those pieces that "worked too soon" and became "structurally hardened."[70] The abridged version which appeared serially in *Maclean's* in 1953–54 is about a third the length of *The Vanishing Point*. While well over half of it reappears in the later novel in identical or recognizable form,[71] the simplicity of *The Alien* throws the technical achievement of *The Vanishing Point* into sharp relief. Comparison also affords one of those rare opportunities to examine a novelist's conscious use of craft by isolating a series of deliberate changes in the development of the same basic situation.

In *The Alien*, Carlyle Sinclair goes to the Paradise Valley reservation as teacher and later Indian Agent because he is himself of mixed blood and feels a responsibility to lead his mother's people out of ignorance, privation, and despair. Though he takes his wife with him, and though he learns the language of his charges, he remains very much an alien, his isolation within himself expressed outwardly in his inability to inhabit either White or Indian world. His considerable success with the Indian people is measured primarily in material terms, but as in *The Vanishing Point* his self-esteem depends upon guiding his protégé, Victoria, through school and nursing training to success in White terms. When she returns to the reservation pregnant and looking like any other Indian girl, he despairs, complaining that his efforts have been "like teaching a bitch to walk on her hind legs."[72] After Carlyle has betrayed the Indians' faith in him by accepting an unsatisfactory land deal, his wife leaves him, temporarily, to find his way out of his self-absorption and self-pity. In a scene in the tribal dance tent closely paralleling that at the end of *The Vanishing Point*, Carlyle is moved from his belief that the Indians have failed him to a realization that he has failed them. "He was truly one of them and of the human race and he had failed them."[73] After dancing with Victoria and being convinced that "There would be other Victorias who would try with his help . . . ,"[74] Carlyle can return to his dedication and his wife.[75]

The contrast in narrative structure between the two novels is striking. Point of view in *The Alien* is third-person limited, the focus confined almost exclusively to Carlyle's consciousness. The narrative covers the ten years on the Paradise reservation in roughly chronological order. The opening of *The Vanishing Point*, with Carlyle's planned visit to Victoria at the training hospital, sets up a number of structural sources of vitality. Beginning *in medias res*, the action is charged with the implications of what has gone before. Carlyle's ten years on the reservation and his childhood experiences all emerge through the narrative foreground of the two weeks of present action. Much that is laid out in thin panoramic narration in *The Alien* is here concentrated in flashbacks sharpened by the selective and shaping powers of recollection and tightened by ironic tensions between present and past consciousness. There are, in effect, three time scales unfolding. Events of childhood, the time on the reservation, and the immediate present interact across the spark-gap between them: Aunt Pearl's compulsive neatness, for example, with Ian Fyfe's regulations, and Carlyle's desperate need to keep Victoria in the White world of the hospital.

Carlyle's verbal sparring with Archie Nicotine as he drives into the city typifies the dramatic structuring of scenes in the novel. The linguistic and temperamental constrictions of communication between agent and Indian both obscure and embody a genuine conflict of outlooks and wills. Throughout the novel, in scenes between Carlyle and the children, Fyfe, the Indians, and between Archie and Heally Richards or Norman Catface, dramatic tensions vitalize the dialogue and work out conflicting forces in the action. Much that appears as inert exposition in the earlier novel, such as the Indians' suspicion of hospitals as fatal to Indians, becomes part of the argument between Archie and Carlyle. The argument also initiates an opposition of characters, but not a simple one. Archie is representative, a band councillor, a character formed in part by a conflation of native characters from *The Alien*. He is in some respects Carlyle's counterpart, approaching the bridge between the races from the other end. He is as blind and stubborn as Carlyle, and has just that wisdom which Carlyle lacks. Commentators inclined to weigh the theme on the Indian side even see Archie as structurally overbalancing the action, drawing the reader's sympathy from Carlyle.[76] Their pairing is part of a series of character oppositions Mitchell sets up intensifying the binary structure, the balance of tensions in the novel.

Both Indian and White worlds are presented more fully in the later novel, and the dualities they represent are more thoroughly internalized in the character of Carlyle. Neither novel offers a naïve pastoral orientation of regenerative nature and corrupt civilization. The Indian characters in *The Alien* are drawn with some sympathy for their generosity and their "vivid need," as Carlyle conceives it. Humorous behaviour, like the sermons of the lay preacher transferred intact to *The Vanishing Point*, is often appealing, but as in the incident of Sam Bear, who can be philosophical about the rape of his daughter but not the theft of his horses, the treatment is generally condescending. It can be inferred that man in a state of nature is living below the proper human level. Old John Roll-in-the-Mud, the prototype for Esau Rider in *The Vanishing Point*, is not sacrificed like Esau but merely degraded. In the dubious land deal with the power company, he sells out his dignity as a tribal elder and is last seen consoling himself with a shackful of tailor-made cigarettes and raisin bread.

In *The Vanishing Point* the world of the reservation is more ambivalent. It represents the irreducible claims of nature more insistently, partly because of the imagery of the natural cycles which pervades it. On the first morning, Carlyle is wakened by the spring mating ritual of the ruffled grouse, "drumming out again and again its invitation to join the living whole."[77] Direct nature description is not extensive, but the reservation has a sensory vividness reminiscent of the prairie in *Who Has Seen the Wind* and in sharp contrast to the city. While smell, as Carlyle observes, is the first casualty of civilization, Old Esau's cabin still has its "smell concert" of buckskin, willow smoke, elk meat, pack rat, and "the roquefort of feet." Beyond the senses there is the suggestion of a spiritual dimension in Old Esau's dream of leading his people back to Storm and Misty canyon, the source of mountain water and the pure, natural life of their forefathers. But Mitchell is presenting a world of experience in which Esau's magic is regarded not simply as impractical but as "green lobotomy," an ineffectual posture from which to contend with a fallen world.

In *The Alien* the basic values of White society are never seriously questioned, only the methods. Carlyle accepts the ethical value of assimilation, though he complains bitterly of the inadequacy of the means provided for the Indian people. The power company which plans to convert hereditary Indian land to its own use is not objectionable because of its callous pursuit of profits, only because it will not trade the band a tract of grazing land on which to raise cattle more profitably. In *The Vanishing Point* the order of the civilized world is represented as essentially life-denying, especially by the imagery applied to it. Carlyle's wise counsellor, Dr. Sanders, describes its difference from the reservation: "These Stonys are aliens, but what are they alienated from, huh? From the rest — from the real aliens — that concrete and asphalt doesn't sprout and turn green in spring for them" (p. 185). Natural imagery sets up ironic resonances between the two: Fyfe's sequestered hot-house flowers, the human excrement Archie finds sterilized, packaged, and sold in the supermarkets. The sterility of civilization is emphasized by a pervasive whiteness extending from Aunt Pearl's white stool to Heally Richards' white suits. The evangelist, his tanned face set off by his lard-white clothing, reminds Carlyle of a photographic negative. Whiteness as negation.

It is at the deeper level of memory, the flashbacks to Carlyle's childhood, that the White, civilized order is represented as a systematic denial of life. The central image is the vanishing point in Old Kacky's perspective exercises.[78] The teacher imposes upon the round world and the minds of the children a linear perspective which rigidly excludes the cyclical life of nature (the trees Carlyle introduces) and the darker primal energies (the tiger he is afraid to introduce). The vanishing point is the completion of that narrowing process where all the lines converge on a point of total negation. Young Carlyle feels its effect: "He was being vanished from himself . . . stepping outside and apart and walking away farther and farther from himself, getting smaller and smaller and smaller . . . dwindling right down to a point" (p. 322). This is the point of fragmentation, where some part of Carlyle is lost. It reveals the cultural heritage Carlyle has brought to his education of the Indians. The end point for the "Vanishing American" is not his physical extinction but the exclusion of his Indian-ness, when the Carlyle Sinclairs have succeeded in turning all the Victoria Riders antiseptically White.

The quest which gives narrative shape to *The Vanishing Point* leads back and forth between the two worlds and among the three periods of Carlyle's life. The motivation for that quest, as for the action of *The Alien*, is the need to overcome alienation, but the meaning of the alienation at the thematic centre of the two novels is very different. In *The Vanishing Point* it is no longer the fate of a mixed-blood caught between two cultures; it is a part of the general human condition. From the way the alienation is explained it appears that Mitchell is returning to a conception of the fall and of human mortality much closer to that in *Who Has Seen the Wind* than that in the two other novels. Alienation is identified explicitly with the fallen state of humanity. Carlyle invokes the biblical archetype in conversation with Sanders:

> Early Winter Knowledge. Try one, Eve, that old serpent said to her. I can recommend it — a hard, tart, good-keeping apple. So she picked one and she tried it and she gave Adam a bite or two and right then they clearly knew — they weren't any osprey or rainbow or fungus after all — they were humans — the only living thing that could look at itself, and there was no way they could get away from it — sure blew the ass off the Garden of Eden, didn't it? (p. 185)

The fall is again the dawning of human moral consciousness; the first effect, alienation, no more "oneness with eternity," hence the burden of time and mortality, "apartness," and isolation. Mitchell first read Erich Fromm's comments on consciousness of self separating humanity from the living whole while he was writing *The Vanishing Point*. He must have recognized that he had articulated the same idea in *Who Has Seen the Wind*, because he described it as "a constant theme" in his work.[79] In both *The Alien* and *The Vanishing Point*, that "apartness' threatens to become total alienation from the "other" or imprisonment in the self. Carlyle reflects upon this imprisonment when contemplating his son in the earlier novel and Victoria in the later: "All communication between all humans was hopeless, wasn't it? Out of my skin and into yours I cannot get — ever — however hard I try — however much I want it."[80] In *The Alien*, as Carlyle's final recognition reveals, this form of alienation is the main problem of the human condition which is resolved.

In *The Vanishing Point*, it is a major theme embodied in the imagery of bridges, but the "Early Winter Knowledge" which separates human beings from the living whole and commits them to a human moral order can also stifle the instinctual side of their being. The paradox is expressed in Mitchell's use of excremental imagery. Excrement becomes a kind of currency of amoral, self-justifying natural process. Carlyle and Sanders watch with a sense of completion as an Osprey shits in the flowing river. But immediately before this, Carlyle has been outraged by Harold Lefthand's revenge of throwing horse shit in the agency water system. Harold has misused the natural process to contaminate the system; he has violated the human moral order. Harold, like Adam and Eve, is not an Osprey. On the other hand, one cannot deny the natural process as Aunt Pearl does by burning string in her sterilized bathroom. One cannot "scare the shit" out of children, as Old Kacky does, without stifling their essential creativity and (incidentally) contaminating the system. The complementary aspects of humanity — rational and instinctual — threaten to become warring dualities. In *The Vanishing Point* these basic dualities of fallen humanity exist in the instinctual and rational sides of Carlyle's fragmented personality and are given concrete expression in the oppositions of reservation and city, Indian and White worlds.

Unlike *Who Has Seen the Wind*, *The Vanishing Point* is committed to providing answers. Carlyle is aware of the questions very early in his quest. Within a page recalling Carlyle's first days on the reservation Mitchell draws together three essential elements of the theme. First, Carlyle experiences his "aching loss of Grace" (p. 135) (the name cannot be fortuitous in either novel); next, he envies old Esau Rider sitting on a rock by the stream and wonders, "Did he achieve oneness with eternity? — what an overblown way to explain sun-warmed stupor. . . . Not too much different from the steers and cows with absently moving jaws — or the bull trout — or the fungus" (p. 136). Then he has his first glimpse of the child, Victoria, helping the old man back along the trail. Here are the conditions of Carlyle's fall and the seeds of his redemption, but in his quest for Victoria he is initially seeking redemption in a vision of lost innocence. It is not until his quest has taken him through the earlier times of childhood and the reservation that Carlyle recognizes the real nature of the answers he seeks:

He knew he was not trying simply to find her. He knew that he must put back together something he had been trying all his life to keep from being splintered — broken beyond repair. It was something mortally important to him, and it had never — ever — been whole for him really; Aunt Pearl and Old Kacky had seen to that. And his father. (p. 323)

By projecting his vision of innocence on Victoria, he had been exploiting her to avoid facing his own fallen state and the world of experience which is the encompassing moral world of the novel. That is where Carlyle must find his wholeness and reconcile the rational and instinctual sides of his being, including the primal energies suppressed by his childhood experiences. Arnold Davidson, in his "Lessons on Perspective: W.O. Mitchell's *The Vanishing Point*," argues convincingly that the governing polarity in the novel is not Indian versus White but "innocence versus experience."[81]

Each world offers a spiritual remedy for human mortality in the form of what Carlyle calls primitive oversimplifications. On the reservation there is the tent where ritual dances invoke the natural religion which is meant to reunite the people with the living whole. In the city there is the evangelist's tent where Heally Richards "promised to shrive them of their mortality, to lift from them the terrible burden of their humanity, the load of their separateness" (p. 358). The two tents, held in opposition throughout, are eventually the settings for the climactic scenes of the novel. White Christianity does not fare any better here than elsewhere in Mitchell's fiction. The fraudulence of Richards' promise is confirmed when he fails to contend with the mortality of old Esau. In the dance tent Carlyle achieves a kind of wholeness, but not a reunion with the living whole in any simple sense.

The Vanishing Point, like Mitchell's earlier novels, has a comic resolution; the quest ends in ritual purification, community, and the promise of marriage, but again the celebration of hope at the end is muted and ironically balanced. In the simplest terms, Carlyle's redemption is sexual. The drums liberate the repressed and subverted life forces which have been associated with sexuality throughout the novel. Accepting Victoria (a fallen woman) frees him from his misleading vision of lost innocence. In an interview Mitchell draws a parallel with Blake's "little girl lost": "the good guardians come and find her in the cave with the beast, and what do you know? The beast is life, and she hasn't been destroyed after all."[82] In the union with Victoria, Carlyle also escapes from the prison of self by giving himself in love. Love, rather than religion or mysticism or science, is the answer to human mortality.[83]

It is significant that Victoria is of the native people, but Carlyle does not "go Indian." Old Esau has died; there is no going back to Beulah. As Mitchell explains, he chose Blake's concept of Beulah to represent the innocence of childhood which would be an intolerable state for adults even if they could achieve it. Carlyle does, however, gain some insight into humanity's place in the whole: "A wild and distant drum had pulsed for him and for Mate, when they had stood with the total thrust of prairie sun upon their defenceless heads. Together they had discovered that they were both alien from and part of a living whole" (p. 384). The reiterative beat of the drum can return Carlyle to contact with the living whole but not to innocence. Human mortality, moral consciousness, sets humanity apart: "The dry husk of a dead gopher, an abandoned garter-snake skin, magpies, undertaker beetles, had taught them the terror of being human. But they knew that they were accountable to each other; the badger, the coyote, the kill-deer, the jack rabbit, the undertaker beetle, could not share their alien terror. They were not responsible for each other. Man was" (pp. 384–85). Carlyle plans his marriage with Victoria fully aware of the consequences in the world of social and moral responsibility.

What Carlyle achieves is what Mitchell would call an act of balance in a world where there are no absolute victories.[84] As the imagery of the last scene reveals, the previously dammed waters can flow from Beulah, the innocence of childhood. Carlyle can cross the bridge to the innocence of experience. He can perform the act of love with Victoria in full knowledge of its consequences. If a person, conscious, separate, mortal, cannot join the living whole like a heron, one can at least join the human community in a state of wholeness. The weight of mortality cannot be lifted, but one can learn to carry it.

How I Spent My Summer Holidays (1981) is at first glance a surprising development in Mitchell's fiction. Here is the familiar prairie boyhood, warmed by Mitchell's sense of humour and his mastery of humorous anecdote, but the plot is tragic rather than comic. Instead of purification and community, the action moves toward progressive corruption of the fictional world and isolation of the protagonist. The other unexpected feature, and this may not be coincidental, is sexuality. On reflection, it is perhaps more remarkable that in forty years of writing about childhood, maturing, and the fall from innocence, Mitchell has preserved such a conspicuous silence about this one central element — sexual maturity and the loss of sexual innocence. Mitchell has typically stopped his major characters just short of puberty or taken them up when they were well clear of it. When, in *How I Spent My Summer Holidays*, he approaches that gap, the mysteries which threaten the passage to maturity are surrounded by an array of demonic imagery: caves, anuses, serpents, madness, depravity, and death. They suggest, as George Woodcock says, "a vision that seems to have stepped straight out of the Puritan nightmare."[85]

One way of placing *How I Spent My Summer Holidays* in Mitchell's work is to compare it with the *Jake and the Kid* stories, which stand at the opposite end of his fiction in time of writing and in treatment of the gulf between childhood and adulthood. Most of the stories collected in *Jake and the Kid* (1961) were published in *Maclean's* between 1942 and 1955.[86] The first-person, innocent-eye narration is reminiscent of Twain, but the irony is gentler, the stories blander. They are not tightly structured short stories but tales following the structure of their plots. The earlier ones in particular have sentimental outcomes which identify them as well-executed popular fiction.[87] The child's dialect is unrecognizable to me (take, for example, "She's real peaceful inside our barn at evening"),[88] but the figurative language is fresh ("I was sad to my stomach" [p. 1]) and the authenticating detail adeptly handled, as when Jake holds the cow's tail against her flank with his forehead while milking. Two sustaining tensions run through the tales: between the child narrator's understanding and the reader's, and between adult historical reality championed by the teacher, Miss Henchbaw, and the poetic truth of Jake's tall tales. In "The Liar Hunter," Mitchell provides a folklorist's justification for the "creative liar." People disarm their worst fears by rendering them ridiculous, as when Jake concocts the tale of the enormous grasshopper which falls in love with a four-engined airplane.

Over the thirteen years of their publication, the stories show signs of development in form and substance. The plotting is tightened up in the later ones. Characters are initiated who later appear in the novels.[89] The stories also become more regionally authentic. While the idolization of a hired man rather than, say, a gunfighter is true to the Canadian West, the earliest stories have an emphasis on tall tales, shrewd deals, and seeking justice by evading rules which make them hard to distinguish from products of the American West. The later stories reflect a more Canadian distance between imaginative and historical truth. In "The Golden Jubilee Citizen," for example, when Repeat Golightly speaks of writing the history of Crocus to bring out "Wild elements — bred in the blood and bone of Crocus citizenry," Jake, the old fabulator, responds with "Most the folks I know — early days — hail from Ontario. They come out for free land or a chance to start out a general store from scratch. They just got Ontario in their blood an' bone. Kind of thin on the wild elements . . ." (p. 175).

The stories depend upon maintaining the gulf between the child and the grown-ups. The Kid's innocence is inviolate; adulthood is an apparently benign condition; sexuality is unimaginable. In the light of the Freudian overtones of Mitchell's later fiction, the absence of all threatening aspects of maturity is faintly ominous. This is a child's world without the authority of a father. Jake is a harmless substitute, too old to compete for the mother's affection, who has adult powers to solve the problems of a child but is not identified with the sober, prosaic truth, propriety, convention, or order of the adult world. The stories function very much as the tall tales of the creative liar, disarming the worst fears of childhood by rendering them ridiculous.

How I Spent My Summer Holidays is also told from a first-person point of view, but the narrative structure is more complicated. The body of the novel, recollections of the narrator's fall from innocence at the age of twelve or thirteen, is viewed from a narrative foreground set off in reduced type at the beginning and end. There the reader is invited to interpret the childhood experiences by the aging narrator's confession that he is haunted by some shadowy significance in those events which he hopes yet fears he may discover. The "it" in the narrator's "There have been times when I have almost caught it"[90] is as elusive, indefinite, and portentous as the "thing" in Brian O'Connal's "The thing could not hide from him forever" at the end of *Who Has Seen the Wind*.

Initially the story has an innocent Huck Finn-Tom Sawyer appeal as young Hughie and his friend Peter dig a secret cave on the prairie. Soon the adult world begins to impinge as King Motherwell encourages them to harbour a dangerous escaped mental patient, Bill the Sheepherder. The mutilated body Hughie later finds in the cave turns out to be King's wife, Bella. The mystery is only partly unravelled when Bill's body is found sunk in the river with a harrow wheel wired to the ankle. The adult world is satisfied with trying King for killing

Bill, presumably in revenge for his wife's murder, and confining him to the mental hospital, but the children share a dark and secret knowledge which the narrator refuses to face until the end of the novel.

In a discernable progression from *Jake and the Kid* through *The Vanishing Point*, the relationship between the child's world and the adult world has become one of mutual deceit and betrayal. Hughie's fall from innocence begins harmlessly enough in the recognition that "Ventrillo" magic devices and *A Thousand Things a Boy Can Do* are frauds upon the child, but ends in unendurable suspicions of human depravity. As a refuge from the adults in their "upper world," the child society has its caves, which become the most ambiguous symbols in the novel. They are dark, womb-like havens, yet like the "mental hole" in which the boys swim, they suggest unconscious depths unacknowledged in the daylight world. Like Plato's cave, they afford the children those limited shadows of reality they can bear, yet they suggest a Plutonian underworld invested with arcane knowledge beyond the mortality of the upper, adult world. Somewhere between and beyond these two societies are the mental hospital and Sadie Rossdance's brothel, confinements for those who cannot make the perilous passage from one world to the other.

As intermediary between the two worlds, the harmless figure of old Jake Trumper has been replaced by King Motherwell, who is young, virile, a war hero, and an athletic star. The children idolize him because he is "both boy and adult" (p. 39), because he "did not seem to approve of too many adults" (p. 32). As Hughie says, "We had King Motherwell on our side against all the other adults in their upper world" (p. 107). As a rum-runner living beyond the law and as keeper of the forbidden pool-hall which Hughie describes as "a dark submarine cave," Motherwell is King of the underworld. His association with a Plutonian underworld is reinforced by a variety of details: the spirits in which he trades are smuggled west in coffins; Hughie describes King's wife as "proserpine lovely"; King's wisdom about death is consistent with classical conceptions: death is "all bad," and the dead are nothing but twittering shades. King dismisses the Christian conception of heaven and hell as "one big load of elderly bullshit" (p. 31). Like the caves themselves, King is an ambiguous figure; the huge tattoo of a serpent on his body he interprets in Judaeo-Christian terms as "another serpent crawling out of the buffalo-berry bush in the Garden of Eden." King is thus both "boy and adult" in the tragic sense of being caught between the heroic age of the child's imagination and the Calvinist age of the adult present.

The fall is again coincident with passage from childhood, but for the first time in Mitchell's fiction, the chief peril in the passage is openly identified as sex. Very early in the action Hughie experiences a flood of guilt and shame when he accidentally discovers masturbation, and at no time does he express a mature erotic interest in females. To him, the bodies of budding female classmates are "nothing to see"; the nakedness of Sadie Rossdance's girls makes him feel sick, "Then — quickly — disappointed." "After all the years of wondering and wanting to see, there was nothing to see! Tits were quite unnecessary. They did not belong there. The whole female form was wrong!" (p. 159). When Hugh returns home at age twenty-five, he dates Sally Gibson because she is compliant, and he wishes that Sadie Rossdance's cottages were still in operation.

It is not surprising that Hugh's sexuality remains at the perfunctory and exploitive level of childhood. The overtones of sexual repression surrounding his adolescence are pervasive enough to suggest the impossibility of successful passage. His mother, the "eminent Victorian" who expresses the moral tone of adult society, is shocked to discover that she has attracted the lesbian advances of Mrs. Kydd, the police inspector's wife. Mrs. Kydd is Diana the huntress seen in the harshest terms as an emasculating female, particularly when she disciplines her stallion's erect penis with a riding crop. She finds her proper quarry in Bella, who takes the liaison as another form of prostitution like her surreptitious work at Sadie Rossdance's and her marriage to King. The prostitutes' bulrush battle at the swimming hole is sexually suggestive, especially when Bella clasps a bulrush phallus between her thighs and brandishes it at the others. Among the boys there is some suggestion of homosexuality in Austin Musgrave's cloying attachment to Hughie. King Motherwell, as his ambivalent name would suggest, acquires overtones of androgyny. Despite his machismo, his love for children is tender and protective. His first name ironically associates him with Mackenzie King, whom Hughie's father describes as a "covert paedophiliac." When King has ducked in the river, he momentarily looks to Hughie "like Colleen Moore with her Dutch bob," then like Rudolph Valentino. The disposition of King's tattooed serpent also suggests androgyny. After emerging from his crotch hair it circles his umbilicus and then both nipples. King again stands between worlds, at that point of sexual differentiation the boys approach.

Ironically, it is through King's agency that Hughie is brought to the traumatic point of his fall from innocence. In a sense, the boys are nurturing in their cave the sick, subterranean soul of man (or child) driven under by war and the other severities of the adult world. Bill's occupation as shepherd raises a wealth of sacrificial implications. Yet in the process King has involved them in what Hughie recognizes as a "fabric of lies, pretense, and dissemblance" which makes the adult world more threatening. The fabric is torn when Hughie discovers Bella's body. At that point, the narrator says, "I stopped being a boy" (p. 173). At the moment of the fall, Hughie is confronted with death, as Brian O'Connal is, but also with sexuality and the depths of human depravity associated with it. Mitchell's uncharacteristically gruesome description of the body is the sensory equivalent of the moral revulsion the child experiences: "Alive with maggots, black with clotted blood, bruised like an apple and keg-swollen, the head was no longer a head, flies wandering in and out of what had once been eyes, nostrils, mouth, ears . . ." (p. 174). The shock is too much for the boy to accept. He cannot until decades later acknowledge the full solution to the mystery: that King has beaten his faithless wife to death "in a drunken rage of frustration" and, finding Bill dead by one of his fits, has used him as a decoy. Hugh cannot acknowledge this because he will not believe that King could dump the hideous corpse of his Proserpine in the underworld cave of the boys' childhood. He can, paradoxically, accept the possibility that King has murdered the hapless lunatic they have protected, but he cannot accept the violation of the cave.

Until late in life Hugh cannot face the disillusionment necessary to maturity, though King has tried to lead him to it. He is furious when King explains that we live by illusions like the Holy Rollers who mistake the mental patient, Blind Jesus, wading the Souris for Jesus walking on the water, or the heroes who blind themselves to the reality of war. He cannot recognize that King himself is a dealer in illusions as public hero, rum-runner, and artist. And illusion is dangerously close to delusion. King's carvings are artistic illusions but also decoys, including the last, the wooden image of Bella, who has lured him to his destruction. King ends in the mental hospital with the others who cannot escape their illusions. Soon after he is confined, Blind Jesus is struck by a train and Buffalo Billy paralyzed by a bull, suggesting the shattering of adult and childhood illusions.

The narrator sees the process as the tragic but inevitable result of the adult world's impingement upon childhood. He cites as the most obvious victim the anal-erotic Austin Musgrave, who has always sacrificed to the puritan gods:

> I had thought that Austin was the only victim. All of us were. We simply hadn't noticed the adult footprints in our child caves, but they were there all the time, left by guardian trespassers.
>
> ... They wanted only to make it safe for the vulnerable young, to clear it of danger. They did not know, nor did we, that they could be carriers, unintentionally leaving serpents behind, coiled in a dark corner, later to bite and poison and destroy. (p. 222)

This is the nearest the narrator comes to a reconciliation to his mortality.

Two passages of the reduced type which establishes the narrative foreground at the beginning of the novel end with "I mourn the loss of an age of innocence" (p. 4) and "Now I want to sing of arms and a man" (p. 17). In this slightly pompous way, the narrator gives the loss of his own innocence epic associations with the fall of man and the passing of an heroic age. King Motherwell, who guards the goal of the "Trojans" hockey team, evidently represents for the narrator a classic heroic age of male excellence, virtue, and love. The destruction of heroes, the fall of man to the mediocrity, propriety, and repression of the Calvinist present he attributes to the intrusion of the female and sexuality. The narrator's memory treats women unkindly, even scurrilously. They are all seen as bluestockings, lesbians, or whores. In the aging narrator's recurrent dream, "a stylishly dressed and vaguely middle-aged woman" invites him to sodomize a row of child prostitutes. The exploitive implications of the offer are extended when the children's anuses suddenly become caves. It is more than their bodies that are to be violated. The woman reminds the narrator of Miss Coldtart, Mrs. Judge Hannah, and his own mother, representing school, church, and home, respectively. The fallen world is female-dominated.

How I Spent My Summer Holidays presents Mitchell's readers with a new problem of interpretation. It does not exhibit the usual disparity between comic form and tragic awareness. The outcome is tragic; the central figure is isolated from natural and human order while his potential community appears to be disintegrating in corruption. The question is where the narrator stands morally in relation to the world he unfolds and how authoritative his judgements are. While the voice is literate, sensitive, even poetic, the character is clearly a bitter, maladjusted old man. He learns from his revaluation of childhood events, thinks in the end that he "may have sorted it out," but his acceptance only softens the dominant tone of bitterness and self-pity: "Poor King!" "Poor me!" (p. 223). He may have stopped being a boy at the age of twelve, but he has passed mid-life without achieving maturity. It is tempting to see the misogyny of the novel as a function of the fallible narrator's bitterness. This view would account for much, even the fact that the dominating woman in the dream wears a leather purse at her loins like a scrotum while Hughie last sees his hero futilely and pathetically clutching an Indian medicine bag that resembles a severed scrotum. It could hardly, however, account for the portrayal of Diana the huntress, in some forms of matriarchal worship the principal deity, as a sadistic bull dyke. The problem is complicated by apparent contradictions among the mythic allusions which are so much more numerous and obtrusive than elsewhere in Mitchell's fiction.

The narrator appears to invoke three contending mythologies of the Near East: the ancient matriarchal; the patriarchal, classical Greek which supplanted it; and the Judaeo-Christian. He says that Hesiod would have compared him and his boyhood companions to "pre-Aryan silver-age heroes: '. . . eaters of bread, utterly subject to our mothers, however long they lived.'" (p. 3). They would thus be close to the soil, worshippers of the eternal earth, as their fascination for caves might suggest. In pre-Aryan matriarchal mythology, the Proserpine figure would be an earth-goddess of fertility, her serpent spouse master of the mysteries of death and rebirth, their worship implying an acceptance of cyclical cosmic process in which the light and dark aspects of life are equally honoured as complementary. Opposed to their claims of "Mother Right" are the Homeric heroes of the Iron Age evoked by the public figure of King Motherwell. In their patriarchal mythology, Proserpine becomes a secondary fertility goddess with morally dubious connections with death and darkness. Their heroism, their slaying of dragons, as Joseph Campbell says, is to assert "a self-moving power greater than the force of any earthbound serpent destiny."[91] Hence King's grim and futile struggle with the serpent. In the Judaeo-Christian mythology of the Calvinist adult world, the Proserpine figure becomes Eve the temptress bringing death to humankind.

The narrator seems to blame his fall and the terrors of guilt and shame which retard his passage from childhood to manhood on matriarchal domination, without recognizing that it is the patriarchal creeds which have set apart the pairs of opposites — light-dark, male-female, good-evil — and generated the doctrine of original sin.[92] He associates Calvinist repression and consequent perversion of sexuality with female domination, though Calvinism expresses the Judaic, patriarchal will to confine the serpent to hell, the female principle to the status of temptation, and humankind to an inheritance of sin. The inconsistency may result from the narrator's *Golden Book of Legends* understanding of mythology, but there is nothing in the novel to establish the limits of his reliability in this respect, and the allusions imbedded in the imagery pull in conflicting directions.

It may be inappropriate to seek absolute consistency in the mythic allusions of the novel, but however casually they may be introduced, there is no escaping the fact that the fall and the attendant sexual sin and guilt which threaten the passage to maturity are patriarchal rather than matriarchal conceptions. This poses a problem for the integrity of the novel. While the structure suggests that the narrator arrives at a condition of tragic awareness, he is actually left in a fundamental confusion about the world he delivers to us.

In *Since Daisy Creek* (1984) and *Ladybug, Ladybug . . .* (1988), Mitchell appears to be moving away from his pattern of related themes. He initiates a new fictional milieu, Livingstone University in the Alberta foothills; his protagonists are well beyond the age of the fall from innocence and less engaged with elemental nature than with the vanities and hypocrisies of urban and academic life. Yet both men, like the children and adolescents of the earlier novels, are navigating difficult passages in life in which they must face a new awareness of their mortality. In effect, Mitchell is extending rather than abandoning his core themes.

Colin Dobbs, the irascible professor of creative writing in *Since Daisy Creek*, is probably the least appealing of Mitchell's protagonists. His mid-life crisis, brought on by a failure of his creative energies and the break-up of his marriage, is aggravated by his response to it. At a time when evidence of his mortal limitations threatens his sense of self, he has chosen aggressive self-assertion, including the hunting of grizzlies to bolster his ego. Having been mauled by the bear he shot on Daisy Creek, Dobbs's mutilated body is a concrete image of his lacerated ego and a mark of his apartness from the rest of humanity. His pain and disfigurement keep him as self-absorbed physically as he is emotionally. In his obsession with the bear's hide as a trophy of his conquest and a confirmation of his manhood, Dobbs resembles a classic figure in western literature: the individualist male seeking to transcend his mortality through symbolic achievements and fleeing from woman as the reminder and agent of that mortality. Mitchell provides signs of the female as a threat to Dobbs's ego not only in his divorce but in his mauling by a female bear, his earlier comic flight from a sexually aggressive female colleague, his need to make sexual objects of the nurses, and his contentious relationship with his daughter, Annie.

The dramatic heart of the novel is in this opposition between Dobbs and Annie, who has returned to help her father recover and face some painful truths. She battles his obsession with what she calls the great white hunter "icon"[93] and his desire to evade responsibility for his life by "load[ing] everything on that bear" (p. 241). Annie recognizes that what is wrong with Dobbs began before, not since, Daisy Creek. Her efforts to draw him out of his closed self focus on his writing as potentially the most effective form of mediation between self and "other." Annie's task is complicated when Dobbs suffers the humiliation of having the taxidermist substitute for his great grizzly the hide of a juvenile brown bear. Dobbs stubbornly insists on suing for the recovery of his trophy even after he learns that the bear was actually killed by his hunting guide and that the suit will shatter the honest old man whose grandson committed the fraud.

According to the philosophical tenets of Mitchell's fiction, Dobbs is wrong in quite specific ways. If, as Mitchell has said, "consciousness of self is the phenomenon which separates man from the living whole,"[94] then Dobbs's preoccupation with self can only aggravate his alienation. His attempt at symbolic domination of nature can even be seen as a petulant assault on the living whole. It is equally clear in Mitchell's fiction from *Who Has Seen the Wind* to *The Vanishing Point* that humanity can be relieved of isolation and reconciled to mortality only by the bond of human community. Family is Mitchell's most common metaphor for community, and Dobbs has violated the bonds of family. It may be significant that Dobbs, a bastard raised by women in Montreal, is Mitchell's only protagonist without the benefits of family or a Western boyhood. At the centre of the quarrels that destroyed Dobbs's marriage were his efforts to lead Annie away from her mother and traditional female roles into a male idyll of fishing. The result was a child thoughtlessly divided by a domestic power struggle. During the five years since the divorce, Dobbs has thought of Annie as his "little lost girl" (p. 6), again selfishly projecting on the child his own longings for a lost innocence. Paradoxically, Dobbs's only hope for redemption rests with the child who has suffered his abuse.

In *Since Daisy Creek* Mitchell returns to elements of form and technique that were the strengths of his earlier novels. After the reflective first-person narration of *How I Spent My Summer Holidays*, he returns to a third-person limited point of view and to developing the action primarily through dramatic scenes as he had most successfully in *The Vanishing Point*. Not only the central opposition between Dobbs and Annie but the contributing conflicts emerge in dialogue. The tensions between self and community, for example, are further explored in verbal sparring between Dobbs and Archie Nicotine, who is brought back as the guide to save Dobbs's life and exasperate him with his combination of mock primitivism and shrewd cultural criticism. Mitchell again shows the story-teller's mastery of control and pacing, the craft of sustaining an anecdote to its predictable conclusion without puncturing the taut surface of expectation. The scenes leading to the court action, for example, generate a sense of impending disaster. We are shown Archie as a less-than-credible witness, just as in the church scene in *Who Has Seen the Wind* we are conscious of the cud of tobacco in the Ben's mouth, destined to shatter Powelly's social illusion. The legal sequence carries a darker set of implications, but it is ultimately as humorous and more significant to the plot. When Archie antagonizes the judge, he is, ironically, furthering the redemption of Dobbs.

Mitchell does return to a comic resolution, though a rather strange one in which the protagonist is his own blocking character and scapegoat. What the trial brings home to Dobbs is that those around him have sacrificed themselves for others while he has clung to aggressive self-assertion. Annie has risked offering her father unwelcome advice; the old taxidermist has sacrificed his self-respect by perjuring himself to save his grandson; Archie, by killing the bear to save Dobbs, has broken a pact he made with the bear spirit to save his daughter's life. Family is again the measure of human community, and Dobbs's pursuit of his legal rights without regard for the common good (the *right*) is characteristic of the individualism that has proven such a destructive response to his human isolation. In the end, Dobbs abandons his quest for the trophy and is presumably resolved to accommodate the demands of self to the need to rejoin the mortal family. Even with such unpromising raw material as Colin Dobbs, Mitchell is once again able to say "yes" to humanity.

At age seventy-seven, Kenneth Lyon faces his mortality in the most literal sense, yet old age is more the vantage point than the subject of *Ladybug, Ladybug* . . . . As Lyon says, "death is not exclusively an adult matter," fate sooner or later flips out the same hole card, "mortality for all,"[95] and in the action, death threatens the young as immediately as the old. Lyon also experiences the most tangible of human isolation — widowed, childless, retired, and newly evicted from his office at Livingstone University — yet the isolation of the younger characters is often more threatening. That Lyon faces only the most obvious forms of humanity's common lot is made explicit in his parting convocation address, as is the remedy: building bridges between lonely human selves, uniting the mortal family. As the nursery rhyme invoked by the title suggests, family is the subject of *Ladybug, Ladybug* . . . , and not family as the site of innocence and primitive unity. More than in any of his previous novels, Mitchell develops family as a paradigm for human community, complete with the delusions, failures, and betrayals that beset human relations.

In *Ladybug, Ladybug* . . . Mitchell relies less on dramatic scenes than on reflective narration. While the omniscient point of view shifts to the consciousness of several characters, the significance of the action emerges primarily in Lyon's ruminations on past and present events, and, in the emptiness of the old man's life, both came to him with a quality of echo or *déjà-vu*. The most poignant of the echoes are haunted by the loss of his only child, Susan (nicknamed "Little Miss Echo" [p. 27]), who disappeared at Banff forty years earlier. When Lyon hires a housekeeper, Nadya, who is about the age his daughter would have been, and she brings a daughter, Rosemary, the age of the lost Susan, the echoes multiply. The recovered sweetness of domestic affection between young and old is sharpened by what Lyon calls "memory ache," as are the echoes that reach him from early married life and childhood. A menacing shadow falls over the innocence of this asexual family when Charles Slaughter, a psychotic graduate student whose sexual advances Nadya once violently spurned, begins stalking Rosemary for revenge. The outward effect is suspense that lies heavily, at times awkwardly, on the subtler action for more than half the novel. Inwardly, because the child is in his care when kidnapped, Lyon experiences the darkest echo: his guilt and sorrow at the loss of his own daughter. Lyon is slow to realize that what chance has restored to him is not the lost child but the experience of loss, with which he must finally come to terms.

Echoes from the past function, along with an unusual number of paired or repeated motifs, to generate resonances, and these lend intrinsic form to the novel just as the dramatic tension of dialogue shaped the action of *Since Daisy Creek*. Lyon's retirement project, for example, is a biography of Mark Twain, or "Sam" Clemens, with whom he carries on familiar conversations. Such conversations are, of course, reverberations rather than dialogues, and Lyon's research draws him into autobiographical reflections which he hopes will give "life resonance" to the biography. In particular, the premature deaths of Twain's daughters are echoed in Lyon's own loss, and he finds himself fighting the same pessimism and despair that darkened the humorist's final years. In other parallels, Slaughter, the child-abuser, was himself an abused child, raised by a puritanical and sadistic mother and sodomized by a minister of the gospel. Lyon, Rosemary, and Slaughter were all left fatherless at an early age; all the main characters are confronted with isolation.

As such parallels suggest, *Ladybug, Ladybug...* focuses especially on the more ambiguous implications of family. In the face of isolation, family is the most vital of human bonds, yet both fragile and perilous, a delicate web of love and obligation in which usually well-intentioned guardians fail in their responsibility to the young. For the reader of Mitchell, many of the resonances are produced by family motifs drawn together from the earlier novels. The disappearing fathers that began innocently in the "Jake and the Kid" stories have gathered increasing overtones of negligence and inadequacy. The archetype of the "terrible mother" suggested in *The Vanishing Point* and *How I Spent My Summer Holidays* is explicit in Slaughter's childhood. At best the guardians are careless. Lyon's daughter slipped away during a moment of his own inattention; Rosemary is hunted because of her mother's past mistake; Nadya is away auditioning for the part of Saint Joan when her child is kidnapped; Lyon is again too self-absorbed to watch over the child. Again, the lost children evoke Mitchell's Blakean "little girl lost" motif, and when Slaughter hides

191

in a cave over a park across from Lyon's house, the caves come to suggest caves of the unconscious, harbouring madness and death, as in *How I Spent My Summer Holidays*. The imagery comes together most expressively in a scene in the park where Lyon nods while Rosemary plays under the eye of Slaughter. We, the old, sleep while the vulnerable young stray toward the dark caves where monsters created by adult desire and repression are lurking.

It would be a mistake to read Mitchell's paradigm in a romantic or sentimental way. Though he resorts to familiar motifs, Mitchell is here positing a more complex relationship between culture and nature than he has offered before. The innocence of the young is not the purity projected on them by adults, and Mitchell is careful to identify the innate savagery of children. In the park, Rosemary wants to stone a squirrel to death as punishment for biting her, and her primitive instinct echoes Slaughter's desire to punish Nadya for biting him. The child and the villain meet on common ground while she is gathering arrowheads left by the primitive people who are Slaughter's fascination. As elsewhere in Mitchell, natural order has no relation to moral order; the natural instincts of the young must be cultivated to civilized forms of expression. Lyon attempts to persuade Rosemary to forgive the squirrel and transform the arrowheads from instruments of death to objects of art, but society in general has not discharged its responsibility. Slaughter is a sociopath because society has perverted his natural savagery rather than transformed it. Even the university, the guardian of culture, has abused its sacred trust, as have Slaughter's family and his church. It has encouraged his violence by granting him a degree for a novel celebrating a violent Indian avenger and his perversion by engaging him in dubious experiments measuring penis expansion as a test of sexual stimuli. The young are vulnerable not simply because they are innocent but because they are human and thus native to the darkness out of which humanity must climb.

Just as *Ladybug, Ladybug* . . . serves as a virtual concordance to Mitchell's favourite motifs, Lyon's convocation address provides the most comprehensive and explicit statement of the philosophy that generates Mitchell's enduring themes. The key passage could be taken as commentary on the earlier novels:

. . . to be human means to be conscious of self and of being separate from all the rest of the living whole. . . . It is impossible to rejoin the living whole to ease the human pain of loneliness except by dying. . . . When you learn you are going to die, you truly understand you are human. . . . It is for this reason that humans build their bridges from lonely human self to lonely human self. This human need to bridge explains wives, mothers, brothers, sisters, regions, nations . . . . (pp. 137–40)

The same need explains the mediating forms of art: "Death and solitude justify art, which draws human aliens together in the mortal family, uniting them against the heart of darkness." And it explains education: "Our schools and universities, through the Arts and Humanities, must teach the young not just how to make a living but how to live, must keep humans from destroying bridges and returning to the heart of darkness" (p. 140).

To effect a comic resolution, Mitchell extends the paradigm of family even beyond region or nation. With the help of his surrogate family, Lyon learns to rebuild his bridges, and he is presumably reconciled to the experience of loss because this time the child returns alive. Lyon is finally alone with his biography, but he has found, through Twain, a kinship with all North Americans, who are particularly exposed to their cosmic isolation by the newness of the New World.

In some respects, *Ladybug, Ladybug* . . . does not compare well with Mitchell's other novels. It has neither the lyricism of *Who Has Seen the Wind* nor the taut dramatic surface of the later novels. The suspense is not handled with Mitchell's usual subtlety, the Freudian machinery of Slaughter's motivation creaks ominously, and the comic resolution is less than compelling. Lyon's ability to identify with the mortal family in its extended form may save him from Twain's despair, but one can question the nurturing power of communities so remote and abstract. Nonetheless, *Ladybug, Ladybug* . . . is still graced by Mitchell's artistry as a prose stylist. It offers a rich sensory world, vivid characterization, and a range of tone from broad humour to pathos. And thematically it is at the heart of Mitchell's fiction where his comic impulse is in tension with a darkening view of the human condition.

Dramatic W.O. Mitchell (1982) raises questions about the author as novelist and as dramatist which are related to the tensions within his fiction. It is not surprising that when Mitchell began moving his drama to the live stage in 1972, he rose swiftly to prominence in

Canadian theatre. His achievements and reputation in radio and television drama had prepared the way. Mitchell was, after all, an actor before he was a writer, and has said that if there had earlier been a live theatre in Canada he might have been a playwright rather than a novelist. In his novels, Mitchell the dramatist is a strong presence in the dramatic structure of scenes and in the evident sense of theatrical values, especially in comic episodes. But Mitchell distinguishes the dramatist's illusion from that of the novelist who "wants his readers not only to watch and to listen but to enter envelopes of consciousness as well, giving the illusion of inner dimension."[96] Diane Bessai, in her "A Literary Perspective on the Plays of W.O. Mitchell," identifies this distinction with two potentially contending modes of narrative in Mitchell's fiction: "the reflective mode . . . exploring the deeper levels of character perception from within, and the dramatic mode, the episodic folklorish scenes primarily of dialogue and physical action that externalize slightly larger than life people and incidents."[97] The two frequently mark the tension between comic form and the tragic implications of theme I have examined in the fiction.

Bessai also sees in Mitchell's distinction an implied hierarchy of literary forms which affects the kind of plays he is inclined to write. The plays, aligned with the "folk parables" of his radio drama, usually pursue relatively simple themes of "the conflict between petty tyrannies of public sanction and the life-affirming assertions of personal judgement."[98] The three plays which were earliest, at least in conception, can easily be seen in this light. *The Devil's Instrument* dramatizes the liberation of a sensitive adolescent from the peculiar constrictions of a Hutterite colony. The dramatic conflicts within and around the boy, between arbitrary authority and love and beauty (represented by the music of a mouth organ) are uncomplicated. The play includes Mitchell's rare portrayal of the tenderness of first love, and it is untroubled by any of the turmoil of adolescent sexual awakening or the darkness of the fall into mortality. *The Black Bonspiel of Wullie MacCrimmon* is a Prairie version of the Faust story, in which Wullie wagers his soul against winning the Mac-Donald Brier, the outcome to be decided by a curling match with the devil. The real, ongoing dramatic conflicts in the play are between Wullie and the forces of piety and propriety in the town. In adapting *The Kite* to the stage, Mitchell has shifted the focus of attention squarely onto Daddy Sherry. The role of David Lang has been absorbed by other characters and by the dramatic medium itself, and the theme of his imprisonment in time and mortality recedes to a minor feature of a romance between Helen and Daddy's doctor. The comedy of the old man's rebellion against all the tyrannies of town and universe is virtually unimpeded.

In these three plays it appears that without the reflective mode of the novelist's "envelopes of consciousness," Mitchell has been disinclined to approach the more serious themes evident in his fiction during the same period. For *Back to Beulah* and *For Those in Peril on the Sea*, the case is not as simple. Both could be called comedies, at least in form, but they portray a dark and morally problematic world previously reserved for Mitchell's reflective mode of narrative. In *For Those in Peril on the Sea*, the "ship" is a West Coast boarding house and its crew an assortment of life's victims. At the centre of the group is the landlady's son Howard, "a twelve-year-old boy trapped within a seventeen-year-old body,"[99] and an aging and infirm boarder named Lon, who professes to be building a sloop to sail them around the world. Their friendship seems a parody of all the fatherless child and older male relationships in Mitchell's work. The dream the old man shares with the boy is revealed to be a dangerous illusion, and the boy's arrested development, in some measure, a function of his delusion. Yet despite the prevalence of illusions, betrayal between generations, marital failure, alcoholism, and failure to pass into maturity, Mitchell is not creating the fallen world of *How I Spent My Summer Holidays*. After the crisis of Lon's death and Howard's attempted suicide, the characters are all redeemed through charity and mutual understanding, but not without some strain between the comic resolution and the actualities suggested by the play.

In *Back to Beulah*, the most complex and suggestive of the plays, the irony of folk parable again gives way to parody. Three women in a half-way house between a mental hospital named Beulah (innocence of childhood) and the outside world (adult reality) are manipulated, like the Indians in *The Vanishing Point*, by well-meaning officialdom in the person of Dr. Anders. The principals have all been denied the sort of family which could have led them to maturity, but instead of a surrogate for family, the grouping becomes a parody of family, subsisting on drugs, fantasy, and manipulation. The singing of "Amazing Grace," the Christmas setting, and the references to the holy family only heighten the parody. The Christ-child in their crèche is a stolen doll, and there is no access of grace. Earlier versions ended with Dr. Anders softening to play the role of compassionate mother. The published ending, in which she breaks down under enforced exposure to her own therapy, can be considered a comic resolution only in the sense that sanctioned authority breaks down in the face of individual rights and freedom. The revelation that Dr. Anders herself harbours pathological resentments for her parents generalizes the impression of a tragic failure of the human family and of the difficulty of moving from delusion to reality. The implications are similar to those emerging from the last three novels, complete with weak and vanishing fathers and poisonous, domineering women. Doctor and patients all retreat toward Beulah rather than advance toward adult reality. It appears that Mitchell is seeking ways of addressing in the dramatic mode the darker reaches of his vision initially reserved for his reflective mode of narrative.

W.O. Mitchell's place in the first rank of Canadian writers now rests on a substantial and increasingly varied body of work. His stage drama can no longer be relegated to the category of popular entertainment along with his "Jake and the Kid" radio plays, though it can not yet compare with his achievement as a novelist. That achievement has a special importance to Canadian literature because it has included holding a wide popular audience while gaining, eventually, the attention and respect of academic critics. And Mitchell has not compromised his artistic principles to seek that popularity; he believes in the balance of appeal it involves. He has said in interviews that *Huckleberry Finn* may be the great American novel because "Twain hit a serious balance of art and leisure-demand,"[100] which may be another way of describing art which endures because it engages its readers at several levels of awareness.

The balance is not easily achieved or described. To the wider audience, though not to the younger critics, it is reassuring that Mitchell is profoundly conservative in his art. He is probably unequalled among Canadian novelists in stylistic grace and technical mastery of his craft. He asserts aggressively the writer's responsibility to sustain the realist's illusion, insisting that what is important and original is not the truth to be arrived at (which is frequently banal) but the journey in the artist's "illusion bubble."[101] It is tempting to shift his criterion to "a serious balance of art and legerdemain." His analogies for the artist are the illusionist, the juggler, the con man.[102] This perception, which has driven younger writers to Post-Realist,

Deconstructionist theories, Mitchell cheerfully accepts among the obligations of his craft. Mitchell has also been popular because of the type of illusion he has chosen: comedy and humour. Despite the fact that the plots of his novels revolve around death, he has usually resolved to say " 'yes' to man," and this has proven the more difficult balance to maintain.

The ascendancy of the darker side of humanity and the abandonment of comic resolution in *Back to Beulah* and *How I Spent My Summer Holidays* may be unexpected, but they fit into a discernible pattern in Mitchell's work as a whole. From the time of *Who Has Seen the Wind*, the comic form has remained in uneasy tension with the tragic inevitability of humanity's fall from innocence which hangs at the centre of Mitchell's novels. Considering the questions about human mortality raised in that first novel, it is not surprising that the answer to humanity should eventually come up "No," at least some of the time.[103] The point at which it does might even have been predictable from certain features of Mitchell's approach to that crisis of the fall from innocence. It is interesting to see that Laurence Ricou, writing four years before the publication of *How I Spent My Summer Holidays*, is lead by the stages of a boy's development in *Who Has Seen the Wind* to consider that "This next stage, of course, is adolescence, a period of sexual awakening, of strong peer pressure, and often of frustration and alienation."[104] Conspicuously absent from Mitchell's consideration of the fall into mortality, to that point, was the loss of sexual innocence and that central rite of passage, the initiation into physical love, which is the logical consequence and the promised relief of human mortality. Mitchell attributes the absence of adolescent principals in his work to a preference for writing about the vivid young and the vivid old, but his inconclusive treatment of pubescence in *How I Spent My Summer Holidays* suggests that it represents a dark abyss opening between childhood and maturity. The pattern is only confirmed by Mitchell's return to comic resolutions in *Since Daisy Creek* and *Ladybug, Ladybug . . .*, where he chooses protagonists well beyond adolescence. The only approach to the loss of sexual innocence in these novels is in the past of Charles Slaughter, and, as in *How I Spent My Summer Holidays*, it is surrounded with imagery of caves, anuses, castrating women, violence, guilt, perversion, and madness.

Mitchell's shift from comedy is not as sudden as it may seem. Comedy for Mitchell is resolved in community, the antidote to existential isolation, and family in various forms is the basic unit of community. At the centre of family is the relationship of faith between child and parent or quasi-parental adult. To trace the deterioration of that relationship in Mitchell's fiction, one need only look from Jake and the Kid or Brian and Uncle Sean to David Lang and Lon, then to Carlyle and his father or Old Kacky or Aunt Pearl, and on to Hughie and King Motherwell or Howard and Lon in *For Those in Peril on the Sea*. The illusions adults share with children gradually become poisonous serpents. In the later comedies, *Since Daisy Creek* and *Ladybug, Ladybug . . .*, the failure of parental figures to protect the vulnerable young remains a central theme.

Finally there is the philosophical form which questions about human mortality are inclined to assume in Mitchell's fiction. Mitchell once thought of himself as "a Platonist with Presbyterian overtones," and those overtones are evident, however Mitchell may use his humour against them.[105] The fall from innocence acquires an increasingly explicit identification with the Fall of humanity. It is doubtful, once the attendant questions have been imbued with the ethical and metaphysical implications of that archetype, whether Mitchell's protagonists can arrive at a final affirmative answer within the purely secular terms they are given for their search. Especially in the later novels with mature protagonists whose time in life heightens the expectation of answers, the secular and psychological form of those answers seems inadequate to the questions Mitchell has raised. It is significant that the fallen state of humanity is a quality of everyday existence Mitchell presents with evident conviction, yet the only time he evokes the archetypes of redemption, in *Back to Beulah*, they are totally ironic.

Mitchell is not, of course, in search of a final answer. He now describes himself as an existentialist (I would add, "with Presbyterian overtones") portraying a world in which there are no final answers. "Existentialism," he says, "is a falling/balancing act with no absolutes."[106] Mitchell's object will continue to be "balance" in his art as in his world view. Considering that he also feels an increasing awareness of what he calls, from Conrad, "the heart of darkness" in humanity, comedy may become increasingly difficult.[107]

NOTES

[1] My main source of data was biographical notes provided by Catherine McLay of the University of Calgary, confirmed and corrected by the author's wife, Merna Mitchell, and his son and biographer, Ormond Mitchell.

[2] The earliest acceptance, again by Salter's arrangement, was actually "Owl and the Bens," a segment of *Who Has Seen the Wind* published in *Atlantic Monthly*, though it did not appear until 1945.

[3] The tally of episodes varies. I take the figure 320 from Sheila Latham, "W.O. Mitchell: An Annotated Bibliography," *The Annotated Bibliography of Canada's Major Authors*, ed. Robert Lecker and Jack David (Downsview, Ont.: ECW, 1981), III, 334.

[4] For a fuller discussion, see my *Unnamed Country: The Struggle for a Canadian Prairie Fiction* (Edmonton: Univ. of Alberta Press, 1977), chapter vi, from which I quote here.

[5] For a discussion of decline in popular fiction, see my "Popular Fiction of the Canadian Prairies: Autopsy on a Small Corpus," *Journal of Popular Culture*, 14 (1980), 326–32.

[6] "On Stephen Leacock," in *Masks of Fiction: Canadian Critics on Canadian Prose*, ed. A.J.M. Smith (Toronto: McClelland and Stewart, 1961), p. 100.

[7] Patricia Barclay, "Regionalism and the Writer: A Talk with W.O. Mitchell," *Canadian Literature*, No. 14 (Autumn 1962), p. 56.

[8] With apologies to New Zealand for appropriating Katherine Mansfield, this list is accumulated from Barclay, David O'Rourke, "An Interview with W.O. Mitchell," *Essays on Canadian Writing*, No. 20 (Winter 1980–81), pp. 149–59, and a personal interview with Mitchell 18 August 1983, from which the views of the author printed here were gathered.

[9] "Romance and Realism in Western Canadian Fiction," in *Another Time* (Erin, Ont.: Porcépic, 1977), p. 57.

[10] Robin Mathews, "W.O. Mitchell: Epic Comedy," in his *Canadian Literature: Surrender or Revolution*, ed. Gail Dexter (Toronto: Steel Rail, 1978), pp. 109–18.

[11] See Diane Bessai, "A Literary Perspective on the Plays of W.O. Mitchell," Association of Canadian Theatre History Conference, Vancouver, 29 May 1983.

[12] "Review of Spring Novels," *Peterborough Examiner*, 12 March 1947, p. 4. Rpt. in his *The Well-Tempered Critic: One Man's View of Theatre and Letters in Canada*, ed. Judith Skelton Grant (Toronto: McClelland and Stewart, 1981), p. 170.

[13] "Novel of Distinction Recalls Saskatchewan's Barren Years," *The Globe and Mail* [Toronto], 1 March 1947, p. 8.

[14] "Canadian Boyhood," *The New York Times Book Review*, 23 Feb. 1947, p. 5.

[15] "First Novel of Boyhood in Saskatchewan Village," *Mayfair*, April 1947, p. 98.

[16] *Creative Writing in Canada: A Short History of English-Canadian Literature*, 2nd ed. (Toronto: Ryerson, 1961), p. 225.

[17] *Canadian Writers* (Toronto: McClelland and Stewart, 1951), p. 96.

[18] Edward McCourt, *The Canadian West in Fiction* (Toronto: Ryerson, 1949).

[19] "Letters in Canada: 1947: II, Fiction," *University of Toronto Quarterly*, 17 (1948), 265–77.

[20] "A Feeling of Completion: Aspects of W.O. Mitchell," *Canadian Literature*, No. 17 (1963), p. 32.

[21] "Wolf in the Snow: Part One: Four Windows on to Landscapes," *Canadian Literature*, No. 5 (Summer 1960), pp. 7–20. Rpt. in *Contexts of Canadian Criticism*, ed. Eli Mandel (Chicago: Univ. of Chicago Press, 1971), p. 233.

[22] Tallman, p. 236.

[23] *Butterfly on Rock: A Study of Themes and Images in Canadian Literature* (Toronto: Univ. of Toronto Press, 1970), pp. 37–38.

[24] In *Another Time*, pp. 45–53. The paper was originally presented to the Consultation on Canadian Plains Research in Regina, 29 April–1 May 1969.

[25] "Children of the Changing Wind," in *Second Image: Comparative Studies in Quebec/Canadian Literature* (Toronto: new, 1971), pp. 92, 98.

[26] "The Eternal Prairie: The Fiction of W.O. Mitchell," in *Vertical Man/Horizontal World: Man and Landscape in Canadian Prairie Fiction* (Vancouver: Univ. of British Columbia Press, 1973), pp. 95–110.

[27] *Unnamed Country*, chapter vi.

[28] "The Universality of W.O. Mitchell's *Who Has Seen the Wind*," *Lakehead University Review*, 4, No. 1 (1971), 39.

[29] Ken Mitchell, p. 37.

[30] Mathews, p. 110.

[31] Mathews, p. 115.

[32] "Surviving Paradise," *Journal of Canadian Fiction*, 3, No. 1 (Winter 1974), 95.

[33] "Jake and the Id," *Books in Canada*, Nov. 1981, pp. 6–8.

[34] "W.O. Mitchell," in his *A Sense of Style: Studies in the Art of Fiction in English-Speaking Canada* (Toronto: ECW, 1989), pp. 62, 68.

[35] Keith, p. 74.

[36] *How I Spent My Summer Holidays* (Toronto: Macmillan, 1981), p. 4.

[37] "W.O. Mitchell: Epic Comedy," p. 111.

[38] Most extensively in O'Rourke, pp. 153–56.

[39] *Who Has Seen the Wind* (Boston: Little Brown, 1947), p. 11. All further references to this work appear in the text.

[40] "Nature," in *The American Tradition in Literature*, ed. Sculley Bradley, Richmond C. Beatty, and E. Hudson Long, 3rd ed. (New York: Norton, 1967), I, 1081–82.

[41] See, for example, Clara Thomas, *Our Nature — Our Voices: A Guidebook to English-Canadian Literature*, Vol. 1 (Toronto: new, 1972), pp. 141–42.

[42] "Notes on Language and Learning in *Who Has Seen the Wind*," *Canadian Children's Literature*, No. 10 (1977–78), p. 12.

[43] Ken Mitchell, pp. 36–37.

[44] "Some of Today's Developers Have the Sensitivity of Fascist Book Burners," *Canadian Heritage*, Dec. 1980, p. 29.

[45] In "A Feeling of Completion: Aspects of W.O. Mitchell."

[46] "W.O. Mitchell: Epic Comedy."

[47] Ken Mitchell, p. 37.

[48] *Vertical*, p. 105.

[49] *The Vanishing Point* (Toronto: Macmillan, 1973), p. 185, and *How I Spent My Summer Holidays* (Toronto: Macmillan, 1981), p. 222.

[50] See E.D. Blodgett, "The Concept of the 'Prairie' in Canadian Fiction," *Proceedings of the 7th Congress of the International Comparative Literature Association, Montreal 1973*, ed. M.V. Dimic and Juan Ferraté, 2 vols. (Stuttgart: Kunst and Wissen and Erich Bieber, 1979), I, 121–26.

[51] New sees the ending as promising a completeness equivalent to the child's earlier transcendental visions. Ricou sees the final whirlwind as "a token both of continuing mystery and of reassurance" [*Vertical*, p. 106].

[52] *Unnamed Country*, p. 179.

[53] Mathews, p. 113.

[54] Mathews, p. 115.

[55] *The Canadian West in Fiction*, rev. ed. (Toronto: Ryerson, 1970), p. 105.

[56] My definition of comic form is adapted from Northrop Frye, "The Mythos of Spring: Comedy," in *Anatomy of Criticism: Four Essays* (Princeton: Princeton Univ. Press, 1957), pp. 163–86.

[57] *Configuration: Essays in the Canadian Literatures* (Downsview, Ont.: ECW, 1982), p. 201.

[58] Blodgett, *Configuration*, p. 200.

[59] Barclay, p. 55.

[60] Barclay, p. 55.

[61] Mitchell, *Who Has Seen the Wind*, epigraph.

[62] *The Kite* (Toronto: Macmillan, 1962), p. 192. All further references to this work appear in the text.

[63] *The Canadian West in Fiction* (1970), p. 108.

[64] New, p. 28.

[65] McLay, "Kite," p. 44.

[66] *Vertical*, p. 106.

[67] McLay, "Kite," p. 47.

[68] George Baldwin identifies this quality in Daddy as a serious weakness in Mitchell's handling of his central idea, that Daddy's secret knowledge manifests itself "in mere eccentricity and whimsicality," rev. of *The Kite, Queen's Quarterly*, 70 (1963), 284.

[69] Bessai, "A Literary Perspective."

[70] O'Rourke, p. 158.

[71] This is not to say that Mitchell merely revised and expanded the earlier novel. He began with a new conception, then later returned to *The Alien* to retrieve usable fragments.

[72] *The Alien*, serialized in *Maclean's*, 15 Dec. 1953, p. 38.

[73] *The Alien*, serialized in *Maclean's*, 15 Jan. 1954, p. 32.

[74] *The Alien*, serialized in *Maclean's*, 15 Jan. 1954, p. 32.

[75] The suspicion that this ending is a compromise between the actualities suggested by the novel and Mitchell's determination to say "yes" to humanity is encouraged by the fact that in an earlier ending, Carlyle pursues a chain of negation to eventual suicide.

[76] See, for example, Gutteridge, "Surviving Paradise."

[77] *The Vanishing Point* (Toronto: Macmillan, 1973), p. 3. All further references to this work appear in the text.

[78] The telephone lines which symbolized the continuity of human generations in *Who Has Seen the Wind* reappear as part of the life-denying linear imagery of the vanishing point.

[79] "Some of Today's Developers."

[80] *The Alien*, serialized in *Maclean's*, 1 Dec. 1953, p. 55. *The Vanishing Point*, p. 216.

[81] Davidson, p. 76.

[82] O'Rourke, p. 152.

[83] O'Rourke, p. 156.

[84] O'Rourke, p. 156.

[85] "Jake and the Id," p. 8.

[86] Much of what is said here would apply to *According to Jake and the Kid: A Collection of New Stories* (1989), which also won the Leacock medal for humour, but this later collection does not exhibit the same development of the stories over time. At least two of its selections were also published in *Maclean's* in the 1940s, but most appear to be later adaptations from the radio plays.

[87] Margaret Laurence, in her review, "A Canadian Classic?" *Canadian Literature*, No. 11 (Winter 1962), says that the sentimentality and the "clearly indicated moral" in each tale make *Jake and the Kid* a book for children.

[88] *Jake and the Kid* (Toronto: Macmillan, 1961), p. 1. All further references to this work appear in the text.

[89] Daddy Johnston, in "The Golden Jubilee Citizen," for example, is a prototype for Daddy Sherry. Moses Lefthand, the Blackfoot who quit being an Indian to become completely Canadian, in "The Princess and the Wild Ones," bears obvious resemblances to Archie Nicotine.

[90] *How I Spent My Summer Holidays* (Toronto: Macmillan, 1981), p. 1. All further references to this work appear in the text.

[91] *The Masks of God: Occidental Mythology* (New York: Viking, 1964), p. 24.

[92] It is impossible to do justice to Campbell's elucidation of the contending mythologies in brief summary, but the key passage here is, "The patriarchal point of view is distinguished from the earlier archaic view by its setting apart of all pairs-of-opposites — male and female, life and death, true and false, good and evil — as though they were absolutes in themselves and not merely aspects of the larger entity of life" (Campbell, pp. 26–27).

[93] *Since Daisy Creek* (Toronto: Macmillan, 1984), p. 179. All further references to this work appear in the text.

[94] "Some of Today's Developers," p. 29.

[95] *Ladybug, Ladybug . . .* (Toronto: McClelland and Stewart, 1988), p. 35. All further references to this work appear in the text.

[96] *Dramatic W.O. Mitchell* (Toronto: Macmillan, 1982), p. 1.

[97] Bessai, "A Literary Perspective."

[98] Bessai, "A Literary Perspective."

[99] *Dramatic*, p. 219.

[100] O'Rourke, p. 159.

[101] Donald Cameron, "W.O. Mitchell: Sea Caves and Creative Partners," in *Conversations with Canadian Novelists — 2* (Toronto: Macmillan, 1973), p. 52.

[102] O'Rourke, p. 150, and elsewhere.

[103] Mitchell was aware that even *The Vanishing Point* represented only a "qualified yes." See O'Rourke, p. 150.

[104] Ricou, "Notes," p. 15.

[105] O'Rourke, p. 153.

[106] O'Rourke, p. 153.

[107] Personal interview with W.O. Mitchell, 18 Aug. 1983.

SELECTED BIBLIOGRAPHY

Primary Sources

Mitchell, W.O. *Who Has Seen the Wind*. Toronto: Macmillan, 1947.

———. *The Alien*. Serialized in *Maclean's*, 15 Sept. 1953, pp. 8–9, 57–62; 1 Oct. 1953, pp. 14, 36–43; 15 Oct. 1953, pp. 22–23, 38–45; 1 Nov. 1953, pp. 16–17, 40–45; 15 Nov. 1953, pp. 24–25, 81–88; 1 Dec. 1953, pp. 24–25, 46–55; 15 Dec. 1953, pp. 30–40; 1 Jan. 1954, pp. 22–23, 31–34; 15 Jan. 1954, pp. 24, 28–31.

———. *Jake and the Kid*. Toronto: Macmillan, 1961.

———. *The Kite*. Toronto: Macmillan, 1962.

———. *The Devil's Instrument*. Toronto: Simon and Pierre, 1973.

———. *The Vanishing Point*. Toronto: Macmillan, 1973.

———. *The Black Bonspiel of Wullie MacCrimmon*. Calgary: Frontier Publishing, 1976.

———. *How I Spent My Summer Holidays*. Toronto: Macmillan, 1981.

———. *Dramatic W.O. Mitchell*. Toronto: Macmillan, 1982.

———. *Since Daisy Creek*. Toronto: Macmillan, 1984.

———. *Ladybug, Ladybug . . .* Toronto: McClelland and Stewart, 1988.

———. *According to Jake and the Kid: A Collection of New Stories*. Toronto: McClelland and Stewart, 1989.

Secondary Sources

Abley, Mark. Rev. of *How I Spent My Summer Holidays*. *Maclean's*, 2 Nov. 1981, p. 66.

Baldwin, George. Rev. of *The Kite*. *Queen's Quarterly*, 70 (1963), 283–84.

Bannerman, James. "First Novel of Boyhood in Saskatchewan Village." Rev. of *Who Has Seen the Wind*. *Mayfair*, April 1947, p. 98.

Barclay, Patricia. "Regionalism and the Writer: A Talk with W.O. Mitchell." *Canadian Literature*, No. 14 (Autumn 1962), pp. 53–56.

Bartlett, Donald R. "Dumplings and Dignity." *Canadian Literature*, No. 77 (Summer 1978), pp. 73–80.

Bessai, Diane. "A Literary Perspective on the Plays of W.O. Mitchell." Association of Canadian Theatre History Conference, Vancouver, 29 May 1983.

———. "Losing Patients." Rev. of *Back to Beulah*. *NeWest Review*, June 1979, p. 5.

Bissell, Claude. "Letters in Canada: 1947: II, Fiction." Includes rev. of *Who Has Seen the Wind*. *University of Toronto Quarterly*, 17 (1948), 265–67.

Blodgett, E.D. "The Concept of the 'Prairie' in Canadian Fiction." *Proceedings of the 7th Congress of the International Comparative Literature Association, Montreal 1973*. Ed. Milan V. Dimic and Juan Ferraté. 2 vols. Stuttgart: Kunst and Wissen and Erich Bieber, 1979, I, pp. 121–26.

———. *Configuration: Essays in the Canadian Literatures*. Downsview, Ont.: ECW, 1982.

"The Bridge Builder: W.O. Mitchell and His Creative Partners." *Heritage Canada*, Dec. 1980, pp. 26–28.

Cameron, Donald. "W.O. Mitchell: Sea Caves and Creative Partners." In *Conversations with Canadian Novelists — 2*. Toronto: Macmillan, 1973, pp. 48–63.

Campbell, Joseph. *The Masks of God: Occidental Mythology*. New York: Viking, 1964.

Coady, Vince. "Films Mean Woe — W.O." *Edmonton Journal*, 29 Oct. 1982, p. C6.

Davidson, Arnold. "Lessons on Perspective: W.O. Mitchell's *The Vanishing Point*." *Ariel*, 12, No. 1 (1981), 61–78.

Davies, Robertson. "On Stephen Leacock." In *Masks of Fiction: Canadian Critics on Canadian Prose*. Ed. A.J.M. Smith. New Canadian Library, No. 2. Toronto: McClelland and Stewart, 1961.

———. "Review of Spring Novels." Rev. of *Who Has Seen the Wind*. *Peterborough Examiner*, 12 March 1947, p. 4. Rpt. in his *The Well-Tempered Critic: One Man's View of the Theatre and Letters in Canada*. Ed. Judith Skelton Grant. Toronto: McClelland and Stewart, 1981, p. 170.

Deacon, William Arthur. "Novel of Distinction Recalls Saskatchewan's Barren Years." Rev. of *Who Has Seen the Wind*. *The Globe and Mail* [Toronto], 1 March 1947, p. 8.

Edinborough, Arnold. "Go Fly a Kite, Daddy." Rev. of *The Kite*. *Toronto Daily Star*, 5 Oct. 1962, p. 22.

Emerson, Ralph Waldo. "Nature." In *The American Tradition in Literature*. Ed. Sculley Bradley, Richmond C. Beatty, E. Hudson Long. 3rd. ed. New York: Norton, 1967, I, 1064–98.

French, William. Rev. of *How I Spent My Summer Holidays*. *The Globe and*

Mail [Toronto], 22 Oct. 1981, p. E1.

Frye, Northrop. "The Mythos of Spring: Comedy." In *Anatomy of Criticism: Four Essays.* Princeton: Princeton Univ. Press, 1957, pp. 163–86.

Gingell-Beckman, S.A. "The Lyricism of W.O. Mitchell's *Who Has Seen the Wind.*" *Studies in Canadian Literature*, 6 (1981), 221–31.

Grady, Wayne. "Life Ain't Art." *Books in Canada*, Nov. 1981, pp. 3–6.

Gutteridge, Don. "Surviving Paradise." Rev. of *The Vanishing Point. Journal of Canadian Fiction*, 3, No. 1 (Winter 1974), 95–97.

Gzowski, Peter. "One Hour in High River, Alberta." In *Peter Gzowski's Book about This Country in the Morning.* Edmonton: Hurtig, 1974, pp. 18–25.

Harrison, Dick. "Popular Fiction of the Canadian Prairies: Autopsy on a Small Corpus." *Journal of Popular Culture*, 14 (1980), 326–32.

———. *Unnamed Country: The Struggle for a Canadian Prairie Fiction.* Edmonton: Univ. of Alberta Press, 1977.

Hornyansky, Michael. "Countries of the Mind." Includes rev. of *The Kite. The Tamarack Review*, No. 26 (1963), pp. 58–68.

Johnson, Bryan. "Back to Beulah: Lots of Laughs, but Fuzzy Core." Rev. of *Back to Beulah. The Globe and Mail* [Toronto], 2 Feb. 1976, p. 15.

Jones, D.G. *Butterfly on Rock: A Study of Themes and Images in Canadian Literature.* Toronto: Univ. of Toronto Press, 1970.

Keith, W.J. "W.O. Mitchell." In his *A Sense of Style: Studies in the Art of Fiction in English-Speaking Canada.* Toronto: ECW, 1989, pp. 61–76.

Latham, Sheila. "W.O. Mitchell: An Annotated Bibliography." *The Annotated Bibliography of Canada's Major Authors.* Ed. Robert Lecker and Jack David. Downsview, Ont.: ECW, 1981, III, 323–64.

Laurence, Margaret. "A Canadian Classic?" Rev. of *Jake and the Kid. Canadian Literature*, No. 11 (Winter 1962), pp. 68–70.

MacLulich, T.D. "Last Year's Indians." Includes rev. of *The Vanishing Point. Essays on Canadian Writing*, No. 1 (Winter 1974), pp. 47–48.

Mandel, Eli. *Another Time.* Erin, Ont.: Porcépic, 1977.

Mathews, Robin. "W.O. Mitchell: Epic Comedy." In his *Canadian Literature: Surrender or Revolution.* Ed. Gail Dexter. Toronto: Steel Rail, 1978, pp. 109–18.

McCaughna, David. "Back to Beulah a Mix That Doesn't Blend." Rev. of *Back to Beulah. The Toronto Star*, 2 Feb. 1976, p. D6.

McCourt, Edward A. *The Canadian West in Fiction.* Toronto: Ryerson, 1949; rev. ed., 1970.

McLay, Catherine. "Crocus, Saskatchewan: A Country of the Mind." *Journal of Popular Culture*, 14 (1980), 333–49.

————. Rev. of *How I Spent My Summer Holidays*. *Prairie Forum*, 7 (1982), 127–29.

————. "*The Vanishing Point*: From Alienation to Faith." In *Modern Times*. Vol. III of *The Canadian Novel*. Ed. John Moss. Toronto: NC, 1982, pp. 243–60.

————. "W.O. Mitchell's *The Kite*: A Study in Immortality." *Journal of Canadian Fiction*, 2, No. 2 (Spring 1973), 43–48.

Mitchell, Barbara. "The Long and the Short of It: Two Versions of *Who Has Seen the Wind*." *Canadian Literature*, No. 119 (Winter 1988), pp. 8–22.

Mitchell, Ken. "The Universality of W.O. Mitchell's *Who Has Seen the Wind*." *Lakehead University Review*, 4, No. 1 (1971), 26–40.

Mitchell, Orm. "Invading Caves: Autobiography and W.O. Mitchell's *How I Spent My Summer Holidays*." In *Reflections: Autobiography and Canadian Literature*. Ed. K.P. Stich. Reappraisals: Canadian Writers, No. 14. Ottawa: Univ. of Ottawa Press, 1988, pp. 141–52.

————. "Tall Tales in the Fiction of W.O. Mitchell." *Canadian Literature*, No. 108 (1986), pp. 16–35.

Monkman, Leslie. *A Native Heritage: Images of the Indian in English-Canadian Literature*. Toronto: Univ. of Toronto Press, 1981.

Morash, Gordon. "Mitchell's Merry Method." *Alberta Report*, Oct. 1979, pp. 31–38.

New, William. "A Feeling of Completion: Aspects of W.O. Mitchell." *Canadian Literature*, No. 17 (Summer 1963), pp. 22–33.

————. Rev. of *The Vanishing Point*. *The Canadian Forum*, May–June 1974, pp. 26–27.

O'Rourke, David. "An Interview with W.O. Mitchell." *Essays on Canadian Writing*, No. 20 (Winter 1980–81), pp. 149–59.

Pacey, Desmond. *Creative Writing in Canada: A Short History of English-Canadian Literature*. 2nd ed. Toronto: Ryerson, 1961.

Peterman, Michael. "'The Good Game': The Charm of Willa Cather's *My Antonia* and W.O. Mitchell's *Who Has Seen the Wind*." *Mosaic*, 14, No. 2 (1981), 93–106.

————. "W.O. Mitchell." *Profiles in Canadian Literature 2*. Ed. Jeffrey M. Heath. Toronto: Dundurn, 1980, pp. 9–16.

Phelps, Arthur. *Canadian Writers*. Toronto: McClelland and Stewart, 1951.

Porter, MacKenzie. "The Man behind Jake and the Kid." *Maclean's*, 13 Sept. 1958, pp. 22, 46–50.

Ricou, Laurence. "Notes on Language and Learning in *Who Has Seen the Wind*." *Canadian Children's Literature*, No. 10 (1977–78), pp. 3–17.

————. "Stages of Language and Learning in W.O. Mitchell's *Who Has Seen the Wind*." In his *Everyday Magic: Child Languages in Canadian Literature*. Vancouver: Univ. of British Columbia Press, 1987, pp. 48–59.

—————. *Vertical Man/Horizontal World: Man and Landscape in Canadian Prairie Fiction*. Vancouver: Univ. of British Columbia Press, 1973.

Roddan, Samuel. Rev. of *Who Has Seen the Wind*. *The Canadian Forum*, April 1947, p. 22.

Scobie, Stephen. "A Wise Indian's Reservations." Includes rev. of *The Vanishing Point*. *Maclean's*, Nov. 1973, p. 118.

"Some of Today's Developers Have the Sensitivity of Fascist Book Burners." *Canadian Heritage*, Dec. 1980, p. 29.

Sullivan, Richard. "Canadian Boyhood." Rev. of *Who Has Seen the Wind*. *The New York Times Book Review*, 23 Feb. 1947, p. 5.

Sutherland, Ronald. "Children of the Changing Wind." *Journal of Canadian Studies*, No. 5 (Nov. 1970), pp. 3–11. Rpt. in *Second Image: Comparative Studies in Quebec/Canadian Literature*. Toronto: new, 1971, pp. 89–107.

Stafford, Ellen. "A Novel To Be Read Aloud." Rev. of *The Kite*. *The Globe and Mail* [Toronto], 6 Oct. 1962, p. 18.

Tallman, Warren. "Wolf in the Snow: Part One: Four Windows on to Landscapes." *Canadian Literature*, No. 5 (Summer 1960), pp. 7–20, and "Wolf in the Snow: Part Two: The House Repossessed." *Canadian Literature*, No. 6 (Autumn 1960), pp. 41–48. Rpt. in *Contexts of Canadian Criticism*. Ed. Eli Mandel. Chicago: Univ. of Chicago Press, 1971, pp. 232–53.

Thomas, Clara. *Our Nature — Our Voices: A Guidebook to English-Canadian Literature*. Vol. 1. Toronto: new, 1972.

Twigg, Alan. "W.O. Mitchell." in *Strong Voices: Conversations with Fifty Canadian Authors*. Madeira Park, B.C.: Harbour, 1988, pp. 202–07.

Williams, David. "The Indian Our Ancestor: Three Modes of Vision in Recent Canadian Fiction." *Dalhousie Review*, 58 (1978), 309–28.

—————. Rev. of *How I Spent My Summer Holidays*. *Winnipeg Free Press*, 31 Oct. 1981, p. L5.

Woodcock, George. "Jake and the Id." Rev. of *How I Spent My Summer Holidays*. *Books in Canada*, Nov. 1981, pp. 6–8.

*Martha Ostenso
and Her Works*

Martha Ostenso (1900–63)

STANLEY S. ATHERTON

Biography

MARTHA OSTENSO (pronounced Austin-so), the eldest of three children of Sigurd Brigt and Olina (née Tungeland) Ostenso, was born 17 September 1900 on a small farm near the village of Haukeland, not far from Bergen, Norway. Haukeland was the home of her mother's parents. The Ostensos came from the township that bears their name, situated beside the hardangerfjord near the coast, where according to family tradition they had lived since the time of the Vikings. Sigurd Ostenso, as a younger son, was not in line to inherit family land, so in 1902 he indulged an adventurous nature and emigrated to North America. He spent two years in Winnipeg, where he was joined by his wife and daughter, and the family then moved to the United States.[1] Settling first in South Dakota, the family soon began a series of moves that would take them from one small town to another in the Dakotas and Minnesota over the next thirteen years while Sigurd sought work as a stationary steam engineer or as a butter maker in one of the many local dairies then flourishing in the area. In the meantime the family continued to grow with the birth of Bjarne (Barney) in 1903 and Oivind (nicknamed Spot) two years later.

In 1915 Sigurd Ostenso's restlessness drove him back to Canada. He had not prospered, and to save money the family travelled from Benson, Minnesota, to Brandon, Manitoba, in a railway boxcar. Fifteen-year-old Martha was soon enrolled at Brandon Collegiate, where attendance records show her as a diligent student from September 1915 through June 1917, when the family moved yet again. When she arrived in Brandon, Martha Ostenso was already a published writer.[2] By the age of eleven she was being paid (at the rate of eighty cents a column) for regular contributions to the Junior Page of the Minneapolis *Journal*.[3] And her only surviving notebook has an entry dated 12 January 1915 indicating that one of her poems, entitled "The Price of War," had won a prize in a contest sponsored by the *Winnipeg Telegram*.[4] The notebook also reveals that even as a schoolgirl she enjoyed casting herself in the role of creative writer: it is entitled "runaway Rhymes: A Book of Spasmodic outbursts from the cranium of ye youthfull poet Laureate of ye Goldenn Schoole Days."

In 1917 the family moved to Winnipeg, where Sigurd had taken employment as a butter maker with the Dominion Produce Company. Martha continued her education at Kelvin Technical High School, where in the winter of 1917-18 it seems likely she earned the credentials for a temporary teaching certificate. In the late summer of 1918 she took a teaching position in the Hayland School District, about a hundred and sixty kilometres northwest of Winnipeg.[5] While living in Hayland, she boarded with the family of Alexander Hay, his wife and four children (two boys and two girls), and it seems likely that she modelled some of the characters in her first novel, *Wild Geese*, on the Hays and half a dozen other families living in the area at the time, including the Sandmoens, Eggertsons, Gudmundsons, and Gislassons. She enrolled for a single course in literature at the University of Manitoba for the spring term of 1919, and began full-time studies there in September, when she took a number of traditional arts courses. Among them were "English Prose" and "English Verse," both taught by an Assistant Professor named Douglas Durkin, a married man sixteen years her senior who was to become her inseparable companion and the most important influence on her literary career. In the spring and summer of 1920 she worked as a reporter for the *Winnipeg Free Press*, but left in the fall to enroll for her second, and last, year of university studies.[6] In the meantime Durkin had moved to New York, leaving his wife and children in Winnipeg, and was teaching extension courses for Columbia University. In the fall of 1921 Ostenso joined him there. It was the beginning of a remarkably successful personal and professional relationship that was to last until Ostenso's death more than forty years later. Durkin had already published two novels, *The Heart of Cherry McBain* (1919) and *The Lobstick Trail: A Romance of Northern Manitoba* (1921), when he was hired by Columbia to teach an evening course in Techniques of the Novel. According to the prescription, it was designed primarily as a creative writing course in which "exercises and class discussions will bear more particularly upon specific technical problems arising out of work submitted by students."[7] In the winter of 1921-22 Ostenso was a student in the course, and may have begun work on *Wild Geese* then, submitting parts of it for assessment under its working title, "The Passionate Flight." For the next two years she earned her living as a social worker on New York's Lower East Side, and continued to write in her spare time. Late in 1923 she returned to Winnipeg, where she spent most of the winter finishing the first full draft of *Wild Geese*.[8] In the spring of 1924 she returned to the United States for good, and later that year her first book was published, a collection of poems entitled *A Far Land*.[9] In the meantime Durkin had published *The Magpie* (1923), a powerful novel set in Winnipeg in the years just after the First World War.

It was not for poetry, however, that the name Martha Ostenso was to become well known. Within a year the manuscript of "The Passionate Flight" was revised, retitled, and submitted in a competition sponsored jointly by the publishing firm of Dodd Mead, *The Pictorial Review*, and the Famous Players Lasky Corporation to find the best first novel by an American author. There were 1389 entries, and *Wild Geese* was chosen to win the $13,500 first prize. It was a remarkable *coup*, and it launched a long and financially rewarding career for Ostenso and for Durkin, her companion and collaborator. The extent to which Durkin had a hand in the composition of *Wild Geese* is unclear, but more than three decades later both writers were willing to sign a legal document admitting him to a collaboration on the novel.[10] What is clear is that after 1925 the name Martha Ostenso became a pseudonym representing the combined and complementary efforts of the two writers. *Wild Geese* quickly became the source of a financial bonanza. The novel went into multiple print runs (twelve within the first year alone), was translated into seven languages and serialized in Norwegian in *Skandinaven*, a Chicago paper, and was turned into a film starring Belle Bennett.[11] It was followed in 1926 by *The Dark Dawn*, and a year later by *The Mad Carews*, both set in rural Minnesota. In 1928 Ostenso was awarded an honorary M.A. from Wittenberg University in Springfield, Ohio, in recognition of her literary achievement.[12] The next novel, *The Young May Moon* (1929), returned to a southern Manitoba setting. Within two months a second printing of the novel was required, and before the year was out it had been translated into a number of languages, including Norwegian. By now the Ostenso name on a novel was a guarantee of commercial success, and the titles proliferated: *The Waters under the Earth* (1930), *Prologue to Love* (1931), *There's Always Another Year* (1933), *The White Reef* (1934), *The Stone Field* (1937), *The Mandrake Root* (1938), *Love Passed This Way* (1942), and *O River, Remember* (1943). In addition to the novels, Ostenso and Durkin were turning out short formula fiction for the mass magazines, and earning between $750 and $1250 for each of them. Financial records, which they kept scrupulously, suggest that their annual income between 1926 and 1939 fluctuated between thirty and forty thousand dollars, even in the depths of the Depression.

By all accounts, Ostenso and Durkin lived fully up to their income. In the fall of 1925 Ostenso made the first of three visits to her old home in Norway. Between 1926 and 1930 the couple maintained a house in Beverley Hills, California, as well as a residence in New Jersey, near Closter on the Hudson River Palisades. During the 1930s they moved back and forth between Hollywood and Minnesota, where they had a succession of homes in Minneapolis as well as a comfortable cabin they had built around 1930 at Gull Lake.[13] Even during the Depression they continued to live flamboyantly, driving expensive automobiles — Reos were their favourites — and travelling widely. Their circle of friends included actors such as Douglas Fairbanks and his wife Mary Pickford, John Barrymore, and Henry Fonda, who played Caleb Gare in the 1941 Hollywood remake of *Wild Geese*.[14] There were also connections with well known writers. They knew Louis Bromfield, Theodore Dreiser, and Thomas Wolfe. Carl Sandburg inscribed copies of at least two of his books to them. and family gossip has it that Sinclair Lewis desperately wanted to marry Martha, and on one memorable occasion came to blows with Durkin over her.[15]

By the end of the Second World War the literary career of Ostenso and Durkin was in decline. *O River, Remember* had been chosen as a Literary Guild selection in 1943, but it was to be the last of their popular successes. They were married in 1944, a year after the death of Durkin's wife, and settled down to a relatively quiet life in Minnesota. Four more books appeared in the forties, one of them a collaboration with Sister Elizabeth Kenny on her "autobiography." The novels — *Milk Route* (1948), *The Sunset Tree* (1949), and *And the Town Talked* (1949) — tried with little success to chart the changing lifestyles of the post-war world. At best they were unremarkable, at worst, potboilers. In 1958 a final novel appeared. Entitled *A Man Had Tall Sons*, it was a throwback to earlier Ostenso work, set in the pre-war world of rural Minnesota. But the market had changed. Novels of life in rural America were no longer fashionable, and the Ostenso name no longer had the power to generate automatic sales. Martha Ostenso herself was now in failing health: the accumulated effects of three decades of indulgent living, and a growing tendency to alcoholism, had begun to take their toll.[16] Late in 1963 she and Durkin decided to move to Washington to be close to two of Durkin's sons. The journey proved too much for her, however, and she collapsed on the train. On arrival in Seattle she was taken to hospital, where she died two days later on November 24. The cause of death "was cirrhosis of the liver."[17] Durkin survived her by nearly five years.

Tradition and Milieu

The fiction that Martha Ostenso produced in collaboration with Douglas Durkin can be located fairly accurately in the literary tradition of its time and place. In Canada *Wild Geese* is usually considered one of the central novels in the rise of realistic prairie fiction, and *The Young May Moon* should be considered in the same light. These two novels, along with Frederick Philip Grove's *Settlers of the Marsh* (1925) and his later fiction, and Robert J.C. Stead's *Grain* (1926), stand out sharply against a background of less distinguished work. Before the appearance of these novels, sustained, accurate representation of life in the region was rare. Although the Canadian west had been a popular setting for tales of adventure and romance since the 1880s, most fiction set on the prairies or in the northwest was weakened by excessive romanticism, didacticism, melodrama, or sentimentality. Before the turn of the century Sir Gilbert Parker and others such as James Oliver Curwood had set a number of stories on the northern prairie before the coming of the railroad. In later books such as *You Never Know Your Luck* (1914) and *The World for Sale* (1916) Parker dealt with the newly established towns of Saskatchewan, a move which allowed him to capitalize on the growing interest in western settlement that was already being used to flavour the romances of Harold Bindloss, Ridgwell Cullum, and Ralph Connor. But there was little sense of real life in the fanciful encounters of Parker's characters even in these late novels, and they seldom rise above the level of romantic melodrama. Bindloss and Cullum were both British, and although they each spent time on the prairies, they too were less concerned with verisimilitude than with developing the romantic potential of what their readers saw as exotic settings. To be fair, Bindloss did make an effort to record geography with precision, and in *A Prairie Courtship* (1911) and *Ranching for Sylvia* (1912) he was able to convey an accurate sense of the physical landscape. Such was not the case with Ralph Connor (the pseudonym of the Reverend Charles William Gordon). Connor was a phenomenally popular writer — his novels sold in the millions — who turned his own experience as a prairie missionary into a series of didactic romances. In *The Sky Pilot* (1899), *The Foreigner* (1909), and *Corporal Cameron* (1912), among others, Connor used many of the ordinary experiences of prairie life to preach a simplistic optimism based on a belief in the inevitable victory of good sense and Christian virtue over various evils encountered in frontier and immigrant societies. However, his improbable plots, one-dimensional characters, and blindness to the effect of landscape on the human psyche mark the failure of his fiction to come to grips with the complexity of human experience in the Canadian west.

Realistic elements had their place, of course, even in some of the most wildly improbable romantic fiction. In some cases, such as in certain novels of Nellie McClung and Arthur Stringer, the effect was especially striking. What makes these works stand out is their attention to psychological interpretation of character coupled with portrayals of strong and independent women. Both McClung's *The Second Chance* (1910) and *Purple Springs* (1921) and Stringer's trilogy, *The Prairie Wife* (1915), *The Prairie Mother* (1920), and *The Prairie Child* (1922) offer compelling precedents for female characters in later prairie fiction, such as Ostenso's Judith Gare in *Wild Geese* and Marcia Vorse in *The Young May Moon*. Another interesting development in the decade preceding the publication of *Wild Geese* was an evolution in the *kind* of fiction produced by a number of prairie writers. Both Douglas Durkin and Robert Stead began by writing romances, but were later able to make the transition to more serious realistic work. Durkin's *The Heart of Cherry McBain* and *The Lobstick Trail: A Romance of Northern Manitoba* were both melodramatic and sentimental, with an emphasis on event rather than characterization. However, *The Magpie* reveals a marked advance on Durkin's earlier work, and offers penetrating, realistic analysis of social conditions and attitudes in post-war Winnipeg as they affected a number of convincingly developed characters. Stead's *The Bail Jumper* (1914), *The Homesteaders* (1916), *The Cow Puncher* (1918), *Dennison Grant* (1920), and *Neighbours* (1922) show a more steady development, away from the stereotypical characters and situations of romantic fiction and towards a more thoughtful presentation of individual character and legitimate regional concerns. This trend culminated in Stead's publication of *The Smoking Flax* (1924) and *Grain* (1926). Elements of romantic fiction did not completely disappear even from *Grain*. However, as Dick Harrison has pointed out in *The Unnamed Country: The Struggle for a Canadian Prairie Fiction*, "on the prairie, of all places, with its precarious balance of dream and nightmare, romance in one form or another is bound to continue showing its value as a way of capturing subjective experience."[18] A similar confluence of romantic and realistic elements appeared in Laura Goodman Salverson's *The Viking Heart* (1923), a compelling examination of Icelandic settlement in Gimli, Manitoba, between 1876 and 1919, and is also evident in *Wild Geese*. But given the setting and the prevailing Canadian literary precedents, this is hardly surprising.

It would be myopic to consider the Ostenso canon only in terms of a Canadian literary milieu. After all, the later novels were all written while Ostenso and Durkin were living in the United States, and there can be little doubt that they were at least aware of significant literary developments in that country. They were personally acquainted with two of the towering figures in the American literary firmament in the twenties, Theodore Dreiser and Sinclair Lewis, and could hardly have failed to read their work. Dreiser's reputation as one of the first great American naturalistic writers had been established with the publication of *Sister Carrie* in 1900 and *Jennie Gerhardt* in 1911, and confirmed with *An American Tragedy* in 1925. His widely read fiction paved the way for a more open treatment of sexuality, a greater recognition of the importance of immigrant life in American society, and an examination of the thesis that all too frequently social forces direct the actions of seemingly independent individuals. Each of these elements would have a part to play in later Ostenso novels, from *The Dark Dawn* to *A Man Had Tall Sons*. Sinclair Lewis based his satiric denunciation of materialism in *Main Street* (1920) and *Babbitt* (1922) largely on his observations of life in small-town Minnesota, a world Ostenso knew well.

His earlier novel, *The Trail of the Hawk* (1915), which explored the difficulties experienced by a second generation Norwegian family in Minnesota, offers an interesting precedent for a number of Ostenso works, including *The Mandrake Root* and *O River, Remember*. It seems likely that Ostenso and Durkin were also familiar with the works of Willa Cather. *O Pioneers!* (1913), Cather's realistic story of a Norwegian peasant girl in Nebraska, was widely read, as were her later studies of immigrant girls in the new world, *The Song of the Lark* (1915) and *My Antonia* (1918). Cather's habit of affirming strong links between the characters with whom she sympathizes and the natural environment finds a consistent echo in the Ostenso novels, from *Wild Geese* on. Ole Rølvaag, a direct contemporary of Ostenso, was known for his fiction about Norwegian immigrants in Minnesota and the Dakotas. In a series of novels, from the highly acclaimed *Giants in the Earth* (1927) through *Peder Victorious* (1929) and *Their Fathers' God* (1931), Rølvaag traces the turbulent history of a pioneering family through three generations. A central concern of these novels, conflict between husband and wife linked with tension between generations, coincidentally occupied Ostenso and Durkin in one novel after another.

It would be fascinating to know what books were in the Ostenso-Durkin library, though it seems unlikely a list of them will ever turn up. Allusions in the novels themselves, though rare, offer some clues to their authors' reading and to possible literary influences on their work. Four Shakespeare plays are alluded to (*Hamlet, Macbeth, The Merchant of Venice,* and *The Tempest*), with a line from *The Tempest* used as an epigraph to *Prologue to Love*. There is a reference to Nathaniel Hawthorne's *The Scarlet Letter* in *O River, Remember*, which may have led Clara Thomas to suggest that Hawthorne may be helpful in reading *Wild Geese* and *The Young May Moon*.[19] A reference to Hans Christian Andersen's *Fairy Tales* led Brita Mickleburgh to a correlation between Andersen's story entitled "The Flax" and the ending of *Wild Geese*.[20] Occasional references to Joseph Conrad may reflect Durkin's admiration: he also used the name Conrad North as a pseudonym.[21] Scandinavian allusions appear to a Norwegian Bible and hymnbook, to Icelandic sagas, and to Ibsen's *A Doll's House*. And literary parallels are now being noticed by critics, including those between *Wild Geese* and R.D. Blackmore's *Lorna Doone*, Emily Brontë's *Wuthering Heights*, and Sir Walter Scott's *Bride of Lammermoor*.[22]

Critical Overview and Context

Published critical reaction to the Ostenso fiction is a fairly recent phenomenon, and it has yet to appear in the quantity a serious reader of the work might expect. Evaluations which have appeared have focussed primarily on *Wild Geese*, though access to the other novels is available through a number of perceptive theses and dissertations, and in a more limited way, through contemporary reviews. For the most part, critical opinion has been in quiet agreement with Desmond Pacey's dismissive remark in the *Literary History of Canada* that "Martha Ostenso's later novels . . . were almost all set in the northern United States, and were more or less unsuccessful attempts to repeat her own achievement in *Wild Geese*."[24] The general failure to recognize that three of Ostenso and Durkin's novels after *Wild Geese* were set in Canada suggests that these works have largely gone unread, and (arguably) that inexpensive new editions are needed to reintroduce them to Canadian readers.

The original reviews of *Wild Geese* were at best lukewarm. Both *The Saturday Review of Literature* and the *Times Literary Supplement* pointed to the requirements of the competition the novel had won — that the book be adaptable as a serial and as a motion picture — and while the *TLS* reviewer felt that the novel was better than one might expect under the circumstances, Rebecca Lowrie of *The Saturday Review* felt that it suffered because of them.[25] Both critics noted the novel's realism (a point Canadian readers have continued to find important); and *The New York Times Book Review* remarked on the novel's "admirable characterization," a point which reviewers of later novels would make repeatedly.[26] Reviews of *The Dark Dawn*, for example, analyzed the novel's main character, Hattie Murker, in some detail, although both *The Canadian Forum* and *The New York Times Book Review* agreed that "Miss Ostenso has, on the whole, sacrificed definition in her other characters for the sake of Hattie Murker."[27] Reviews of *The Young May Moon* and *The Waters under the Earth* also focussed on the portrayal of central characters in the novels, though they disagreed on the effectiveness with which the characters were developed. For the most part, reviewers of the first five novels saw Martha Ostenso as a serious writer, and discussed the fiction accordingly. They made comparisons between one Ostenso novel and another, pointed to the possible influence of earlier writers, and isolated flaws and strengths in plotting, point of view, characterization, and treatment of ideas. But after 1930, and particularly after the publication of *Prologue to Love* and *There's Always Another Year*, in which romantic elements were dominant, reviewers were increasingly unwilling to engage in serious discussion of technique. With the notable exception of the detailed and generally positive reaction to *O River, Remember* in 1943, reviewers confined themselves to extended plot summaries and vague or neutral assessments of the works.

Apart from the reviews, there were a number of early reactions to *Wild Geese* which are of interest to Canadian readers. Shortly after the announcement that the novel was a prize winner, Morris Colman, "an intimate friend" of Ostenso, wrote a largely biographical "appreciation" of her work in *Maclean's*.[28] The following year W. E. MacLellan wrote a stirring essay for the *Dalhousie Review* castigating the Canadian reading public for its failure to appreciate "the most striking and by far the best literary work that any one of its children has yet done."[29] The assessment was echoed in the pages of *The Canadian Bookman*, where the novelist Georges Bugnet said that "for a first novel, *Wild Geese* may well be called a masterpiece."[30] In 1926 William Arthur Deacon was at pains to point out to misguided American reviewers that the setting of *Wild Geese* was Canadian, and at the same time he offered a brief comparison of the novel to Grove's *Settlers of the Marsh*.[31] Grove's own reaction to *Wild Geese* was memorable: in a letter to Austin M. Bothwell (18 November 1925) he damned the novel thoroughly, concluding that "only trash wins a prize."[32] As Desmond Pacey pointed out in his Introduction to Grove's *Letters*, there was "perhaps a certain amount of jealousy involved" in Grove's analysis.[33]

Masterpiece or trash, *Wild Geese* (along with other Ostenso fiction) was mainly ignored by both Canadian and American critics for the next thirty years. Edward A. McCourt barely mentioned Ostenso in his pioneer study, *The Canadian West in Fiction* (1949), and Desmond Pacey devoted only eight lines to *Wild Geese* in *Creative Writing in Canada* (1952), although he did place Ostenso with Grove and Stead as a significant contributor to the advent of realism in modern Canadian fiction.[34] The 1960s saw the beginning of renewed attention, initiated by the 1961 New Canadian Library edition of *Wild Geese* with an Introduction by Carlyle King.[35] King's brief two-part commentary includes a biographical sketch coupled with an attempt to place Ostenso in a North American literary tradition, and a balanced analysis of the novel's strengths and weaknesses. The following year S.G. Mullins offered a tentative look at the novel's integration of theme and structure in a short article in *Culture*.[36] More telling commentary appears in Roy W. Meyer's *The Middle Western Farm Novel in the Twentieth Century* (1965), which isolates a number of repetitive patterns in character relationships and plot in the later fiction.[37] In 1965 the landmark *Literary History of Canada* appeared, and in the essay entitled "Fiction 1920–1940" Desmond Pacey concludes that *Wild Geese* "is the single most consistent piece of western realism to appear before the novels of Frederick Philip Grove, and has a niche of its own in . . . our literary development."[38] Also in 1965, on 2 April, a ninety minute radio version of *Wild Geese* was aired on "CBC Stage."[39] In 1968 Stanley C. Stanko completed the first thesis on the Ostenso fiction. Entitled "Image, Theme, and Pattern in the Works of Martha Ostenso," it divides the novels into three groups: works dealing with tyranny and guilt, works which exhibit a pattern of decline, fall, and regeneration, and three novels which explore relationships between "vital male" and "creative female" figures.[40]

Since 1970 the pace of critical response has gradually quickened, marked by the appearance of half a dozen articles, two substantive sections of books on prairie literature, a full doctoral dissertation and part of another, and more M.A. theses. The main focus of these works, taken collectively, is still on *Wild Geese*, but two of the articles deal with *The Young May Moon*, and two others make more than passing reference to later fiction. Both Alexander H. Jones, whose thesis "Martha Ostenso's Novels: A Study of Three Dominant Themes" was completed in 1970, and Becky-Jean Hjartarson, whose "A Study of Conflict in the Major Novels of Martha Ostenso" was finished in 1976, look at particular themes which appear in many of the novels.[41] Like Stanko, each of these writers pays attention to the recurrent concept of tyranny, though Jones sees it as one of three sources of family tension (along with incompatibility and isolation) and Hjartarson views it in terms of conflict between parent and child, man and woman, and between the potentially independent woman and her society. Joan Buckley's dissertation, "Martha Ostenso: A Critical Study of Her Novels," also completed in 1976, offers an overview of the Ostenso canon from a remarkably similar perspective.[42] The study's central focus is on conflict, both within families and in terms of male-female relationships, but it goes beyond this to take into account man in conflict with himself and with the land.

Buckley also comments on technical shortcomings in the fiction, such as the frequent use of sentimental endings and the too-often unfocussed point of view. The dissertation has a useful bibliography, including information about elusive short stories published in unindexed periodicals. A 1978 thesis by Rosaleen McFadden is more specialized. In "Icelandic Edda and Saga in Two Prairie Novels: An Analysis of *The Viking Heart* . . . and *Wild Geese*," she explores mythopoeic patterns in *Wild Geese* based on the *eddas*, the principal source of Norse myth.[43] She argues that the central characters each have their counterparts in myth: Judith is linked to the Norse fertility goddess Freyja, Amelia with the goddess of motherhood Frigga, and Caleb with Loki, the devil.

Recent published criticism is generally more tightly knit than the unpublished studies, although Brita Mickleburgh's "Martha Ostenso: The Design of Her Canadian Prose Fiction," which looks at related images in three novels (*Wild Geese*, *The Dark Dawn*, and *Prologue to Love*), is a rather uncoordinated application of some of Northrop Frye's critical apparatus.[44] M. G. Hesse's "The Endless Quest: Dreams and Aspirations in Martha Ostenso's *Wild Geese*" also pays some attention to *The Dark Dawn*, as well as to *The Waters under the Earth* and *O River, Remember*, in an attempt to reinforce observations about thematic patterns in *Wild Geese*.[45] Essays by Stanley S. Atherton ("Ostenso Revisited") and Clara Thomas ("Martha Ostenso's Trial of Strength") move from discussion of *Wild Geese* to examine *The Young May Moon*, but are not concerned with the other novels. Both critics focus on the protagonist in *The Young May Moon*, Marcia Vorse, and the living nightmare of her desperate search for inner strength and peace; and both essays comment on narrative technique, agreeing that *The Young May Moon* is "a novel whose seriousness of theme is more satisfyingly matched by its tightness of structure and total artistic consistency" than is the case in *Wild Geese*.[46]

The approaches to *Wild Geese* in some articles reveal the beginnings of a critical dialogue on the novel. Laurence Ricou devotes one of the eight chapters in *Vertical Man/Horizontal World* ("Man and Landscape in Canadian Prairie Fiction") to *Wild Geese*.[47] Entitled "The Obsessive Prairie: Martha Ostenso's *Wild Geese*," the chapter offers a perceptive look at Ostenso's "serious and comprehensive vision" in terms of an imaginative response to the physical environment.[48] Ricou pays a lot of attention to Caleb Gare's relationship to the land, and his analysis of Caleb's death has led to an alternative reading in my own "Ostenso Revisited." Robert G. Lawrence takes Ricou's interest in landscape a step further in "The Geography of Martha Ostenso's *Wild Geese*," an essay in which he innovatively maps the layout of the Gare farm and the community of Oeland from clues scattered throughout the novel.[49] In *Unnamed Country: The Struggle for a Canadian Prairie Fiction*, Dick Harrison argues from a different perspective. In his view, *Wild Geese* "could be seen as a demonic counterpart to the idyllic romances [of earlier writers such as Connor and McClung], a wholesome antidote because it grants the true power to some of the dark forces in human and external nature."[50] In this frame of reference, Caleb Gare becomes "a creature of romance" with "the larger-than-life dimensions of a romantic villain."[51] In this original interpretation (which includes a look at Caleb's biblical ancestry), Harrison not only enriches our understanding of the novel's imaginative resonances, but also suggests the wealth of interpretive possibilities implicit in *Wild Geese*. David Arnason's dissertation, "The Development of Prairie Realism: Robert J.C. Stead, Douglas Durkin, Martha Ostenso and Frederick Philip Grove," agrees with Clara Thomas and Dick Harrison that the novel is a blend of realistic and romantic elements, though he questions Harrison's casting of Caleb Gare in the role of romantic villain.[52] W. J. Keith, in "*Wild Geese*: The Death of Caleb Gare," engages both Grove's early assessment ("Caleb's end is twaddle") and Dick Harrison's interpretation of the event, and offers two surprisingly similar literary antecedents for Caleb's horrible death.[53] More recently, Barbara Godard has brought feminist criticism to bear on *Wild Geese* in a conference paper entitled "The View from Below: The Female Novel of the Land."[54] In summary, recent and continuing critical attention paid to *Wild Geese* confirms its acceptance as an important landmark in our literary tradition. The position of later Ostenso fiction, though it offers fertile ground for analysis and evaluation, remains obscured.

Ostenso's Works

To put the fiction in perspective, it is useful to have an overview of the literary career carved out together by Martha Ostenso and Douglas Durkin. Although we can not be certain how much Durkin worked with Ostenso on *Wild Geese*, circumstantial evidence suggests that he was somehow involved in its creation.[55] If the collaboration was at all extensive, then the novel clearly had an unfair advantage over the other 1388 entries in the contest. Whether the novel would have attracted as much attention if it had not won the well-publicized competition is open to debate; but it seems likely that the subsequent careers of Ostenso and Durkin would have turned out differently. But *Wild Geese* did win, whether there was deliberate fraud involved or not. And what happened after that is more a story of commercial shrewdness than anything else. The market for Ostenso's fiction had been established — additional novels under her name were expected — and together she and Durkin set out to satisfy the demand. Novels followed one another in rapid succession: by 1930 there were five of them, by 1938 another five, and so on. The quality was distinctly uneven. For the most part the novels were flawed, sometimes badly so, because they were written quickly for an assured and essentially unsophisticated market. In a few instances they transcended the conventions of popular fiction and rose to the level of competent, even challenging, writing. But with one notable exception, Ostenso and Durkin had completed their best work by 1930. After that, most of the novels smacked of commercialism, the most obvious example being the release in 1933 of *There's Always Another Year*, with its hopeful title, hopeful heroine named Silver, and silver-coloured cover to cater to the escapist dreams of Depression-weary readers. After the War, sensing the sweeping changes that were reforming North American tastes, Ostenso and Durkin tried to write new kinds of novels. They began to use urban settings and to explore new patterns of relationships with more sophisticated characters; the novels took on a tone of muted hectoring, rejecting the rapidly changing present in favour of a more stable, ordered past; but none of it worked. The authors were simply out of touch with the times, and the novels were not well received. Their final novel, *A Man Had Tall Sons*, returned to the rural setting and characters of pre-War novels, but it too was a commercial and critical disappointment.

It seems sensible in this brief evaluation to concentrate on the best of the Ostenso fiction: *Wild Geese*, *The Young May Moon*, and *O River, Remember*. Succinct comments on the other novels (with particular reference to the Canadian works) will round off the study. For Canadian readers, *Wild Geese* has always been the most accessible of the Ostenso novels, and it has received the most critical attention. It is also, arguably, the best in the canon, though increased accessibility to *The Young May Moon* and possibly to *O River, Remember* could alter the ranking. In some ways *Wild Geese* stands as a model for later Ostenso novels: there are a number of integrated patterns — in theme, structure, and character relationships — which appear in this novel and reappear frequently in the later fiction. The common denominator for these patterns is confrontation, usually manifested in battles between life-affirming and life-denying forces, and worked out in bitter conflicts between individual characters. In *Wild Geese* and many of the other novels the family occupies centre stage, and traditional familial conflicts (parent-child, husband-wife) dominate the action. The conflicts worked through in this sharply focussed environment are neither limited nor petty, however: the antagonists represent forces and principles which extend far beyond their individual lives to touch us all. So the monstrous tyranny exerted over his family by Caleb Gare, one of the principal characters in *Wild Geese*, dramatizes our concern with universal principles of freedom and bondage; and the guilt that paralyses communication between family members leads us to consider the implications of all forces which isolate one human being from another. In most Ostenso novels such conflicts provide the dynamics of plot, allowing the reader to chart graphically the ebb and flow of battle and the peaks and valleys of success and failure for individual characters.

Wild Geese chronicles the events of a single summer — between the coming and going of the geese that give the novel its title — in the northern Manitoba farm community of Oeland. Told mainly (though not exclusively) through the perceptions of Lind Archer, a school teacher from outside the community, the story centres on Caleb Gare, his family, and his farm. Caleb tyrannizes his wife, Amelia, with the threat that he will reveal the secret of an illegitimate son she bore to a fiancée who was killed before she met Caleb, thereby shaming her and branding her son a bastard. Caleb reinforces his hold over Amelia when her son, Mark Jordan, turns up in Oeland and begins courting Lind Archer, who boards with the Gares. Caleb also brutalizes his children, forbidding them all social and civilizing influences and forcing them to work incessantly to satisfy his greed for ever more land and wealth. Only one of them, seventeen-year-old Judith, rebels at the oppression. Her pregnancy, the result of an affair with Sven Sandbo, a young man from the neighbouring farm, provides the catalyst for her escape from Caleb's domination. Judith's resolve galvanizes her mother to stand up to Caleb as well, and the resulting confrontation provides the novel with its most dramatic scene. At the moment when Amelia forces Caleb to face the truth about himself and his life, he must also confront a natural disaster when a sudden brush fire threatens to destroy his painstakingly tended crops. Temporarily unbalanced by this double blow to his self-esteem, Caleb discounts the danger of crossing a piece of muskeg as he hurries to save his precious field of flax. But the ineluctable pull of the muskeg draws him in: he is caught and dies, horribly and alone.

The bare facts of plot can only hint at the nature and scale of human confrontation in the novel. Virginia Woolf pointed out in her famous essay, "Mr. Bennett and Mrs. Brown," that the most important thing in a novel is the portrayal of character. On the evidence of *Wild Geese*, it is clear that Ostenso agreed, for the characterization of Caleb Gare makes him one of the most memorable figures in Canadian fiction.[56] As I have mentioned elsewhere, Caleb is at the centre of *Wild Geese*, a mad and monstrous being who terrorizes his wife and children, cheats and bullies his neighbours, and is seen as "a spiritual counterpart of the land, as harsh, as demanding, as tyrannical as the very soil from which he drew his existence."[57] The source of Caleb's malevolence is his lust for power, his insensate need to dominate; and it is exercised over his family through the unwilling help of his wife, who will do anything to stop him revealing the parentage of her illegitimate son. According to Dick Harrison, Caleb "is a creature of romance," described initially in such a way as to give him "the larger-than-life dimensions of a romantic villain."[58] While not wholly convincing (partly because it relies only on the initial description of Caleb, partly because it discounts the precise nature of Ostenso's adjectives), Harrison's argument is provocative. For the characterization of Caleb Gare clearly partakes of both naturalism and romance. Although later in the novel we see him in a number of naturalistic poses (dodging an axe flung by Judith, stealthily caressing his flax, whipping Amelia), he retains an extra dimension as representative of evil forces. If there is a problem in characterization in *Wild Geese* (and to a greater or lesser extent in the later fiction), it is that one character often overwhelms the novel and other characters are relegated to roles in which their function is more important than their individuality. So Caleb's children become unnatural caricatures, subjugating their dreams and desires to his will, beaten into passive acceptance of their lot by his unquenchable appetite for power, wealth, and land. Ellen, the elder daughter, "reasoned only as Caleb had taught her to reason, in terms of advantage to the land and to him" (*WG*, p. 96); her twin brother Martin "worked with the bowed, unquestioning resignation of an old unfruitful man" (*WG*, p. 36). Judith is an exception, however, and as a more fully developed character provokes our interest and invites our sympathy.

This is as it should be, for it is in the confrontation between Judith and Caleb that the important issues of *Wild Geese* are dramatized and its structural patterns developed. Their struggle is a contest of individual wills; but it is also a collision between the life-denying forces embodied by Caleb and the life-embracing and affirming forces which Judith represents. The opposition is clearly apparent in their differing reactions to the land. For Caleb the land is something to be owned and dominated. It is above all else "*his* land," and whatever it produced is the "result of *his* industry" (*WG*, p. 249). Although for him the time of growth in the fields is "a terrific, prolonged hour of passion," it is a passion perverted:

> while he was raptly considering the tender field of flax — now in blue flower — Amelia did not exist to him . . . . Caleb would stand for long moments outside the fence beside the flax. Then he would turn quickly to see that no one was looking. He would creep between the wires and run his hand across the flowering, gentle tops of the growth. A stealthy caress — more intimate than any he had ever given to woman. (*WG*, p. 171)

"The land has become a substitute for Caleb's wife," as Laurence Ricou has pointed out, and like Amelia, the land must be bent to his will.[59] It remains an implacable adversary, however, offering him only the perennial challenge "to force from the soil all that it would withhold" (*WG*, p. 250). Blinded to other considerations, Caleb comes to see the land (even his favoured field of flax) only in terms of profit, as a means to secure ever greater amounts of the wealth and power he obsessively craves.[60]

In sharp contrast, Judith's relationship with the natural world is one of passionate kinship. Early in the novel she lies naked on the warm spring earth, revelling in "the waxy feeling of new sunless vegetation under her," knowing intuitively that she had been "singled

. . . out from the rest of the Gares" to apprehend the mystery of life, "something forbiddenly beautiful, secret as one's own body" (*WG*, p. 67). Judith embraces the natural world, literally and figuratively, in a scene that is powerfully reminiscent of D.H. Lawrence:

> At the spring . . . she threw herself upon the moss under the birches, grasping the slender trunks of the trees in her hands and straining her body against the earth. She had taken off the heavy overalls and the coolness of the ground crept into her loose clothing. The light from the setting sun seemed to run down the smooth white bark of the birches like gilt. There was no movement, except the narrow trickle of the water from the spring, and the occasional flare of a bird above the brown depth of the pool. There was no sound save the tuning of the frogs in the marsh that seemed far away, and the infrequent call of a catbird on the wing. Here was clarity undreamed of, such clarity as the soul should have in desire and fulfillment. Judith held her breasts in ecstasy. (*WG*, p. 216)

Judith's openness, her ability to accept and respond to the elemental rhythms of the natural world, stands in direct opposition to the perverted responses of Caleb, who must turn everything he touches to his own unnatural ends.

Physically as well as spiritually, Caleb and Judith are poles apart. Caleb is physically repulsive. His "tremendous and massive head" at first "gave him a towering appearance. [But] when attention was directed to the lower half of his body, he seemed visibly to dwindle" (*WG*, p. 5). "Broad and bent over," he moves with a "dragging step," "his top-heavy body forming an arc toward the earth" (*WG*, pp. 262, 269, 270). Other characters in the novel see him as a hypocrite, "too sly for honest people," an insane egoist, and a murderer (*WG*, p. 286). In extra-human terms he is "demoniacal," "an old satyr," and "the devil himself" (*WG*, pp. 8, 36, 104). Judith, on the other hand, is a sensual passionate beauty, "the embryonic ecstasy of all life" (*WG*, p. 35). She is "like some dark young goddess," and sees herself as "an alien spirit . . . in no way related to the life about her," unwilling to submit like her mother and siblings to a "meager and warped" life under her tyrannical father (*WG*, pp. 97, 124, 332).

She defies him openly, denouncing his insatiable demands on members of the family, and clandestinely, in meetings with her lover

Sven Sandbo, a young Norwegian "god" from the neighbouring farm (*WG*, p. 216). When Caleb threatens to beat her into submission, after spying on her love-making with Sven, she flings an axe at him, narrowly missing his head. The scene is superbly drawn, and provides the novel with a memorable metaphor for the fundamental antagonism of the forces Judith and Caleb represent. The confrontation is not climactic: Caleb has yet to provoke the terrible defiance of Amelia. But it does dramatically reinforce the patterns of conflict — repression and freedom, denial and affirmation — which are at the heart of *Wild Geese*. After the attempt to kill her father, Judith is virtually imprisoned on the farm and Caleb's tyranny seems unassailable. A resolution is achieved when Judith, who is bearing Sven's child, is helped to escape by Lind Archer and by Amelia, who is unwilling to let Caleb destroy her daughter's life as he had her own. Caleb's death, which swiftly follows Judith's flight into life, is both appalling and ironically appropriate.[61] Laurence Ricou has argued that the resolution of *Wild Geese* is too compressed, that "the suddenness with which the fire follows Amelia's critical defiance and Caleb's moment of 'shame and self-loathing' is inconsistent with the subtle development of the novel to this point."[62] Such a reading fails to take into account the enormity of Caleb's transgressions, which require a retributive devastation of his being that must be swift and complete to achieve the optimum dramatic effect. So it is appropriate that man and nature combine in a single powerfully drawn sequence of events to annihilate him — spiritually through the knowledge of Judith's escape and the harrowing impact of Amelia's defiance, physically by earth, air, fire, and water.

The dramatically different reactions to the land exhibited by Caleb and Judith point to a pattern which Ostenso and Durkin used in many of the later novels. When battle is joined between two central characters, the reader's sympathies are always directed towards the character who has a strong affinity for the land and to the natural rhythm of the seasons. The technique is not only used with major figures; in fact, one of the predictable pleasures of reading the Ostenso novels grows from the authors' ability to capture in a few sure strokes the elements in the natural world which complement and highlight the emotional situation of even minor characters. One of the finest examples of this linkage is the description of Anton Klovacz' final journey in *Wild Geese*, as Mark Jordan and the farmer's eldest son take his body to the Catholic mission for burial.

The passage (in chapter xx, pp. 301–03) is marked by a mood of great loneliness, which echoes the feelings of the characters and the emptiness of the landscape. It also offers an intriguing paradigm of the entire novel. For *Wild Geese* might finally be read as a superb study of isolation: each of the central characters (and many of the minor ones as well) is touched by loneliness and forced in some way to explore its mystery. It is a powerful vision, reinforced by skillful repetition of the words "alone," "lonely," and "loneliness" in one scene after another to create an effect that is almost incantatory. The reader, caught up in the novelist's fascination with the "unmeasurable Alone surrounding each soul," is left at the end with the indelible, haunting image of the wild geese, whose "cry smote upon the heart like the loneliness of the universe . . . a magnificent seeking through solitude — an endless quest" (*WG*, pp. 57, 356).

Isolation and the concomitant problems of failures in communication are explored again in *The Young May Moon*, published four years after *Wild Geese*. The romantic title (taken from one of Thomas Moore's poems) is clearly inappropriate, as a number of contemporary reviews pointed out. Clara Thomas has suggested that "The Ordeal of Marcia Vorse" would have been more fitting, and her suggestion has merit.[63] For *The Young May Moon* focusses on the development through suffering of a single personality, and the conflicts it presents are essentially internal. While for Ostenso and Durkin the exigencies of story-telling required a number of other characters who either assist or obstruct the protagonist, the spotlight shines steadily throughout the novel on Marcia Vorse, illuminating her personal ordeal and the qualities which enable her to survive.

For the setting of *The Young May Moon* Ostenso and Durkin returned to the Lake Manitoba country which had provided the background for *Wild Geese*. The fictional town in which most of the action takes place is called Amaranth, and Marcia Vorse arrives there as the twenty-year-old bride of Rolf Gunther, a mother's boy and local lumber dealer.[64] After a winter of living in the house of Dorcas Gunther, the dominating, repressive mother-in-law who has hung a sampler above the young couple's bed with *"Repent Ye!"* "worked in red wool against a white background," Marcia is reduced to pleading with Rolf to make love to her.[65] After a passionate argument she runs away, returning a few hours later to find her husband drowned, a probable suicide. She stays on with Dorcas, partly to atone for the guilt she feels over Rolf's death, and submits to a soul-destroying regimen of domestic and spiritual tyranny. With the painful recognition that her life has become "dwarfed and twisted under the old woman's blighting intolerance," Marcia is finally able to confess her "responsibility" for Rolf's drowning to Dorcas, and to leave the house, taking her young son with her (YMM, p. 102). Her departure marks a turning point in the novel. In self-imposed isolation in a ruined house at the edge of town, she wrestles with her special demons, by turns exultant and terrified at what is happening to her. In the end, after a harrowing journey through self-reproach, denial, doubt, and fear, she comes to terms with herself and her obsession, helped in so small way by the young doctor Paul Brule, who has survived a similar crisis of his own.

The structure of The Young May Moon consists of a series of interlocking patterns of denial and affirmation. In the six-year time span of the novel, Marcia Vorse moves hesitantly but in clearly defined stages from guilt-ridden isolation to an acceptance of the life-affirming impulses within her and a recognition of her value to the community in which she lives. At the same time the lives of other characters which touch hers reflect complementary patterns of repression and denial, conviction and assertion. Intriguingly, the transformation of Marcia Vorse stands in direct contrast to the course of Caleb Gare's life. In both Wild Geese and The Young May Moon the central characters are obsessed with unacceptable variations of the most basic human events, a birth that is illegitimate and a death that is premature, but in coming to terms with their obsessions, the protagonists move in opposite directions on a moral spectrum. Caleb Gare sees himself as a victim and turns into a vengeful, life-denying tyrant, while Marcia Vorse, at first an apologist for atonement, rids herself of the "recurrent obsession" and joyously reaffirms life: at the end of the novel "all eternity was [for her now] but a single fierce stroke of rapture" (YMM, p. 298).

The road to self-assertion and fulfillment is not an easy one for Marcia Vorse. Buffeted by external influences and internal conflicts in the early months of marriage as her ebullient personality is gradually suppressed by the "prim patterns of denial" forced on her by Rolf's mother, she at first tries to accommodate herself to the situation (YMM, p. 73). She stops singing the carefree songs her father had taught her, and turns her gift for music into a "consecrated voice" in the church choir (YMM, p. 6). For a time she even denies her need for love-making — Dorcas's repressive motto over the bed having had its effect. But inevitably her vital impulses reaffirm themselves, and in the passionate outburst in which she pleads with Rolf for attention ("I want to be loved — to have a lover, Rolf. I want you for my lover.") she also threatens to leave him for another admirer (YMM, p. 8). Although she does leave, to spend an agonizing night alone appraising the strength of her feelings, she returns to a far worse situation than the one she had left.[66]

Trapped in Dorcas Gunther's house, largely because of her assumption of moral responsibility for Rolf's death and her need to atone for it, but also because she is pregnant and has very little money, Marcia becomes the semi-acquiescent victim of her mother-in-law's puritanical repression. It is clear that Dorcas Gunther's unwavering and perverted sense of moral righteousness (which echoes that of Caleb Gare) is meant to represent the darker side of the Puritan consciousness, and its manifestation is devastating. For Dorcas not only recognizes the symptoms of guilt in others, she manipulates them shamelessly to maintain her domestic and spiritual control. As a result, her home becomes Marcia's prison, and her "passion for curbing growth" defines Marcia's death-in-life existence for four years behind "the closed gate" from which she can only watch "all of April . . . young and wild and strange, shut out" (YMM, p. 73). When Dorcas' intolerance extends beyond the house, however, and affects an innocent child whose mother is the focus of malicious gossip, Marcia is moved to protest, and so begins the long road back to independence and self-respect. " 'I'm not surprised that little Hally's mother left,' " she tells Dorcas and her friends (YMM, p. 110). " 'She left because she wasn't strong enough to stay and work while women like you . . . flayed her with your tongues. She couldn't bear up under it. But I — I wouldn't go, I'll tell you. I'd stay — no matter what I had done — and no matter what you had to say about me. I'd stay until I starved to death rather than give you the satisfaction of thinking you had run me out of town' " (YMM, p. 110). Marcia's awakening recognition of the need to take her life into her own hands is reinforced by Paul Brule's forceful criticism of her existence with Dorcas:

"I have watched you . . . for four years — suffering remorse — doing penance — making a little hell for yourself and shutting yourself in. You think you are paying the price of your error. What you are really doing is losing your interest in living, letting yourself go to pieces, physically and morally, living a selfish, self-centered existence concerned only with your own little difficulties and never giving a thought to anyone else." (*YMM*, pp. 123–24)

Brule's argument, ostensibly on behalf of "Rolf Gunther's son," in whom he has taken a great interest, has a telling effect on Marcia, and she returns home to a shattering confrontation with Dorcas (*YMM*, p. 125).

In admitting her part in Rolf's death to Dorcas, Marcia is able to free herself physically and spiritually from the old woman's control. She also recognizes that release from the need of forgiveness by Dorcas Gunther's Puritan God offers no final absolution, and as she takes up residence in a ruin at the edge of town she begins a fresh and prolonged self-appraisal. There are moments of great joy in her new life: she learns to sing again, to share precious moments of make-believe with her little boy, and to take pride in the skills she acquires in creating a home out of the hillside ruin she had bought for a few dollars from local farmers. But the demons of doubt remain, challenging her need for a productive, useful life and a sharing, supportive relationship with another human being. For nearly two years the pendulum swings between denial and affirmation as Marcia "nurses her fear, her remorse, her inescapable loneliness" (*YMM*, p. 154). On the one hand, she worries about becoming known as a witch, like a Valkyrie "out of the mists of . . . Norse lore . . . [whose] rare singing on nights of rain or very clear starlight was an omen that bore hearkening to" (*YMM*, p. 153). On the other, she experiences days "when the future was a vital hope that sent her singing to the work that awaited her" (*YMM*, p. 155). She is physically attracted to Paul Brule at the same time as she is repelled by his assumption of knowledge of an emotional and spiritual condition she is unable or unwilling to define for herself. When she learns by chance of Rolf's pre-marital affair with a local girl, Rosina Machlet, Marcia realizes that her own needs and loneliness are not unique — that even Rolf, whom she had turned into a kind of saint before whose memory she measured her own unworthiness, was in his own way also "utterly alone" and weak (*YMM*, p. 186).

The recognition is a kind of epiphany for Marcia, and opens the way for her acceptance of Paul Brule's diagnosis of her situation. For Brule, who had suffered (and finally overcome) his own obsession for a wife who had divorced him, speaks with authority when he tells her that ultimately each of us is

"alone. So damned alone . . . . We fill our lives with ideas — loves, hates, ambitions — thinking to make companions of them, so to speak. But something in us always remains separate, nevertheless, unapproachable. You, now — you and your puny, stubborn will — you've been deceiving yourself with the belief that all life hangs on this something you call atonement — nothing but an illusion — a companion in your own peculiar aloneness. There is no such thing."
Marcia laughed sharply.
"No such thing as atonement, you mean?"
"Of course. If there were, there would be a point, wouldn't there, indicating a place where atonement was achieved? It's nothing but a device by which you shield yourself from the unbearable truth."
"And that is — " Marcia looked down at her hands, lying tightly folded on the table.
"That you have done something irrevocable. Atonement, remorse, repentance, all hokum." (*YMM*, pp. 242–44)

Intellectual acceptance of such an explanation is one thing, but as Marcia points out, such powerful ideas are not so easily dismissed: " 'they can cast a spell over you' " (*YMM*, p. 244). The breaking of the spell involves a final trial for Marcia, and in a sense it is the most severe of her long ordeal. When Paul later tells her of his agony in laying to rest the ghost of passion for his ex-wife, he offers persuasive proof " 'that it's possible for a man to find his way back — back to the tangle — and unravel it' " (*YMM*, p. 292). But it is only when he asks Marcia to marry him that he forces her to travel her own road back, to find and unravel the tangle of her own emotional and spiritual past. For Marcia will not accept Paul, or life either for that matter, until she can come to terms with herself. Unwilling to compromise herself for what she thinks is only sexual desire, her first impulse is to leave Amaranth at once and for good. Then, in a dramatic re-enactment of the novel's opening scene, she returns to Bethune, the nearby village where she grew up, and walks back along the railway track to Amaranth. Only in this way could she "trace the thread of life — find the knot — untangle it" (*YMM*, p. 298).

Alone in the prairie night, she lays the ghost of Rolf Gunther to rest, and comes to see that her place is with life and the living. Back in town, she stops at the house where Dorcas Gunther had lived and recently died, and in her old room finds that darkness had swallowed up the flaming motto over the bed. At peace, with her past exorcised and her re-entry into life confirmed, Marcia can finally go home.

> The length of the path to her own doorway dwindled under her feet . . . . In the morning she would go down to the Stornos', and bring little Rolf home . . . . Before noon, old Jonas would wander up to begin cutting the birch from that new hillside acre. Also, there were those new potatoes she had promised to take to Herb Lundy's; she would have to send Jonas down with them in the afternoon. In the evening Paul Brule would come once more up the pathway. He had said he would . . . .
> She rested her head back against the tree trunk and closed her eyes. A slight wind moved through the thorn-apple tree; it moved across darkness and sleep, on and on. (*YMM*, p. 301)

The final paragraphs of *The Young May Moon* echo a narrative pattern established in *Wild Geese*: a compelling account of intense struggle is followed by a sense of calm and a final reassurance of life's continuity. It is a pattern as old as the story-teller's art, but one which remains remarkably satisfying, despite its conventionality. Ostenso and Durkin favoured endings like this, but they were not locked into the pattern, and later novels ended in a variety of ways. Nonetheless, one constant in all the Ostenso fiction is a strong sense of continuity in the sweep of human history. Many of the novels, especially those set on the prairies, deal with family life extending over a number of generations. Most of the half-dozen American works classified by Roy W. Meyer as middle-western farm novels, for example, deal with two generations and have characters from a third making cameo appearances. *O River, Remember*, the most memorable of the American novels, is structured in terms of the generations, with a time sequence which moves from a present generation now (1941) back through grandparents in the 1870s and forward again to focus on parents ("those who were young then: 1888–1902").[67]

O River, Remember traces the lives of Magdali and Ivar Vinge, a Norwegian couple who immigrate to Minnesota in the 1870s. They settle on the banks of the Red River and prosper as hard-working pioneers. Their five children grow up in a mid-west that is transformed in the course of the novel from prairie wilderness to a milieu of well-established farms and thriving towns. A second family, the Shaleens, counterpoints the material success of the Vinges (who soon change their name to Wing) with a more relaxed attitude to "getting ahead" and a corresponding emphasis on achievement in the worlds of music and art. For two generations the families live in uneasy proximity, troubled by a series of romantic and star-crossed relationships. Only in the third generation is a love affair between a Wing and a Shaleen allowed to run its natural course. The force that keeps the families apart as much as possible is the powerful personality of Magdali Wing, and *O River, Remember* is essentially her story. As in earlier Ostenso fiction, a single character casts a shadow over the entire novel: in this case, the character's strength is such that "a dozen assorted Wings and Shaleens are needed to serve adequately as her foil."[68] For Magdali Wing is an accomplished and manipulating tyrant, and *O River, Remember*, like *Wild Geese* and so many other Ostenso novels, is a full-scale study of the devastation such a character can wreck on the lives of those around her.

As Richard Cordell pointed out in *The Saturday Review of Literature*, Magdali Wing represents "the pioneer spirit in its least glamorous and lovely aspects: in her steady advance from the sod-house to her vast country house . . . she brushes aside as ridiculous or sentimental any distinction between private enterprise and exploitation, success and happiness, bad luck and shiftlessness."[69] Like Caleb Gare, she is consumed with "building a little empire," exploiting land and neighbour alike (*ORR*, p. 221). Early in the novel, Magdali (along with her equally unscrupulous brother Roald) takes advantage of a neighbour's ignorance of the coming railway and escalating land values to buy him out cheaply. A short time later they resell the land at enormous profit. When Magdali's fair-dealing husband hears of the transactions and protests, she distracts his attention and neutralizes his dissent by succumbing to a sudden weakness brought on by advanced pregnancy. Although in this instance the illness may have been real (we are never sure), Magdali uses the same technique on a number of later occasions when she feigns or exaggerates illness to manipulate both Ivar and their children in order to get her own selfish way. Direct confrontations between Magdali and Ivar are rare, however: we usually learn about his reactions to her schemes through the omniscient narrator. Nonetheless, Ivar continues to function as a moral corrective to Magdali's unprincipled activities, representing as he does a genuine love of the land, honest vision, and an incorruptible sense of fairness. He outlives her by more than a dozen years, and is still alive at the end of the novel when the story of his generation merges with that of his grandchildren.

Although Ivar is by turns angry, frustrated, and depressed by Magdali's schemes to advance the family fortunes (she has the Presidency for a child or grandchild as the ultimate goal), he suffers less than a number of other victims of his wife's machinations. Their children in particular are all spiritually or psychologically damaged, as are a number of the Shaleen children who fall in love with them. The Shaleens are perceived by Magdali as shiftless and impious (they drink, sing secular songs on Sundays, and their "flower garden, though things grew luxuriantly there, had no order to it"), and they are clearly excluded from her grand design (ORR, p. 259). When Karsten Wing, who wants to become a painter, falls passionately in love with Rose Shaleen, he makes the mistake of informing his mother, who promptly invites Rose for coffee and a private chat. Surely and cleverly, she convinces the impressionable Rose that her deceased parents' occupation as saloon-keepers could be used to compromise Karsten's future career in the legal profession Magdali has chosen for him. If Rose really loves Karsten, Magdali tells her, she must protect him by giving him up. To close the interview she gives Rose "a scarlet banner of silk" with which to make a party dress (ORR, p. 323). Rose throws the material away as soon as she discovers its colour, but it is taken by the wind and catches in the branches of a tree. It is also caught in the reader's consciousness, and provides an ironic prophecy of subsequent events. Although Magdali has her way — Rose refuses to see Karsten, who later becomes a lawyer and marries his partner's daughter — Karsten's loveless marriage ends in divorce, and his subsequent affair with Rose, who has married an insipid bank clerk, leads to her violent death at the hands of her estranged husband. Later, when childhood friendship between the Wing's youngest daughter, Olina, and David Shaleen grows into love, it too is frustrated by Magdali's calculated opposition.[70] David returns from a year studying sculpture in Paris, and asks Olina to marry him and leave for New York at once. But as the last daughter at home, Olina feels constrained to tell her mother first. Magdali is in bed, "recovering" from a simulated illness brought on by the elopement two weeks earlier of another daughter, Solveig. On hearing Olina's news, Magdali feigns a relapse, but recovers momentarily to tell Olina that her marriage to David "would kill me" (*ORR*, p. 351). Overwhelmed by guilt, Olina rejects David's offer and her own chance for happiness. Once again, the consequences of Magdali's manipulation are disastrous. Olina is manoeuvred into a marriage of convenience with a well-off man twice her age, and within a year she dies in child-birth in the local hospital. The other Wing children are molded in Magdali's own image: Arne turns into a spiritually stunted, unscrupulous real estate broker, and Magdis becomes an unimaginative Puritan drudge, whose "reverence for work, inherited from her mother, might have been called a virtue if it had been even lightly tinctured with joy" (*ORR*, p. 236).

Curiously, because she clearly dominates the novel, Magdali Wing is a far more shadowy figure than other Ostenso protagonists such as Caleb Gare or Marcia Vorse. There are two main reasons for this elusiveness: first, we see Magdali almost completely from the outside through the perceptions of the narrator or the eyes of other characters; second, much greater emphasis is placed on the *effects* of her activity rather than on the moments in which she initiates a chain of events. Yet despite these barriers to our direct apprehension of her, Magdali Wing comes alive with an undeniable power to move us, to engage our interest and provoke our response.[71] Other technical paradoxes mark the novel. The point of view is clearly inconsistent, for example, and therefore potentially disconcerting to the sophisticated reader. Yet in *O River, Remember* the shifts in and out of the consciousness of various characters, the comments of an omniscient narrator, and even clichéd means of establishing credibility, such as having young Olina eavesdrop on a conversation between Magdali and Rose Shaleen, blend harmoniously to create a convincing sense of verisimilitude. The novel's plot is not particularly coherent; in fact the only real sense of order outside the repetitive pattern of Magdali's machinations is provided by the passage of time, and even that is dislocated by the inclusion of chapters which comment from the perspective of time present on events which happen later in the novel but in an earlier time frame. Yet despite this, *O River, Remember* succeeds, moving forward in a series of brilliant, related vignettes which focus and bring to life the recurring dramas that take place within Magdali Wing's sphere of influence. One is reminded in reading it of the panoramic novels of Dickens, which also transcend technical imperfections — too frequently flat characters, improbable coincidences, excessive sentimentality, and so on — yet continue to work their magic on our sensibilities.

O *River, Remember* is a special case, however, and Ostenso and Durkin's other novels are considerably more pedestrian. Of the thirteen, eleven are set in the United States and two in Canada. One of the Canadian novels, *Prologue to Love*, is interesting for its insights into the social history of the Okanagan Valley, even though it has little literary merit. The novel is a formulaic romance in which a twenty-three-year-old beauty, Autumn Dean, comes back to live with her widowed father, Jarvis, on a ranch near Kelowna. Years before, Jarvis Dean had accidentally killed Geoffrey Landor, the man with whom his wife was in love, and though he was never found out, the man's wife suspects him and allows a bitter hatred to grow and fester inside her. When Autumn falls in love with the dead man's son, Bruce, the stage is set for a series of melodramatic confrontations, but the inevitable happy end is predictable. Still, the novel has its place in Canadian literary history, both as a fictional record of the lives of well-off British-born ranchers in the Okanagan region during the 1920s, and as a document attesting to Ostenso and Durkin's interest in maintaining a connection with Canada long after the success of their American careers was assured.

The White Reef, published three years after *Prologue to Love*, is a much better novel. Set in a fishing village near Port Alberni on the Pacific shore of Vancouver Island, it explores the pride and passion of Nona Darnell, an independent twenty-six-year-old single parent. The first three of the novel's nineteen chapters narrate the events that led to Nona's present situation, and the rest of the novel takes place during a single summer and fall. At the age of nineteen, Nona had fallen in love with Quentin Wingate, the son of a wealthy Vancouver businessman who owns the local fish processing plant. She runs off with him to Vancouver, where they plan to marry. But when Quentin's mother and sister patronize Nona and tell her that Quentin is engaged to the wealthy daughter of family friends, she leaves in rage but with her pride intact, and returns to the village. When she has an illegitimate son, she refuses to be intimidated by scandalized relatives and local gossips, and turns down an offer of marriage that would make her respectable in the eyes of the village. Six years later, Quentin returns. Guilt ridden at his treatment of Nona, and fed up with letting himself be controlled by his wife's money — his own family had lost everything in the Depression — he is determined to reactivate the fish plant and also to repay the villagers money which his father had swindled out of them years before in a get-rich-quick scheme. Ironically, Quentin only learns of his son's existence the day after the boy drowns. Nona's grief at her son's death is intense: she temporarily loses her reason, and her recuperation is long and difficult. An encounter with Quentin rekindles her pride and her ambivalent feelings about him, and after initially rejecting him, she comes slowly to the recognition that his struggle has been no less harrowing than her own. In the end she allows him to re-enter her life; and the final chapter of the novel reaffirms the strength of their renewed commitment and the sense of equality which is at its core.

Unlike Autumn Dean and other romantic heroines of the Ostenso canon, Nona Darnell is a spiritual sister to Marcia Vorse; and *The White Reef* is reminiscent of the earlier novel in a number of ways. In both novels the protagonist loses a lover and suffers intensely because of it. Each woman must cope with being socially ostracized, and must bear her suffering alone. In each case the situation is made doubly difficult by the responsibilities of single parenthood. Each woman must go through an agonizing personal reappraisal as the result of the death by drowning of an important male figure in her life. And in the end both Marcia and Nona not only survive their ordeals, but emerge from them reaffirming an inner strength and sense of independence while at the same time recognizing the value of an intense commitment to another human being.

All this is not to say that *The White Reef* is as good a novel as *The Young May Moon*. It is not; and there are notable differences in the way similar raw material is handled in the two books. *The White Reef* suffers from the lack of a single consistent point of view, and from a certain blurring of focus which is caused partly by the attempt to present Quentin's struggle as a counterpoint to Nona's. We learn a great deal about Quentin's situation, for example, through the omniscient narrator or through Quentin's conversation with Timothy Entwhistle, an elderly villager. In *The Young May Moon*, on the other hand, we know as little as Marcia about Paul Brule's agony until he tells her about it. *The White Reef* also descends occasionally into melodrama, and more than one scene is marred by dramatic posturing and overwrought dialogue. There are also too many minor characters who have little direct effect on Nona's situation, and who get in the way of a clear exposition of her dilemma. Still, the novel does have a number of solid virtues. It deals at length with the struggle of an independent woman against social prejudices of her time and place in ways which make it remarkably apposite to our own. The dialogue (with the exceptions just noted) is generally crisp and credible; and the descriptions of the coastal environment are both evocative and memorable. On balance, *The White Reef* stands up surprisingly well, and deserves to be more widely known.

The same can not be said of Ostenso and Durkin's other eleven novels, most of which should be left to gather dust on library shelves. Some, like the proverbial curate's egg, are good in parts, but none of them comes consistently near the level of achievement represented by *Wild Geese, The Young May Moon,* and *O River, Remember.* Six of them might conveniently be called border novels, since they are set in rural areas in states which have a common boundary with either northwestern Ontario, Manitoba, or Saskatchewan, and usually include some reference to Canadian connections or experience. They are *The Dark Dawn, The Mad Carews, There's Always Another Year, The Stone Field, The Mandrake Root,* and *A Man Had Tall Sons.* Two of these, *The Mad Carews* and *The Stone Field,* present a situation in which a poor but clever farm girl marries into a prominent local family whose power comes from extensive land holdings. In each case the girl identifies with an older family member who represents solid values now in danger of being lost, and in the end, after much sound and fury, things turn out well for her and her husband. While not dull, these novels are unsatisfying because of their predictable plots and stereotypical characters. An air of fairy tale unreality pervades both of them; or as Johan Smertenko suggested in his review of *The Mad Carews,* "the aristocratic Carews ... form an improbable and impossible group out of Mrs. Radcliffe's romances. They neither win conviction nor awaken sympathy."[72] The comment applies equally, with suitable change of family name, to *The Stone Field.*

Two other novels, *The Dark Dawn* and *A Man Had Tall Sons,* have some interest as tentative studies of sexual politics. In both of them a battle for control, based on conflicting definitions of appropriate sexual roles, extends beyond domestic confines and into the community. *The Dark Dawn* presents a strong but predatory woman named Hattie Murker who seduces an idealistic young farmer named Lucian Dorrit, who in turn feels compelled to marry her. Lucian's predictable rebellion against Hattie's domestic tyranny and her use of him to consolidate control over others in the community quickly turns either into silliness (when he marks his rebellion by re-labelling her milk cans with his name) or melodrama (when he threatens to move to the attic and she retaliates with a suicide attempt which she bungles). Although Hattie is bedridden and paralyzed, she continues to rule "despotically, from the minutest detail in the running of the house to the most important business transaction in the managing of the farm," and every day "Lucian talked with her in her room, as a hireling might talk with his employer."[73] Unfortunately Lucian never becomes a credible or adequate opponent for Hattie, and the rich potential of their conflict is never developed. He is freed from her tyranny only at the end of the novel, when she dies. *A Man Had Tall Sons* explores the emotions of Luke Darr, a fifty-two-year-old widower who had always resented his wife's dominance. He marries twenty-five-year-old Bess, planning to mold her into his image of what a wife should be. Conflict quickly develops, and there are some remarkably effective confrontations as Luke and Bess struggle to achieve a balance of power. Unhappily the conflict is complicated by the presence of Luke's three grown sons, who resent his attempt to control their lives as well. The suicide of one of them initiates a sudden alteration in Luke's behaviour as he comes to see the grave risks of attempting to control the lives of others. The resolution is too neat, and too clearly imposed from outside, and because of this the novel loses much of its impact. Disappointingly, neither *A Man Had Tall Sons* nor *The Dark Dawn* develops the rich potential of the subject they begin to explore with such promise.

The *Mandrake Root* is the best of the border novels, and prefigures *O River, Remember* in its treatment of Norwegian pioneers in Minnesota. The novel recounts the tragic consequences of Eric Stene's return to the farm where he had grown up, to write a book about his pioneer grandfather. The couple now renting the farm, Andrew and Lydie Clarence, are childless, and Lydie decides to use Eric as a mandrake root to remedy the situation. Although she is successful in seducing him and in conceiving a child, Andrew learns of her adultery and commits suicide. Eric fails in his attempt to get Lydie to leave the farm with him and start a new life elsewhere, and the novel ends on an unusually ambiguous note. In some ways, *The Mandrake Root* is stronger than anything since *The Young May Moon*. The use of passages from the diary of Eric's grandfather (the farm's original owner) to comment obliquely on the action is particularly effective;

and occasional scenes, such as the one describing Andrew's confrontation with Eric over the adultery, show how well Ostenso and Durkin could write when they chose. One of the novel's main weaknesses lies in its clutter, in the frequent appearances of peripheral characters in scenes which have virtually nothing to do with the development of the principal figures. Another serious problem is the curious division of the reader's sympathy, which is directed haphazardly toward either Lydie or Eric through most of the novel, but also sometimes toward Andrew. So at the end, when Eric invites Lydie to leave with him and she refuses, the reader is uncertain whether her response is meant to be appropriate, and if so, what it signifies. *The Mandrake Root* provokes a more ambivalent response from the reader than any of Ostenso and Durkin's novels, and unhappily the confusion is not resolved by a second reading.

What is left in the canon is a ragbag of half a dozen novels, none of which is worth much attention from the serious reader. At worst they are potboilers; at best they make occasional pretense to serious writing. *There's Always Another Year* is a superficial western romance in which a lovely girl with a slightly shady past comes "home" to inherited land and finds love, after suitable difficulties have been overcome, with her aunt's stepson, who happens to be farming the land she had inherited. *And the Town Talked* trades in the clichés of small town romance and big city dreams. In this novel a beautiful orphan runs off to New York to become a dancer, much against the wishes of her elderly guardians. When she is badly injured, she returns home, where her recuperation is greatly helped by the handsome doctor who has always quietly loved her. The novel has a certain bibliographic interest, since it was only published in a paperback edition in Toronto, and is not listed in any of the standard bibliographies or catalogues.[74] *Love Passed This Way* deals with a female novelist from South Dakota who has found a measure of fame in New York. The novel begins promisingly with teasing references to the career of a woman who had been a social worker in New York slums and whose first novel had made "quite a stir."[75] There is even a spoof of early critical reaction to *Wild Geese*: " 'This cannot be from the pen of a young woman of twenty-six!' " (*LPTW*, p. 13). The novel's promise is not fulfilled — this is not a novel about how novels are written — and it sinks very quickly to the level of shallow romance in which the writer returns to the farm to find true love with a childhood sweetheart. *Milk Route* uses the delivery pattern of a milkman to comment from the outside on the disparate lives of various characters in a small town just after the War. *The Sunset Tree* has a tighter focus, and offers a retrospective self-examination of a singer whose relationships with men have all gone wrong. It is memorable only for an extended analogy between the singer and a parasitic slime mould called *mycetozoa* that feeds on other living things. The title of *The Waters under the Earth* seemed fair game for Anne Wilson, who headed her review in *Saturday Night* with the words "Only a Puddle."[76] Although the novel has superficial similarities with *Wild Geese* — the major character, Matthew Welland, is a domestic tyrant who ruins the lives of all but one of his seven children — the novel never comes to life. The stunted lives of Matthew's children seem appropriate reward for their unwillingness to rebel, and the one child who does escape from her father's domination "was so instinctively governed by her natural impulses that it never occurred to her to fight or rebel; she simply lived."[77]

Martha Ostenso's literary career began with great promise, but the promise was only intermittently fulfilled. The overwhelming success of *Wild Geese* created demands which any writer would have found difficult to satisfy, and Ostenso, even with Douglas Durkin as a silent partner, was simply unable to meet them. It might be argued persuasively that instant access to large amounts of money was at the root of her inability to develop as a serious novelist. Her financial commitments to her extended family and her quickly acquired taste for an expensive lifestyle, as well as the demands of her publishers and her readers for new works, created intense personal and professional pressures which resulted in the writing of too many novels too quickly. By 1943, just eighteen years after the publication of *Wild Geese*, she was burned out. Though she would live for another twenty years and publish four more novels, her career as a serious writer was effectively finished. What is remarkable, in the final analysis, is that she and Durkin produced as much good work as they did. Three of their sixteen novels continue to repay as much time as serious readers wish to spend on them, and two others can still be recommended without embarrassment. All things considered, it's not a bad score.

NOTES

¹ Joan N. Buckley, "Martha Ostenso: A Critical Study of her Novels," Diss. Univ. of Iowa 1976, p. 2. All further references to this work (Buckley) appear in the text.

² Although she was bilingual, and remained so throughout her life, Ostenso did all her creative work in English.

³ Grant Overton, *The Women Who Make Our Novels* (New York: Essay Index Reprint Series, 1967), p. 247.

⁴ Manuscript note dated 12 Jan. 1915 beside poem entitled "The Price of War" in Ostenso's notebook. The only fiction it contains is an eight-page section from chapter III of *Wild Geese*, showing only minor variations from the printed text. The notebook was made available to me through the kindness of Prof. Stanley C. Stanko, London, Ontario, Ostenso's literary executor.

⁵ Dates of Ostenso's teaching stint in Hayland (Sept.–Dec. 1918) confirmed by Shirley Morrish, Manitoba Department of Education, in a letter to the author, 19 March 1982. Hayland was changed to Oeland in *Wild Geese*: the two words have similar pronunciations in Norwegian and Icelandic.

⁶ University enrolment information supplied by J. Brian Salt, Director of Student Records, University of Manitoba, in a telephone conversation, 20 Aug. 1984.

⁷ Information supplied by Columbia University and quoted in Brita Mickleburgh, "Martha Ostenso: The Design of Her Canadian Prose Fiction," *Alive*, No. 35 (1973), p. 17. All further references to this work (Mickleburgh) appear in the text.

⁸ Buckley, p. 11; also in Lyn Tallman, "Martha Ostenso: The Interesting Beginnings of a Writer," *The Western Home Monthly*, March 1927, p. 30.

⁹ Martha Ostenso, *A Far Land* (New York: Thomas Seltzer, 1924). The collection includes forty-three short poems on a wide range of subjects. "Wasteland" (pp. 26–27) and possibly one or two others are worth anthologizing; the others are generally undistinguished.

¹⁰ The document, dated 11 Feb. 1958, has to do with copyright, and was shown to the author by Prof. Stanko. It contains the following clause: "whereas, all of the literary works of Martha Ostenso commencing with the publication of 'Wild Geese' in 1925 were the results of the combined efforts of Douglas Leader Durkin and Martha Ostenso . . . . "

¹¹ The film in turn spawned one of the earliest "film editions" of a novel: the Grosset and Dunlap edition (New York, 1925) as "illustrated with scenes from the photoplay." The translations were in Danish, Dutch, Finnish, German, Norwegian, Polish, and Swedish: a separate English edition was entitled *The*

Passionate Flight.

[12] Confirmed by administrative staff of Wittenberg University by telephone, 6 Aug. 1984. If Ostenso had been a man, the University would have given her a doctorate. Happily this policy was abandoned a short time later.

[13] During this period they also helped to support Ostenso's extended family, including her parents and siblings as well as Durkin's wife and children (Buckley, p. 17; confirmed by Prof. Stanko).

[14] The film was entitled *Wild Geese Flying*, and is said to have taken great liberties with the novel.

[15] Information from Prof. Stanko, who has interviewed a number of family members at length. Presumably this was before 1928, when Lewis married his second wife, Dorothy Thompson.

[16] Buckley, p. 21.

[17] Buckley, p. 21.

[18] Dick Harrison, *Unnamed Country: The Struggle for a Canadian Prairie Fiction* (Edmonton: Univ. of Alberta Press, 1977), p. 108. All further references to this work (Harrison) appear in the text.

[19] Clara Thomas, "Martha Ostenso's Trial of Strength," in *Writers of the Prairies*, ed. Donald G. Stephens (Vancouver: Univ. of British Columbia Press, 1973), pp. 39–50. All further references to this work (Thomas) appear in the text.

[20] Mickleburgh, p. 17.

[21] David Arnason, "The Development of Prairie Realism: Robert J.C. Stead, Douglas Durkin, Martha Ostenso and Frederick Philip Grove," Diss. New Brunswick 1980, p. 131. All further references to this work (Arnason) appear in the text.

[22] See Mickleburgh; also W.J. Keith, "*Wild Geese*: The Death of Caleb Gare," *Studies in Canadian Literature*, 3 (Summer 1978), 274–76.

[23] Arnason, p. 229.

[24] Desmond Pacey, "Fiction 1920–1940," *Literary History of Canada: Canadian Literature in English*, gen. ed. and introd. Carl F. Klinck (Toronto: Univ. of Toronto Press, 1965), p. 678.

[25] Rev. of *Wild Geese*, *Times Literary Supplement*, 24 Dec. 1925, p. 898; Rebecca Lowrie, "A Prize Novel," *The Saturday Review of Literature*, 28 Nov. 1925, pp. 335–36.

[26] Rev. of *Wild Geese*, *The New York Times Book Review*, 18 Oct. 1925, pp. 335–36.

[27] Rev. of *The Dark Dawn*, *The Canadian Forum*, Jan. 1927, pp. 121–22; rev. of *The Dark Dawn*, *The New York Times Book Review*, 24 Oct. 1926, p. 6.

[28] Morris Colman, "Martha Ostenso, Prize Novelist," *Maclean's*, 1 Jan. 1925, pp. 56–58.

[29] W.E. MacLellan, "Real Canadian Literature," *Dalhousie Review*, 6 (Oct. 1926), 18–23.

[30] George Bugnet, "Two New Western Books," *The Canadian Bookman*, 7 (Dec. 1925), 203.

[31] William Arthur Deacon, "A Letter from Canada," *The Saturday Review of Literature*, 6 March 1926, p. 614.

[32] Frederick Philip Grove, *The Letters of Frederick Philip Grove*, ed. Desmond Pacey (Toronto: Univ. of Toronto Press, 1976), pp. 25–26.

[33] *The Letters of Frederick Philip Grove*, p. xx.

[34] Edward A. McCourt, *The Canadian West in Fiction* (Toronto: Ryerson, 1949); Desmond Pacey, *Creative Writing in Canada* (Toronto: Ryerson, 1952), p. 223.

[35] Carlyle King, Introd., *Wild Geese*, by Martha Ostenso, New Canadian Library, No. 18 (Toronto: McClelland and Stewart, 1961), pp. v–x.

[36] S.G. Mullins, "Some Remarks on Theme in Martha Ostenso's *Wild Geese*," *Culture*, 23 (1962), 359–62.

[37] Roy W. Meyer, *The Middle Western Farm Novel in the Twentieth Century* (Lincoln: Univ. of Nebraska Press), 1965, pp. 150–51, 224–26.

[38] Desmond Pacey, "Fiction 1920–1940," *Literary History of Canada: Canadian Literature in English*, gen. ed. and introd. Carl F. Klinck (Toronto: Univ. of Toronto Press, 1965), pp. 678–79.

[39] Martha Ostenso, *Wild Geese*, adapted for radio by Len Peterson, music composed by Morris Surdin, broadcast nationally on "CBC Stage," 2 April 1965. Tommy Tweed appeared as Caleb Gare, Frances Hyland as Amelia, Pegi Loden as Judith, and Beth Lockerbie as the narrator.

[40] Stanley S. Stanko, "Image, Theme, and Pattern in the Works of Martha Ostenso," M.A. Thesis Alberta 1968.

[41] Becky-Jean Hjartarson, "A Study of Conflict in the Major Novels of Martha Ostenso," M.A. Thesis Regina 1976.

[42] Joan N. Buckley, "Martha Ostenso: A Critical Study of Her Novels," Diss. Iowa 1976.

[43] Rosaleen McFadden, "Icelandic Edda and Saga in Two Prairie Novels: An Analysis of *The Viking Heart* by Laura Goodman Salverson and *Wild Geese* by Martha Ostenso," M.A. Thesis Concordia 1977.

[44] Brita Mickleburgh, "Martha Ostenso: The Design of Her Canadian Prose Fiction," *Alive*, No. 35 (1973), pp. 17–19.

[45] M.G. Hesse, "The Endless Quest: Dreams and Aspirations in Martha Ostenso's *Wild Geese*," *Journal of Popular Culture*, 15, No. 3 (Winter 1981), 47–52.

[46] Stanley S. Atherton, "Ostenso Revisited," in *Modern Times*, Vol. III of The

Canadian Novel, ed. John Moss (Toronto: NC, 1982), pp. 57–65; Clara Thomas, "Martha Ostenso's Trial of Strength," in *Writers of the Prairies*, ed. Donald G. Stephens (Vancouver: Univ. of British Columbia Press, 1973), pp. 39–50.

[47] Laurence Ricou, *Vertical Man/Horizontal World: Man and Landscape in Canadian Prairie Fiction* (Vancouver: Univ. of British Columbia Press, 1973), pp. 74–80.

[48] Ricou, *Vertical Man/Horizontal World*, p. 74.

[49] Robert G. Lawrence, "The Geography of Martha Ostenso's *Wild Geese*," *Journal of Canadian Fiction*, No. 16 (1976), pp. 108–14.

[50] Dick Harrison, *Unnamed Country: The Struggle for a Canadian Fiction* (Edmonton: Univ. of Alberta Press, 1977), p. 109.

[51] Harrison, *Unnamed Country*, p. 108.

[52] Arnason, pp. 153–54.

[53] W.J. Keith, "*Wild Geese*: The Death of Caleb Gare," *Studies in Canadian Literature*, 3 (Summer 1978), pp. 274–76.

[54] Barbara Godard, "The View from Below: The Female Novel of the Land," paper read at "Intersections," Univ. of Nebraska, Lincoln, Neb., 18 March 1982. Eight pages are devoted to an analysis of *Wild Geese*.

[55] In addition to the document referred to earlier, there is David Arnason's assertion, presumably based on his extensive interview with Barney Ostenso, that "Ostenso wrote the first draft . . . [and] Durkin rearranged and revised the manuscript" (Arnason, p. 132).

[56] On the evidence of the later fiction in general and *The Young May Moon* and *O River, Remember* in particular, it is clear that Durkin was also in accord with Woolf's view.

[57] Martha Ostenso, *Wild Geese* (New York: Dodd, Mead, 1925), pp. 35–36. All further references to this work (*WG*) appear in the text. Portions of my analysis of *Wild Geese* and some comments on *The Young May Moon* have appeared in an earlier version in my "Ostenso Revisited," in *Modern Times*, Vol III of The Canadian Novel, ed. John Moss (Toronto: NC, 1982).

[58] Harrison, *Unnamed Country*, p. 108.

[59] Ricou, *Vertical Man/Horizontal World*, p. 75.

[60] The obsession is underscored by Caleb's name: Caleb is associated with land-holding in the Bible (see Numbers: 13 and 14), while Gare in Old Norse meant covetous or greedy.

[61] Judith's escape, or "passionate flight," gave the novel its working title.

[62] Ricou, *Vertical Man/Horizontal World*, p. 79.

[63] Thomas, "Martha Ostenso's Trial of Strength," p. 43.

[64] The choice of Amaranth was probably a private joke for the collaborators, since Durkin's birthplace was in the Ontario township of Amaranth.

[65] Martha Ostenso, *The Young May Moon* (New York: Dodd, Mead, 1929), p. 21. All further references to this work (*YMM*) appear in the text.

[66] Marcia's appraisal takes place as she walks back along the railway line from Bethune, the nearby village where she had grown up. This sequence, which opens the novel, is repeated in the novel's closing pages, when Marcia undergoes her final ordeal of self-examination.

[67] Martha Ostenso, *O River, Remember* (New York: Dodd, Mead, 1943), p. 229. All further references to this work (*ORR*) appear in the text.

[68] Richard A. Cordell, rev. of *O River, Remember*, *The Saturday Review of Literature*, 13 Nov. 1943, p. 8.

[69] Cordell, rev. of *O River, Remember*, p. 8.

[70] Karsten and Olina are Ivar's favourites; and the pattern of their relationships with the Shaleens is prefigured by Ivar's romantic yet platonic admiration for Kate Shaleen, who taught in the first school in the area until Magdali engineered her dismissal.

[71] A third reason is that there are no parallels for the scenes in *Wild Geese* in which the protagonist comes to see and suffer for his actions. Magdali dies in relative spiritual and physical comfort, of old age.

[72] Johan J. Smertenko, "Mixed Elements," rev. of *The Mad Carews*, *The Saturday Review of Literature*, 15 Oct. 1927, p. 197.

[73] Martha Ostenso, *The Dark Dawn* (New York: Dodd, Mead, 1926), p. 267.

[74] The novel was originally published in an abbreviated version in *McCalls* 65 (Feb. 1938). The only known copy is in the Thomas Fisher Rare Book Library at the University of Toronto.

[75] Martha Ostenso, *Love Passed This Way* (New York: Dodd, Mead, 1942), p. 13. All further references to this work (*LPTW*) appear in the text.

[76] Anne Wilson, "Only a Puddle," rev. of *The Waters under the Earth*, *Saturday Night*, 6 Dec. 1930, p. 9.

[77] "A Tyrannical Father," rev. of *The Waters under the Earth*, *The New York Times Book Review*, 23 Nov. 1930, p. 6.

SELECTED BIBLIOGRAPHY

Primary Sources

Books

Ostenso, Martha. *A Far Land*. New York: Thomas Seltzer, 1924.
——— . *Wild Geese*. New York: Dodd, Mead, 1925.
——— . *The Dark Dawn*. New York: Dodd, Mead, 1926.
——— . *The Mad Carews*. New York: Dodd, Mead, 1927.
——— . *The Young May Moon*. New York: Dodd, Mead, 1929.
——— . *The Waters under the Earth*. New York: Dodd, Mead, 1930.
——— . *Prologue to Love*. New York: Dodd, Mead, 1932.
——— . *There's Always Another Year*. New York: Dodd, Mead, 1933.
——— . *The White Reef*. New York: Dodd, Mead, 1934.
——— . *The Stone Field*. New York: Dodd, Mead, 1937.
——— . *The Mandrake Root*. New York: Dodd, Mead, 1938.
——— . *Love Passed This Way*. New York: Dodd, Mead, 1942.
——— . *O River, Remember!* New York: Dodd, Mead, 1943.
——— , and Elizabeth Kenny. *And They Shall Walk: The Life Story of Sister Elizabeth Kenny*. New York: Dodd, Mead, 1944.
——— . *Milk Route*. New York: Dodd, Mead, 1948.
——— . *The Sunset Tree*. New York: Dodd, Mead, 1949.
——— . *And the Town Talked*. News Stand Library, No. 69. Toronto: Export Publishing Enterprises, 1949.
——— . *A Man Had Tall Sons*. New York: Dodd, Mead, 1958.

Contribution to Periodicals

Ostenso, Martha. "A Man I Would Marry." *Pictorial Review*, 27 (June 1926), 4, 64, 66.

Secondary Sources

Arnason, David. "The Development of Prairie Realism: Robert J.C. Stead, Douglas Durkin, Martha Ostenso and Frederick Philip Grove." Diss. New Brunswick 1980.

Atherton, Stanley S. "Ostenso Revisited." In *The Canadian Novel: Modern Times*. Ed. John Moss. Toronto: NC, 1982, pp. 57–65.

Baldwin, Charles C. *Martha Ostenso: Daughter of the Vikings*. New York: Dodd, Mead, 1930.

Buckley, Joan N. "Martha Ostenso: A Critical Study of Her Novels." Diss. Iowa 1976.

Bugnet, George[s]. "Two New Western Books." *The Canadian Bookman*, 7 (Dec. 1925), 203.

Colman, Morris. "Martha Ostenso, Prize Novelist." *Maclean's*, 1 Jan. 1925, pp. 56–58.

Cordell, Richard A. "Wings and Shaleens." Rev. of *O River, Remember!*, by Martha Ostenso. *The Saturday Review of Literature*, 13 Nov. 1943, p. 8.

Deacon, William Arthur. "A Letter from Canada." *The Saturday Review of Literature*, 6 March 1926, p. 614.

"A Domineering Woman." Rev. of *The Dark Dawn*, by Martha Ostenso. *The New York Times Book Review*, 24 Oct. 1926, p. 6.

"Earth Hunger." Rev. of *Wild Geese*, by Martha Ostenso. *The New York Times Book Review*, 18 Oct. 1925, pp. 8, 16.

"Four Novels." Rev. of *The Dark Dawn*, by Martha Ostenso. *The Canadian Forum*, Jan 1927, pp. 121–22.

Godard, Barbara. "The View from Below: The Female Novel of the Land." Paper read at "Intersections," Univ. of Nebraska, Lincoln, Neb., 18 March 1982.

Grove, Frederick Philip. *The Letters of Frederick Philip Grove*. Ed. Desmond Pacey. Toronto: Univ. of Toronto Press, 1976.

Harrison, Dick. *Unnamed Country: The Struggle for a Canadian Prairie Fiction*. Edmonton: Univ. of Alberta Press, 1977.

Hesse, M.G. "The Endless Quest: Dreams and Aspirations in Martha Ostenso's *Wild Geese*." *Journal of Popular Culture*, 15, No. 3 (Winter 1981), 47–52.

Hjartarson, Becky-Jean. "A Study of Conflict in the Major Novels of Martha Ostenso." M.A. Thesis Regina 1976.

Keith, W.J. "*Wild Geese*: The Death of Caleb Gare." *Studies in Canadian Literature*, 3 (1978), 274–76.

King, Carlyle. Introd. *Wild Geese*. By Martha Ostenso. New Canadian Library,

No. 18. Toronto: McClelland and Stewart, 1961, pp. v–x.

Lawrence, Robert G. "The Geography of Martha Ostenso's *Wild Geese*." *Journal of Canadian Fiction* 16 (1976), pp. 108–14.

Lowrie, Rebecca. "A Prize Novel." Rev. of *Wild Geese*, by Martha Ostenso. *The Saturday Review of Literature*, 28 Nov. 1925, pp. 335–36.

MacLellan, W.E. "Real 'Canadian Literature.'" *Dalhousie Review*, 6 (Oct. 1926), 18–23.

McCourt, Edward A. *The Canadian West in Fiction*. Toronto: Ryerson, 1949.

McFadden, Rosaleen. "Icelandic Edda and Saga in Two Prairie Novels: An Analysis of *The Viking Heart* by Laura Goodman Salverson and *Wild Geese* by Martha Ostenso." M.A. Thesis Concordia 1977.

Meyer, Roy W. *The Middle Western Farm Novel in the Twentieth Century*. Lincoln: Univ. of Nebraska Press, 1965.

Mickleburgh, Brita. "Martha Ostenso: The Design of Her Canadian Prose Fiction." *Alive*, No. 35 (1973), pp. 17–19.

Mullins, S.G. "Some Remarks on Theme in Martha Ostenso's *Wild Geese*." *Culture*, 23 (1962), 359–62.

Overton, Grant. *The Women Who Make Our Novels*. 1918; rpt. New York: Essay Index Reprint Series, 1967.

Pacey, Desmond. *Creative Writing in Canada: A Short History of English-Canadian Literature*. Toronto: Ryerson, 1952.

———. "Fiction (1920–1940)." In *Literary History of Canada: Canadian Literature in English*. Gen. ed. and introd. Carl F. Klinck. Toronto: Univ. of Toronto Press, 1965, pp. 658–93.

Rev. of *The Passionate Flight*, by Martha Ostenso. *Times Literary Supplement*, 24 Dec. 1925, p. 898.

Ricou, Laurence. *Vertical Man/Horizontal World: Man and Landscape in Canadian Prairie Fiction*. Vancouver: Univ. of British Columbia Press, 1973.

Smertenko, Johan J. "Mixed Elements." Rev. of *The Mad Carews*, by Martha Ostenso. *The Saturday Review of Literature*, 15 Oct. 1927, p. 197.

Stanko, Stanley C. "Image, Theme, and Pattern in the Works of Martha Ostenso." M.A. Thesis Alberta 1968.

Tallman, Lyn. "Martha Ostenso: The Interesting Beginnings of a Writer." *The Western Home Monthly*, March 1927, p. 30.

Thomas, Clara. "Martha Ostenso's Trial of Strength." In *Writers of the Prairies*. Canadian Literature Series. Ed. Donald G. Stephens. Vancouver: Univ. of British Columbia Press, 1973, pp. 39–50.

"A Tyrannical Father." Rev. of *The Waters under the Earth*, by Martha Ostenso. *The New York Times Book Review*, 23 Nov. 1930, p. 6.

Wilson, Anne. "Only a Puddle." Rev. of *The Waters under the Earth*, by Martha Ostenso. *Saturday Night*, 6 Dec. 1930, p. 9.

Sinclair Ross and His Works

Sinclair Ross (1908–   )

MORTON L. ROSS

Biography

In order to rescue Sinclair Ross from what one reviewer called "the prominent obscurity"[1] granted him by readers, three investigators sought him out during his years of retirement in Spain — Myrna Kostash in 1972, William French in 1974, and Lorraine McMullen in 1977. Each of them reported that while Ross was cooperative and friendly during the interviews, his discussions of his life and work were modest, unassuming, and finally reticent, and there seems general agreement with French's summary characterization: "He's a reclusive bachelor, a loner who cherishes his privacy."[2] Never seeking the public eye except for his fiction, and persistently discouraged by its public reception, Ross may deserve the biographer's tact more than those writers following the model of Norman Mailer's *Advertisements for Myself* (1959). The most complete biographical information about Ross available to date has been collected by Lorraine McMullen and published in her TWAS series volume on Ross in 1979.[3]

James Sinclair Ross was born, the third child and second son, on 22 January 1908, to Peter Ross and Catherine Foster Fraser Ross on a 160-acre homestead twelve miles from Shellbrook, Saskatchewan. Catherine Fraser, her father a university educated clergyman, had been born in Edinburgh and had come to Prince Albert, Saskatchewan, with her mother and stepfather. There she married Peter Ross who had come west from the Owen Sound area of Ontario. They permanently separated when Sinclair was about seven years old and he alone of the three children remained with his mother who supported them by working as a housekeeper on various farms. He completed grade eleven at age sixteen in 1924 at Indian Head, Saskatchewan, and began his long career with the Royal Bank of Canada, first at the Union Bank of Abbey, then in 1928 at Lancer and in 1929 at Arcola until transferred to Winnipeg in April of 1933. He joined the Canadian Army in 1942, was sent overseas with the

Ordnance Corps, and served with Army Headquarters, London, until he was demobilized and returned to Winnipeg and the Royal Bank in 1946. In April of that year, the bank transferred him to its headquarters in Montreal where he lived and worked until his retirement on 31 January 1968. In March of 1968 he moved to Athens, Greece, living there for three years, then in 1971 to Barcelona and in 1973 to Malaga, on Spain's Costa del Sol. Ken Mitchell reports that Ross returned again to live in Montreal in 1980,[4] and recent reports have him living in Vancouver.

Professor McMullen records Ross's interest in writing fiction as early as his tenth year and an unsuccessful submission of a story for publication at age sixteen; Ross was twenty-six before his first story, "No Other Way," was published in the English *Nash's Pall-Mall* in October of 1934, after it had received third prize in Nash's short story competition for previously unpublished writers from a reported eight thousand entries. Over the next eighteen years, Ross published fifteen stories, all but three of them in the *Queen's Quarterly*. Ten of these were carefully revised to form the collection titled *The Lamp at Noon* in 1968, and since that date two more stories have been published, the last in 1972. Ross's first novel, *As for Me and My House*, was published in 1941 in New York to a North American audience deeply preoccupied with yet another world war; the result, as French reports, was a few hundred copies sold and "exactly $270" for Ross, all in advance royalties.[5] *The New Yorker* noted the book in four sentences, concluding that, "Some good things here, but the book is very gloomy."[6] Another New York critic persisted in referring to the author as Miss Ross.[7] The public's response to *The Well* in 1958 and *Whir of Gold*, rewritten in Greece and published in 1970, was little better. During the decade of the seventies, Ross's work was beginning to receive belated critical attention and one consequence may have been a more sympathetic reception for *Sawbones Memorial* when it appeared in 1974, but there has been nothing since. Seventeen years between his first and second novels, twelve between it and his third, and four years of productive retirement issuing in his fourth and shortest novel, and then silence — these long intervals may be mute testimony to Ross's repeated frustrations and disappointments, perhaps another reason for his career-long concern with the figure of the outsider or exile struggling to maintain his independence and self-respect in a particularly obdurate world. But the intervals may also testify to Ross's persistent need for expression, a need captured in *Sawbones Memorial* by Harry Hubbs's memory of his own behaviour in isolation: "I'd get a feeling sometimes that I had to tell somebody, write a letter, tell what it was really like, the prairie and the Pims and the horses with their sores, but there was nobody to write to, not a letter telling those things. So I'd get a piece of paper and just sit looking at it for a while, sort of wondering, and then not knowing what else to write I'd make a list . . . things I'd no intention of doing, couldn't do, but just writing them down sort of gave me a feeling I was still all right."[8]

Tradition and Milieu

William French reports that Ross's boyhood was marked by feelings of "rootlessness"; moving with his "strong-willed" mother among the farms where she worked as housekeeper, Ross "always felt like a visitor or boarder."[9] This sense of being an outsider may have been both relieved and exacerbated, as Lorraine McMullen reports it,[10] by Mrs. Ross's determination to give her son, despite their reduced rural situation, an education or at least a cultivation consistent with her own family background; she early encouraged Ross in what he has described as a life-long habit of voracious and eclectic reading. One effect must have been something like the alluring echoes of a more spacious world beyond the Prairies imagined by Ross for the sensitive young people in stories like "Cornet at Night" and "Circus in Town." But if such echoes were alluring, they might also have underscored the relative cultural poverty of his boyhood surroundings. In a taped interview with Earle Toppings in 1971, Ross insisted that "my failure to make an impact is because I'm a western Canadian," citing in support Pearl Buck's remark to the effect that a writer is handicapped by an unpropitious birthplace. Later in the interview, Ross first disclaims any awareness of literary influence on his work: "I've always read a great deal. I don't know any that have influenced me; I suppose they have, but I'm not aware of any particular influence"; he then adds: "there wasn't very much western Canadian writing *to* influence me,"[11] and then, pressed a bit by Toppings' encouraging silence, lists Scott, Dickens, and Conrad, and with some emphasis, Hardy's *Return of the Native*. Ross has confessed an impact on him by Martha Ostenso's *Wild Geese*, but after noting this, McMullen takes the occasion to state flatly: "He has not read Frederick Philip Grove."[12] Ross seems to have made no public mention of some other early regional writers whose works might have been of interest and available to him, writers like R.J.C. Stead, Arthur Stringer, or Laura Salverson. There is also no mention, in published accounts, of the American midwestern regionalists closest to his own work. Hemingway is there, but not Hamlin Garland, whose stories of harsh farm life in *Main-Travelled Roads* (1891) anticipated Ross's own; Faulkner is there, but not Sinclair Lewis, whose portrait of Carol Kennicott in *Main Street* (1920) at least remotely prefigures Mrs. Bentley. E.K. Brown, the most perceptive of Ross's early reviewers, began by stating that "This novel, Mr. Ross's first, owes nothing to any other work of Canadian fiction."[13] If Brown is right, it is more relevant to speak here of his influence rather than influences upon him. Certainly Margaret Laurence may have voiced the indebtedness of other western writers like W.O. Mitchell, Robert Kroetsch, Rudy Wiebe, and Ken Mitchell to Ross's lonely part in initiating a tradition of serious fiction about the Canadian west: *As for Me and My House* "had an enormous impact on me, for it seemed the only completely genuine one [novel] I had ever read about my own people, my own place, my own time. It pulled no punches about life in the stultifying atmosphere of small and ingrown towns, and yet it was illuminated with compassion."[14]

McMullen also records that at about age twenty, Ross had been impressed by Aldous Huxley's *Point Counter Point*. His early interest in this portrait of an urbane coterie of London intellectuals may hint at his own natural hopes for a sustaining circle of friends and fellow writers, but his own testimony indicates that he remained the outsider, even in the urban midst of Winnipeg and Montreal. Responding in 1970 to an invitation from the editors of *Mosaic* "for a comment on the effect of Manitoba as a literary environment," Ross wrote: ". . . I couldn't write three hundred words on the influence of Manitoba on my work, much less three thousand, for the simple reason that it had no influence whatsoever." Ross seems to be thinking of influence on his stories' settings, but the remark is also a bleak register of what one might expect to have been the stimulation, after so many Saskatchewan small towns, of a nine-year residence in Winnipeg, a period in which he did much of his best work, and there seems a faint note of envy for Margaret Laurence and Adele Wiseman who, unlike himself, experienced there, he says, "any number of influences."[15] In 1966, Ross had been invited by the editors of *The Tamarack Review* to comment on what Montreal and French-Canadian culture might mean to an English-Canadian novelist. He began his response by recalling that his initial hopes for Montreal as "a French city" had been quickly disappointed, adding somewhat wistfully: "I knew no artists or intellectuals who might have helped me see a little further."[16] McMullen reports that Ross did meet, "very briefly,"[17] Hugh MacLennan and Ralph Gustafson, and that he met another expatriate, Mavis Gallant, on several occasions during her visits to Montreal, but William French records: "When I asked him why he hadn't been involved in the Montreal literary scene, he said: 'I flee from the literary scene. Then I don't have to defend myself.' " A defensive non-defence, evidence perhaps for French's judgement that "he is still oddly defensive about his Grade 11 education."[18] But despite such defence, and against all odds, all accounts agree that Ross has become what his mother had hoped, a thoroughly cultivated gentleman, fluent in French and Spanish, and familiar with a great range of the world's literature.

It is not surprising, I think, that when asked to name and explain the sources of and influences upon their work, writers will tend to respond with their current preoccupations. The existing and very limited list of such sources and influences named by Ross for his work was compiled by inquiries undertaken in the 1970s when Ross himself was preoccupied by the writing, publication, and reception of *Sawbones Memorial*. It seems likely, therefore, that this short list will be most revealing for this novel. In 1941, R.S. Stubbs had reported that Ross's "favorite authors were Ernest Hemingway, Richard Hughes, and H.E. Bates."[19] In the middle years of his career, Ross had moved beyond the subjects of his early short stories and *As for Me and My House* to explore a new interest in what he described to Earle Toppings as "the criminal mentality," an interest informing both *The Well* and *Whir of Gold* and the later short stories, "Spike" and "The Flowers That Killed Him." Had inquiry into sources begun during this period, one would have expected more authors and titles from among Ross's reading to match McMullen's report of the influence of Dostoyevsky, "especially *Crime and Punishment* and *The Brothers Karamazov*."[20] But in fact such inquiry began in earnest only when Ross was striking out in the new direction represented by *Sawbones Memorial* and his new technical concern for devices like multiple voices, embedded stories, and interior monologues, all designed to reveal not a single individual, but a community, seems reflected in the authors and titles he chose to offer investigators. Lorraine McMullen has made clear, for instance, that Claude Mauriac's *Dîner en Ville* (1959) was a direct model for this most recent novel, thus linking Ross with the tradition of the French *nouveau roman*. The shared concerns of technique and the focus on a group portrait may also account not only for the unexpected mention of *Point Counter Point*, but for the specific inclusion of Faulkner's *As I Lay Dying* and *The Sound and the Fury*, Joyce's *Ulysses*, Hemingway's *The Sun Also Rises*, and works by such South American writers as García Marquez and Vargas Llosa. In fact, although Robert Kroetsch fails to include Ross in his supporting list of writers, *Sawbones Memorial* fits neatly within a recent tradition Kroetsch has characterized as follows: "The compounding of genealogical relationship, in the Canadian novel of the seventies, manifests itself in complex narrative structure;... In these novels we have not only myriad embedded stories, but also embedded voices."[21] It is thus encouraging to suspect that Ross, publishing his most recent novel at age sixty-six, is fit for the contemporary company Kroetsch names, a group which includes not only those linked with Ross before, Margaret Laurence and Rudy Wiebe, but also Dave Godfrey, Audrey Thomas, Michael Ondaatje, and Jack Hodgins.

Critical Overview and Context

Public comment on Ross's work began with reviews of *As for Me and My House* in 1941. The best of these is E.K. Brown's, a remarkably cogent survey of the novel's technical features; Brown commends its "taut psychological conflict" and firmness of design, yet points out the dangers of repetitive detail and certain lapses from "unity of tone," and he concludes with some apt praise: "He has contrived with amazing success to be both local and universal, to write a book which is, within its narrow limits, a realistic representation of a community and a way of living, and no less an insight into powerful and permanent emotions."[22] Brown's judgements, especially his reservations about the use of repetition, shaped an initial consensus about the book's technical merits as they were essentially agreed to by Edward McCourt in 1949, by Roy Daniells in 1957, and encapsulated as a quasi-official view by Hugo McPherson in the *Literary History of Canada* in 1965: "Ross does not always escape the trap of a reiteration which is merely reflex, yet in technique his book remains one of the most finished works that Canada has produced."[23]

However, between 1941 and 1957, when Ross's first and still lone novel was reissued in paperback by New Canadian Library, comments on Ross's works were so rare and so scattered that Edward McCourt, after a necessarily brief but favourable description of the novel and Ross's early short stories within his survey of *The Canadian West in Fiction* (1949), could lament that "in Sinclair Ross we may, through indifference and neglect, have permitted a fine artist to perish."[24] But Roy Daniells' introduction to the new edition of *As for Me and My House* was to provide an issue that would generate some energetic debate, even though it was to be eight years more before such debate began. Daniells both summarized and exceeded the early critics' generally sympathetic view of the novel's narrator: "Mrs. Bentley, in whose words the whole is recounted, through whose eyes, by whose sensibility, all is seen and realized, she it is who engrosses the reader's interest and regard. . . . She is pure gold and wholly credible." Daniells apparently realized his position was extreme; he prefaced this judgement with a warning: "About the characters there is room for some friendly critical disagreement."[25] The disagreement began in 1965 when Donald G. Stephens warned the reader of some dangers in taking Mrs. Bentley's narration as wholly credible, and it deepened in 1968 when W.H. New argued that the deliberate aim of the novel is ambivalence, ". . . emerging out of a carefully constructed web of viewpoints, Mrs. Bentley's and ours, pitted ironically against each other so that we come to appreciate not only the depth and complexity of the narrator and her situation, but also the control in which Ross artistically holds his words."[26] As New's remarks suggest, this accelerating stress on the unreliability of the narrator obliges the critic to identify those devices by which Ross might continue to control the novel's effects. Efforts to do this were accompanied by further exposures of Mrs. Bentley's unreliability as a narrator in essays by Wilfred Cude and Laurence Ricou in 1973, and by John Moss and David Stouck in 1974. I offered a case study of the criticism of *As for Me and My House* in 1978, arguing that these critics' attacks on the narrator's unreliability had produced a debunking of Mrs. Bentley's moral character that seemed like calumny, and charged that the arguments finding Mrs. Bentley imperceptive, fallible, limited, or contradictory were too often taken as license for the reader, freeing him or her to supply what Mrs. Bentley does not or can not or what Ross may not. One form in which this debate continues is in recent efforts to redress the moral balance, to rehabilitate Mrs. Bentley, as in D.J. Dooley's chapter on the novel in 1979: "All the altruism, the generosity, the willingness to make sacrifices for the other person, are to be found on the wife's side."[27] Another sort of resolution was offered by Paul Denham in 1980: "If we examine this technique carefully, it appears that Ross does not have his materials entirely under control," and he concludes: "There is, ultimately, no way of knowing what to make of Mrs. Bentley, and therefore no way of knowing what to make of her narrative."[28]

Another line of inquiry, one concentrating on Philip rather than on Mrs. Bentley, was begun in 1960 by Warren Tallman who characterized the novel as "a study of a frustrated artist — actually, a non-artist — one unable to discover a subject which will release him from his oppressive incapacity to create,"[29] and the clear implication of Tallman's judgement was soon announced by Hugo McPherson in the *Literary History of Canada*: "Ross's central theme is the imagination and its failure in Canada."[30] In *Survival* (1972), Margaret Atwood placed it among those Canadian novels that have "created memorable works of art out of the proposition that such a creation, in their environment, is impossible,"[31] and in 1974, David Stouck took the novel beyond regional or national considerations by emphasizing "the artist's story theme which gives the novel its universal interest."[32] That this line of inquiry continues to be promising is indicated by Barbara Godard's perceptive and searching essay in 1981, opening the novel both as "a portrait of the artist and a discovery of the esthetic by which the portrait is painted."[33]

Another line of inquiry that has proved useful in moving critical attention beyond its heavy concentration on Ross's first novel was articulated by Henry Kreisel in 1968: "All discussion of the literature produced in the Canadian west must of necessity begin with the impact of the landscape upon the mind"; Kreisel goes on to claim: "It is because *As for Me and My House* contains the most uncompromising rendering of the puritan state of mind produced on the prairie that the novel has been accorded a central place in prairie literature."[34] Sandra Djwa traced "this puritan state of mind" and its implications in two essays in 1972 and 1973, but Kreisel's formulations also pointed a way to investigate Ross's techniques for revealing the consciousness of his characters: ". . . Mrs. Bentley uses the prairie constantly as a mirror of her own fears, frustrations, and helplessness."[35] Most commentators since have travelled over this mirrored way, explored most fully by Laurence Ricou in 1973, and by Lorraine McMullen in 1979.

Aside from Keath Fraser's survey of the short stories in an essay in 1970 and a great deal of incidental mention, Ross's other work has had to wait until 1975 for a meaningful fraction of the attention paid his first novel. In that year Robert D. Chambers devoted half a short book to a critique of all of Ross's work except *Sawbones Memorial*, and in 1979 Lorraine McMullen covered his career and work in the first book-length study. This careful and perceptive undertaking, particularly useful in its approach to Ross's most recent novel, was followed in 1981 by Ken Mitchell's trenchant *Sinclair Ross: A Reader's Guide*. Despite the burden of extra-critical responsibilities — the provision of biographical notes and other scholarly apparatus, the more or less necessary inventories of plot and theme, and (in Mitchell's case) the reprinting of some fugitive texts — each of these helps fill the need for a more comprehensive assessment of Ross's achievement. Thus encouraged, we could have expected more studies to match Gail Bowen's sensitive essay in 1979, a reading that reaches beyond his first novel to embrace everything indicated by its title, "The Fiction of Sinclair Ross," but only one such essay has appeared: Paul Comeau's 1984 survey of Ross's use in his major works of the modes of tragedy, irony, and comedy.

The focus for Ross studies in the 1980s remained firmly upon *As for Me and My House*, although some critics moved beyond its interpretation to its place within world literature. Robert Thacker, in two essays, has assessed Ross's novel against Steinbeck's *Grapes of Wrath*, Hamlin Garland's *The Moccasin Ranch*, and Ole Rølvaag's *Giants in the Earth*, in each case finding Ross's book the "most artful" of these treatments of prairie and depression subjects. In 1986 Pamela Banting offered a subtle comparison of *As for Me and My House* with Hawthorne's *The Scarlet Letter*, and in the same year Frances Kaye argued that Ross used George Sand and Frederic Chopin as models for the Bentleys, but most studies in the 1980s continued to worry about the question of how to read *As for Me and My House* properly. Beginning with essays by Wilfred Cude and Ryszard Dubanski in 1979, critics continued the efforts to find ways that would permit the reader to compensate for Mrs. Bentley's unreliability as a narrator. Cude and Dubanski both found a corrective for Mrs. Bentley's narration in a careful reading of Philip's activities as an artist. In 1984 Lorraine York studied the interrelationship of verbal and non-verbal means of communication in the novel, and in the same year David Williams opened a new issue by arguing for the probability that Philip is innocent of the act of adultery and claiming that this allows the problem of perspective in the novel to be resolved. In 1987 Beverley Mitchell agreed with Williams, arguing that Mrs. Bentley suffers from clinical depression and thus believes, erroneously, that Philip is the father of Judith's baby; Mitchell believes there is evidence that the real father is Paul. This concern with the kinds and qualities of evidence necessary to correct an unreliable narrator has extended beyond Ross's first novel to a mini-controversy about his short story, "One's a Heifer." In 1982 F.H. Whitman argued that to see the whole story of the girl as anything other than "a fiction in Vickers' mind" is a mistake that comes from accepting the opinions of a narrator who is unreliable. In 1984 Marilyn Chapman took up Whitman's point, arguing that there is *no* conclusive evidence in the story either to establish that the girl is Vickers' hallucination or that she is real. The question of evidence with which to correct Mrs. Bentley's mistakes was further tangled (perhaps with tongues-in-cheek) by an essay from Evelyn Hinz and John Teunissen in 1986; they argue that Percy Glenn, not Philip, was the father of Mrs. Bentley's stillborn child; they exonerate both Philip and Paul from the charge of fathering Judith's child, finally fingering Mr. Finley, Chairman of the Church Board, as "the likely suspect." Given these multiplying possibilities for a correct understanding of what happens in *As for Me and My House*, we can expect that such debate will continue in the 1990s.

Ross's Works

In his story "September Snow," first published in 1935, Sinclair Ross described his protagonist struggling through a blizzard: "Passive for a minute with weariness, he felt the full sweep and power of the wind, heard its sob and suck, and suddenly a maddening sense of helplessness and isolation beat down on him. It was the immensity and wildness of the night — an intuitive, bolt-like conviction of combat, of hostile, implacable force opposed to him."[36] This is the mark of a naturalistic writer, as shrill and as unmistakable as anything in Jack

London. But in revising "September Snow" — it became part II of "Not by Rain Alone" in the 1968 New Canadian Library collection of his short stories — Ross simply omits this passage. And the pattern of such revision is consistent for this and other early stories. Images of nature "screaming in derision of his labour"[37] and of man "against its frozen, blizzard-breathed implacability"[38] are removed, and descriptive tone deliberately lowered by the omission of grandiloquent modifiers like "incredible," "immeasurable," "overpowering," "impenetrable," "irresistibly," and "strangely." Ross's revisions here suggest that, however belatedly, he recognized and backed away from the naturalists' version of the pathetic fallacy, that easy and portentous personification of nature as a hostile or malignantly indifferent antagonist for humanity. The truth is that nature functions most effectively in Ross's early stories when he conceives it not as cause or antagonist, but rather as condition or occasion for human action, and his revisions are consistent with this less cosmic, and ultimately less sentimental view.

In "Not by Rain Alone," a young farmer contemplates his drought-threatened crop: "It was such niggard land. At the best they would grub along painfully, grow tired and bitter, indifferent to each other. It was the way of the land. For a farmer like him there could be no other way."[39] Ross's most characteristic early stories are contrived to bring the way of the land into dramatic collision with values associated with other ways, collisions which expose the human costs of prairie farming. By any means of counting, the tally of such costs is impressive. At the extreme they are the loss of life itself; three of the early stories recount needless deaths, but these are offered as culminating events in patterns of repeated disappointments and frustrations, protracted into hopeless bitterness and the erosion of imagination, trust, communication, and love. Given the range and intensity of such human costs, it has been tempting to read Ross's displays of the way of the land as an indictment of cosmic injustice, pity-inducing views of humanity as the helpless victim of nature or of nature's god. This sort of reading continues to tempt recent commentators; in 1975 Robert D. Chambers: "Here the landscape has a brooding, threatening quality, as though just beyond the horizon a malevolent God is preparing horrors of nature to hurl against an embattled people";[40] in 1979 Lorraine McMullen: "Here nature is revealed as beautiful but indifferent, serenely uncaring about the havoc it has wrought";[41] and in 1981 Ken Mitchell: "The effect is to give us a microcosm of suffering mankind, caught in the grinding wheels of a universe beyond human understanding or control."[42] The revisions which I began by citing suggest that while Ross may have originally shared these naturalistic views, he deliberately removed from his stories much of the evidence upon which such readings can be based, and Ross himself comments wryly on such readings. Some characters in *Sawbones Memorial* are arguing about the song "Redwing," and one asks for an interpretation of the line "The sun is shining and Redwing's pining": "Why should she be pining when the sun is shining, what's the connection?" Nellie Furby answers: "Perhaps it's intended as a comment on the indifference of nature to the human predicament. Very Canadian."[43]

Ross's revisions further suggest that he was seeking means to sharpen his stories' focus on the intricate and purely human reactions to the way of the land. In his interview with Earle Toppings in 1971, Ross explained that the struggle for survival was part of the universal human condition, "only in the case of a man on the land, it is thrown up in relief so that you can see it and are aware of it as a struggle for survival." Ross's use of the painter's term "thrown up in relief" is apt here, for the early stories typically emphasize a short, but intense arc of human feeling against a dramatic natural background, and they often end with a landscape tableau throwing into relief the exhausted emotions of the characters. The terrifying hail-storm and the brilliant cloudscape it leaves at the end of "A Field of Wheat" is the best example here, and its effects may be compared with advantage to the carefully etched beauty of Sherwood Anderson's "Death in the Woods."

What gives Ross's fiction its energy, I believe, is his craftsman's interest in the dramatization of human consciousness, and I mean to trace this concern through the course of his career. In moving beyond the essentially static and pictorial device of sudden bursts of emotion thrown into relief against landscape tableaux, Ross clearly faced an initial problem in dramatizing the kind of consciousness associated with the way of the land. How does a writer enact, for instance, and particularly within the limits of a short story, the endlessly repetitious accretions of conditioning produced by the laborious rounds of the way of the land? Can such representation be anything other than expository or summarily descriptive? This problem — and his first attempt at a solution — can be illustrated by Ross's first published story, "No Other Way." The protagonist is Hatty Glenn, a farm wife grown old, ugly, and shrewish in the course of creating a successful farm. Her crisis occurs as she discovers, despite her habitual scorn for her husband as "a lazy good-for-nothing," that she still loves him. After a pathetic and unsuccessful attempt to reclaim his love, she resolves to kill herself: "This was the best way. She would save herself years of misery, and give Dan a chance of happiness. . . . This was the only way."[44] But the stronger ways of work and prudential habit reassert themselves at the provocation of cows loose in her garden, and the story ends with "And then in a flash she was clutching a broom and swooping into the garden. 'Get out, you greedy old devils!' . . . Butter twenty-five cents a pound. There was no other way" (p. 94). Hatty's character is defined for us as animated by

An old struggle, for years now an inseparable part of her life. Love against a sense of injustice — duty against something that kept saying she was a fool — loyalty and sympathy trying to oust the fear that she was making only a dog of herself. A useless, wearying struggle, making her harsh and sour and old, and always ending just where it had begun. (p. 80)

Here Ross simply enumerates the vectors of force that over Hatty's years have intersected to form her character. And I mean these mathematical terms to emphasize Ross's initial use of the naturalistic conception of a web or matrix of restraints which determine action and character. The action of the story, moving within this matrix, and reported by Ross as a third person who assumes limited omniscience, is a sequence of reactions by Hatty to her sudden and inexplicable break with a dominant habit. Her crisis begins when her habitual nagging is ". . . suddenly checked. It was queer — something that had never happened before, and that her understanding did not even attempt to pierce" (p. 83). Only gradually does she discover the import of this apparently unprecedented "something": "With the sight of Dan shaving there had come a sharp, revealing flash that wakened her" (p. 84). She has discovered that she still loves her husband, and resolves to fight in order to keep him: "She had not thought out her sudden resolution. It was just instinct . . ." (p. 84). After an evening party in town has convinced her that she is helpless to recover his love, "All night she lay awake, and each hour

brought a more clear and inescapable understanding of herself"
(p. 89). The result of this understanding is her resolution to kill
herself, but the adjectives become ironic because she does escape her
choice — presumably the last dictate of a clear and inescapable
understanding — when the force of original habit reasserts itself at
the story's conclusion. As these passages indicate, the theatre of
Hatty's consciousness arrays an activating sequence of impulse,
instinct, sudden insight, and momentary understanding against the
conditioning of habit. If the gain for Hatty seems at least a momentary self-knowledge, the clear victor in this drama of consciousness
is the dominant force of habit, broken to begin the action, but
re-asserting itself to conclude it. This resolution invites naturalistic
phrases like reversion to type or the snap of a behavioural trap; the
trouble is that finally this sort of closure undermines and makes
specious what might have originally seemed a genuine drama of
consciousness. No matter how "sharp" and "revealing" the flash of
awakening is alleged to be, no matter how "clear and inescapable"
the understanding, they are revealed as insubstantial and perhaps
even illusory against the inexorable force of habit. The effect is
schematic, even mechanical; it's as if Ross had begun to temper Jack
London's deterministic psychology with Henry James's possibilities
of informed understanding, but in the end had awarded the palm to
London. What gave promise of being a victim's emancipation,
however limited, into self-awareness becomes simply an illustrative
episode confirming the narrator's remark that Hatty's was "A useless, wearying struggle, making her harsh and sour and old, and
always ending just where it had begun" (p. 80).

But that Ross was moving away from the mechanical matrices of
deterministic psychology to a more spacious exploration of the
intricacies of human choice is indicated by the achievement of "The
Painted Door," which appeared in 1939, five years after "No Other
Way." Like his first story, "The Painted Door" reveals the human
costs exacted by a conflict between the way of the land and the ways
of love, but here the costs are subtly and richly balanced by some
clear human gains. The story records the complex responses of a
young farm wife to the necessary absence of her husband during a
day which promises and a night which brings an intense winter
storm. Much of this complexity is generated by Ann's passionate act
of infidelity and its ironic confrontation with her husband John's
willed act of almost perfect constancy. Ann's crisis occurs within

what may also be termed a web of forces, but unlike the deterministic matrix of sudden reactive or reflexive impulse or the eruptions of memory that agitated but failed to change Hatty's conditioning, Ann's choices are constrained but informed, not determined by her understanding and insight. She is portrayed as correctly estimating her husband's defining virtue, both appreciating his constancy and self-sacrifice, and suffering an awareness of its defect, his persistent drudgery in improving their lot:

> ... the only real difference that it all made was to deprive her of his companionship, to make him a little duller, older, uglier than he might otherwise have been. He never saw their lives objectively. To him it was not what he actually accomplished by means of the sacrifice that mattered, but the sacrifice itself, the gesture — something done for her sake.
>
> And she, understanding, kept her silence. In such a gesture, however futile, there was a graciousness not to be shattered lightly.[45]

Touched by his devotion, she is constrained and finally frustrated in protesting its excess. And Ross continues to explore the resonant contrarieties of Ann's understanding. We sense, for instance, the troubled combination of judgements as her gratitude for John's solicitous invitation to young Steven to keep her company contends with exasperation at her husband's failure to understand the handsome neighbour's erotic appeal; we are thus prepared for the mixture of motives that leads to her infidelity — her relief in Steven's presence from her day-long loneliness and sense of deprivation, and her appraisal and deliberate acceptance of the erotic challenge posed by his self-assured and arrogant masculinity. The descending action of the story opens as Ann lies dozing beside the sleeping Steve. Dreaming, or imagining she dreams, she sees John standing over the bed, in his face "only calm, and stonelike hopelessness" (p. 115). Awakening, she measures her guilt, and after a momentary hope of concealing it from John, she acknowledges it. And in her reflections, "She re-lived their seven years together and, in retrospect, found them to be years of worth and dignity" (p. 116). She then recognizes that she has deceived herself in doubting John's constancy: "John always came. There could never be a storm to stop him" (p. 117). Appraising again the sleeping Steven, she realizes his shallowness and re-dedicates herself to her husband: "John was the man. With him lay all the future. For tonight, slowly and contritely through the day and years to come, she would try to make amends" (p. 118). Having in effect performed the traditional ritual of penitence — acknowledge-ment of guilt, contrition, and a resolve for restitution — Ann can now recognize, without minimizing her infidelity, that her act of passion was false to her own best understanding, principally an understanding of John's constancy. John's effort, before his depar-ture, to reassure her of his return becomes, in this retrospect, an ironic measure not of her sin, but of her lapse of understanding: " 'You ought to know by now I wouldn't stay away,' he tried to brighten her. 'No matter how it stormed' " (p. 100). But there is one final section; John is found frozen to his own pasture fence, "erect still, both hands clasping fast the wire" (p. 118). And Ann endures a final discovery, a tell-tale smear of fresh paint on John's hand exposing what had seemed her dream image as his actual presence, his mute discovery of her infidelity. Ross leaves us to imagine Ann's subsequent response, but it is the measure of both his craft and control in this story that he has given us, I believe, clear direction for our imagining. Ken Mitchell imagines Ann "facing an indescribably tormented future of guilt, for her one lapse of conviction."[46] My own view is that Ross has created a character that we have become convinced is capable of something transcending victimage, fully capable of rising above whatever reaches of shock, guilt, and regret she may traverse, to recover the quality of understanding from which she had lapsed, that quality of understanding of her husband's final act already so clearly voiced for her: "To him it was not what he actually accomplished by means of the sacrifice that mattered, but the sacrifice itself, the gesture — something done for her sake. And she, understanding, kept her silence. In such a gesture, however futile, there was a graciousness not to be shattered lightly" (pp. 103–04). We can never, of course, know whether Ann will recover this understanding, but her capacities have been established, and the possibility dignifies both characters — he for willing the gesture and she for the ability to understand it. Whatever else may be said about this story, it displays a depth and sophistication of character conception and the nature of consciousness well in advance of "No Other Way," an advance that was to continue in *As for Me and My House.*

As for Me and My House

In my 1978 case study of the criticism of *As for Me and My House*, I argued that efforts to assess her reliability as a narrator had produced a debunking of Mrs. Bentley that seemed very like calumny, and illustrated this contention by a list of character flaws compiled from the critics, which I here repeat: "arrogant, obtuse, stubborn, hypocritical, manipulative, smug, dowdy, petty, deceptive, self-indulgent, jealous, mean, bitchy, self-dramatizing, bitter, subject to delusions, fussy, morose."[47] Additions to update this list from subsequent studies, one even charging "slovenly housewifery,"[48] make it now seem even more like character assassination, especially with Ken Mitchell's blunt reference to "the conventional view; that is, that Philip Bentley is a misunderstood hero-artist and his wife a nagging bitch." Mitchell may be a bit wry here, for his own reading does something to rehabilitate Mrs. Bentley, but one wonders again when he begins by claiming that "at the outset, we must forsake all credence in Mrs. Bentley as a reliable or honest narrator."[49] If we forsake *all* credence in her narration, what's left? By choosing a completely unreliable narrator, hasn't Ross abandoned all authorial direction for or control of what his reader is to believe; hasn't he in effect licensed the reader for every and any interpretive flight?

But, having complained at length of other readings of this novel, it seems only fair to sketch my own, not only as a contribution to what now seems a necessary critical rebalancing, a further rehabilitation of Mrs. Bentley, but also in aid of what must continue to be a collaborative enterprise, the identification of the means by which Ross retains and exerts authorial direction and control in the absence of a reliable narrator.

The most fruitful line of inquiry into such means pursued in recent essays about the novel has been exploration of its concerns about art and artists. Mrs. Bentley is of course and by her own account a more or less accomplished musician, but there is even more abundant evidence to indicate that Ross conceives and displays her activities as an artist under definitions of the term that are at once older, humbler, and broader than its post-Renaissance connotations frame, conceptions that recover the word's root meanings of artificer and maker. Ross's conception is evident in her very first entry, a remarkable characterizing device for establishing the quality of his narrator's consciousness. Reread this short passage and notice that its apparently random or associative details are in fact carefully organized by the speaker's preoccupation with the techniques, lessons, and rules of a curious, but thoroughly familiar sort of craft. The passage has the flavour of a self-scrutinizing, but generally satisfied review of a performance, here the crucial opening performance "at home" to the audience of their new Horizon congregation. In her evening's reflection, we are in effect backstage with her, invited by Ross to share her tart and unsparing critique. She recalls, for instance, that she had to interrupt her husband, to step on his lines, in order to bring them up to the level of piety expected by their first visitor: "Poor Philip — for almost twelve years now he's been preaching in these little prairie towns, but he still hasn't learned the proper technique for it. He still handicaps himself with a guilty feeling that he ought to mean everything he says. He hasn't learned yet to be bland."⁵⁰ She articulates the conventions dictating the roles she plays and relishes her stratagems for meeting them. Claiming that "I could use the pliers and hammer twice as well myself, with none of his mutterings or smashed-up fingers," she has "let him be the man about the house, and sat on a trunk among the litter serenely making curtains over . . ." (p. 3), in obedience to a lesson learned twelve years before about the community's expectations. We even catch a glimpse of her skills at improvisation as, in a moment of affectionate concern for Philip, she rehearses a rapid sequence of quick changes: "broodless old woman that I am, I get impatient being just his wife, and start in trying to mother him too" (p. 4). Although she records her on-stage management of Philip's performance, we also learn that the demands of their public roles are no less exacting, no less directed by the close tolerances within which she must perform than are the roles she plays for her husband. Moved by her concern for Philip, she had kissed him, but only "Lightly, for that is of all things what I mustn't do, let him ever suspect me of being sorry" (p. 4). The images and figures by which Ross embodies his conception of his narrator are not, however, exclusively theatrical. Alert to the task of shaping her husband, she is quick to recognize a fellow craftswoman in Mrs. Finley, their last visitor, and as quick to assess her work:

The deportment and mien of her own family bear witness to a potter's hand that never falters. Her husband, for instance, is an appropriately meek little man, but you can't help feeling what an achievement is his meekness. It's like a tight wire cage drawn

over him, and words and gestures, indicative of a more expan-
sive past, keep squeezing through it the same way that parts of
the portly Mrs. Wenderby this afternoon kept squeezing through
the back and sides of Philip's study armchair. (pp. 5–6)

Her mention of Mrs. Finley's sons reminds her of her own stillborn
son and prompts a sudden change of tone from the mild bawdy of
Mrs. Wenderby's backside to a sombre and touching moment of
empathy with or perhaps self-projection into Philip's imagination.
Ross again varies the figures, but retains the conception underlying
the whole entry: "He likes boys — often, I think, plans the bringing-
up and education of *his* boy. A fine, well-tempered lad by now, strung
just a little on the fine side, responsive to too many overtones. For I
know Philip and he has a way of building in his own image too"
(p. 6).

In the novel Paul earns Philip's scorn for characterizing one of his
sketches as *"Humanity in microcosm"*; I risk less in claiming that the
book's first entry offers us the narrator in microcosm, for Ross has
taken great care to organize seemingly disparate details by a principle
of selection that leaves a coherent — and I will argue — definitive
impression of his narrator: her mind, the quality of her consciousness,
is organized primarily as that of an artificer, practising an intricate
set of crafts deliberately, self-consciously, and with a hard-won, but
still zestful sense of their demands, possibilities, and limits. It is not
so much that Ross creates Mrs. Bentley within the métier or by means
of technical vocabularies associated with any particular craft; it is
rather that he endows her with the characteristic perceptions, aspirations, energies, and concerns of the craftsman, the artisan, or the
maker, in brief with the active sensibility of a certain kind of artist.

One implication of this reading is that the first entry may serve as
prologue or overture for the subsequent work, announcing key
motifs then developed and counterpointed against each other. For
instance, the conception made explicit in the image of Mrs. Finley's
"potter's hand" is repeated with variations to establish that a wife's
need to manage or shape her husband is a commonplace in this
community. The bias of Mrs. Bentley's habit of mind may account
for her description of Mrs. Lawson of Partridge Hill, ". . . a sharp,
stirring, rather pretty woman, hurrying and managing her long lean
husband like a yelping little terrier round a plodding Clyde" (p. 20),
but we hear the same intent in the voices of the most commendable

women in the novel. Mrs. Bird, the doctor's wife, is a self-professed expatriate: "Provincial atmosphere — it suffocates. The result is it's always a man's world I live in" (p. 21). And later we get her "formula for marital success" in such a world. "But you shouldn't distress him this way, letting him see you cry. He'll never forgive you for it. . . . Always let a man think how fine and tolerant he is to put up with you" (p. 86). And Laura, the independent ranch wife who takes an "unaccountable dislike" to Philip, puts it straightforwardly and a bit ominously: "I wish I had the handling of him for a day or two" (p. 102). This motif reveals that some of the shaping arts Mrs. Bentley practises are as much martial as marital.

A related motif introduced in the first entry and later developed is Mrs. Bentley's attribution to or perhaps recognition in Philip of the shaping intent she shares with the community's women. She describes Philip's reaction to their adoption of Steve: "He hasn't seen him with his eyes yet, just his pity and imagination. An unwanted, derided little outcast, exactly what he used to be himself. . . . After a while the pity and imagination are going to run out; and there's going to be left just an ordinary, uninspiring boy" (p. 53). Later she identifies ". . . a strange arrogance in his devotion to Steve, an unconscious determination to mold him in his own image, even though it's an image in which he himself must find little satisfaction; and stubborn still he keeps on trying to make an artist of the boy . . ." (p. 112). If Philip's determination in this respect is "unconscious," her own, as she admits, is fully conscious: "Philip will forget the real Steve before long, and behind his cold locked lips mourn another of his own creating. I know him. I know as a creator what he's capable of" (p. 119).

Their rivalry over Steve is part of another pattern of figures which casts the relationship between the sexes as contest. Mrs. Bentley characteristically expresses her sense of her marriage with images of a combat not so much violent as chivalric, and at least evoking the ritualized, paradoxical, and erotic potential of such figures so fully exploited in the English tradition by Donne and Shakespeare. "It's a woman's way, I suppose, to keep on trying to subdue a man, to bind him to her, and it's a man's way to keep on just as determined to be free" (p. 64). These subduing and binding ways, "a woman's ways," seem to require techniques more appropriate to the guerrilla than to the knight, but like a knight, she can occasionally vaunt: "Now sometimes I feel it a kind of triumph, the way I won my place in his life despite him . . ." (p. 33). More often, however, she understands the strategic dangers of tactical victories: "For when he gives himself to me like that, when we come close to each other, always to follow is a sudden mustering of self-sufficiency, a repudiating swing the other way" (p. 23), or again: "He would just half-yield himself to me, then stand detached, self-sufficient" (p. 33). And she has learned the logistics of affection, has learned to temper her sense of triumph with a special kind of husbandry: "It was more of him than I had had in weeks, but afraid to be spendthrift with such a moment I slipped away from him again" (p. 23), or again: "And then, still to be frugal with the moment, I let him go back to his study" (p. 24). As these passages suggest, Mrs. Bentley's entries sometimes have the air of reports from the front, assessing the strengths and weaknesses of her forces in these battles of the heart.

Perhaps the greatest irony of Mrs. Bentley's understanding of this chivalric contest is her full awareness that both her greatest risks and her greatest chances for a victory lie in submission. She contests with an opponent she has long ago submitted to as her lord and master: "For right from the beginning I knew that with Philip it was the only way. . . . Submitting to him that way, yielding my identity — it seemed what life was intended for" (p. 16). She also realizes the risks of unconditional submission, for she has become dependent upon her loving enemy for the very resources that energize her as a worthy opponent: "To have him notice me, speak to me as if I really mattered in his life, after twelve years with him that's all I want or need. It arranges my world for me, strengthens and quickens it, makes it immune to all other worlds" (p. 16). If the engagements of this contest are reported with some quickened zest, there are also casualty reports: "I must still keep on reaching out, trying to possess him, trying to make myself matter. I must, for I've left myself nothing else. I haven't been like him. I've reserved no retreat, no world of my own. I've whittled myself hollow that I might enclose and hold him, and when he shakes me off I'm just a shell" (p. 75). I find this one of the most moving of Mrs. Bentley's confessions even as I despair of untangling its close weave of pathos and the grotesque, of genuine pain, firm resolve, and self-dramatizing pride. But at least part of its affective power comes from Ross's deft use of one of the homeliest of crafts, whittling, to image his narrator's ruling habit of mind, her shaping sensibility even as it works to create her own enclosing self. This shaping sensibility directs us, finally, to comprehend Mrs.

Bentley's major actions in the novel as the activities of a home-maker in a way well beyond the literal. Having realized that the House of Bentley has become another false front, she marshals her skills and energies to restore its substance, not only shaping herself and her husband to that end, but also ruthlessly expropriating first Steve and then Judith's son to restore the lineage. The novel's title, given this understanding, acquires a fine ironic ring: the lord Mrs. Bentley serves is her husband, and her service is in restoring his failing house.

It is just here that the major critical issue about this novel has been drawn. What is the proper way to respond to this spectacle? In my case study, I identified one emerging consensus that would have us distance ourselves from it. These critics warn us to be wary and suspicious of Mrs. Bentley so that we may recognize and compensate for her unreliability as a narrator. In this view we must resist immersion or too intimate a share in her narrative perspective, must almost immediately disengage ourselves from her consciousness in order to assume a position from which we can second-guess or sit in judgement upon her. I then tried to uncover the critical difficulties and dangers of such a course. Let me here make two additional points. While such distancing may eventually be necessary for the reader, done prematurely it risks a failure to appreciate the intricate dynamics of Mrs. Bentley's world as she both suffers and seeks to shape it; a failure, in short, to undergo the experience of this novel. Moreover, because the case against Mrs. Bentley's unreliability has almost invariably been prosecuted by means of allegations of her failings in manners and morals, we may have overlooked another direction offered by Ross's controlling conception of his narrator for a proper judgement of Mrs. Bentley.

If I'm right about this conception and its authority for the reader, at the very least the novel suggests that she be judged primarily by the measures of successful craftsmanship, the measures of competence like ingenuity, aptness, efficiency, cleverness, and so on — measures she is by no means always successful in meeting. In fact Mrs. Bentley's practice as an artificer and maker renders her particularly liable to the strictures of traditional codes of manners and morals, a liability common to a line of makers tracing back to the poets Plato banned from his republic for lying. She *is*, undeniably, a dissembler; she *is* self-dramatizing; she *is* manipulative, but Ross's authorial procedures seem designed to raise some thorny questions about exactly what standards become most appropriate and relevant in judging such activities. Is the artist to be held to the moral standards imposed by and on ordinary men, or can he claim a latitude by virtue of his special calling? Ross poses this question — and gives it considerable ironic potential — by means of Mrs. Bentley's frequent estimations of Philip as artist. Although she makes little or no claim for moral licence on behalf of her own activities as artificer, she makes every such claim for her husband. She habitually defines Philip as an artist by nature, as a "born dreamer"; "He believed he could paint — with the passion and extravagance that are natural to a boy sometimes, believed that he was meant to paint. The important thing was to fulfill himself, let the end justify the means" (p. 18). However boyish the belief imputed here to Philip, it is certainly her own, and she easily adapts this justifying formula to excuse everything from his bad manners to his bad faith with his God and his congregation: "It was temperament, I said, the artist in him" (p. 64). In part her defence is based on awe for his artist's calling, her conviction that he is in quest of something more worthy than her own considerable understanding of ordinary reality; Philip "pierces this workaday reality of ours" (p. 101), and she cites with approval his contention that art, like religion, is "a rejection of the material, common-sense world for one that's illusory, yet somehow more important" (p. 112). Intent on shaping only the human clay of the material world, she is chagrined to discover that she may have reduced the very moral latitude required for Philip's artistic or self-fulfilment: "But it was all wrong. Comfort and routine were the last things he needed. Instead he ought to have been out mingling with his own kind. He ought to have whetted himself against them, then gone off to fight it out alone. He ought to have had the opportunity to live, to be reckless, spendthrift, bawdy, anything but what he is, what I've made him" (p. 103). This is licence indeed and whether or not Philip merits it, we must ask, I think, whether Ross may intend some reflexive ironies here. Should Mrs. Bentley's claims for Philip, and by extension for art and the artist, have any bearing on our moral judgements of her own character? Might not simple justice require that we now extend to Mrs. Bentley, humble artificer though she is, some of the mitigating moral latitude she — and some of her detractors — claim only for her husband?

In any event, the cumulative effects of Ross's controlling conception of Mrs. Bentley add a dimension to her characterization and to narrative missing in his previous works. In "No Other Way," his first effort to shape a drama of consciousness, the portraiture of Hatty Glenn is handicapped by deterministic psychology, a conception of character finally dominated by her conditioning. In "The Painted Door," Ross advanced to a credible drama resolved by his protagonist's achieved, but tragically interrupted awareness. In his first novel, Ross abandons the intervention of a third-person reporter to offer us the direct spectacle of a remarkably active, complex, and dynamic consciousness, a shaping intelligence fully engaged, not to say embattled, with her world.

The Well

In his second novel, *The Well* (1958), Ross continues to centre his narrative attention on the revelation of one character's consciousness. Perhaps having discovered the limit of first-person narrative that Henry James called "the terrible *fluidity* of self-revelation,"[51] Ross now returns to the method he had used in most of the early short stories, a third-person narrator whose omniscience is confined to reporting the central character's psychic experience. Unfortunately, Ross's deployment of this method over a long narrative results in some unresolved problems that weaken this novel considerably.

Ross's protagonist, young Chris Rowe, has taken flight from a life of petty crime in Montreal and has found what first seems refuge as a hired man on a prosperous prairie farm. But refuge quickly threatens to become a trap as Chris discovers demanding new roles he is expected to play. Old Larson, the farm's owner, fitfully sees in Chris a substitute for his dead son, and Larson's young and predatory wife sees a conspirator, first in her bed and then in her plot to do away with Larson. And Chris is responsive to each of these demands; hardened as an urban predator by his Boyle street conditioning and yet still softened by the early loss of his own father and the promiscuity of his mother, he becomes a more-or-less willing pawn in the bitter contest between Larson and Sylvia. Robert D. Chambers has described the resulting narrative plan quite precisely: "Chris' character is shaped to fit with great structural neatness into the polarities represented by Sylvia and Larson. The basic development of the book sees Chris vacillating between these two centres of contrasting values."[52]

Chambers' use of "vacillating" here is neutral, but the pejorative connotations of the word may also be used to define the first of the problems disfiguring this novel. Because so much of the narrator's activity is devoted to reports of Chris's inner states, it seems clear that Ross had hoped to achieve dramatic energy and intensity by making the stage of his protagonist's consciousness a particularly busy place. Certainly the cast of emotions, memories, inclinations, and moods that are said to move Chris Rowe is remarkably active, suddenly appearing, vigorously interacting for a moment, and then quickly succeeding each other off stage. Chapter five, in which Ross uses the occasion of Chris's introduction to Larson's skittish stallion, North, to explore the boy's feelings about the older man, is a good illustration of this method. Confronted by the stallion, "Chris quailed a moment . . . but his vanity, the need to live up to Larson's praise, regained control swiftly."[3] A page later, "A sudden hot rage filled him and he had to bite his lip a moment to control himself" (p. 43). But shortly after this, "Chris watched and listened respectfully. It was acceptance again. Like a boy, he wanted to please Larson now, prove himself worthy" (p. 45). And then, "But with the wish came the realization of what happened, where he was, and his elation collapsed as quickly as it had soared. . . . His mind made another leap, this time to the futility of possession" (p. 45). A page later, "For a moment he hated Larson," but "Again the implication was acceptance, and Chris, forgetful that a moment before he had been hostile and withdrawn, swung back impulsively" (p. 46). And the action of the chapter finally concludes with "Chris softened again. To be preferred, singled out for a favor . . . it gave him a feeling of place and acceptance. It was a kind of fulfilment, a licence to relax and trust. But it was also a threat to his self-reliance, to the tough hard strength in which he took such pride. He half yielded a moment, then thrust it away scornfully" (pp. 47–48).

These reports of Chris's rapid succession of mood swings are meant not only to promote some illusion of intense psychic action, but also to generate a certain suspense about Chris's eventual choice as the contest between Larson and Sylvia moves to its violent climax. Unfortunately the accumulation of these reports works against these intentions. Because the polarities of feeling and Chris's vacillations among them become so familiar and predictable as their patterning is repeated throughout the novel, the impression is not one of growth or change in Chris, but rather of a character that seems remarkably shallow, passive, irresolute, and unstable. On occasion Ross even

removes the interval between contrary feelings so that Chris is said
to experience them simultaneously, and the result is a virtual paralysis of consciousness: "There was one impulse to respond, and
another to flare up and ask him what he meant. They neutralized
each other. He flushed, then half-smiled, then stood silent and
abashed" (p. 106). Robert Chambers believes that "we can see Ross
gradually inching Chris toward regeneration";[54] again his use of
"inching" is neutral, but that is exactly the impression left, progress
so barely perceptible that it seems more like stasis. Rather than
learning from the succession of his emotions, Chris comes to seem
doomed to their endless round, an impression the narrator strengthens with suggestions that Chris has been bewitched or enchanted:
"He was repelled and fascinated. At the same time he rejected and
believed. He wanted to break the spell and he wanted to remain
possessed by it. He lay still and taut now, drawn back a little, scarcely
touching her" (p. 184). Chris is said to be released from this stasis
when, at the novel's climax, he suddenly realizes that he has not
obeyed Sylvia's order to shoot Larson: "He was free — there was
room for nothing else. He had been living under a spell — of what
he was, always had been, always must be, a doom of Boyle Street
cheapness and frustration — and now the spell was broken" (p. 236).

Some of the critics' dissatisfaction with what Ken Mitchell has
called the book's "drawn-out, flabby resolution"[55] may occur
because what seems a climax for Chris, his sense of being freed, is
almost immediately exposed as illusory as he wavers once again,
submitting to Sylvia's direction in disposing of Larson's body. It takes
some sixteen more pages for Chris again to muster strength enough
to resist her: "And somehow, in asserting his own strength, he had
defeated her completely" (p. 252). After the voluminously recorded
minutiae of Chris's mental and emotional states, the "somehow"
here is vastly inadequate; the narrator's usual care with dissection
has turned evasive at a most crucial juncture. Although Chris's voice
is said to be "clear and resolute" in the novel's last paragraph,
"somehow" can do little to change what has come to be our
understanding of Chris's character, our expectation that, given the
long record of his experience, he will likely vacillate again from his
"final" decision, irresolute to the end.

The narrator's crucial lapse during the novel's climax points further
to some unresolved tensions within his role in the novel. Protected
by the convention of third-person omniscience from the charges of

incompetence brought against Mrs. Bentley, the narrator of *The Well* has generous licence from the reader to be the probing, but essentially self-effacing reporter of the novel's central consciousness. However, Ross indulges this licence so extensively that even dialogue comes to seem intended as illustration for the narrator's analysis. In fact the narrator's penetrating voice sounds so insistently throughout the novel that it often calls attention to itself in ways that compromise the narrative authority sanctioned by convention. Lorraine McMullen, for instance, has noted a use of figures that necessarily reflects on the narrator's own habits of perception: "When colorful metaphor is occasionally employed it seems inappropriate, too precious for the harshness of theme and action and the personality of the central character."[56] And one can easily find other kinds of examples that raise questions about the narrator's sensibility: "The inherent softness of his nature, everything immature that had been held in place by nerve and vanity as a rupture is held in place by a truss, was swollen out painfully in need of protection and security" (pp. 6–7), this time a figure not too precious, but too crude for its subject. Occasionally the reader feels the burden the narrator carries in trying to record a sensibility less articulate than his own. After reporting a paragraph of questions that Chris seems to be asking himself, the narrator adds: "Something like this, swift and confused, went through Chris's mind . . ." (p. 140). On other occasions, the reader is simply unclear about what role the narrator is playing. He shows Chris once again musing over his predicament and then adds parenthetically: "(This, perhaps, because his conscience was so little accustomed to being deferred to that it made only modest claims, and accepted what he had already suffered as settlement in full; or because its mechanism and functioning were of so rudimentary a nature that the slight counterweight of rejecting Sylvia's scheme had been sufficient to restore its equilibrium)" (p. 201). Is this the voice of a reporter, or a speculative analyst scrupulous in offering alternative possibilities? Is the consciousness being recorded here suddenly impenetrable, or is the analyst uncertain about the terminology appropriate to its description, or is the tone simply condescending? It is impossible for the reader to be sure, and the uncertainty compromises the narrator's authority.

I agree with Chambers that this novel continues to show ample evidence of Ross's "keen psychological insight,"[57] but here it is so earnestly, even doggedly deployed that it threatens to impede rather than facilitate the novel's drama of consciousness. The flaws of this novel indicate that, despite the relative success of *As for Me and My House*, Ross had not yet mastered the crafts for adequately translating his psychological insights into effective characterization over a long narrative, that he was still experimenting in search of appropriate form.

Whir of Gold

In *Whir of Gold* (1970), Ross's narrator/protagonist, the young musician Sonny McAlpine, recalls "days when the major-minor diatonic forthrightness of 'Old Black Joe' and 'Rock of Ages' was a strait jacket into which I couldn't fit, neither I nor the prairie world around me; and at such times, like a cat trying the furniture for the right texture to scratch on, to ease the itch in its claws, I would leave off practising and for a few minutes go exploring on my own."[58] In effect this passage also voices Ross's own decision to break from the restraint of convention, to "go exploring on my own." The next seven chapters of the novel, 21 through 27, are unlike anything he had previously written; in this sequence Sonny reports his preparation for, participation in, and escape from the scene of a robbery and records the experience with a style that seeks to convey both its immediacy and its precise affective texture: "Lucky — such a lot of snow. . . . Hidden in it — lost, alone . . . . Couldn't have picked a better night. . . . Starting to thicken, gain, clogging the eyes and nostrils as if I were venturing too far, into forbidden territory. A flick at my ear and then away, another, sharper, on my cheek; then a thick hard slap to cut my breath and fill my mouth —" (p. 145). There is nothing particularly innovative about this style; it employs variations on stream-of-consciousness techniques, but its departure from Ross's usual habits of reflective narration is vivid enough to have attracted critical comment ranging from Ken Mitchell's approval of the "tight, blistering pace"[59] of the robbery scene to Robert Chambers' complaint about that style's "cryptic shorthand whose meaning occasionally eludes the reader."[60]

But the most serious consequence of the style is what Lorraine McMullen has called "a structural imbalance"[61] in the novel. The seven-chapter sequence focusing on the robbery is set within a plot that repeats the basic situation of *The Well*: Mad, "A big, warm lump of a woman who would never grow up and never grow bad" (p. 86), competes with Charlie, a small-time grifter, for Sonny's loyalties. As in *The Well*, these two flanking figures come to embody conflicting values between which Sonny vacillates — here the possibilities of Mad's love and the claims of her domesticity opposed by Charlie's lure of easy money and its promise of freedom. Sonny is more mature and sensitive than Chris Rowe of *The Well*, more intelligent than the characters his narration creates; his vividly empathic portraits of Mad and Charlie convince us that he fully understands both their natures and the values they offer. The opening pages of chapter four, in which Sonny feigns sleep in order to observe Mad's strategies of delay in departing his room after what he had insisted was only a one-night stand, is a deft and touching display of his imaginative abilities to penetrate the motives of another, and it is testimony that Ross at least began this novel with his attention firmly fixed on the drama of consciousness. Sonny's skills as a narrator are further attested to by the risks he takes with language in order to convey the exact quality of his impressions: "Charlie was a sandy, thin man with a double-take face that ran the gamut of age. Sometimes you caught the callow, awkward look of an adolescent — wanting approval, watching for signs of it; sometimes the craftiness of an old man, isolated in suspicion and defeat. . . . The lips were red and full, almost a pout: a late raspberry on a dry stalk; and the eyes peered cautiously from deep, dirty-finger sockets. A spoiled, ill-tempered little boy, trying to scare you with a skull" (pp. 41–42). Given this range of narrative abilities, it is surprising, and finally disappointing, that in reporting his own decision to join Charlie in the robbery, the choice that resolves the plot's initial conflict, Sonny must confess an almost complete ignorance about his motives: "There must have been a moment when the key clicked and turned — a moment of decision, involving *me* — but when I go back I find only the door, first closed, then open, never the act of opening it" (p. 114). He makes the point not to excuse himself: "Morally, I take my medicine" (p. 114), but in genuine perplexity. In the 1970 interview with Earle Toppings, Ross spoke of Sonny's crucial lapse in a way that suggests he himself was uncertain about its reasons: ". . . he puzzles himself over why he did it; and he makes plausible suggestions; probably they're not right. . . ." The novel itself suggests that Sonny's inability to recover the moment of choice may have affinities with the existentialists' "gratuitous act" as used by Gide and Camus; it may also be the result of conflicting narrative demands, the need to transform Sonny rather suddenly from a reflective intelligence into a sensate locus of direct experience. Whatever the reasons, the effect is to compound what Ken Mitchell has seen as "too many unresolved contradictions" in Sonny's character: "We are asked, at some points, to see Sonny McAlpine as a gawky, naive farmboy fighting the asphalt jungle; at others, he is depicted as street-wise and cagey."[62] The point can be extended to unresolved contradictions among Sonny's functions as a narrator; in the opening sequence, he is clearly the perceptive observer creating the world of the novel with a touch of the poet, but at the plot's turning point, he suddenly disclaims the ability to understand and consequently to inform, and thereafter his function is reduced to little more than a reflexive register of immediate experience. Here, Ross's promising beginning for a drama of consciousness is threatened by a new departure in mid-novel, an experiment with techniques for the rendition of what might be called pre-conscious experience, a sequence of sensation unmediated by the narrator's mind. Both narrative levels are vividly and carefully done, but they work against each other in this novel.

Sawbones Memorial

In *Sawbones Memorial* (1974), Ross abandons for the first time the use of a single narrator, organizing the work dramatically as a series, by Lorraine McMullen's count, "of forty individual episodes which vary in length from a few lines to twelve pages, including six interior monologues, two speeches, one dramatic monologue, snatches of conversation, and more extended conversations between two or more individuals";[63] we hear or overhear, by my count, at least twenty-one identifiable voices and a small chorus of anonymous ones. The novel's present consists of a few hours at an evening party where the community of Upward, Saskatchewan, has gathered to honour Doc Hunter, retiring after forty-five years as the town's sole physician, and to celebrate the opening of a new hospital bearing his name; the date is 20 April 1948, Doc's seventy-fifth birthday and the anniversary of his arrival in Upward in 1903. Ross successfully exploits this public occasion of nostalgic reminiscence, credibly demonstrating that the life of this community quite literally creates and sustains itself in the stories its citizens tell. Ross not only records their stories, but with some neat touches reveals the conventions which govern their telling. Some stories, for instance, may be worn and familiar: "I wasn't there but I've often heard you tell it,"[64] but innovation is both permitted and subject to exasperated complaint: "I've heard you tell it many many times and there's never been a word before about an injection . . ." (p. 18), and ". . . Ida's experiences never lost anything in the telling" (p. 25). Most of the stories centre on Doc Hunter, but they reach out to embrace his patients, lovers, critics, protégés, and friends, absent and present, living and dead: "What a lot of stories Doc could tell" (p. 70), and the community's voices join him in telling them. Dan Furby, the editor of the town's *Chronicle*, is instructed by his wife, Nellie, who edits the "Nosy Parker" column, to "draw out an anecdote or two, something to reveal the warmth and humanity of the man" (p. 81), and the citizens comply, but they are also ready with "A lot of stories, Doc, that you used to have a pretty good way of fiddling round yourself" (p. 9), or with "the stories he was such a hard collector" (p. 93). The stories multiply and this balance is maintained as the town reveals its pettiness and bigotry as well as its good will, its earthy humour as well as the rigid curbs of its respectability.

The cumulative effect of these interweaving stories is engaging rather than dramatically intense or powerful; our curiosity is aroused and adroitly satisfied, but the experience is muted and distanced, certainly less intense than the response reported to Doc by another outsider, Caroline Gillespie, who has come to Upward as the English war bride of the town's leading citizen: "You and Grandmother Robinson — the stories began to haunt me, until suddenly one day it was clear, and I said to myself that's what I want too" (p. 24). Those stories were about pioneer hardships, the town's heroic past, and Caroline has quickly discovered their discrepancies with Upward's present and pervasive gentility, but story-telling works in other ways to draw her into the community: "Caroline, this is terribly nervy of us but we're curious — just how did you and Dunc ever get to know each other?" (p. 76). She complies, and is rewarded with: "Now isn't that a story!" (p. 77). The exclamation seems excessive for the commonplace anecdote she has related, nor are we completely convinced by Nellie Furby's judgement of her husband's report of Doc's stories about difficult medical and moral decisions from his professional past: " 'Now isn't that drama for you?' 'Not just drama, Dan, *high* drama' " (p. 97). Nellie's earlier comment —

"He's likely done all sorts of things like that, played a part in countless little dramas" (p. 80) — seems more accurate as a description of the novel's stories. Because the scale of so many "little dramas" tends toward the diminutive, they also tend to be adumbrated rather than developed, sketched rather than enacted.

A related reason for the muted quality of *Sawbones Memorial* is that, by his choice of technique, Ross has virtually abandoned plot as a source of the reader's interest. Aside from some comic bickering, there are no human conflicts in the novel's present that might generate significant action. What potential there is for such action is left unexploited. For instance, Benny Fox, the town's discreet homosexual, asks what might first seem a crucial question: "Doc, you're leaving and I may not have another chance to ask you: did my mother kill herself?" Doc's answer is unpromising — "I don't know, Benny" (p. 100) — but the subsequent conversation suggests that Benny doesn't seem to care very much anyway. The stories, of course, allude to conflict and action aplenty. Lorraine McMullen reminds us that "Beneath the surface he reveals a tumultuous Dostoyevskian activity — including murder, suicide, incest, attempted rape, abortion, euthanasia — all aspects of the past of this seemingly ordinary little community. . . ."[65] But most of these stories are about conflicts long since resolved if only by the passage of time, actions completed in the past and now preserved in the retelling. This patina of reminiscence leeches both force and colour from the stories; as Nellie says of the town's notorious Maisie Bell, now "Fifty-five if she's a day": "The scarlet by this time must be faded to a pretty pale pink" (p. 20).

Finally, because the stories work as distillations of the town's past, tending to preserve an event by the shorthand of its public evidence and external configurations, we are only invited or left to infer the nature of the actors' psychological participation — its contours, qualities, and costs — a narrative concern that has given much energy, however sporadically realized, to Ross's previous work. The exceptions permitted by this novel's form are the six interior monologues, one of which, Sarah Gillespie's extended reminiscence about the problems of adolescent female sexuality on the Prairies, forms perhaps the liveliest passage in the work. But again, because the monologues are private meditations upon associative memories triggered by the occasion, the reader's share in the experience is reflective rather than dramatically urgent or empathic. Doc's mono-

288

logue, which concludes the novel, is typical; there he muses on his still secret, but long past adultery with Big Anna, the fruit of which is Nick Miller, raised by Anna and her tubercular husband as their own son. Nick has been a butt of Upward's bigotry against "hunkies" and Doc recalls his covert efforts, covered in part by his avuncular role in the town, to protect Nick, eventually sending his protégé to medical school, and Doc ends with quiet satisfaction that Nick is returning to Upward as his successor. Because the monologue confirms that Doc is Nick's father, something the town, and the reader, only dimly suspect, it offers one kind of closure, but it raises a troubling question as well, for Doc is silent even to himself about his motives for so long concealing, and continuing to conceal Nick's identity as his son, presumably even from Nick himself. Because the stories have revealed Doc as otherwise forthright, outspoken, and independent, we are left to speculate about his motives here — is it fear of exposure, or necessary deference to community standards, a case, as Doc phrases it earlier, of "Upward . . . imposing its will" (p. 25)? But the novel also offers a clue that restrains such speculation. At one point Dan Furby asks old Harry, Doc's crony, whether he has ever wondered about what, although Harry cuts him off before he can name it, they both surmise is Doc's relationship with Nick, and Harry later says: "Even supposing what's on your mind is true, what difference does it make now? Why snoop around to start another story" (p. 96). Whatever else Harry may mean, I take his remark as confirmation that in *Sawbones Memorial*, Ross has deliberately transferred his narrative attention from the theatre of private consciousness to the public stage of story telling, a stage where the conventions permit only limited access to the private soul.

Although *Sawbones Memorial* is Ross's shortest novel, it displays and celebrates the plenitude and diversity of social life more fully than any of the others. It is, furthermore, a particularly well-made work and deserves much of the praise that Lorraine McMullen's careful analyses have sought for it. But its achievement is quieter, certainly less intense or powerful, perhaps safer than that of *As for Me and My House,* and its techniques, for all the new direction they represent in Ross's career, not only abandon, but tend to seal off the experiments with the revelation of human consciousness conducted in *The Well* and *Whir of Gold.*

In a short essay titled "On Looking Back" in 1970, Ross refused to speculate about "his sensibility and creative processes," on grounds that "artists themselves as well as psychologists seem pretty well agreed that the 'creative sources' are in the subconscious, and the psychologists are also agreed that self-analysis can seldom do more than scrape the surface. . . . So if I don't understand myself — my 'creative processes' if you like, why I did this and not that — how could I possibly write about them?"[66] Despite his refusal to inquire into them, it seems clear that Ross's creative processes have concentrated, over the course of his career, on the exploration and exposure of the inner life of his characters. Beginning with the limited possibilities of deterministic psychology, the sequence of his fiction records the patient efforts, the risks taken in searching for means to delineate and dramatize the vagaries of human consciousness, even to the latest reticence about its deeper secrets in *Sawbones Memorial*. If the record is uneven, if *The Well* and *Whir of Gold* represent unsuccessful experiments, Sinclair Ross's success is to be measured by the superb vitality of the inner life realized in "The Painted Door" and in *As for Me and My House*.

NOTES

[1] Mark Sarner, "Whore with a Heart of Golda," *Books in Canada*, Nov. 1974, p. 9.

[2] William French, "Too Good Too Soon, Ross Remains the Elusive Canadian," *The Globe and Mail* [Toronto], 27 July 1974, p. 25.

[3] Lorraine McMullen, *Sinclair Ross*, Twayne's World Author Series (Boston: Twayne, 1979). Unless otherwise specified, all biographical information has been taken from Chapter i of this book.

[4] Ken Mitchell, *Sinclair Ross: A Reader's Guide* (Moose Jaw: Thunder Creek Publishing Co-operative, 1981), p. iii.

[5] French, p. 25.

[6] Rev. of *As for Me and My House*, *The New Yorker*, 22 Feb. 1941, p. 72.

[7] Rose Feld, rev. of *As for Me and My House*, *New York Herald Tribune Book Review*, 23 Feb. 1941, p. 14.

[8] Sinclair Ross, *Sawbones Memorial* (Toronto: McClelland and Stewart, 1974), p. 89.

[9] French, p. 25.

[10] McMullen, p. 16.

[11] Earle Toppings, "Canadian Writers on Tape: Sinclair Ross," Ontario Institute for Studies in Education, 1971.

[12] McMullen, p. 22.

[13] E.K. Brown, rev. of *As for Me and My House*, *The Canadian Forum*, July 1941, p. 124.

[14] Margaret Laurence, "Introduction" to *The Lamp at Noon and Other Stories*, New Canadian Library, No. 62 (Toronto: McClelland and Stewart, 1968), p. 7.

[15] Ross, "On Looking Back," *Mosaic*, 3, No. 3 (Spring 1970), 93.

[16] Ross, "Montreal and French-Canadian Culture," *The Tamarack Review*, No. 40 (Summer 1966), p. 46.

[17] McMullen, p. 21.

[18] French, p. 25.

[19] R.S. Stubbs, "Presenting Sinclair Ross," *Saturday Night*, 9 Aug. 1941, p. 17.

[20] McMullen, p. 22.

[21] Robert Kroetsch, "Beyond Nationalism: A Prologue," *Mosaic*, 14, No. 2 (Spring 1981), vi.

[22] Brown, p. 125.

[23] Hugo McPherson, "Fiction, 1940–1960," in *Literary History of Canada: Canadian Literature in English*, gen. ed. and introd. Carl F. Klinck (Toronto: Univ. of Toronto Press, 1965), p. 706.

[24] Edward McCourt, *The Canadian West in Fiction* (Toronto: Ryerson, 1949), p. 99.

[25] Roy Daniells, "Introduction" to *As for Me and My House*, New Canadian Library, No. 4 (Toronto: McClelland and Stewart, 1957), pp. vi–vii.

[26] W.H. New, "Sinclair Ross's Ambivalent World," *Canadian Literature*, No. 40 (Spring 1969), p. 27.

[27] D.J. Dooley, *Moral Vision in the Canadian Novel* (Toronto: Clarke, Irwin, 1979), p. 44.

[28] Paul Denham, "Narrative Technique in Sinclair Ross's *As For Me and My House*," *Studies in Canadian Literature*, 5 (1980), 118–19.

[29] Warren Tallman, "Wolf in the Snow: Part One: Four Windows on to Landscapes," *Canadian Literature*, No. 5 (Summer 1960), p. 15.

[30] McPherson, p. 705.

[31] Margaret Atwood, *Survival: A Thematic Guide to Canadian Literature* (Toronto: House of Anansi, 1972), p. 191.

[32] David Stouck, "The Mirror and the Lamp in Sinclair Ross's *As for Me and My House*," *Mosaic*, 7, No. 2 (Winter 1974), 143.

[33] Barbara Godard, "El Greco in Canada: Sinclair Ross's *As for Me and My House*," *Mosaic*, 14, No. 2 (Spring 1981), 56.

[34] Henry Kreisel, "The Prairie: A State of Mind," *Transactions of the Royal*

Society of Canada, 4th ser., 6 (June 1968), 173.

[35] Kreisel, pp. 175, 178.

[36] Ross, "September Snow," *Queen's Quarterly*, 42 (1935), 455. I am indebted to May Diver for her careful collation of the variant texts of Ross's stories.

[37] Ross, "The Lamp at Noon," *Queen's Quarterly*, 45 (1938), 39.

[38] Ross, "The Painted Door," *Queen's Quarterly*, 46 (1939), 165.

[39] Ross, "Not by Rain Alone," in *The Lamp at Noon and Other Stories*, New Canadian Library, No. 62 (Toronto: McClelland and Stewart, 1968), p. 57.

[40] Robert D. Chambers, *Sinclair Ross & Ernest Buckler* (Vancouver: Copp Clark, 1975), p. 11.

[41] McMullen, p. 50.

[42] Ken Mitchell, p. 5.

[43] Ross, *Sawbones Memorial*, p. 108.

[44] Ross, "No Other Way," in Ken Mitchell, *Sinclair Ross: A Reader's Guide*, pp. 91–92. All further references to this work appear in the text.

[45] Ross, "The Painted Door," in *The Lamp at Noon*, pp. 103–04. All further references to this work appear in the text.

[46] Ken Mitchell, p. 16.

[47] Morton Ross, "The Canonization of *As for Me and My House*: A Case Study," in *Figures in a Ground: Canadian Essays on Modern Literature Collected in Honor of Sheila Watson*, ed. Diane Bessai and David Jackel (Saskatoon: Western Producer Prairie Books, 1978), p. 194.

[48] Denham, p. 121.

[49] Ken Mitchell, p. 28.

[50] Ross, *As for Me and My House* (Toronto: McClelland and Stewart, 1957), p. 4. All further references to this work appear in the text. I have elected to use this edition rather than the comparatively rare first edition of 1941. My colleague, Professor B.J. Mitchell, has recently completed a comparison of the texts of the two editions, and reports that for all practical purposes, the texts are identical.

[51] Henry James, "Preface" to *The Ambassadors* (New York: Scribner's, 1909), p. xix.

[52] Chambers, p. 42.

[53] Ross, *The Well* (Toronto: Macmillan, 1958), p. 42. All further references to this work appear in the text.

[54] Chambers, p. 43.

[55] Ken Mitchell, p. 57.

[56] McMullen, p. 98.

[57] Chambers, p. 46.

[58] Ross, *Whir of Gold* (Toronto: McClelland and Stewart, 1970), p. 126. All further references to this work appear in the text.

59 Ken Mitchell, p. 61.

60 Chambers, p. 50.

61 McMullen, p. 113.

62 Ken Mitchell, p. 62.

63 McMullen, p. 119.

64 Ross, *Sawbones Memorial*, p. 18. All further references to this work appear in the text.

65 McMullen, p. 121.

66 Ross, "On Looking Back," p. 94.

SELECTED BIBLIOGRAPHY

Primary Sources

Books

Ross, Sinclair. *As for Me and My House.* New York: Reynal and Hitchcock, 1941.

——. *As for Me and My House.* New Canadian Library, No. 4. Toronto: McClelland and Stewart, 1957.

——. *Au Service du Seigneur?* Trans. Louis-Bertrand Raymond. Montréal: Fides, 1981.

——. *The Well.* Toronto: Macmillan, 1958.

——. *The Lamp at Noon and Other Stories.* New Canadian Library, No. 62. Toronto: McClelland and Stewart, 1968.

——. *Whir of Gold.* Toronto: McClelland and Stewart, 1970.

——. *Sawbones Memorial.* Toronto: McClelland and Stewart, 1974.

——. *Sawbones Memorial.* New Canadian Library, No. 145. Toronto: McClelland and Stewart, 1978.

Short Stories

(Stories collected in *The Lamp at Noon and Other Stories* are indicated by an asterisk.)

Ross, Sinclair. "No Other Way." *Nash's Pall-Mall* (1934), pp. 16, 80–82, 84; rpt. in Ken Mitchell, *Sinclair Ross: A Reader's Guide.* Moose Jaw: Thunder Creek Publishing Co-operative, 1981, pp. 79–94.

——. * "A Field of Wheat." *Queen's Quarterly,* 42 (1935), 31–42.

——. * "September Snow." *Queen's Quarterly,* 42 (1935), 451–60.

——. * "Circus in Town." *Queen's Quarterly,* 43 (1936–37), 368–72.

——. * "The Lamp at Noon." *Queen's Quarterly,* 45 (1938), 30–42.

——. "A Day with Pegasus." *Queen's Quarterly,* 45 (1938), 141–56; rpt. in

Stories from Western Canada. Ed. Rudy Wiebe. Toronto: Macmillan, 1972, pp. 106–18.

———. * "The Painted Door." *Queen's Quarterly*, 46 (1939), 145–68.

———. * "Cornet at Night." *Queen's Quarterly*, 46 (1939–40), 431–52.

———. "Nell." *Manitoba Arts Review*, 2, No. 4 (1941), 32–40.

———. * "Not By Rain Alone." *Queen's Quarterly*, 48 (1941), 7–16.

———. * "One's a Heifer." In *Canadian Accent*. Ed. Ralph Gustafson. Harmondsworth: Penguin, 1944, pp. 114–28.

———. "Barrack Room Fiddle Tune." *Manitoba Arts Review*, 5, No. 3 (1947), 12–17.

———. "Jug and Bottle." *Queen's Quarterly*, 56 (1949–50), 500–21.

———. * "The Outlaw." *Queen's Quarterly*, 57 (1950), 198–210.

———. "Saturday Night." *Queen's Quarterly*, 58 (1951), 387–400.

———. * "The Runaway." *Queen's Quarterly*, 59 (1952), 323–42.

———. "Spike." Trans. Pierre Villon. *Liberté*, 11, No. 2 (1969), 181–97; in English, in Ken Mitchell. *Sinclair Ross: A Reader's Guide*. Moose Jaw: Thunder Creek Publishing Co-operative, 1981, pp. 95–107.

———. "The Flowers That Killed Him." *Journal of Canadian Fiction*, 1, No. 3 (1972), 5–10.

Articles

Ross, Sinclair. "Montreal and French-Canadian Culture: What They Mean to English-Canadian Novelists." *The Tamarack Review*, No. 40 (Summer 1966), pp. 46–47.

———. "On Looking Back," *Mosaic*, 3, No. 3 (Spring 1970), 93–94.

Secondary Sources

Atwood, Margaret. *Survival: A Thematic Guide to Canadian Literature*. Toronto: House of Anansi, 1972.

Banting, Pamela. "Miss A and Mrs. B: The Letter of Pleasure in *The Scarlet Letter* and *As for Me and My House*." *North Dakota Quarterly*, 54, No. 2 (Spring 1986), 30–39.

Bowen, Gail. "The Fiction of Sinclair Ross." *Canadian Literature*, No. 80 (Spring 1979), pp. 37–48.

Brown, E.K. Rev. of *As for Me and My House*. *The Canadian Forum*, July 1941, pp. 124–25.

Chambers, Robert D. *Sinclair Ross & Ernest Buckler*. Toronto: Copp Clark, 1975.

Chapman, Marilyn. "Another Case of Ross's Mysterious Barn." *Canadian Literature*, No. 103 (Winter 1984), pp. 184–86.

Comeau, Paul. "Sinclair Ross's Pioneer Fiction." *Canadian Literature*, No. 103 (Winter 1984), pp. 174–84.

Cude, Wilfred. "Beyond Mrs. Bentley: A Study of *As for Me and My House*." *Journal of Canadian Studies*, 8, No. 1 (1973), 3–18; rpt. in his *A Due Sense of Differences: An Evaluative Approach to Canadian Literature*. Lanham, MD: Univ. Press of America, 1980, pp. 31–49.

————. "Turn It Upside Down: The Right Perspective on *As for Me and My House*." *English Studies in Canada*, 5 (1979), 469–88; rpt. in his *A Due Sense of Differences: An Evaluative Approach to Canadian Literature*. Lanham, MD: Univ. Press of America, 1980, pp. 50–68.

Daniells, Roy. "Introduction." *As for Me and My House*. New Canadian Library, No. 4. Toronto: McClelland and Stewart, 1957, pp. v–x.

Denham, Paul. "Narrative Technique in Sinclair Ross's *As for Me and My House*." *Studies in Canadian Literature*, 5 (1980), 116–24.

Djwa, Sandra. "No Other Way: Sinclair Ross's Stories and Novels." *Canadian Literature*, No. 47 (Winter 1971), pp. 49–66.

————. "False Gods and the True Covenant: Thematic Continuity Between Margaret Laurence and Sinclair Ross." *Journal of Canadian Fiction*, 1, No. 4 (Autumn 1972), 43–50.

Dooley, D.J. *Moral Vision in the Canadian Novel*. Toronto: Clarke, Irwin, 1979.

Dubanski, Ryszard. "A Look at Philip's 'Journal' in *As for Me and My House*." *Journal of Canadian Fiction*, No. 24 (1979), pp. 89–95.

Fraser, Keath. "Futility at the Pump: The Short Stories of Sinclair Ross." *Queen's Quarterly*, 77 (1970), 72–80.

French, William. "Too Good Too Soon, Ross Remains the Elusive Canadian." *The Globe and Mail* [Toronto], 27 July 1974, p. 25.

Godard, Barbara. "El Greco in Canada: Sinclair Ross's *As for Me and My House*." *Mosaic*, 14, No. 2 (Spring 1981), 55–75.

Harrison, Dick. *Unnamed Country: The Struggle for a Canadian Prairie Fiction*. Edmonton: Univ. of Alberta Press, 1977.

Hicks, Anne. "Mrs. Bentley: The Good Wife." *Room of One's Own*, 5, No. 4 (1980), 60–67.

Hinz, Evelyn J., and John J. Teunissen. "Who's the Father of Mrs. Bentley's

Child?: *As for Me and My House* and the Conventions of Dramatic Monologue." *Canadian Literature*, No. 111 (Winter 1986), pp. 101–13.

Kaye, Frances W. "Sinclair Ross's Use of George Sand and Frederic Chopin as Models for the Bentleys." *Essays on Canadian Writing*, No. 33 (Fall 1986), pp. 100–11.

Kostash, Myrna. "Discovering Sinclair Ross: It's Rather Late." *Saturday Night*, July 1972, pp. 33–37.

Kreisel, Henry. "The Prairie: A State of Mind." *Transactions of the Royal Society of Canada*, 4th ser., 6 (June 1968), 171–80; rpt. in *Contexts of Canadian Criticism*. Ed. Eli Mandel. Chicago: Univ. of Chicago Press, 1971, pp. 254–66.

Kroetsch, Robert. "The Fear of Women in Prairie Fiction: An Erotics of Space." In *Crossing Frontiers: Papers in American and Canadian Western Literature*. Ed. Dick Harrison. Edmonton: Univ. of Alberta Press, 1979, pp. 73–83; rpt. in *The Canadian Forum*, Oct.–Nov. 1978, pp. 22–27.

––––––. "Beyond Nationalism: A Prologue." *Mosaic*, 14, No. 2 (Spring 1981), v–xi.

Latham, David. "Sinclair Ross: An Annotated Bibliography." In *The Annotated Bibliography of Canada's Major Authors*, Vol. 3. Ed. Robert Lecker and Jack David. Downsview, Ont.: ECW, 1981, 365–93.

Laurence, Margaret. "Introduction." *The Lamp at Noon and Other Stories*. New Canadian Library, No. 62. Toronto: McClelland and Stewart, 1968, pp. 7–12.

McCourt, E.A. *The Canadian West in Fiction*. Toronto: Ryerson, 1949; rev. ed., 1970.

McMullen, Lorraine. "Introduction." *Sawbones Memorial*. New Canadian Library, No. 145. Toronto: McClelland and Stewart, 1978, pp. 5–11.

––––––. *Sinclair Ross*, Twayne's World Authors Series. Boston, Twayne, 1979.

McPherson, Hugo. "Fiction, 1940–1960." In *Literary History of Canada: Canadian Literature in English*. Gen. ed. and introd. Carl F. Klinck (Toronto: Univ. of Toronto Press, 1965), pp. 693–731.

Mitchell, Beverley. "Depression in *As for Me and My House*." *Canadian Issues/Thèmes Canadiens*, 3 (1987), 205–18.

Mitchell, Ken. *Sinclair Ross: A Reader's Guide*. Moose Jaw: Thunder Creek Publishing Co-operative, 1981.

Moss, John. *Patterns of Isolation*. Toronto: McClelland and Stewart, 1974.

New, W.H. "Sinclair Ross's Ambivalent World." *Canadian Literature*, No. 40 (Spring 1969), pp. 26–32; rpt. in *Writers of the Prairies*. Ed. Donald G. Stephens. Vancouver: Univ. of British Columbia Press, 1973, pp. 183–88.

Ricou, Laurence. *Vertical Man/Horizontal World: Man and Landscape in*

Canadian Prairie Fiction. Vancouver: Univ. of British Columbia Press, 1973.

Ross, Morton. "The Canonization of *As for Me and My House*: A Case Study." In *Figures in a Ground: Canadian Essays on Modern Literature Collected in Honor of Sheila Watson.* Ed. Diane Bessai and David Jackel. Saskatoon: Western Producer Prairie Books, 1978, pp. 189–205. Rpt. in *The Bumper Book.* Ed. John Metcalf. Toronto: ECW, 1986, pp. 170–85.

Sarner, Mark. "Whore with a Heart of Golda." *Books in Canada*, Nov. 1974, p. 9.

Stephens, Donald. "Wind, Sun, and Dust." *Canadian Literature*, No. 23 (Winter 1965), pp. 17–24; rpt. in *Writers of the Prairies.* Ed. Donald G. Stephens. Vancouver: Univ. of British Columbia Press, 1973, pp. 175–82.

Stouck, David. "The Mirror and the Lamp in Sinclair Ross's *As for Me and My House.*" *Mosaic*, 7, No. 2 (Winter 1974), 141–50.

Stubbs, R.S. "Presenting Sinclair Ross." *Saturday Night*, 9 Aug. 1941, p. 17.

Tallman, Warren. "Wolf in the Snow: Part One: Four Windows on to Landscapes." *Canadian Literature*, No. 5 (Summer 1960), pp. 7–20. *Canadian Literature*, No. 6 (Autumn 1960), pp. 41–48.

Thacker, Robert. "The Grapes of Dearth: Steinbeck, Ross, and the Dustbowl '30s." *Canadian Issues/Thèmes Canadiens*, 3 (1987), 193–203.

———. " 'twisting toward insanity': Landscape and Female Entrapment in Plains Fiction." *North Dakota Quarterly*, 52, No. 3 (Summer 1984), 181–94.

Toppings, Earle. "Canadian Writers on Tape: Sinclair Ross." Toronto: Ontario Institute for Studies in Education, 1971.

Whitman, F.H. "The Case of Ross's Mysterious Barn." *Canadian Literature*, No. 94 (Autumn 1982), pp. 168–69.

Williams, David. "The 'Scarlet' Rompers: Toward a New Perspective in *As for Me and My House.*" *Canadian Literature*, No. 103 (Winter 1984), pp. 156–66.

Woodcock, George. *Introducing Sinclair Ross's As for Me and My House.* Canadian Fiction Studies, No. 6. Toronto: ECW, 1990.

York, Lorraine M. "Its Better Nature Lost: The Importance of the Word in Sinclair Ross's *As for Me and My House.*" *Canadian Literature*, No. 103 (Winter 1984), pp. 166–74.

INDEX